Internationalizing China

A volume in the series

CORNELL STUDIES IN POLITICAL ECONOMY

Edited by Peter J. Katzenstein

A full list of titles in the series appears at the end of the book.

Internationalizing China
Domestic Interests and Global Linkages

David Zweig

CORNELL UNIVERSITY PRESS

ITHACA AND LONDON

First published 2002 by Cornell University Press
First printing, Cornell Paperbacks, 2002

Printed in the United States of America

Library of Congress Cataloging-in-Publication Data

Zweig, David.
    Internationalizing China : domestic interests and global linkages /
David Zweig.
        p. cm.—(Cornell studies in political economy)
Includes bibliographical references and index.
    ISBN 0-8014-3967-1 (cloth : alk. paper)—ISBN 0-8014-8755-2 (pbk. :
alk. paper)
        1. China—Foreign economic relations. 2. China—Commercial policy.
3. China—Economic policy—2000-4. Investments, Foreign—China. 5.
Globalization—Economic aspects—China. I. Title. II. Series.
    HF1604 .Z395 2002
    337.51–dc21

                                                2001008500

Cornell University Press strives to use environmentally responsible suppliers and materials to the fullest extent possible in the publishing of its books. Such materials include vegetable-based, low-VOC inks and acid-free papers that are recycled, totally chlorine-free, or partly composed of nonwood fibers. For further information, visit our website at www.cornellpress.cornell.edu.

Cloth printing   10 9 8 7 6 5 4 3 2 1
Paperback printing   10 9 8 7 6 5 4 3 2 1

*To Joy, who has shared China's
internationalization with me*

Contents

Illustrations

Tables

Acknowledgments

This project has been more than a decade in the making, and many debts that have accumulated along the way must be acknowledged. In 1987 and 1988, funding from both the Kearney Foundation, administered by Merle Hinrichs, and the Sackler Foundation paid for summer travel to Wujiang County, in southern Jiangsu Province, where I first investigated the impact of foreign trade and internationalization on rural China. That research was the first step toward a broader study of China's internationalization. Then, in 1991–92, with a fellowship from the Committee on Scholarly Communication with the People's Republic of China (CSC-PRC), in Washington, D.C., my wife and I lived at the Nanjing University–Johns Hopkins University Center for one year. With the help of Xie Naikang, deputy director of Nanjing University's Foreign Students and Scholars Department, I lived in Zhangjiagang and Nantong, at which time much of the research for chapters 2 and 3 was carried out. I also thank the directors of the foreign affairs offices in both Zhangjiagang and Nantong, who arranged all my interviews. Those weeks in Zhangjiagang were particularly tense because the Soviet Union had recently collapsed; it was a courageous act to host a foreigner at that time and give him access to Chinese society. Naikang also helped arrange interviews in some universities in Sichuan Province. I thank the staff of the CSC-PRC who helped in various ways, including giving me access to their files on Chinese educational exchanges. The Committee's work was directed by Robert Geyer, with help from Kathlin Smith, Megan Close, Ellen Catz, Pam Pierce, and Keith Clemenger.

Internationalization takes many forms, one of which is the flow of information among scholars from different countries. I owe a huge debt to my colleague Chen Changgui, with whom I have had a remarkably successful collaboration for the past ten years. Since the early 1990s, we have shared data, worked on surveys and interview projects, and co-authored several articles and one book, *China's Brain Drain to the United States: The Views of China's Scholars in the 1990s*. I have used data from that study here, as well as data on returnees collected by Chen in 1997, and I express my debt to Changgui for his generosity, his insights, and his energy. Also I extend special thanks to my dear friend Stan Rosen, who has been a great source of intellectual, moral, and material support. My research on China's open door in education could not have occurred without the help of the directors of the foreign affairs offices at the eight universities where Chen and I carried out interviews. The 1993 survey in the United States of overseas Chinese scholars carried out by Chen, Stan Rosen, and me was funded by the Ford Foundation office in Beijing, and we owe special thanks to Peter Harris, director of the Beijing office at the time, who supported our efforts financially. Ruth Hayhoe's support for Chen in Toronto allowed us to pretest the survey instrument.

My research in China was also funded by a grant in 1991–94 from the Social Sciences and Humanities Research Council of Canada (SSHRC), which supported my study of the Canadian International Development Agency (CIDA) in China. At CIDA, Hausing Tse took a risk when he provided me with a remarkable degree of access to the archives, files, and staff. Thereafter the staff at CIDA were extremely responsive, meeting with me and sharing their insights on Canada's aid to China. My old friend Sandra Pookhay, at CIDA, introduced me to Cao Zhenxiang of the Special Economic Zone Office (SEZO) and Xia Keqiang, vice-mayor of Pudong. I also thank Y. C. Pan, Henri-Paul Normandin, Kent Smith, Graham Schatz, David Yasui, Scott Wade, and Alex Volkhoff. And I thank the staff at the various executing agencies that ran CIDA projects, including John Knight and Brock Carlton, at the Federation of Canadian Municipalities, and Vic Falkenheim, who helped on the Coastal Open Cities Project. At the Association of Community Colleges of Canada I was given great assistance by Najat Gorica, Diane Tyler, Sue Carey, and Harold Golden.

Some people helped me along the way, but their names do not appear here. I do not want to link them to the interview information I was able to collect.

Interviews are the heart and soul of my research, making access and introductions critical to its success. My former student Zhang Xian helped me make contacts with the Ministry of Foreign Economic Relations and Trade and Zhang Guanghui at the China International Center for Economic and Technical Exchange (CICETE). Other people at CICETE were extremely helpful and open as well. CIDA officials, including Alison Nankivell, introduced me to the All-China Women's Federation, the Anhiu Management Development Center, the Special Economic Zone Office, and the Changzhou Entrepreneur's Center, and I thank all the people I interviewed at those organizations.

I owe an enormous debt to the officials and staff at the UNDP headquarters in New York and Beijing, including Nessim Shallon, Benjamin Brown, Herb Berhstock, Roy Morey, Jan Mattson, Richard Conroy, Jordan Ryan, and Arthur Holcombe. I apologize if things I have said were not as favorable to these organizations as their officials had hoped when they gave me access; I went in with no predetermined viewpoints and simply tried to reflect reality as I saw it. At the World Bank, I also acknowledge the assistance of Peter Harold, Christine Wong, Rajiv Lall, Austin Hu, and Anthony Ody.

I also received financial assistance in the form of two Direct Allocation Grants from the Research Grants Council of Hong Kong, administered by the Hong Kong University of Science and Technology. This money helped me visit Beijing, carry out interviews in both Zhangjiagang and Nantong in 1997, and also look at the impact of the East Asian financial crisis on rural industrial exports.

People to whom I have a particular intellectual debt include Iain Johnson, for a long and clarifying phone call on the U.S. Thanksgiving; Tom Gottshaung and Tom Moore, who gave the manuscript an incredibly helpful reading; Constance Lever-Tracy, Erik Baark, Yang Dali, and Lucian Pye for comments on parts of the manuscript; Susan Shirk, who has led the study of China's internationalization; and two unnamed reviewers for Cornell University Press. I also thank Muriel Bell for her consideration. Others who helped intellectually along the way include Pitman Potter, Sam Ho, Steve Goldstein, Jonathan Kirshner, Jeremy Paltiel, Matt Evangelista, Kyna Rubin, Rod MacFarquhar, Noel Tracy, Tony Kane, Don Waterfall, Ed Tower, Ding Jingping, Nicholas Lardy, Steve Newman, Vivienne Shue, Thomas Christensen, Rick Baum, Samuel Kim, Michael Johnston, Hao Yufan, Pete Suttmeier, Cong Cao, Denis Fred Simon, Joe Fewsmith, David Goodman, Mark Selden, the late Gerald Segal, John Gruetzner, Diana Lary, John Wong, Gao Xin, Margaret Pearson, Merit Janow, Steve McGurk, Tony Saich, Y. Y. Kueh, David Dapice, Dirck Stryker, Peter Geithner, Bob Meagher, Charles Pentland, Steve Page, He Gaochao, Leonard Cheng, Bob Ross, Merle Goldman, Bernie Frolic, Andrew Walder, Larry Liu, François Gipouloux, Durwood Marshall, and Yue Xiaodong. I acknowledge in particular the help of Wu Changqi of Hong Kong University of Science and Technology, who provided me with a great database on rural exports and then guided me through the data.

Parts of several chapters have appeared as papers in journals and occasional papers series including *China Quarterly, Comparative Politics, Universities Services Centre Occasional Papers Series, Washington Journal on Chinese Studies,* and *In Depth,* and in an edited book by Jae-Ho Chung. Comments on those papers helped me refine my ideas, and in particular I thank Tom Bernstein, Dorie Solinger, Madelyn Ross, Maurice Brosseau, and Jae Ho Chung.

Many friends in China have helped along the way. They include Zhao Shuming, Sang Bingnan, Zhang Roncun, Luo Xiaopeng, Wang Zhenyao, Zhao Yang, Li Na, Zhu Jiaming, Zhang Wei, Ke Gao, Chen Yongxiang, Han Zhun, Zhang Mingquan, Wei Wei, Fan Yongmin, Xia Keqiang, Hui Haiming (who was particularly helpful in getting me access to the Kunshan Development Zone), and Bai Nansheng.

In Hong Kong, I acknowledge the assistance of Jean Hung, deputy director of the Universities Services Centre and its wonderful collection of journals and statistical yearbooks, as well as the support of the Center's director, Kuan Hsin-ch'i.

I have had many research assistants including Zachary Abuza, Shu Yuan, Howard Yao, Yu-Wing Yat, Zhang Lihui, Brent Fulton, Kimberley Silver, John Auerbach, Lai Ho-sze, Dia Warren, Adam Segal, Anna Ng, Shirley Fraser, Chung Him, Shen Yifei, Wang Wei, Chau Man Chao, Choi Kai Hang, and David Rankine. I want particularly to highlight the assistance and intellectual help of Chung Siu Fung and to thank Alvin So, my department head in Hong Kong, who helped provide research support.

Although he did not have a direct impact on this book, I owe an intellectual debt to the late Mike Oksenberg, who has inspired me throughout my academic career. My lifelong teacher and mentor Dan Tretiak warned me on a memorable junk ride in Hong Kong in 1991 that the scope of this study was too big—I trust I have convinced him that these diverse cases can be incorporated under one common theme and theory.

I thank both Peter Katzenstein and Roger Haydon for their interest and confidence in the project and their assistance in making this manuscript into a better book. I also thank Karen Hwa and Julie Nemer for their help on the manuscript. That the final outcome of all this work was a book published in Peter's esteemed series makes the decade-long struggle almost worthwhile.

Finally, I thank my mother who has always been in my corner; my children, Rachel and Aaron, who had to see less of me as I worked on this book—I hope they will read it some day with pride; and my dear wife, Joy, who understood that it would take sacrifice on everyone's side to get this book done. As I have studied China's internationalization, she has experienced it herself through her own business ventures in Guangdong. I dedicate this book to her.

DAVID ZWEIG

Hong Kong

Internationalizing China

Introduction: China's Internationalization in Context

The Cultural Revolution sealed China from the outside world, and almost all transnational exchanges ground to a halt. Only links to revolutionary movements persisted. Although trade with the West, particularly Japan, had expanded in the early 1960s, by the middle of that decade autarky and a strict code of self-reliance had come to characterize China's external relations. In the early 1970s, Mao Zedong legitimized burgeoning contacts with foreign countries. Secret negotiations with the United States and Canada presaged a new turn outward. The great chess game of strategic balance and international politics was Mao's concern, but these decisions would turn the lives of the Chinese and the Chinese economy on their heads.

After 1978 and Deng Xiaoping's opening to the outside world, global exchanges became a key growth sector in the Chinese economy. People skilled in facilitating transnational exchanges suddenly found new opportunities. Foreign language capabilities, a cause of suspicion and banishment during the Cultural Revolution, became capital, dividend checks for a new future. Overseas Chinese networks, long scorned as the tools of capitalist invasion, became channels for an export-led development strategy. Universities, the battleground for reactionary and revolutionary ideologies, turned into conduits for technological, managerial, and personal exchanges. New ideas and funds flooded in; intellectuals flooded out. Peasants, chastised for their petty bourgeois ideology and unskilled labor, soon became industrial soldiers, cannon fodder (and a critical component of China's comparative advantage) for the People's Republic's export boom as their inward-looking, local communist leaders became directors of transnational corporations. China was opening to the outside world with alacrity, bringing economic growth and political change.

Two stories reflect the microlevel drama generated by Mao's decision and the benefits that global linkages brought to individuals and communities.

The first begins in 1968, at the peak of the xenophobic Cultural Revolution, when a couple in the Foreign Ministry was banished to Hunan Province. Having spent years in Europe, they lost their Beijing residence permits and were sent to one of the poorest sections of south-central China to remold themselves by laboring and by learning from the "poor and lower middle peasants," as Mao had advocated in 1968. Trapped in the countryside, they wondered if they would ever escape what Karl Marx, in his essay "The Eighteenth Brumaire" once called "the idiocy of rural life." But suddenly an outward-oriented China needed translators to facilitate global exchanges. Soon after the 1972 Nixon visit, they joined a university's new foreign language department situated in a drab and dreary city in central China. Not heaven, but a step up from the cattle pen that had been their home in their May 7th Cadre School. As the opening expanded, a large state-owned enterprise, in the midst of heated negotiations with British and Americans, needed its contracts and technical agreements translated. Personal friends intervened, and this couple moved to Beijing's western suburbs. Perched on the edge of their former domicile, they waited with their temporary residence permits because few people had been allowed to return permanently to the capital. Finally, after 1978, when China decided to publish an English language newspaper, this couple reestablished their permanent residency status in Beijing, where they worked until retirement.

The second is a personal experience of the impact of internationalization. I lived in China as an exchange student from 1974 to 1976, one of the first foreigners to penetrate the Celestial Empire after the Cultural Revolution. Yet, despite state propaganda that China's "friends are everywhere under the heavens," China remained impenetrable, even to those who traversed its borders. My roommate at Beijing University in 1975–76 was a local resident; but not only did I never visit his home, his father's job was treated as a state secret. But five years later, in summer 1981, a stranger on the train to Quanzhou, a city on the south coast of Fujian Province famous for historical overseas linkages, invited me to visit Stone Lion, the governmental seat of nearby Jinjiang County. After a one-hour bike ride, I discovered that there the outside world was pouring in. An imported stereo in a new ice cream parlor threw the voice of Deng Lijun, Taiwan's pop singing sensation, into the street. Seiko watches were ubiquitous. The most popular t-shirt read, "I love Hong Kong." China's internationalization was under way.

China Opens Up

Since 1978, China has shifted from an autarkic relationship with the international system, characterized by low levels of trade, scientific exchange, foreign investment, tourism, and shipping, to become a state that, for a large country, is quite engaged in global commerce and quite active in transnational exchanges of all sorts. Yet this transition has been gradual, with the state maintaining regulatory controls to monitor the changes. New linkage channels of global transaction, such as joint ventures, export-processing zones, educational exchanges, foreign affairs offices, and a variety of counterpart agencies (*duikou danwei*) established to control foreign donors have emerged in most sectors. Through these channels have passed a rapidly expanding quantity of goods, services, capital, and people.

But this leap in transnational exchanges raises several issues. Why did a communist country, and a leadership so long committed to Maoist autarky, increase the level of global transactions and reduce the level of regulatory controls? What was the driving force behind this opening and the deeper levels of internationalization that have ensued?

If we define *internationalization* as the expanded flows of goods, services, and people across state boundaries, thereby increasing the share of trans-national exchanges relative to domestic ones,[1] along with a decline in the level of regulation affecting those flows, then many sectors in China's society and economy and have become increasingly more internationalized (table I.1). And even in those sectors where the ratio of foreign to domestic transactions has not increased, the level of global transactions has risen dramatically. Compared to many other countries in the world, such as the United States or Japan, China as of 1992 had become much more internationalized (table I.2; unless indicated, all dollar amounts in this book are in U.S. dollars.). But what was the role of international economic, strategic, and political forces in the decision to open up, compared to the role of domestic politics? How did domestic political and economic structures shape the process of internationalization? Given our definition of inter-nationalization, we must address adjustments in the regulatory controls imposed by the state on transnational exchanges. Bureaucrats under planned socialist economies have formidable powers and generally resist deregulation, export promotion, and an expanded role for global market forces.[2] So how did China open up its economy to an increasing market-governed flow of goods and services? Did regulated barriers decrease and, if so, why? How did China's leaders overcome entrenched bureaucratic interests? Were bureaucrats bought off or did they transform themselves? How did bureaucratic regulations affect the process by which China opened? And, what role did society and the local state play in decreasing the central state's regulatory powers and deepening the level of interna-tionalization? Did global market opportunities create a strong lobby that

1. Keohane and Milner see internationalization as "a process that can be empirically meas-ured by the growth in the proportion of international economic flows relative to domestic ones." Helen V. Milner and Robert O. Keohane, "Internationalization and Domestic Politics: An Introduction," in *Internationalization and Domestic Politics*, ed. Robert O. Keohane and Helen V. Milner (Cambridge, UK: Cambridge University Press, 1996), p. 4.
2. Josef C. Brada, "The Political Economy of Communist Foreign Trade Institutions and Policies," *Journal of Comparative Economics* 15 (1991): 211–38.

Table 1.1 Indicators of China's Global Integration, 1978–2000

	1978	1980	1982	1984	1986	1988	1990	1992	1994	1996	1997	1998	1999	2000
Total foreign trade (billion $)	20.6	38.1	41.6	53.5	73.8	99.8	115	166	237	290	325	324	360.6	474.3
Total exports (billion $)	9.8	18.1	n.a.	n.a.	30.9	47.5	62.1	84.9	121	151	183	184	195	249
Exports by foreign-invested firms (billion $)	n.a.	n.a.	n.a.	n.a.	0.48	2.46	7.80	17.4	34.7	61.5	74.9	80.9	88.6	119.4
(Exports by foreign-invested firms, % total exports)					(1.6)	(5.2)	(12.6)	(20.5)	(28.7)	(40.7)	(40.9)	(44.0)	(45.5)	(48.0)
Cargo handled at principal ports (million tons)	198	217	237	275	344	438	483	603	744	851	908	922	1,052	1,256
Number of ports opened to foreign trade[a]	51	n.a.	n.a.	n.a.	n.a.	35	143	162	201	n.a.	n.a.	n.a.	n.a.	n.a.
Number of deep-water berths in principal seaports (10 thousand tons)[b]	85	n.a.	n.a.	178[c]	n.a.	n.a.	282	n.a.	359	406	449	468	490	518
Number of foreign tourists (thousands)[d]	n.a.	529.1	764.5	1,134	1,482	1,842	1,747	4,006	5,182	6,744	7,428	7,108	8,430	10,160
International air routes	n.a.	n.a.	n.a.	24	17	40	44	58	84	98	109	131	128	133
Number of foreign hotels	n.a.	203	362	505	974	1,496	1,987	2,354	2,995	4,418	5,201	5,782	7,035	10,481

Sources: *China Statistical Yearbook,* 1978 to 2001. For data on foreign hotels 1980–90, *China's Foreign Economic Statistics,* 1979–1991 (Beijing: China Statistics Information and Consultancy Service Center, 1992), p. 761.

Note: n.a., not available.

[a] This indicator is not reported in the yearbooks after 1994.

[b] These harbors are referred to as "Berths of Principal Seaports" without specifically mentioning 10,000-ton berths.

[c] This is 1985—not 1984—data, presented here to give a sense of the overall trends between 1978 and 1990.

[d] Does not include overseas Chinese and Chinese from Hong Kong and Macau.

Table 1.2 Comparison of China's Global Integration, 1992 versus 1997

	China		Brazil		India		Indonesia		Japan		Nigeria		United States	
	1992	1997	1992	1997	1992	1997	1992	1997	1992	1997	1992	1997	1992	1997
Trade (billion $)	166	325	59	118	43	74	61	95	573	760	21	n.a.	1,002	1,588
GDP (billion $)	469	918	405	804	272	n.a.	139	215	3,719	4,193	32	n.a.	6,244	8,111
Trade (as % GPD)	35	35	15	15	16	n.a.	44	44	15	18	66	n.a.	16	20
Share of world trade (%)	2.2	3.0	0.8	1.1	0.6	0.7	0.8	0.9	7.7	7.0	0.3	n.a.	13.4	14.7
External debt (% GNP)	13	15	31	23	26	18	62	62	n.a.	n.a.	108	72	n.a.	n.a.

Sources: Data for GDP and trade from Editorial Board of the Almanac of China's Foreign Economic Relations and Trade, ed., *Almanac of China's Foreign Economic Relations and Trade, 1999* (Hong Kong: China Resources Advertising Co., 2000). Data for external debt from the World Bank, *World Development Report, 1994, 1999* (New York: Oxford University Press, 1994 and 1999).

Note: n.a., not available. The *World Development Report* did not report external debt as % GNP for the U.S. and Japan.

demanded greater internationalization? With collective action illegal under China's communist system,[3] did the demands for access to the international system by a multitude of nonorganized interests propel this process forward? Did variations in the impact of internationalization on domestic China—in particular the generation of differential growth rates in different localities or economic sectors—serve as a feedback loop, influencing the pace and process of the opening since the 1980s?

Importance of China's Internationalization

China's internationalization is a key event in the late twentieth century, second only to the collapse of communism in Europe and the end of the Cold War. First, when China sneezes, the world shakes. When decollectivization in 1978 enriched rural households and 80 percent of China's farmers improved their housing, 16 percent of the world's total population undertook the largest housing boom in world history! If rural China, with 20 percent of the world's population, continues to expand its exports, the results will deeply affect manufacturers, consumers, and importers worldwide.

Second, China's apparent economic success, and the gradual shift from planned economy to market economy without a big bang, has enormous theoretical and practical significance. Was China's ability to overcome bureaucratic entrenchment and expand its foreign sector just another example of "growing out of the plan"?[4] Can other states follow suit? And just how serious are the distortions generated by the regulatory regime during the process of liberalization?

Third, most studies of China's global transition eschew the broader literature in international political economy and institutional economics.[5] As a result, international relations generalists find little to which they can relate in the studies of China's internationalization. Moreover, China is rarely used as a case study because it is often presented as sui generis, too complex for any comparativist to handle. But China's story speaks to key issues of interest to generalists in international political economy: Are domestic coalitions necessary for a society to shift from autarky to inter-

3. For a study on how collective action emerges from unorganized interests under state socialism see Zhou Xueguang, "Unorganized Interests and Collective Action in Communist China," *American Sociological Review* 58 (February 1993): 54–73.

4. Barry Naughton, *Growing Out of the Plan: Chinese Economic Reform, 1978–1993* (New York: Cambridge University Press, 1995).

5. Major exceptions are Susan L. Shirk, *How China Opened Its Door: The Political Success of the PRC's Foreign Trade and Investment Reforms* (Washington, D.C.: Brookings Institution, 1994); Margaret Pearson, *Joint Ventures in the People's Republic of China* (Princeton: Princeton University Press, 1991); Tom Moore, *China in the World Market: Chinese Industry and International Sources of Reform in the Post Mao Era* (Cambridge, UK: Cambridge University Press, 2002).

dependence? Is leadership activism enough? Can states permit extensive transnational relations without ceding a large degree of central control? Can regulatory controls be maintained during the process of internationalization without bureaucrats becoming predatory? And even if they become somewhat predatory, can rent seeking and growth coexist? Do internationalization and decentralization strengthen the local state vis-à-vis the central state or society? Can an authoritarian state open its economy and polity to international forces without collapsing?

Finally, what does greater involvement in the global economy mean for China's foreign and domestic behavior? Does internationalization increase interdependence, leaving China more vulnerable to global shocks? China was clearly affected by the East Asian financial crisis, although the shock would have been far greater had China already deregulated its currency controls. Will interdependence increase the ability of countries, such as the United States, to influence China's foreign (and even domestic) behavior?[6] Will it constrain an otherwise assertive foreign policy, brought on by heightened nationalism and a sense of increased national power? Or will internationalization simply increase China's global economic power, allowing it to be more assertive in the foreign policy realm? Looking at how China has managed the gradual process of internationalization since the 1980s should yield some important clues about China's ability to manage the first decades of the twenty-first century, as it enters the World Trade Organization (WTO) and a more open trade regime.

Explaining Internationalization: Four Views from the Field

Four models are relevant to understanding the process by which states interact with the international system: (1) explanations that focus on the power of regulatory regimes to limit or skew the pattern of global interaction, (2) neoliberal explanations that stress the role of global market forces and suggest that domestic coalitions of trade beneficiaries (or trade opponents) influence national policy and the state's level of internationalization, (3) the East Asian model, or state-led development explanations that characterize bureaucrats as successfully managing the transition to a more internationalized economy by creating comparative advantage, and (4) a network capital model that stresses horizontal linkages by smaller ethnic Chinese firms that carry out successful transnational exchanges with a modicum of central state interference.

6. Thomas W. Robinson, "[In][ter]dependence in China's Post-Cold War Foreign Relations," in *China and the World*, 4th ed., ed. Samuel Kim (Boulder: Westview Press, 1998), pp. 193–216; Elizabeth Economy and Michel Oksenberg, "Introduction: China Joins the World," in *China Joins the World: Progress and Prospects*, ed. Elizabeth Economy and Michel Oksenberg (New York: Council on Foreign Relations Press, 1999), pp. 1–41.

REGULATORY CONTROLS

The first model addresses the level of administrative constraints in the domestic economy, as well as the regulations or "separation fences" established by the state for managing transnational exchanges.[7] It also focuses on domestic political and economic structures, such as political coalitions or previous patterns of investment that create path dependence and mediate the impact of global pressures for internationalization.[8] These political and economic institutions limit internationalization and/or distort the workings of the international and domestic markets, as well as popular perceptions of the opportunities available under internationalization.

Communist foreign-trade systems undermine internationalization by favoring capital-intensive state-owned industries over light-industrial labor-intensive exports.[9] Also, the common interest of state bureaucrats and industrial managers in protecting state-owned enterprises should prevent deregulation of the foreign trade and foreign investment regimes.[10] Communist ideology also favors the state monopoly of foreign trade, rejecting even a shift to tariff controls (which could not protect domestic industries from industrial capitalism).[11]

For Douglass North and institutional economists, collectivist norms and the dominance of public over private property in socialist systems create high transaction costs and undermine international economic activity in the medium or long term.[12] Similarly, Ziya Onis sees the private sector as crucial to global competitiveness.[13] But publicly owned firms, with their soft-budget constraints, could have an insatiable hunger for international goods; once regulations are eased, or the means are established to circumvent the regulations, unbridled demand, in the form of investment fevers,

7. This is a concept used by the World Bank and is cited in Shirk, *How China Opened Its Door*, p. xiii.
8. Geoffrey Garrett and Peter Lange, "Internationalization, Institutions, and Political Change," in *Internationalization and Domestic Politics*, ed. Robert O. Keohane and Helen V. Milner (Cambridge, UK: Cambridge University Press, 1996), pp. 48–75. For "path dependence," see David Stark, "Path Dependence and Privatization Strategies in East Central Europe," *East European Politics and Society* 6, no. 1 (1991): 17–54.
9. Brada, "Political Economy," p. 238.
10. Janos Kornai, *The Socialist System: The Political Economy of Communism* (Princeton: Princeton University Press, 1992).
11. Hough quotes Lenin: "No tariff policy can be effective in the epoch of imperialism. . . . Our border is maintained not so much by customs or border guards as by the monopoly of foreign trade." Jerry Hough, "Attack on Protectionism in the Soviet Union? A Comment," *International Organization* 40 (spring 1986): 495.
12. Douglass C. North, *Structure and Change in Economic History* (New York: W. W. Norton, 1981).
13. Ziya Onis, "The Logic of the Developmental State," *Comparative Politics* 24 (October 1991): 109–26.

could emerge.[14] Based on these institutionalist assumptions, China's international transactions, tightly limited by central or local administrators, should remain relatively stagnant; the easing of constraints can be expected to trigger bursts of almost uncontrollable demand.

Finally, for Gordon Tullock and James Buchanan, state actors enact regulations to create a rent-seeking society in which they can maximize their own benefits.[15] These regulations distort the impact of relative prices, constrain economic choices, and channel benefits to state bureaucrats. Anne Krueger's pioneering work shows how transnational constraints, such as tariffs and quotas, abet the emergence of a predatory, rent-seeking bureaucracy that misdirects entrepreneurship into nonproductive activity, inflating transaction costs and generating enormous economic inefficiency.[16]

But China's behavior since 1979 highlights the dilemmas of an explanation based primarily on institutional constraints. If regulatory controls and the interests of state bureaucrats undermine the benefits of international exchanges, why did China's transnational transactions boom for two decades? Yes, the corruption, smuggling, and rent seeking predicted by this model have become scourges that threaten China's political system, and these problems are the product of a highly regulated trade regime; yet they do not seem to have had a significant impact on the scale of transnational exchanges. Between 1978 and 1997, foreign trade increased 16 percent annually (figure I.1). Moreover, imports have kept pace with exports, despite cries from the U.S. trade representative that China maintains a closed economy. In fact, many indicators of internationalization (see table I.1) show remarkable and consistent growth. Ironically, a country long seen as totalitarian and in complete control of its borders has allowed almost 400,000 of its brightest students and scholars to leave the country, and some 250,000 remain abroad.[17]

Also, since 1978, China's shift from relying primarily on quotas to more formal tariff and nontariff barriers has decreased regulatory controls and increased the role of market forces in foreign trade.[18] Clearly China has

14. Janos Kornai, "Hard and Soft Budget Constraints," in *Contradictions and Dilemmas: Studies on the Socialist Economy and Society*, ed. Janos Kornai (Cambridge, Mass.: MIT Press, 1986), pp. 33–51.
15. See James M. Buchanan, "Rent Seeking and Profit Seeking," in *Towards a Theory of the Rent-Seeking Society*, ed. James M. Buchanan, Robert D. Tollison, and Gordon Tullock (College Station: Texas A&M University Press, 1980), pp. 3–15.
16. Anne O. Krueger, "The Political Economy of the Rent-Seeking Society," *American Economic Review* 64, no. 3 (June 1974): 291–303.
17. "China Encourages Students Overseas to Serve in Various Ways," Beijing, Xinhuanet, http://www.cnd.org/Global/01/08/20/010820-9.html.
18. Nicholas R. Lardy, *Foreign Trade and Economic Reform in China, 1978–1990* (Cambridge, UK: Cambridge University Press, 1992); Daniel H. Rosen, *Behind the Open Door: Foreign Enterprises in the Chinese Marketplace* (Washington, D.C.: Institute for International Economics and Council on Foreign Relations, 1999).

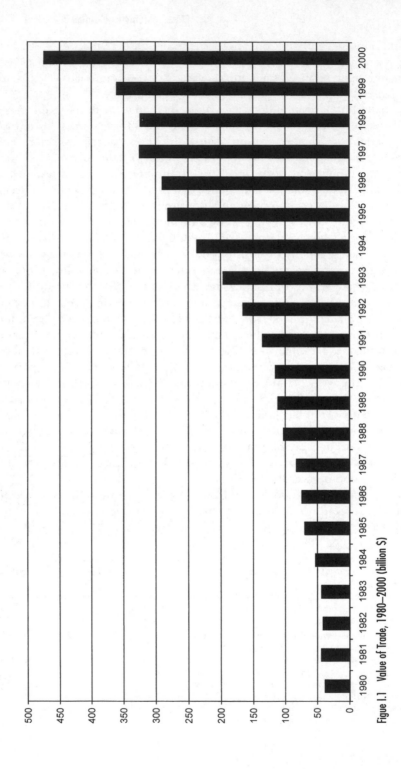

Figue I.1 Value of Trade, 1980–2000 (billion $)

often re-regulated sectors, establishing new agencies to control transactions, even as it liberalized a specific sector,[19] and these regulations greatly influence the pattern or process of internationalization in China. But, market forces, not just regulatory constraints, must be incorporated into an explanation of China's process of internationalization.

NEOLIBERAL EXPLANATIONS

Specialists in international political economy, particularly advocates of liberal trade theory, stress the impact of international forces on domestic behavior and government policy.[20] Both Ronald Rogowski and Helen Milner explain internationalization by asserting that those who possess factors of production that are in surplus in the domestic economy, the potential export firms, will act collectively to try to liberalize the state's trade regime.[21] To create a broader theory that explains change, Jeffry Frieden and Rogowski argue that decreases in the costs or increases in the rewards of international exchange, which they call "exogenous easing," change the relative prices of resources and create new opportunities for domestic actors who push for liberalization, regardless of the regime's domestic structure.[22]

Other authors suggest that the impact of international market forces on domestic interests cannot explain a country's internationalization. Matthew Evangelista has found that regulations in the USSR's foreign-trade system erected strong barriers between domestic and international economies and stopped price signals from reaching domestic actors, preventing them from "knowing their interests."[23] Similarly, Susan Shirk argues that China's tight political institutions prevented changes in relative prices from influencing domestic prices, so that the type of domestic behavior hypothesized by Freiden and Rogowski did not occur.[24] Moreover, with

19. Steven K. Vogel, *Freer Markets, More Rules: Regulatory Reform in Advanced Industrial Countries* (Ithaca: Cornell University Press, 1996).
20. Peter Gourevitch, "The Second Image Reversed: The International Sources of Domestic Politics," *International Organization* 32 (autumn 1978): 881–911.
21. Ronald Rogowski, *Commerce and Coalitions: How Trade Affects Domestic Political Alignments* (Princeton: Princeton University Press, 1989); Helen V. Milner, *Resisting Protectionism: Global Industries and the Politics of International Trade* (Princeton: Princeton University Press, 1988), respectively.
22. Jeffry A. Frieden and Ronald Rogowski, "The Impact of the International Economy on National Policies: An Analytical Overview," in *Internationalization and Domestic Politics*, ed. Robert O. Keohane and Helen V. Milner (Cambridge, UK: Cambridge University Press, 1996), pp. 25–47.
23. Matthew Evangelista, "Stalin's Revenge: Institutional Barriers to Internationalization in the Soviet Union," in *Internationalization and Domestic Politics*, ed. Robert O. Keohane and Helen V. Milner (Cambridge, UK: Cambridge University Press, 1996), pp. 159–85.
24. Susan Shirk, "Internationalization and China's Economic Reforms," in *Internationalization and Domestic Politics*, ed. Robert O. Keohane and Helen V. Milner (Cambridge, UK: Cambridge University Press, 1996), pp. 186–206.

interest group activity and collective action illegal in China, how could domestic beneficiaries of open trade pressure the state to lower the trade barriers? Particularly in the early days of the reform, China was a very centralized political system, so which sectors or regions were opened to international prices was decided by the top elites, who were only marginally affected by lobbying from below.[25] Finally, because liberals believe all states respond to the international market regardless of domestic structure, if we can show that domestic structure, not just comparative advantage, caused localities to respond differently to international opportunities, we can challenge that aspect of the neoliberal perspective.

EAST ASIAN MODEL

The East Asian model of development asserts that bureaucrats are not rent seekers, but are enlightened directors of industrialization who manage the market and successfully promote development.[26] And as long as the state maintains a close, but relatively autonomous link to domestic economic interests, which Peter Evans calls "embedded autonomy," it can organize the captains of domestic industry for shared projects of national development without falling prey to predatory, rent-seeking behavior.[27] By targeting export subsidies, punishing enterprises that did not conform to the state's rules,[28] and creating comparative advantage, rather than passively responding to global markets as envisioned by the liberals, late developers such as Korea, Taiwan, and Japan, experienced decades of rapid growth.

However, China's reality is far from the ideal type posed by the East Asian model. Until the late 1990s, elite conflict has made it inordinately difficult for China's leaders to set a clear industrial policy. Unlike Korea, the key growth sectors have not been centralized; every province has an auto and electronics industry. Efficiency has come more from interprovincial competition than from the state pushing large corporations into the international market. The Chinese state has largely protected its loss-generating state sector, responding more to domestic pressures than global ones, suggesting that the Chinese state of the 1980s and 1990s was weaker than the Korean state of the 1970s. Only in the mid-1990s did China enunciate a clear industrial strategy and only since 1998 has Zhu Rongji aggressively pushed the state sector into the global marketplace. Finally, the

25. See Dorothy J. Solinger, *From Lathes to Looms: China's Industrial Policy in Comparative Perspective, 1979–1982* (Stanford: Stanford University Press, 1991); Joseph Fewsmith, *Dilemmas of Reform in China* (Armonk: M. E. Sharpe, 1994).
26. Robert Wade, *Governing the Market: Economic Theory and the Role of Government in East Asian Industrialization* (Princeton: Princeton University Press, 1990).
27. Peter Evans, *Embedded Autonomy: States and Industrial Transformation* (Princeton: Princeton University Press, 1995).
28. Alice Amsden, *Asia's Next Giant: South Korea and Late Industrialization* (New York: Oxford University Press, 1989).

enlightened bureaucrats of the Maoist era, necessary for successful late industrialization, have since 1978 become increasingly rapacious, expending enormous energy seeking rents.

NETWORK CAPITAL MODEL

The final model, also sensitive to external forces, stresses the role of network capitalism, particularly overseas Chinese business networks that have facilitated East Asia's economic dynamism and China's global economic linkages.[29] Until the mid-1990s, somewhere between 70 and 80 percent of all foreign investment in China came from overseas Chinese who are seen as the major global force driving China's economic development.[30] Although much attention has focused on the large overseas Chinese families,[31] the structure of the East Asian economy is more horizontal than vertical or hierarchical, based on networks among family businesses[32] and composed of many small-scale overseas Chinese investors seeking export markets and cheap offshore centers for export processing. This competition for low-cost export production leads to a beelike swarming effect, whereby tens of thousands of small private companies rapidly move into a country in response to changes in the relative price of labor.[33] And given rudimentary capital markets and a weak legal system, large amounts of capital, information, and trade follow transnational, personal relationships (*guanxi*) among people of Chinese ancestry. Much of this network capitalism originates from Taiwan, with its small-scale but densely networked export-oriented economy, but much investment also comes from Hong Kong.

Therefore, first, although each Taiwanese investment project in China may be relatively small and low tech, the total number of such projects can

29. See S. Gordon Redding, *The Spirit of Chinese Capitalism* (New York: Walter de Gruyter, 1993); George L. Hicks and S. G. Redding, "Culture and Corporate Performance in the Philippines: The Chinese Puzzle," in *Essays in Development Economics in Honor of Harry T. Oshima*, ed. George L. Hicks and S. Gordon Redding (Manila: Institute of Developmental Studies, 1982), pp. 199–215.

30. Constance Lever-Tracy, David Ip, and Noel Tracy, *The Chinese Diaspora and Mainland China: An Emerging Economic Synergy* (New York: Macmillan, 1996).

31. The top 500 overseas Chinese families control over U.S.$500 billion. See James R. Lilley and Sophia C. Hart, "Greater China: Economic Dynamism of the Overseas Chinese," in *China's Economic Future: Challenges to U.S. Policy*, ed. Joint Economic Committee (Armonk: M. E. Sharpe, 1997), pp. 423–50.

32. Redding refers to a new breed of multinational corporations, "not organized hierarchically or coordinated by bureaucratic control mechanisms. It is instead a looser web organized horizontally, and leaving a great deal of autonomy in the local units." Gordon Redding, "Overseas Chinese Networks: Understanding the Enigma," *Long Range Planning* 28, no. 1 (1995): 67.

33. Gary G. Hamilton, "Organization and Market Processes in Taiwan's Capitalist Economy," in *The Economic Organization of East Asian Capitalism*, ed. Marco Orru, Nicole Woolsey Biggart, and Gary G. Hamilton (Thousand Oaks: Sage, 1997), p. 254.

be quite large, playing a major force in China's export-led growth. Second, the impact of culture will push most of these projects into the home regions of overseas Chinese, affecting the geographic spread of this form of foreign direct investment (FDI). Finally, network capital may be critical for circumventing central regulatory controls if personal relations emerge between overseas Chinese investors and local state agents in China who are responsible for development.

EXPLANATIONS FROM THE CHINA FIELD

China scholars prefer elite, domestic political or network explanations[34] for China's post-Mao foreign economic policy. They generally downplay external factors, particularly global economics—hence this book.

Nevertheless, people who believe that global factors have affected domestic China and its policy making have been on the scene since 1990. In a classic article on *kaifang* (opening) James Townsend calls on readers not to underestimate the role that foreign interests—strategic, economic, ethical, intellectual, and cultural—play in keeping China open.[35] He also sees "new social forces produced by the introduction of modern technology and organization" as one of two deep structural influences on the opening, the other being the elite's century-long drive for modernization. Nicholas Lardy, too, sees China's foreign trade regime responding to international pressures,[36] while Margaret Pearson believes that once China decided to use FDI, state sovereignty and control were undermined by competing government elites, declining state control over the economy, and foreign investors who, similar to a domestic lobby, forced the central government to soften its foreign exchange regulations.[37] Thus, despite their apparent strong bargaining power with foreign investors, even socialist states cannot resist the power of international regimes and norms.

Tom Moore employs a classic international political economy perspective to show how the international market affects China's domestic development.[38] Import quotas on China's textile exports under the Multi-Fibre Agreement and surplus capacity in the global shipbuilding industry forced China to reform both sectors, and, in the case of textiles, to shift to higher value-added products. The textile sector was particularly vulnerable to global economic structures due to intense domestic competition and hard-budget constraints within the industry; economic failure meant closing

34. Moore, *China in the World Market*.
35. James Townsend, "Reflections on the Opening of China," in *Perspectives on Modern China*, ed. Kenneth Lieberthal et al. (Armonk: M. E. Sharpe, 1991), p. 406.
36. Lardy, *Foreign Trade and Economic Reform*.
37. Pearson, *Joint Ventures*.
38. Moore, *China in the World Market*.

shop. In contrast, the silk industry, which retained its state subsidies and soft-budget constraints and whose exports were not subject to international quotas, did not reform its productive processes.

Several scholars now stress the role of network capitalism to explain the pattern and depth of China's internationalization. For Constance Lever-Tracy, David Ip and Noel Tracy, "diaspora capitalism" from Taiwan, Hong Kong, and East Asia in general was the key form of FDI in the early 1990s.[39] Yuen-Fong Woon shows how villagers' interest in opening businesses was affected by whether they received remittances from overseas relatives.[40] Ironically, those with direct overseas links and large amounts of capital were less willing to engage in long-term investment projects and risky businesses than residents of the same village without such ties. Although Woon shows how network capital strengthened the local state's capacity to supply its citizens with public goods, Kuo Cheng-Tian shows how Xiamen municipality's hunger for Taiwanese capital made it less willing to follow central directives to impose political constraints on Taiwanese capitalists.[41] Similarly, You-tien Hsing shows how, when it relocated into south China, the Taiwanese shoe industry linked with local government and circumvented central regulations that were supposed to limit the autonomy of foreign capital.[42]

Among the domestic explanations for the opening, Shirk's political bargaining model has been quite influential outside the China field. She argues that through particularistic contacting, China's central elites let some coastal leaders link with the global economy in return for support for impending political battles.[43] But political explanations ignore the coast's comparative advantage in foreign trade, which is the real explanation why the center favored it over the inland areas. Comparative advantage also explains why Shirk's "communist coalition" of inland provinces failed to stem the tide of pro-coastal policies until 1995,[44] when threats of social unrest, triggered by fifteen years of pro-coastal policies, finally led the center to dismantle many benefits bestowed on the coast.[45] In fact, central

39. Lever-Tracy, Ip, and Tracy, *Chinese Diaspora and Mainland China.*
40. Yuen-Fong Woon, "International Links and the Socioeconomic Development of Rural China: An Emigrant Community in Guangdong," *Modern China* 16 (April 1990): 139–72.
41. Kuo Cheng-Tian, "The PRC and Taiwan: Fujian's Faltering United Front," *Asian Survey* 32 (August 1992): 683–95.
42. You-tien Hsing, *Making Capitalism in China: The Taiwan Connection* (London: Oxford University Press, 1998), pp. 130–31.
43. Shirk, *How China Opened Its Door.*
44. Susan Shirk, "The Domestic Political Dimensions of China's Foreign Economic Relations," in *China and the World*, 4th ed., ed. Samuel S. Kim (Boulder: Westview Press, 1984), pp. 57–81.
45. Dali Yang, *Beyond Beijing: Liberalization and the Regions in China* (New York: Routledge, 1997). See also Hu Angang, "Why I Am for 'No Preferential Treatment' for Special Economic Zones," *Ming bao*, 23 August 1995, reprinted in *Foreign Broadcast Information Service* (hereafter *FBIS*), no. 188 (28 September 1995): 36–40.

leaders did not have to buy off coastal leaders because they were the natural beneficiaries of internationalization. Instead, reformers had to placate state bureaucrats, whose monopolies on China's transnational exchanges were suddenly at risk.

Robert Kleinberg presents a Machiavellian view of China's government and bureaucracy, and suggests that they were unaffected by global forces.[46] Openings occur at the state's whim to entice foreign investors; once investments are sunk, mercantilist impulses tighten the regulatory reins on foreign funds. But, although Chinese elites have been quite mercantilist and retrenchments have followed periods of liberalization, unless he recognizes the role of international and local pressures Kleinberg cannot explain why China continues to deregulate control over most global transactions.

Combining economic and political logic makes Jude Howell's cyclical explanation of China's internationalization very useful.[47] Decentralized control over global exchanges and weak economic norms allow strong domestic demand for international commerce and resources to overheat the economy each time liberalization occurs, forcing the state to clamp down on domestic and international transactions. But new beneficiaries of internationalization, created during each outward stage of the cycle, resist retightening, leaving China more open at the end of each cycle than at the beginning. Howell, however, understates the administrative interests in the process of internationalization, overstates the political ones, and largely ignores the role of foreign capital and foreign markets in promoting China's internationalization.

Two more recent contributions to the debate are from Dali Yang and Daniel Rosen. Yang, recognizing the importance of local government initiative in opening China, suggests that competitive liberalization is driving the process. Each locality offers to dismantle administrative constraints in its region in order to attract foreign investors.[48] However, Yang ignores the role of the central state, which must approve these local initiatives and, in fact, encourages them by granting local governments exemptions from regulatory controls, or what it calls preferential policies. Finally, Rosen argues that the regulatory regime is breaking down because, as of 1997, foreign businesses were free to establish wholly owned foreign enterprises rather than being compelled to form joint ventures with Chinese partners. These freedoms, however, were limited to specific sectors.[49]

---

46. Robert Kleinberg, *China's "Opening" to the Outside World: The Experiment with Foreign Capitalism* (Boulder: Westview Press, 1990).
47. Jude Howell, *China Opens Its Door: The Politics of Economic Transition* (Boulder: Lynne Rienner, 1993).
48. Yang, *Beyond Beijing*.
49. Rosen, *Behind the Open Door*.

Domestic and Global Linkages

Chapter one details my argument; here I briefly introduce my views on the forces that brought down the barriers in China. First, I believe that explanations that rely solely on either the international or the domestic structure to explain internationalization are insufficient[50]—particularly in the Chinese case. We need an explanation that recognizes that significant opportunities are generated by relative prices and the global market because, after so many years of economic isolation, the differences in the values of goods and services inside and outside China were often significant. Those who could transfer resources across China's borders reaped huge benefits. Second, without central initiatives, the opening could not have begun; elite developmental strategies created the rules within which local governments, firms, organizations, and individuals made their allocative decisions.[51] But the organizational or administrative structure of a sector,[52] its property rights, and the sector's level of decentralization all affect how global factors meshed with domestic interests to create constraints and incentives for individuals, firms, and communities who sought global linkages.

Such an explanation must incorporate incentives generated by the regulatory regime, which I call channels of global transaction, erected by the state to control transnational exchanges. Whereas liberals see the strength of at-the-border regulations as the outcome of domestic collective action or changes in international relative prices, boundaries and the incentives they create are also independent variables affecting domestic behavior, much as the rent-seeking analysis suggests. Thus although external forces and changes in relative prices can create a strong demand for dismantling institutional barriers, those barriers also affect the value of goods and services that can be transferred across China's borders and allow regulators to charge fees or rents for facilitating exchanges.

But above all, my explanation emphasizes the role that the local state, local communities, organizations, and individuals played in bringing down institutional barriers to transnational exchanges. The pattern of development under China's open policy depended greatly on the entrepreneurship of local bureaucrats or leaders of organizations and their ability to manipulate or evade centrally erected barriers to global transactions. Citizens, too, who saw benefits from global exchanges pursued their individual interests through widespread unorganized efforts to establish global links that undermined the barriers to internationalization.

50. Robert O. Keohane and Helen V. Milner eds., *Internationalization and Domestic Politics* (Cambridge, UK: Cambridge University Press, 1996), pp. 5–6.
51. Stephan Haggard, *Pathways from the Periphery: The Politics of Growth in the Newly Industrializing Countries* (Ithaca: Cornell University Press, 1990).
52. Vogel, *Freer Markets, More Rules.*

Therefore, I propose four general arguments or hypotheses that reflect the role of external forces, bureaucratic agents, domestic structure, and a feedback loop based on the distributional consequences of internationalization. First, states can constrain the impact of global forces (and relative prices) through strong institutional barriers; but once central leaders let internationalization begin, members of the bureaucracy, local governments, individuals, and corporate entities will discover whether they have interests that can be advanced due to the gap in relative prices. If so, they have incentives to establish global linkages. Second, bureaucrats and their bureaus, which monitor transnational exchanges, must benefit from global transactions through expanding their resources, rent seeking, corruption, or doing business; otherwise they will strongly resist the loosening of regulatory controls. But over time, as they see that their interests are maximized by facilitating rather than blocking global transactions, the level of exchanges will increase. Third, if the central government introduces regulations that vary the level of institutional constraints on global exchanges faced by different regions, the regulations themselves become a target of political activity as individual localities lobby the central government and pursue policies, not just wealth. By easing the administrative controls (or transaction costs) in some localities but not others, the state creates comparative advantage and determines which localities or sectors will benefit from internationalization. These factors, as well as the entrepreneurship of local leaders, explain which regions, industrial sectors, types of enterprises, and perhaps even which individuals will respond most rapidly to internationalization. Finally, internationalization affects economic growth, inequality, and the locus of domestic investment; so, potential beneficiaries of internationalization should push the state to deregulate its boundaries or try to circumvent those barriers. But given China's authoritarian regime, domestic actors cannot pursue their interests collectively. Nonetheless, popular perceptions that others are benefiting from deregulation and global linkages, and popular concerns that phases of liberalization and opportunities for linking may be short-lived, may lead localities to engage in feverish efforts to establish global linkages right after the state deregulates its transnational boundaries. Thus a disequilibrium emerges between mercantilist efforts by the state to control exchanges and the domestic and international demands that barriers to exchanges be lowered and interdependence deepened.

Structure of the Book

This book employs a comparative case study approach. It examines four sectors of China's political economy to test hypotheses I derive inductively from the Chinese case, based on concepts from international political economy, positive political economy, and institutional economics. In each case I seek answers to the same general questions:[53] (1) Why and how was the sector initially opened? Did central leaders respond to international and/or domestic forces? (2) What were the key domestic and international resources in that sector? Did the opening affect their value and did demand for them increase? (3) What legal or administrative institutions did the state establish to control global exchanges in this sector? Was control over these channels to the international system decentralized? (4) Who were the potential beneficiaries of internationalization in that sector? What constraints did they face in pursuing these interests? Were they able to circumvent those constraints and, if so, how? (5) Did the pursuit of transnational exchanges take on a feverish pitch? Why? and (6) Did these fevers and other efforts at global linkage undermine the state's control over the boundaries between that sector and the international system?

Most international political economy studies compare responses across industrial sectors,[54] or nation-states;[55] I look at internationalization in different sectors or policy arenas: urban internationalization, rural internationalization, the internationalization of universities and research institutes, and foreign assistance to government institutions and local communities. These sectors share some qualities. First, all began the reform era under tight bureaucratic controls; all were starved for resources, but state leaders gave them all the opportunity to interact with the international system. Second, in all sectors the channels of global transaction cushioned the impact of international forces and insured continued bureaucratic control. Third, in each sector, domestic reforms and new property rights arrangements created a powerful profit incentive for some organizations to link globally.

In addition, according to Theda Skocpol, sector analysis is important when assessing state power (or its decline) because "one of the most important facts about the power of a state may be its unevenness across policy areas."[56] Thus differences in the level or process of internationalization among the sectors may let me compare the impact of my independent variables on the responses of local actors and the state's ability to maintain its regulatory regime. These variables include the state's policy or strategy for opening the sector, particularly the extent of decentralization; the admin-

53. I employ what George calls "structured, focused comparison." Alexander L. George, "Case Studies and Theory Development: The Method of Structured, Focused Comparison," in *Diplomacy: New Approaches in History, Theory, and Policy*, ed. Paul G. Lauren (New York: Free Press, 1979), pp. 43–68.
54. Moore, *China in the World Market*.
55. D. Michael Schafer, *Winners and Losers: How Sectors Shape the Developmental Prospects of States* (Ithaca: Cornell University Press, 1994).
56. Theda Skocpol, "Bringing the State Back In: Strategies of Analysis in Current Research," in *Bringing the State Back In*, ed. Peter B. Evans, Dietrich Rueschemeyer, and Theda Skocpol (Cambridge, UK: Cambridge University Press, 1985), p. 17.

istrative structure and constraints within the sector at the beginning of the reform era; the level or nature of external interests in that sector; the strength of the regulatory regime in the sector; and the type of linkage channel created by the state. These all affected the level of popular demand for linkages, the way in which linkages occurred, and the ability of the state to control that sector's global ties.

Much of my argument and the analysis of the sectors is based on extensive interviews carried out in the field. I spent 1991–92, the summer of 1993, and several weeks in 1994, 1997, and 1998 visiting Zhangjiagang, Nantong, Kunshan, Beijing and Nanjing, development zones in numberous cities in Jiangsu and Shandong provinces, as well as Shanghai; eight universities in four cities in four different provinces; and five foreign aid projects in three different provinces. Without frank discussions with Chinese citizens my research would have been impossible. But one of the hazards and responsibilities of such a research methodology is the obligation to protect one's sources. Therefore, in all cases, when I quote directly from an interview, I employ my own coding system that allows me to cite my informants without revealing their identity.

THE SECTORS

Communist planners starved their cities, preferring to expand industrial output and avoid investment in what appeared to them to be nonproductive infrastructure. But as China's economy turned outward, coastal and riverine cities and counties with geographically comparative advantage in foreign trade lacked the harbors, roads, airports, bridges, power plants, potable water, telecommunications, and other modern conveniences for the efficient movement of goods and services. Internationalization became a major strategy through which the cities could promote urban development. To attract foreign funds, the central government deregulated the constraints on international commerce for certain locations—special economic zones (SEZs), coastal cities, and various development zones—creating a less regulated, more tax-free environment within these enclaves, where the transaction costs of doing business were much lower. Suddenly, whether a locality was declared open to foreign investment and became the beneficiary of deregulation—which the Chinese call preferential policies— had enormous implications for the inflow of both domestic and foreign capital that saw economic benefits from working in a deregulated environment. Regional and local leaders competed to have their locality (or part of it) declared open in order to receive favorable policies and the opportunities openness entailed. They expended enormous energy and funds pursuing policies, lobbying central leaders to internationalize their locality. With development zones a key channel of global transaction through which cities could gain preferential policies and lower transaction costs, a zone fever emerged in the early 1990s that weakened institutional boundaries between China's cities and the world. Equally important, zone directors offered access to the domestic market to foreign investors in return for the capital needed to develop the zone, further undermining the regulatory regime separating domestic China and the global economy.

Township and village enterprises (TVEs) responded with alacrity to the opportunities generated by internationalization. In 1984–85, TVEs earned only 4 percent of China's total foreign exchange, and in 1985 supplied 4.8 percent of the total commodities purchased by state-owned trading companies for export. By 1993, TVEs earned almost 33 percent of China's total foreign exchange and supplied almost 54 percent of the export commodities purchased in the domestic economy. Similarly, between 1991 and 1995, the number of rural joint ventures (JVs) jumped from 7,000 to 35,000. Why did this shift occur? As chapter 3 shows, by establishing equity JVs, TVEs and the local governments that owned them circumvented institutional constraints placed on their involvement with the global economy, purchased advanced technology that increased their international competitiveness, and earned rents in the domestic economy that were available to those with access to foreign technology. Through rural JVs, overseas Chinese network capital gained access to low-cost export platforms and to China's domestic market, avoiding constraints imposed by the state and furthering the process of internationalization. Access to these rents for TVEs and network capital led to a JV fever in rural China in the early 1990s.

Maoism also starved China's universities, ended scholarly exchanges with the West for thirty years, and depressed the wages of university employees by world standards. When international linkages offered universities access to global resources and gave individuals opportunities to improve their status, income, and life chances through overseas travel, the demand for overseas contacts exploded. Within the universities, access was constrained by foreign affairs offices and other bureaus that monitored and controlled transnational exchanges, but interuniversity competition and the demands of students and scholars for more exchanges forced university administrators to expand the opening. This sector is enriched by the individualistic nature of the benefits of internationalization. Although communities, local governments, collectivities, and their leaders were major actors in the first two sectors, the rewards from internationalization in higher education were also reaped by individual scholars and students whose feverish desire to go abroad propelled the process of internationalization. Also, after 1989, their collective refusal to return to China unless the regulations controlling exchanges were revised helped deregulate the entire sector.

Finally, overseas development assistance (ODA) supplied enormous amounts of international resources, training, and travel opportunities to collectivities and individuals. To control the opening, the Chinese state established a coterie of counterpart agencies (*duikou danwei*) within the bureaucracy in Beijing to funnel funds and projects to central and local bureaus, territorial governments or local organizations. These bureaucrats were the prototypical linkage agents, whose prosperity depended on controlling and facilitating transnational exchanges. By observing their behavior we discern the impact of international stimuli and opportunities on administrative behavior. Also, special to this sector is that although aid helped local actors who hungered for global linkages, the center did not decentralize the channels of global transaction, so no linkage fever emerged. Nevertheless, in the 1990s, foreign nongovernmental organizations (NGOs) used a weak regulatory regime to work directly with local governments and Chinese society. This de facto deregulation and decentralization weakened the institutional constraints that were expected to limit China's internationalization.

This, then, is my key goal: to explain the how and why of China's internationalization over the last two decades of the twentieth century. Why did the barriers come down and why do they remain? What role did state leaders, global forces, and domestic actors play in this process? As China deepens its economic links to the outside world, we need to understand more clearly why the shift from mercantilism to interdependence took place and how that process has created the Chinese system that we see today. This book sheds some light on this historic transition.

1

Explaining Internationalization: Channels, Resources, and Fevers

In 1978 China decided to increase the number of its transnational interactions. Under a mercantilist strategy, China's leaders created new at-the-border institutions, channels of global transaction, through which all foreign transactions had to flow, including special economic zones (SEZs), high-tech or export-processing zones, joint ventures (JVs), and various types of foreign affairs offices. The state granted them regulatory powers and special privileges, which the Chinese call preferential policies, that facilitated exchanges and often decreased the transaction costs of international business. The subsequent expansion in the flow of goods and services under these bureaucratic constraints created a new political economy that reconstituted the incentives to which bureaucrats, local officials, ordinary citizens, enterprise managers, collectivities, and foreign investors responded.

Differences in the relative values of many goods and services on either side of the border offered people who could move goods across China's borders the rents and extra-normal profits that come with regulated markets and limited competition. China's bureaucrats, who were responsible for monitoring and controlling transnational transactions but whose positions at the nexus of the international and domestic market gave them important rent-seeking positions, found that they could benefit more from facilitating rather than blocking such exchanges. The state's decision to deregulate global linkages for some localities, sectors, or organizations while preventing other actors from engaging in transnational exchanges—a process I call segmented deregulation—had distributional consequences: growth in most deregulated or internationalized sectors or regions greatly outpaced growth in closed ones. As a result, Chinese citizens, collectivities, and local governments lobbied the state to grant them control over a channel of global transaction, to deregulate or internationalize their locality or parts of it, or simply to give them some preferential policy that would increase their comparative advantage over others who lacked such privileges. Those with a real comparative advantage in some form of international exchange also sought ways to carry out such transfers. All this microlevel behavior created unorganized but feverish demands for global linkages that pushed on the boundaries of the system, weakening China's regulatory regime and strengthening the degree of internationalization.

This chapter explains the generation of this disequilibrium between state control and demands for deregulation that resulted in China's pattern of internationalization. The views of China's elites and bureaucrats toward internationalization are one key to the story. How tradable goods and services mobilized the Chinese to expand global exchanges and how channels of global transaction shaped their responses are another. Also, the policy process by which China distributed these preferential policies determined the nature of domestic political activity under the open policy. I introduce the leading actors in our drama, the linkage agents who carried out the transactions, and discuss briefly how China's decentralization influenced local responses to global opportunities. Finally, I explain how feverish efforts to expand global links undermined China's regulatory regime and deepened its level of internationalization.

Controlling the Opening: Mercantilism versus Internationalization

Throughout its history, China, although not closed to all foreign influences, has sought to control them.[1] Traditional strategies included geographic separation, the granting of trade monopolies to Chinese officials, forcing foreigners to live outside the capital and deal through official "barbarian handlers," ideological expressions of self-sufficiency, eschewing foreign trade and the advantages of comparative advantage altogether, and ritualizing China's foreign affairs. In the 1950s, the People's Republic combined many of these traditions using a communist system adapted from the Soviet Union. Foreign trade became a state monopoly managed by a handful of foreign trade companies who followed a central plan replete with quotas and tight foreign trade controls.

After 1978, elites and bureaucrats sought to benefit from transnational exchanges, while at the same time protecting the domestic economy from unwanted global competition. Figure 1.1 presents a visual representation of the book's overall argument. Here, the empirical definition of internationalization involves two components: an expanded number of transnational exchanges (movement from left to right on the horizontal axis) and a decrease in the barriers or regulations limiting such exchanges (movement downward on the vertical axis). As we outline later, movement along the horizontal axis was propelled by China's comparative advantage in foreign trade, an easing of the costs of international trade through the

1. Joanna Waley-Cohen, *Sextants of Beijing: Global Currents* in *Chinese History* (New York: W. W. Norton, 1999).

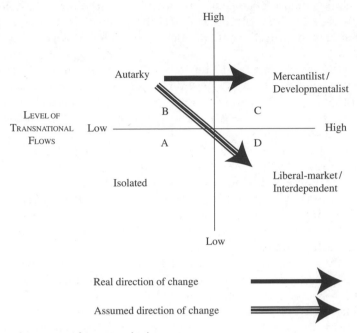

LEVEL OF REGULATORY CONSTRAINTS

High

Autarky

Mercantilist /
Developmentalist

LEVEL OF
TRANSNATIONAL   Low
FLOWS

B   C

High

A   D

Isolated

Liberal-market /
Interdependent

Low

Real direction of change

Assumed direction of change

Figure 1.1   China's Pattern of Transnational Linkages

expansion of ports and other infrastructure facilities, which Frieden and Rogowski call "exogenous easing,"[2] as well as the significant gap between the values of goods and services on either side of the border that galvanized domestic and international actors to move goods across the border to reap the rents and extra-normal profits created by the regulatory constraints. Movement on the vertical axis, however, was the result of elite policies, the decentralization to local governments of authority over the formal and informal rules governing exchanges, the incentives for the state's bureaucrats to facilitate rather than limit exchanges, the demand for deregulation generated by unorganized domestic interests favoring expanded unfettered exchanges, and pressures from the international environment. Based on these two continua, I differentiate four development strategies: quadrant A, isolated, with low levels of transnational flows and little need for regulation; quadrant B, autarky, with low flows due to high levels of

2. Jeffry A. Frieden and Ronald Rogowski, "The Impact of the International Economy on National Policies: An Analytical Overview," in *Internationalization and Domestic Politics*, ed. Robert O. Keohane and Helen V. Milner (Cambridge, UK: Cambridge University Press, 1996), pp. 25–47.

bureaucratic regulation; quadrant C, a mercantilist, economic nationalist, or developmentalist perspective, in which global transactions increase markedly but the state strictly controls those flows; and quadrant D, a liberal-market or interdependent model, in which flows are high and regulation is low.[3]

China, in 1978, decided to move out of quadrant B and engage the world economy more fully. However, whereas neoliberal assumptions predict that as states expand the scale of global transactions (move from left to right on the horizontal axis) deregulation, due to international norms, domestic interest groups, and the need for economic efficiency pushes the state into quadrant D, in reality enormous elite and bureaucratic interests actually moved China into quadrant C. With more regulations, the Chinese state could protect its domestic market, maximize its ability to extract taxes,[4] and hope to control its agents. By maintaining regulatory controls, bureaucrats could earn rents and charge fees for allowing transactions to go forward; so their preferences, too, moved the system into quadrant C, not D.

Since the 1980s, however, regulatory constraints have lessened as the flow of goods and services have intensified, moving China down the vertical axis, deepening its level of internationalization. Two aspects of this transition from quadrant C to D form the subject of this book. First, I explain why, despite the initial preferences of China's elite and bureaucrats, China's level of internationalization deepened and to what extent international versus domestic and regulatory versus market forces propelled this process forward. Second, I explore how the fact that China first adopted a mercantilist strategy, with high levels of regulation and expansive transnational flows, and then moved into quadrant D has affected China. Again, the liberal hypothesis focuses primarily on the end point, liberalization; a more process-sensitive approach focusing on the changes in the domestic political economy generated by internationalization explains more clearly how the opening occurred and the impact of that process on China's political economy, leaving us with a richer, more robust portrait of the contours of the Chinese state at the end of the twentieth century.

---

3. Although the level of regulation may decrease, it may also increase somewhat in order to insure an orderly market. See Steven K. Vogel, *Freer Markets, More Rules: Regulatory Reform in Advanced Industrial Countries* (Ithaca: Cornell University Press, 1996).

4. "Perhaps one key to global liberalization should be sought . . . in the recognition by predatory rulers that they can manipulate the terms of international exchanges. Positioned at the nexus of the domestic and global political economies, such rulers control profitable international connections and skim off profits from the world economy without having to tax their subjects directly." Robert O. Keohane, "Problematic Lucidity: Stephen Krasner's 'State Power and the Structure of International Trade,'" *World Politics* 50 (October 1997): 170.

Role of Elites in Internationalization

When countries undergo what Charles Hermann calls a "fundamental change in a country's international orientation," the role of the leaders is critical.[5] Their goals and strategies define the rules, laws, or regulations to which local and external actors must respond.[6] Because bureaucrats kept domestic actors in China in the dark about the benefits of transnational exchanges and because ideological norms justified such constraints, elite activism in opening up a closed sector was absolutely necessary if domestic actors were to learn how they might benefit from internationalization.

Thus, preferences among Chinese elites played a leading role in opening China to the outside world. No sector could be deregulated without strong support from a coalition of top leaders, although Deng Xiaoping did have the charisma to push openings forward even when resistance among conservative leaders was strong. So, although the structure of elite conflict in China (based on factions, policy packages, or political coalitions) and its influence on policy making has been hotly debated in the China field, competing elite visions over how to manage China's external economic relations, shifts in political influence among those elites, and changes in elite perceptions about the risks of opening to the outside world—a process called "elite learning"[7]—determined the pace and breadth of deregulation.[8]

Most senior leaders generally favored engaging the outside world. Yet we can posit two elite views: a mercantilist view that was deeply concerned about protecting China from the dependence that might ensue from economic integration, and a second, more liberal view that recognized that only through broad-based involvement with the outside world could China gain access to the resources, capital, and technology needed for rapid modernization.[9]

---

5. Charles F. Hermann, "Changing Course: When Government's Choose to Redirect Foreign Policy," *International Studies Quarterly* 34 (March 1990): 3.
6. Stephan Haggard, *Pathways from the Periphery: The Politics of Growth in the Newly Industrializing Countries* (Ithaca: Cornell University Press, 1990).
7. Alastair Iain Johnston, "Learning versus Adaptation: Explaining Change in Chinese Arms Control Policy in the 1980s and 1990s," *China Journal* 35 (January 1996): 27–62.
8. China's successful integration through 1994 was due to "the dominance within the Chinese leadership of reformers committed to the Open Policy." Margaret Pearson, "China's Integration into the International Trade and Investment Regime," *in China Joins the World: Progress and Prospects*, ed. Elizabeth Economy and Michel Oksenberg (New York: Council on Foreign Relations, 1999), p. 175.
9. According to Robinson, the regime tried to strike a balance between the two, albeit favoring the first view in what he called "independence as a basis for interdependence." Thomas W. Robinson, "[In][ter]dependence in China's Post-Cold War Foreign Relations," *China and the World*, 4th ed., ed. Samuel Kim (Boulder: Westview Press, 1998), p. 203. Pearson differentiates between a "full integration" and "partial integration" model. Under the latter,

Chen Yun, China's economic czar throughout the 1980s and into the 1990s, fought to maintain regulatory controls on internationalization.[10] Believing that foreigners would use interdependence to weaken China, he opposed dismantling China's external and domestic controls. Because he "abhorred inflation, government deficits, and foreign debts,"[11] Chen prevented China's foreign debt and trade balance from ballooning, all the while defending the interests of the central administration. In 1979, after a wave of foreign purchases by overzealous bureaucrats threatened China's capital account, he insisted on the widespread cancellation of billions of dollars in contracts with Japan.[12] Until his death in 1995, Chen remained a lightening rod for bureaucratic and regional concerns about equity, the role of central planning in foreign economic policy, and the need for fiscal redistribution from wealthy to poorer areas. Others who shared this perspective included Peng Zhen,[13] Yao Yilin, Li Peng, and Deng Liqun (who offered the ideological rationale for intermittent efforts to limit dramatically the influence of global economic and political forces on China's development).[14] Their views remained relatively fixed and their support for internationalization limited; so when their influence dominated, the center asserted its controls over global transactions and deregulation was less likely.

Yet despite periodic tightening, China continued to deepen its level of internationalization, due in part to three leaders, Deng Xiaoping, Zhao Ziyang, and Zhu Rongji, who saw benefits in transnational exchanges. Believing that China must master international management skills and science and technology in order to increase national power and welfare,[15] Deng became the patron saint of China's opening in science and technology and higher education. In a temporary alliance with Chen Yun, Deng precipitated and steered the 1978–81 opening, with new regulations allowing SEZs, foreign direct investment (FDI) under China's first JV law, and

China's leaders see participation in the global economy as practical and desirable but want to control those influences. In 1997, Pearson saw this strategy as dominant. See Pearson, "China's Integration," p. 162.

10. David Bachman, "Differing Views of China's Post-Mao Economy: The Ideas of Chen Yun, Deng Xiaoping, and Zhao Ziyang," *Asian Survey* 26 (March 1986): 292–321; Joseph Fewsmith, *Dilemmas of Reform in China* (Armonk: M. E. Sharpe, 1994).

11. Kenneth Lieberthal and Michel Oksenberg, *Policy Making in China: Leaders, Structures, and Processes* (Princeton: Princeton University Press, 1988).

12. Ryosei Kokubun, "The Politics of Foreign Economic Policy Making in China: The Case of Plant Cancellations with Japan," *China Quarterly* 105 (March 1986): 19–44.

13. Peng Zhen, "Guanyu 'Zhonghua Renmin Gongheguo waizi jingying qiye fa (cao'an)'" [Explanations for the draft joint venture law of the PRC], in *Peng Zhen wenxuan* [Collected works of Peng Zhen] (Beijing: People's Press, 1991), pp. 378–82, cited in Pitman Potter, "Foreign Investment Law in the People's Republic of China: Dilemmas of State Control," *China Quarterly* 141 (March 1995): 167.

14. Richard Baum, *Burying Mao* (Princeton: Princeton University Press, 1994).

15. Deng Xiaoping, "Why China has Opened Its Doors," reprinted in *Foreign Broadcast Information Service* (hereafter *FBIS*) (12 February 1980): L1–5.

China's induction into key international economic organizations. After reading a study by his advisor, Huan Xiang, about the yawning technology gap between China and the West, Zhao Ziyang, supported by Deng, Hu Yaobang, Hu Qili, and a host of economic advisors, inaugurated a massive "second wave of reform" in 1984, including the opening of fourteen coastal cities, twelve economic and technical development zones (ETDZs), and three coastal delta regions, as well as the decentralization of science and technology, educational exchanges, harbor management, and foreign trade.[16] In 1987, concerned that China had missed the export boom of the 1970s and 1980s that had enriched the four Asian tigers[17]—Taiwan, Hong Kong, Singapore, and South Korea—Zhao, with Deng's approval, introduced the Coastal Development Strategy, which further decentralized foreign trade, turned Hainan Island into a fifth SEZ, opened the entire coast and its 300 million residents to FDI, and propelled China's rural industries into the maelstrom of global market competition and export-led growth. In 1988, China also began to experiment with high-tech development zones (HTDZs), granting them special import-export privileges. Then two and a half years after the Tiananmen crackdown destroyed Zhao's political career and his reform faction, and following the collapse of the Soviet Union, Deng, believing that economic stagnation was a greater risk to the security of the Communist Party than further economic deregulation and deeper internationalization, traveled to south China and called on local officials to be bold and to link to the outside world. The result was a new wave of deregulation and expanded global exchanges.

Finally, in 1998–2000, Premier Zhu Rongji and President Jiang Zemin faced down enormous domestic opposition and offered the United States a remarkable package of concessions that brought China into the WTO in mid-2001. Zhu, although initially lukewarm to joining the WTO,[18] eventually saw internationalization as a cudgel with which to force through the reform of state-owned enterprises and to decrease corruption by cutting back on regulatory controls governing China's transnational exchanges.[19]

Bureaucratic Forces Favoring Mercantilism

Throughout much of China's opening, most bureaucrats preferred monopolies and regulatory controls over deregulation and competition.

---

16. Carol Lee Hamrin, *China and the Challenge of the Future* (Boulder: Westview Press, 1990).
17. "Zhao on the Coastal Area's Development Strategy," *Beijing Review*, 8–14 February 1988, pp. 18–23.
18. Joseph Fewsmith, *China and the WTO: The Politics Behind the Agreement* (Seattle: National Bureau of Research Publications, November 1999).
19. David Zweig, "The Stalled Fifth Wave: Zhu Rongji's Reform Package of 1998–2000," *Asian Survey* 41, no. 2 (March–April 2001): 231–47.

For foreign-trade bureaucrats, internationalization and the proliferation of channels of global transaction were threats to their power. According to Yu Boge, general manager of China Resources Textiles, "the existence of various export channels will only result in disrupting the market order and eventually cause losses to the state. . . . under socialist public ownership, it is not proper to introduce free competition in foreign trade."[20] In 1992, one Chinese observer called on the state to participate in collusion and prevent Chinese enterprises from fighting one another on the world market, arguing that "the practice of harmonizing enterprises' foreign relations, importing technologies, and fixing prices of imports and exports by non-governmental commercial chambers and associations will be acceptable to GATT."[21] And even in 1999, Wu Jichuan, Minister of Information Industries, tried to override Premier Zhu Rongji's efforts to deregulate the communications sector and open it to foreign competition.

Western analysts highlight the bureaucracy's efforts to control transnational exchanges. For Pitman Potter, "state control over foreign business has remained a singular norm of the regulatory regime. In fact, the continued expansion of the Chinese legal system regarding foreign investment has been meant to strengthen the state's managerial role," not weaken it.[22] Rosen, too, believes that regulators had an enormous interest in preventing the transparency of rules, regulations, and business opportunities because a lack of transparency kept foreigners dependent on them.[23] Even in 1997, China's acceptance of JV trading companies was characterized as "token liberalization" because the state was expected to limit severely the number of JVs that would be approved.[24]

A debate in the late 1980s and early 1990s shows the strong base of support for a mercantilist strategy.[25] For some, lowering tariff barriers to maximize trade opportunities would harm domestic industries, particularly heavy industry, telecommunications, pharmaceuticals, chemicals, and machinery, which with their higher value-added should be the basis of China's future export strategy. Therefore, import substitution and protec-

20. Quoted in "Yu Boge, a China Trade Official in Hong Kong Calls for Strengthening the Management of the Channels for Exporting Textiles to Hong Kong," *Zhongguo xinwen she*, 12 September 1989, reprinted in *FBIS*, no. 185 (26 September 1989): 43. By "market order," Yu means planned, not free market, exchanges.

21. Zhao Xiaodi, "A New Task for Participating in International Economic Competition," *People's Daily*, 4 September 1992, p. 5, reprinted in *FBIS*, no. 181 (17 September 1992): 26–27, cited in Donald C. Clarke, "GATT Membership for China?" *University of Puget Sound Law Review* 17 (spring 1994): 517–31.

22. Potter, "Foreign Investment Law," pp. 167–68.

23. Daniel H. Rosen, *Behind the Open Door: Foreign Enterprises in the Chinese Marketplace* (Washington, D.C.: Institute for International Economics, 1999), pp. 31–32.

24. T. K. Chang, "Token Liberalization Limits Foreign Interest in Investment," *China Law and Practice* (February 1997): 19.

25. See Robert C. Hsu, *Economic Theories in China, 1979–1988* (Cambridge, UK: Cambridge University Press, 1991), pp. 134–42.

tionism were necessary to make these sectors competitive.[26] In the mid-1990s, this debate was couched in nationalistic rhetoric,[27] and many economists supported an industrial policy, similar to that of South Korea, in order to build globally competitive industries. In 1998, researchers in Jiangsu's Academy of Social Sciences argued unabashedly that China should limit JVs to sectors in which China experienced shortages, such as computers, and not allow them in sectors where China should promote its own national industries, such as pharmaceuticals, advanced equipment, and the chemical industry.[28] And, writing in May 1999, two Chinese analysts referred to the "three lines of defense" against global forces in response to China's WTO accession: (1) adopting adequate measures of trade protectionism; (2) increasing the strength and awareness of tariff and non-tariff barriers; and (3) restricting the volume and arenas of FDI.[29]

Constraints as Incentives under Regulated Internationalization

Due to this preference for mercantilism, the Chinese state established an array of regulatory constraints whose goal was to help bureaucrats control foreign and domestic forces. Thus, China's opening to the outside world was not a free-market one. Administrative units and legal institutions—the channels of global transaction—constrained the way domestic interests pursued global transactions. Factories wanting linkages had to establish equity JVs; except for self-paying students, most overseas scholars had to exit China through formal exchanges managed by foreign affairs offices, teacher quality offices, or other bureaus in the school. Municipalities that wanted to deregulate their ties to the outside world could do so by becoming SEZs, open coastal cities (OCCs), or by establishing ETDZs that were bequeathed special tax privileges by the central government. Finally, as we see later in our final sector, foreign donors who wanted to help China had to work through counterpart agencies (CPAs), whose task was to control their activities. These institutional boundaries and the incentives created by regulations affected the behavior of domes-

---

26. Liu Changli, "Import Substitution Is China's Long-Term Strategy for Catching up with or Surpassing the Developed Countries," *Jingji yanjiu* [Economic research] 8 (1987): 34–44, cited in Hsu, *Economic Theories in China*, p. 137. See also He Lianchan, Zhou Dongtao, and Yan Qiubao, "On China's External Development Strategy and the Strategy of External Competition," *Zhongguo jingji wenti* [Economic problems in China] 2 (1991): 1–6.
27. Yongnian Zheng, *Discovering Chinese Nationalism in China: Modernization, Identity, and International Relations* (Cambridge, UK: Cambridge University Press, 1999).
28. Interviews in Nanjing at the Jiangsu Academy of Social Science, summer 1998.
29. Di Yingqing and Zheng Gang, "The Key Is to Control the Initiative in Economic Development: An Analysis of the Problem of China's Joining the WTO," *Gaige neican*, no. 11 (20 May 1999): 35–39, translated in *The Chinese Economy, China and the WTO, Part II* 33, no. 2 (March–April 2000): 29.

tic actors and therefore must be part of our explanation of the process of internationalization.

The government's decision to establish these channels, even as the flow of goods and services across China's borders increased dramatically, makes the process of internationalization very powerful, and herein lies one of the key ideas behind my theory—that control over an expanding flow of highly valued resources in a partially regulated system became a critical source of power, influence, and wealth. Actors developed an enormous interest in gaining access to external or domestic resources whose value was changing under the open policy, as well as vying for control over these channels of global transaction, because they brought rents, fees and added opportunities to those who managed them. Thus although scholars such as Milner and Rogowski treat the regulatory regime as a dependent variable whose shape is determined by international pressures or domestic politics, national boundaries, the ways in which they are regulated, and the scale of goods flowing across them constitute an independent variable that creates incentives for individual and collective behavior in the domestic system.[30] Defining boundaries as "marked discontinuities in the frequency of trans-actions,"[31] Karl Deutsch asserts that one measure of power is the ability to affect the rate of change in transnational flows. Therefore, particularly under conditions of large-scale resource transfers, the ability to control boundary channels between the state and the outside world became an immense source of power and influence.[32] Similarly, boundary controls are intervening variables, constraining responses and influencing how the attributes of the international system—its structure, resources, prices, and norms—affect domestic social, political, and economic behavior.

Political economists have long understood that the ability to disrupt the flow of goods and services creates rent-access positions,[33] which endow regulators with enormous opportunities for expanding their power and wealth.[34] By restricting transnational flows, regulatory controls keep the

30. One study that influenced my thinking on this is William Zimmerman, *Open Borders, Nonalignment, and the Political Evolution of Yugoslavia* (Princeton: Princeton University Press, 1987).
31. Karl W. Deutsch, "External Influences on the Internal Behavior of States," in *Approaches to Comparative and International Politics*, ed. Barry Farrell (Evanston: Northwestern University Press, 1966), p. 5.
32. According to J. P. Nettl, the classic locus of state power is the regulation of relations with the external world. J. P. Nettl, "The State as a Conceptual Variable," *World Politics* 20 (1968): 559–92.
33. James M. Buchanan, "Rent Seeking and Profit Seeking," in *Towards a Theory of the Rent-Seeking Society*, ed. James M. Buchanan, Robert D. Tollison, and Gordon Tullock (College Station: Texas A&M University Press, 1980), pp. 3–15.
34. Regulation is a "self-interested exercise by politicians and regulators who use their power over industries to win reelection or to keep lucrative jobs." Martin Neil Baily, "Summary of the Papers," in *Brookings Papers on Economic Activity: Microeconomics, 1989*, ed. Martin Neil Baily and Clifford Winston (Washington, D.C.: Brookings Institution, 1989), p. x.

value of resources, skills, and information at above-market prices, earning those who controlled those resources extra-normal profits or rents.[35] In the case of extra-normal profits, competition undermines these profits; in the case of rents, regulations limit competition or allow regulators to impose levies for not stopping flows. Thus, for example, rents in India's export sector were over 7 percent of GNP in 1964, and in Turkey were about 15 percent of GNP in 1968.[36] In China, rents created by the difference between free-market and planned commodity prices, foreign exchange, and low credit interest rates accounted for 20–25 percent of GNP in 1981–89,[37] while the quotas needed for marketing textiles internationally were on average 20–25 percent of the selling price of a good.[38] No wonder government-related businessmen who earned rents "try by every means to maintain the existing rent system and establish a new rent system to expand the scope of rents."[39]

How does all this relate to the China's open policy? Regulatory constraints allow communities, collectivities or productive enterprises that gain access to valuable international resources to increase their global or domestic competitiveness; their wealth, power, and status; and their access to other domestic resources, precisely because of the limited flow created by those constraints. Similarly, people who exited the system to attain information, technology, or skills enhanced their position on returning because of constraints on the inward flow of such resources. These regulatory controls, therefore, led many organizations, individuals, and communities to seek control over these channels of global transaction (e.g., development zones, JVs, foreign affairs offices, and CPAs), which became nodes of power under the open policy because they were the key channels through which most global resources flowed and the key pathways by which people realized their comparative advantage in global exchanges.

Moreover, the policy process by which China's leaders opened society to the outside world, which I call segmented deregulation, greatly affected the way internationalization occurred.[40] Rather than suddenly dismantling all

35. I thank Tom Gottschang, who clarified this difference. Political economists differentiate between natural *economic rents*, which stimulate competition, market entry, and eventually dissipate, and *rent seeking*, in which people spend resources to capture contrived economic transfers, the result of monopolies or regulation. Robert D. Tollison, "Rent Seeking: A Survey," *Kyklos* 35, no. 4 (1982): 575–602.

36. Anne O. Krueger, "The Political Economy of the Rent-Seeking Society," *The American Economic Review* 64, no. 3 (June 1974): 291–303.

37. Interview with Wu Jinglian, *Jingji ribao* [Economic daily], 6 April 1993, p. 7, reprinted in *FBIS*, no. 82 (30 April 1993): 17.

38. Thomas Moore, *China in the World Market: Chinese Industry and International Sources of Reform in the Post-Mao Era* (Cambridge, UK: Cambridge University Press, 2002).

39. Wu, *Jingji ribao*.

40. The classic article on how the policy process determines the nature of politics is Theodore J. Lowi, "American Business, Public Policy, Case Studies and Political Theory," *World Politics* 16 (July 1964): 677–715.

bureaucratic regulations cotrolling global linkages, which would have triggered enormous collective resistance by government officials, reformers deregulated exchanges between the international system and specific locations, industrial sectors, universities, or enterprises, even as they maintained constraints on global transactions in other sectors or regions of the country. In deregulated locales or industries that were granted preferential policies (*youhui zhengcê*)—exemptions from import duties, tax exemptions for foreign investors, tax rebates on exports, or exclusions from labor regulations and salary caps—transaction costs were considerably lower than in the rest of the country.[41] Therefore, units and localities in highly regulated regions had great incentives to try to gain these preferential policies or to move their enterprises or branch plants into these deregulated environments.

The political result of segmented deregulation was a pattern of central-local politics whereby localities pleaded and lobbied the central administration to grant them these exemptions. Local leaders also eased economic constraints in their own localities through competitive liberalization, granting foreign and domestic investors special privileges that were often not theirs to grant.[42] However, because it was illegal under China's authoritarian political system to advocate openly changes in the state's boundaries (or tariff policy), regional leaders did not lobby for the deregulation of an entire sector (e.g., the rules governing foreign trade); instead, they lobbied for specific benefits for their locality or the right to have their locality deregulated.

The bifurcated legal and tax-exemption system established under segmented deregulation made deregulated or internationalized territories or sectors a focal point of opportunity for domestic actors. They developed enormous powers of attraction, drawing domestic resources and actors into their special environment. Because economic development in deregulated areas greatly outpaced growth in closed areas and as the state demonstrated some willingness to consider further deregulation, more and more domestic actors sought global linkages, generating an enormous domestic demand for easing the constraints on transnational exchanges.[43]

---

41. Salacuse describes the liberalization process as one of legal exemptions. Jeswald W. Salacuse, "Foreign Investment and Legislative Exemptions in Egypt: Needed Stimulus or New Capitulations," in *Social Legislation in the Contemporary Middle East*, ed. Laurence O. Michalak and Jeswald W. Salacuse (Berkeley: Institute of International Studies, University of California, 1986), pp. 241–61.

42. Dali Yang, *Beyond Beijing: Liberalization and the Regions in China* (New York: Routledge, 1997).

43. This appears to be a general pattern. For example, under Egypt's open policy, granting exemptions to foreign investors led domestic producers to demand equal rights, further weakening the state's control over FDI. John Waterbury, "The 'Soft State' and the Open Door: Egypt's Experience with Economic Liberalization, 1974–1984," *Comparative Politics* 18 (October 1985): 65–83.

Global Forces and China's Internationalization

What role have external forces played in moving China from quadrant C to quadrant D (figure 1.1)? According to Robert Gilpin, the structure of the international system, including international norms, the global capital regime, the organization of international markets, and the relative value of international resources, constrains the choices of a country's leaders and creates incentives for domestic actors to seek greater internationalization.[44]

The strategic environment had its influence. Deng's 1978 decision to strengthen China's security vis-à-vis the Soviet Union and to seek capital and technology from the West forced China to work within the rules of the world capitalist system, which differed significantly from the trade regime within the Soviet bloc. Whereas transactions among socialist economies were based on centralized bargaining, the westward opening was more influenced by global market forces, particularly the power of relative prices, the hegemonic influence of the United States, and the network capitalism of the overseas Chinese.

Membership in international organizations and regimes or trade dependence may lead states to adjust their regulations controlling exchanges with the international system. The most obvious examples are structural adjustment loans under which the International Monetary Fund (IMF) forces states to end domestic subsidies. What the World Bank calls "deep integration" may even lead states to make domestic laws consonant with international norms.[45] Thus accepting aid from international organizations, including the World Bank and United Nations Development Program (UNDP), as well as bilateral assistance, opened China to pressure on an array of policy issues.[46] However, foreign donors, hungry to get into the China game, imposed less onerous demands on China than those placed on most developing countries. In part, China had already instituted many of the structural adjustments preferred by the IMF and the World Bank on its own. But also, while officials in many developing countries advocated trade liberalization and economic restructuring,[47] the Chinese were cautious in adopting foreign views that challenged established positions.

44. Robert Gilpin, *The Political Economy of International Relations* (Princeton: Princeton University Press, 1987), p. 81.

45. Susan L. Shirk, *How China Opened Its Door: The Political Success of the PRC's Foreign Trade and Investment Reforms* (Washington, D.C.: Brookings Institution, 1994), p. 6.

46. Only after joining the World Bank did China begin to use the concept of GNP; similarly, to gain access to World Bank assistance, China had to become more transparent in giving the World Bank access to data about the domestic economy. Harold K. Jacobson and Michel Oksenberg, *China's Participation in the IMF, the World Bank, and GATT* (Ann Arbor: University of Michigan Press, 1990), p. 151. China also had to introduce environmental impact studies as part of its plans for infrastructure development.

47. Robin Broad, *Unequal Alliance: The World Bank, the International Monetary Fund, and the Philippines* (Berkeley: University of California Press, 1988).

But reliance on the U.S. market and efforts to join the WTO did alter China's foreign trade and investment regime. In the 1980s, the desire to enter the General Agreement on Tariffs and Trade (GATT) "propelled China towards a more decentralized trade regime in order to ease import restrictions."[48] To make its trading system more congruent with international practice, China shifted from planned foreign trade to a tariff system.[49] In 1992, 1995, and 1996, China signed three bilateral agreements on Intellectual Property Rights with the United States, promising to lower its tariffs, increase the transparency of its regulations, and improve market access for foreign goods. No doubt, China's implementation of these agreements fell far short of expectations. But throughout the second half of the 1990s, China announced major cuts in its tariffs, so that China's average tariff rate soon reached 15 percent.[50] Finally, in early 1999, during intense negotiations surrounding Premier Zhu Rongji's visit to the United States, and in subsequent negotiations in November 1999, China agreed to open many protected sectors as the price of membership in the WTO.

Peter Gourevitch has shown that changes in the structure of the international system can affect the distribution of power in regimes.[51] Along these lines, changes in the international lending regime led China to switch from commercial loans to FDI,[52] which had a profound impact on China's transnational relations by opening China to investment by tens of thousands of smaller overseas Chinese firms from Hong Kong and Taiwan. Whereas loans from commercial banks, multilateral agencies, or foreign governments are more easily managed by the central bureaucracy, relying on FDI in an economy where almost all enterprises were owned by different levels of the government forced the state to decentralize authority over foreign investment to the lower levels of the state bureaucracy. A large amount of foreign capital fell into the hands of local governments, empowering local communities along the Chinese coast and undermining the central government's control over its foreign exchange regime. Foreign

---

48. Jacobson and Oksenberg, *China's Participation*, p. 130.
49. Nicholas R. Lardy, *Foreign Trade and Economic Reform in China, 1978–1990* (Cambridge, UK: Cambridge University Press, 1992), p. 46.
50. Chang, "Token Liberalization," p. 20.
51. Peter Gourevitch, "The Second Image Reversed: The International Sources of Domestic Politics," *International Organization* 32 (autumn 1978): 881–911.
52. Commercial loans, as a share of capital flows to the Third World, dropped from 50.8 percent in 1980, to 37.6 percent in 1985, to 8.9 percent in 1989. FDI hovered at 16 percent in 1980 and 1985, but jumped to 36.8 percent by 1989. Similarly, multilateral loans grew from 12.7 percent in 1980 to 36.4 percent by 1989. Barbara Stallings, "International Influence on Economic Policy: Debt, Stabilization, and Structural Reform," in *The Politics of Economic Adjustment*, ed. Stephan Haggard and Robert R. Kaufman (Princeton: Princeton University Press, 1992), p. 57. Although commercial loans, by 1979, made up over one-third of China's foreign capital, China shifted to FDI and multilateral borrowing in the early and mid-1980s. Jude Howell, *China Opens Its Door: The Politics of Economic Transition* (Boulder: Lynne Reinner Publishers, 1993).

investors demanded the right to expatriate profits and called for new regulations that clearly stipulated the terms under which they could sell in the
domestic market;[53] the central state then had to respond to these demands.
By establishing JVs with local governments, network capital surreptitiously
gained access to China's domestic market.[54] Also, to facilitate exports, the
central government increased the number of local foreign trade companies and allowed JVs direct import-export powers. The result was a multiplication of local channels to the global system, strong incentives for local
governments to ally with foreign investors rather than the central state, and
a decreased administrative capacity to control China's foreign trade and
investment regime.

The relative value of goods and services on either side of the border
mobilized internal and external actors to engage in transnational exchanges. When a good's domestic price is below its world price, global
demand pushes that good into the tradable sector where it can earn more
profits.[55] But when a good's domestic price is above world prices, the
Chinese have strong incentives to import it, despite efforts by the state to
limit such inflows, often resulting in corruption.

The Yuanhua Company in the city of Xiamen in 2000 is a case in point.
Because state quotas on the importation of oil kept domestic oil prices
higher than international ones, this company could smuggle oil into
China, pay off dozens of customs agents, establish brothels to maintain
their loyalty, and still make a profit selling the oil on the domestic market.
Thus, although the central government's goal was to limit the flow of goods
and services, the relative price of oil created strong incentives for the
Yuanhua Company to smuggle it into the country.

Similarly, because of constraints on technology imports, the price of
certain products in the Chinese marketplace was artificially high. Foreign
investors, aware of these price differentials, saw China's domestic market as
a golden opportunity for extra-normal profits. Chinese rural enterprises,
therefore, had strong incentives to establish joint manufacturing facilities
with these foreign manufacturers and help them sell these technologies in
the domestic market, despite central government opposition to such sales;
as partners in the JVs, local governments shared any profits that were
earned.

The relative value of labor on either side of the border created strong
incentives for people to work overseas. For example, in the 1980s, a
Chinese professor teaching in China might earn 6,000 RMB per year

53. Margaret Pearson, "The Erosion of Controls over Foreign Capital in China,
1979–1988," *Modern China* 17 (January 1991): 112–50.
54. You-tien Hsing, *Making Capitalism in China: The Taiwan Connection* (London: Oxford
University Press, 1998).
55. Ronald Rogowski, *Commerce and Coalitions: How Trade Affects Domestic Political Alignments*
(Princeton: Princeton University Press, 1989).

($1,500), but his or her pretax income would increase thirty times by teaching the same courses in the United States! So, a Chinese professor working in the United States for just two years could earn the equivalent of thirty years salary in China. Not surprisingly, as constraints on going overseas were relaxed and new opportunities emerged, an enormous fever to go abroad erupted. Moreover, gatekeepers charged fees or received gifts for granting these opportunities. Clearly, without the initial lowering of barriers to trade, the differences in relative prices would have had no domestic impact and domestic actors would not have known their interests.[56] But once barriers were eased, international market prices altered the domestic value of those resources and the opportunity structures, incentives, and activities of those who controlled them.

With China's currency nonconvertible, and as the scale of global transactions boomed, foreign exchange was in great demand at all levels of the system. It greased the wheels of internationalization, and without it access to foreign goods, technology, information, travel, and most other transnational exchanges was impossible. The value of foreign exchange could be magnified if it were traded for scarce foreign goods that had enormous domestic value under a regulated foreign trade system.[57] Also, the state's hunger for foreign exchange allowed units or localities that could assert that their development project would generate foreign exchange to jump the queue for state investment, beating out projects that were unrelated to transnational exchanges. This "power of attraction of things foreign," which increased the perceived comparative advantage of domestic programs that had global links over projects that did not, led units to compete vigorously for transnational connections that improved their negotiating position.

Demand for a new category of transnational goods that eased global exchanges jumped: these instruments such as quotas, visas, and permits that allowed exchanges despite regulatory constraints became marketable commodities. Chinese with foreign language skills,[58] and even foreigners, themselves, became critical goods in the burgeoning transnational economy. As conduits for information, management techniques, language skills, business networks, foreign exchange, and channels through which Chinese could exit the system, foreign connections, which under Mao had made people political targets, increased in value dramatically.

56. Matthew Evangelista, "Stalin's Revenge: Institutional Barriers to Internationalization in the Soviet Union," in *Internationalization and Domestic Politics*, ed. Robert O. Keohane and Helen V. Milner (Cambridge, UK: Cambridge University Press, 1996), pp. 159–85.
57. Josef C. Brada, "The Political Economy of Communist Foreign Trade Institutions and Policies," *Journal of Comparative Economics* 15 (1991): 218.
58. In 1987, the demand for graduates in English and other foreign languages was five to ten times greater than the supply. "College Graduate Shortage Eased," *China Daily*, 17 October 1987, p. 3.

Role of Linkage Agents

The relative value of goods and services on both sides of the border and the opportunities for extra-normal profits and rents for those who engaged in transnational exchanges mobilized a proliferation of linkage agents who helped propel China further down the road of internationalization.[59] These include the leaders of local territorial governments, semipublic companies, development zones, enterprises, universities, laboratories, bureaucratic agencies, as well as overseas Chinese and local Chinese with overseas networks.

Due to policies that allowed territorial governments to keep more and more of the profits of their enterprises, many communities along the coast saw trade and FDI as major engines of economic growth. Reflecting what Evans calls the "third view of the state," developmental communities along China's coast (townships, counties, or small cities possessing industrial capacity, a disciplined workforce, and administrative networks extending into higher levels of the state bureaucracy) mobilized the entire locality for export-oriented growth and energetically sought FDI.[60]

Similarly, ETDZs, SEZs, and HTDZs were institutional innovations in which the external and internal world met in a less regulated environment. By building an inviting physical, legal, and tax environment for FDI, these zones were expected to create incentives for foreigners to invest in China, all the while containing most foreign economic activity in closely monitored locations. Zone directors were expected to act as government agents and control the flows, but, as we will see in chapter 2, many of them granted foreigners access to the domestic market, all the while giving domestic investors tax exemptions and import-export powers if they invested in their zone.

Foreign capital creates incentives for the emergence of new organizations.[61] Thus, reforms in the 1980s and transnational capital flows created

59. Actors in "linkage politics" function in both the domestic and international system. James N. Rosenau, *Linkage Politics* (New York: Free Press, 1969), pp. 1–17. For Stallings, "linkage agents"—academics trained overseas who prefer neoliberal norms of free global markets over neomercantilist protectionism—weaken regulatory boundaries in the Third World. See Stallings, "International Influence on Economic Policy." Townsend refers to the "agents of *kaifeng*" who were formed by modernization and the opening. James Townsend, "Reflections on the Opening of China," in *Perspectives on Modern China*, ed. Kenneth Lieberthal et al. (Armonk: M. E. Sharpe, 1991), p. 408.

60. Developmental communities challenge the liberal view, in which the state is purely an arena for contesting interest groups, the rent-seeking perspective, in which the state is a predator, and the dependency model, in which the state is the helpless subject of global capitalism. Peter Evans, "The State as Problem and Solution: Predation, Embedded Autonomy, and Structural Change," in *The Politics of Economic Adjustment*, ed. Stephan Haggard and Robert R. Kaufman (Princeton: Princeton University Press, 1992), pp. 139–81.

61. See Robert H. Bates, "Macropolitical Economy in the Field of Development," in *Perspectives on Positive Political Economy*, ed. James E. Alt and Kenneth A. Shepsle (Cambridge, UK: Cambridge University Press, 1990), pp. 31–56.

new organizations that participated in and transformed the nature of China's internationalization. Moreover, as the central government shrank the formal state bureaucracy in the 1980s, officials created new organizations and companies that would insure incomes for the newly laid-off bureaucrats.[62] This search for soft landings triggered company fevers (*gongsi re*) in 1984–85 and 1992–93.[63] In 1992 alone, following Deng's southern trip, 229,000 new companies were established, an 88.8 percent increase over 1991. Many of these companies used the deregulation of global transactions to become local foreign trade companies (FTCs).[64]

Producers and end users, such as enterprises, research labs, hotels, and individual scientists and scholars, used linkage channels to contact the outside world, access foreign technology or capital, or sell their products.[65] Much of the FDI that flowed into China in 1993–95 targeted state-owned enterprises (SOEs) whose competitiveness improved due to foreign assistance. Similarly, under the internationalization of the education system, university exchange programs came under the control of administrators, many of whom were able to create new specializations in foreign trade or training centers whose income was derived from faculty exchanges and preparing students to go overseas. Finally, one group not addressed by this study, but which made up a larger and larger share of China's exports in the late-1990s, are the wholly owned foreign enterprises, which have no formal links with any Chinese organization but serve as important channels for inflows of technology and information.

The opening also led to a proliferation of bureaucratic agencies to monitor and control global transactions. Most important, the opening increased the authority of foreign trade officials at all levels of the system, including those in the Customs Bureau. Most ministries established a bureau (*chu or ke*) or department (*ju or si*) to mediate international exchanges. For example, in 1987 the Ministry of Commerce dispersed its foreign links among several departments: the General Office had a foreign affairs bureau, the Department of Planning had an import-export bureau, and the Supply and Marketing Cooperation Leading Department had a foreign liaison bureau. By 1989, these bureaus were incorporated into a higher-ranked International Cooperation Department, and two new departments also got involved in imports and exports.

By 1987, perhaps 17 percent of all central government bureaus were

62. Yi-min Lin and Zhanxin Zhang, "The Private Assets of Public Agencies," in *Property Rights and Economic Reform in China*, ed. Jean C. Oi and Andrew Walder (Stanford: Stanford University Press, 1999).
63. Su Qinfu et al., eds., *Wu ci lang chao* [The five waves] (Beijing: Zhongguo renmin daxue chubanshe, 1989).
64. Dali Yang, "China Adjusts to the World Economy: The Political Economy of China's Coastal Development Strategy," *Pacific Affairs* 64 (spring 1991): 42–64.
65. Grow sees end users in China as critical actors in the transfer of transnational resources. See Roy F. Grow, "Acquiring Foreign Technology: What Makes the Transfer Process Work," in *Science and Technology in Post Mao China*, ed. Denis Fred Simon and Merle Goldman (Cambridge, Mass.: Harvard Contemporary China Series), pp. 342–43.

Table 1.1   China's Externally Oriented Bureaucracy, 1987

	Personnel		Departments		Bureaus	
	Total	Externally Oriented[a]	Total	Externally Oriented[b]	Total	Externally Oriented
All Institutions[c]	42,966	8,429 (19.6%)	1,150	154 (13.4%)	4,797	799 (16.6%)
Without MFA, MOFERT, and Customs Bureau[d]	38,179	3,642 (9.5%)	1,079	61 (5.6%)	4,519	334 (7.4%)

Source: Zhonghua Renmin Gongheguo Guowuyuan zuzhi jigou gaiyao [Essential organizational setup of the State Council of the People's Republic of China, 1987] (Beijing: Gongren chubanshe, 1988). I thank Zachary Abuza for his help in building this table.

Note: Includes people, departments, and bureaus involved in imports; exports; the transfer and acquisition of foreign technology; sending people abroad for conferences, educational programs, or study tours; contacting international NGOs, MEIs, and other multilateral development agencies; controlled and allocated foreign capital and foreign exchange; approved or controlled FDI and the establishment of JVs; foreign economic research offices; and the foreign cooperation (guoji hezuo) and foreign affairs (waishiban) bureaus found in most ministries. FDI, foreign direct investment; JVs, joint ventures; MEIs, multilateral economic institutions; MFA, Ministry of Foreign Affairs; MOFERT, Ministry of Foreign Economic Relations and Trade; NGOs, nongovernmental organizations.

[a] If a department (si) has bureau (chu) that are externally oriented, the number of the people in the department is divided by the number of bureaus in the department to derive the number of people involved in foreign affairs.

[b] This figure is extremely conservative in that only departments (si or ju) that were completely externally oriented are included (i.e., departments having one external bureau (chu) are not included).

[c] MFA, MOFERT, the Customs Bureau, and other ministries and commissions that are externally oriented by their very nature are included. Information is not provided for the military, security, and intelligence bureaucracies.

[d] A more accurate figure might be obtained by not including MFA, MOFERT and the Customs Bureau.

involved in foreign affairs of some kind, and even if we remove the ministries responsible for foreign affairs, foreign trade, and customs, approximately 7 percent of bureaus were linked to transnational exchanges (table 1.1). Between 1987 and 1989, some offices (ban'gongshi) handling foreign affairs were elevated to department-level offices. If we include provincial-, municipal-, and county-level organizations involved in transnational ties, an astonishing number of bureaucrats now drew their sustenance from some aspect of China's internationalization.

Domestic reforms altered the interests of these bureaucrats. Initially, many who sat astride the domestic and global system fought to limit transnational exchanges. They favored state interests over societal pressures, but may also have been constrained by path dependence and their responsibilities to protect social groups who had been beneficiaries of the Maoist planning system.[66] However, as the 1980s progressed, their needs and the needs of their organization or their community took precedence

66. David Stark, "Path Dependence and Privatization Strategies in East Central Europe," East European Politics and Society 6, no. 1 (1991): 17–54.

over state goals.[67] These bureaucrats learned that foreign connections increased the establishment (the number of formal positions in the bureau), raised the status of the bureau in the official hierarchy, or strengthened the institutional capacity of the bureau. Global transactions included perquisites—trips overseas, access to JV hotels, gifts, better meals, or opportunities to send their children to foreign universities. Thus most bureaucrats learned that stopping transnational exchanges was not as beneficial as allowing them to go forward—no flow, no dough!

Finally, as China moved from quadrant B to quadrant C (figure 1.1), enormous opportunities emerged for entrepreneurs who could fill structural holes between domestic and international networks.[68] Whereas in 1978 bureaucrats dominated the few channels that linked the international and domestic system, thereafter entrepreneurs with social capital filled some of these holes. Companies created by ministries had insider information on prices, projects, and opportunities, as well as the ability to move goods across national borders. Mayors and local officials introduced foreign investors to their city's firms. The children of high-ranking officials, benefiting from "nomenklatura nepotism,"[69] had access to people of high status on both sides of the border. Mainlanders with families on Taiwan organized "family visits," which were really scouting tours for business opportunities. Bureaucrats in foreign trade bureaus, overseas Chinese offices, and United Front organizations dealing with Taiwan also became public entrepreneurs.

IMPACT OF DECENTRALIZATION

The ways in which domestic or global actors responded to these international opportunities was deeply affected by China's domestic political and economic institutions, and the ongoing reforms in China.[70] The salience of domestic factors is particularly high for transitional states, in which domestic economic institutions may be quite powerful and yet vary from the

67. Victor Nee and Peng Lian, "Sleeping with the Enemy: A Dynamic Model of Declining Political Commitment in State Socialism," *Theory and Society* 23 (1994): 253–96.
68. Ronald S. Burt, *Structural Holes: The Social Structure of Competition* (Cambridge, Mass.: Harvard University Press, 1992).
69. Brada, "Political Economy," p. 218.
70. Geoffrey Garrett and Peter Lange, "Internationalization, Institutions, and Political Change," in *Internationalization and Domestic Politics*, ed. Robert O. Keohane and Helen V. Milner (Cambridge, UK: Cambridge University Press, 1996), pp. 48–75. According to Milner and Keohane, countries do not respond to changes in the global economy "simply as a function of its effects on their relative prices. . . . this impact is mediated by domestic political factors, which reflect diverse historical experiences." Helen V. Milner and Robert O. Keohane, "Internationalization and Domestic Politics: An Introduction," in *Internationalization and Domestic Politics*, ed. Robert O. Keohane and Helen V. Milner (Cambridge, UK: Cambridge University Press, 1996), p. 10.

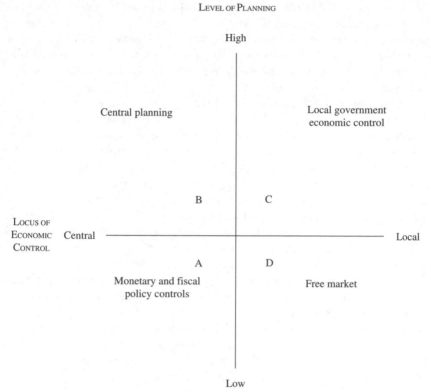

LEVEL OF PLANNING

High

Central planning

Local government
economic control

B   C

LOCUS OF
ECONOMIC   Central
CONTROL

Local

A   D

Monetary and fiscal
policy controls

Free market

Low

Figure 1.2   Impact of Economic Decentralization

norms of the capitalist world with which they seek to interact.[71] The most
important domestic reform for this book was the level of economic decentralization in a sector. The impact of decentralization is illustrated in figure
1.2. The vertical axis, the Level of Planning, represents the extent to which
economic transactions are controlled by the plan or the market, with movement downward on the vertical axis representing an increased role for the
market. The horizontal axis, on the other hand, represents a continuum
running from Beijing to the localities and reflects where economic deci-

71. In communist and capitalist systems, strong political institutions, political coalitions,
economic conditions, and ideas already in force distort the transfer process. See Peter
A. Hall, ed., *The Political Power of Economic Ideas* (Princeton: Princeton University Press,
1987); Judith Goldstein and Robert O. Keohane, "Ideas and Foreign Policy: An Analytical
Framework," in *Ideas and Foreign Policy: Beliefs, Institutions, and Political Change,* ed. Judith
Goldstein and Robert O. Keohane (Ithaca: Cornell University Press, 1993); Thomas Risse-
Kappen, "Ideas Do Not Float Freely: Transnational Coalitions, Domestic Structures, and the
End of the Cold War," *International Organization* 48 (spring 1994): 185–214.

sions are made. Thus in quadrant B we find a high level of economic plan-ning with control vested in Beijing; in quadrant C, high levels of planning persist, but local governments are in control; in quadrant D, there is no planning and no central controls, reflecting a free market; and in quadrant A, the center has some economic levers, but they would not really be seen as a form of economic planning.

Decentralization, then, transferred the authority over many channels of global transaction to territorial governments, development zones, and uni-versities. Again, although the liberal hypothesis assumes that abrogating central planning will transfer controls over all economic decisions to the independent producers and consumers who make key decisions in a market economy (figure 2.1, quadrant D),[72] in reality, much of the decision-making authority over the economy was first transferred to local governments (figure 2.1, quadrant C) and corporate entities, such as zones.[73] These corporate entities, who had planning authority, were in a powerful position to expand the number of horizontal linkage channels, and, as we have seen, had strong incentives to do so.[74]

Similarly, the changing property rights regime mobilized new corporate entities that could establish global links under a decentralized political economy. Therefore, as we discuss each of the sectors, we pay particular attention to the domestic political and economic structures at the dawn of the reform era to reveal how they constrained or energized domestic actors to pursue or eschew global linkages and how changes in those structures and norms affected the depth of China's internationalization.

Feverish Demand for Global Linkages

Foreign trade, foreign investment, technology transfer, and other global transactions have distributive implications for a country's political econo-my and for the individuals, organizations, and communities who engage in these activities. As opportunity costs push resources from the domes-tic economy into the export sector, those who possess more of the resources valued by the global economy are likely to prosper under internationalization. Moreover, the shift in China's development strategy

72. Schurman differentiates between Decentralization I and Decentralization II. Under the first, decision-making power passes to production units, who respond to market signals; in the second, authority is transferred to local governments where decisions remain a function of local planner's preferences, rather than to producers and consumers. Franz Schurman, *Ideology and Organization in Communist China* (Berkeley: University of California Press, 1968).
73. Christine P. W. Wong, "Between Plan and Market: The Role of the Local Sector in Post-Mao China," *Journal of Comparative Economics* 11 (1987): 385–98.
74. According to Grow, less central control over technology transfer meant initially more agencies, not more markets. Grow, "Acquiring Foreign Technology," p. 336.

from redistribution to comparative advantage,[75] the expansion of trade opportunities,[76] increased investment in trade-oriented infrastructure in coastal cities, and the bequeathing of preferential policies to coastal regions rather than inland regions, triggered a major flow of domestic and foreign resources into the coastal regions, whose share of China's gross value of industrial output (GVIO) jumped by 10 percent between 1984 and 1994.[77]

Great domestic demand for global opportunities resulted. Particularly after Deng's 1992 southern trip, organizations and municipalities that had hesitated to think globally were now taking greater political and economic risks.[78] As entrepreneurial leaders in rural and urban centers recognized that access to international markets and FDI was critical for growth and development in an internationalizing China, demand for external links increased dramatically.

Many attempts to establish global ties took on feverish proportions. Fevers, according to Thomas Schelling, are the collective or macrolevel outcome of individual microlevel actions that result from the anticipated action of everyone else.[79] Fevers arise because individuals believe that many other people will react quickly to an emerging opportunity and that those who enter a new market first will reap the largest benefits.

In China, cycles of openings and closings taught citizens the high cost of hesitation. As a mixed economy, driven by both administrative controls and market forces, China's economy remained quixotic; opportunities for rapid development emerged during waves of liberalization and deregulation, but the subsequent periods of retrenchment lasted for several years. After the 1987–88 liberalization, China's economy remained in cold storage until 1992. Thus, missed opportunities in one year had long-term implications because the beneficiaries of deregulation in this period could consolidate their market position and earn extra-normal profits before the next round of liberalization allowed new competitors to emerge. Similarly,

75. Terry Cannon, "Regions: Spatial Inequality and Regional Policy," in *The Geography of Contemporary China: The Impact of Deng Xiaoping's Decade*, ed. Terry Cannon and Alan Jenkins (London: Routledge, 1990), p. 32.
76. Coastal cities may have benefited from the "grand advantages" of access to the entire international market, compared to the "petty advantages" available to border provinces, which had trade links with only one country. Brantly Womack and Guanzhi Zhao, "The Many Worlds of China's Provinces: Foreign Trade and Diversification," in *China Deconstructs: Politics, Trade and Regionalism*, ed. David S. G. Goodman and Gerald Segal (London: Routledge, 1994), pp. 131–76.
77. Y. Y. Kueh, "Foreign Investment and Economic Change in China," *China Quarterly* 131 (September 1992): 637–90.
78. Jae Ho Chung, "Preferential Policies, Municipal Leadership and Development Strategies: A Comparative Analysis of Qingdao and Dalian," in *Agents of Development: Sub-Provincial Cities in Post-Mao China*, ed. Jae Ho Chung (London: Routledge, 1999), pp. 105–40.
79. Thomas C. Schelling, *Micro-Motives and Macro-Behavior* (New York: W.W. Norton, 1978), pp. 17, 77–78.

students and scholars feared that China would suddenly tighten the rules governing who could go overseas to study.

Due to socialism's soft-budget constraint,[80] there was no real cost to capital or real financial limits on demand for global goods. Only administrative constraints (e.g., a lack of foreign exchange, lack of import licenses, or other limits on transnational exchanges) kept domestic actors who had no bottom line from accumulating international resources. Thus, when liberalization occurred, feverish hoarding of resources ensued.

China's government contributed to the fevers by using administrative authority, including Communist Party propaganda and organizational institutions, to mobilize people to participate in economic programs. For example, to promote township and village enterprise (TVE) exports and rural JVs, the central government gave local leaders quotas that had to be filled before promotions or salary increases were given. But, according to Hu Angang, local demand quickly outdistanced the state's expectations, creating a disequilibrium between central goals and local behavior and forcing the state to resort to its "emergency braking mechanisms," which shut the system down entirely.[81] The actors understood this process, and it gave them an incentive to move quickly, if not rashly; cadres were not held responsible for losses that resulted from bad investments.

Under all these conditions, the sudden removal of transnational constraints or the expansion of opportunities for global linkages dramatically increased the number of actors who tried to respond to the new opportunities, generating what Zhou Xueguang calls "collective action based on unorganized interests" which, like interest group behavior in the West, pressured the state to deregulate transnational controls.[82] For example, as interregional competition to attract FDI intensified, local governments deregulated their own economies in a liberalizing rush because the last to liberalize would receive no benefit.[83] Thus while local state agents should have buttressed China's regulatory regime, the opportunities for growth through transnational exchanges led many collectivities to defect and undermine the central state's controls.

80. Janos Kornai, "Hard and Soft Budget Constraints," in *Contradictions and Dilemmas: Studies on the Socialist Economy and Society*, ed. Janos Kornai (Cambridge, Mass.: MIT Press, 1986), pp. 33–51.
81. Hu Angang, "Why China's Economy Consistently Experiences Wide Fluctuation," *Gaige neican* [Internal reference materials on reform] 15 (August 5, 1995): 6–9, reprinted in *Chinese Economic Studies* 29 (May–June 1996): 59–64.
82. Zhou Xueguang, "Unorganized Interests and Collective Action in Communist China," *American Sociological Review* 58 (February 1993): 70.
83. Yang, *Beyond Beijing*, pp. 44–46. Although Yang's model of competitive liberalization explains the willingness of local government to sell out the domestic market to foreign investors, it does not include the impact of retrenchments or the fact that local governments had to lobby the center for the formal right to liberalize their locality.

The global economy reinforced fevers in two ways. Dramatic differences between the price and quality of foreign and Chinese goods and services, created by decades of isolation and maintained by regulatory barriers, meant that extra-normal profits went to those who swiftly traversed China's borders. Thus, network capital, such as Taiwanese traders, swarmed to the mainland in search of cheap labor and a largely untapped domestic market, generating a JV fever in rural China in 1992–93. In 1992–95, multinational corporations, fearful that the Chinese government would suddenly close access to the domestic market, leaving enormous profits in the hand of early entrants who had established their relationships, created a FDI fever, establishing tens of thousands of JVs in just four years.[84]

Conclusion

China's leaders decided to open China gradually but to keep tight regulatory control over the process. To accomplish this task, they forced transnational exchanges to pass through "channels of global transaction" that were to be monitored by their bureaucratic agents. The large gap in the relative values of goods and services on either side of the border created enormous opportunities for domestic actors who could bring in foreign resources and for foreign interests who gained access to China's domestic market. Controlling the channels through which resources flowed became a profitable avocation for millions of Chinese, because those who engaged in global transactions had to work through, work around, or pay off these gatekeepers. Also, opening China through segmented deregulation led local governments and organizations to lobby the center for preferential policies or exemptions from regulatory constraints, placing demands on the central government that it could not ignore entirely. And although decentralization facilitated exchanges, it placed authority over those exchanges in the hands of bureaucratic agents whose preferences had changed and whose behavior could not be so easily controlled.

Although this development strategy slowed the pace of internationalization and helped the state maintain some control, it created uneven patterns of development; areas that were allowed to link or who chose to link grew much faster than those that did not. Chinese collectivities, organizations, and individuals, motivated by property rights clarified in China's reforming domestic economy and hungry for global linkages, responded feverishly to each lifting of regulatory constraints, placing great, albeit unorganized, pressure on the state to deregulate transnational exchanges

---

84. Rosen, *Behind the Open Door*. The 216,692 contracts signed in 1992–95 made up 65.3 percent of the total number of contracts signed between 1979 and 1999.

further. A tremendous disequilibrium emerged between the state goal of maintaining regulatory controls and local self-interested efforts to undermine or circumvent those controls. In the end, domestic and global market forces played a much larger role than political factors in internationalizing China. But government policy, regulatory constraints, and domestic political and economic structures gave shape and content to the opening, defining the nature of the Chinese state at the end of the millennium.

2

Segmented Deregulation and the Politics of Urban Internationalization

In 1978, China began to reduce the barriers between its cities and the global economy. Starting with four special economic zones (SEZs) on its southern coast, China's leaders by 1994 had opened 311 cities and counties as well as 114 open zones to foreign investment, trade, and technology. What role did international market forces, including domestic demand for foreign direct investment (FDI) and other global resources, play in this process? How did elite policy and the center's mercantilist urges skew the process of internationalization? Did bureaucrats and local administrators resist the opening and, if not, what benefits did they earn from the internationalization of China's territory? How did domestic structure—institutional constraints left over from the Maoist era as well as the ongoing domestic reforms—affect the interests of bureaucrats and local actors? Did the potential beneficiaries of internationalization push this process forward, and, if so, through collective action or unorganized individual initiatives? And finally, how did the responses of local governments affect the state's ability to monitor and control its own boundaries?

Spatial Deregulation as an Explanation for the Process of Internationalization

The two major explanations outlined in chapter 1 predict very different patterns and politics for the process of internationalization. The neoliberal model predicts that the potential beneficiaries of internationalization, aware of their comparative advantage in foreign trade and in attracting foreign investment, will collectively lobby the central government to lower barriers to trade and investment.[1] As China opens, capital should flow into infrastructure projects, such as bridges, harbors, and roads, which further

1. Jeffry A. Frieden and Ronald Rogowski, "The Impact of the International Economy on National Policies: An Analytical Overview," in *Internationalization and Domestic Politics*, ed. Robert O. Keohane and Helen V. Milner (Cambridge, UK: Cambridge University Press, 1996), pp. 25–47; Helen V. Milner, *Resisting Protectionism: Global Industries and the Politics of International Trade* (Princeton: Princeton University Press, 1988).

reduces transaction costs and improves China's trade competitiveness. On the other hand, the regulatory controls model predicts that changes in relative prices will have little impact on local actors who, due to tight controls on the foreign trade system, did not know their interests.[2] Cities with a comparative advantage in foreign trade can remain captive to bureaucratic forces or supralocal authorities[3] whose political and administrative interests, rather than market forces, direct domestic and international capital flows. And even within communities, vested political and economic interests (pre-reform or early reform decisions on the allocation of resources) should create path dependence that complicates resource reallocations.[4] Rigid regulatory controls on land sales and population transfers should also constrain resource allocations from moving in ways market forces predict. Finally, the illegitimacy of subnational interests should prevent local and regional officials from pursuing their interests collectively, even after they become clearer.

The reality, not surprisingly, was much more complex, incorporating aspects of both models but, more important, reflecting what I call the segmented deregulation model. Rather than opening all of China immediately to global exchanges, China's leaders removed regulatory constraints from specific localities while maintaining those controls over other localities. These open localities received preferential policies (*youhui zhengce*)— including tax breaks for foreign and domestic investors, easier access to domestic capital, greater freedom in foreign trade, increased local authority over domestic resources, foreign capital and investment, higher salaries, greater labor mobility, the right to issue bonds, and the ability to establish new organizations—that dramatically lowered transaction costs, allowing the state, not just the market, to determine which localities had a comparative advantage in foreign and domestic trade.[5]

This strategy had two consequences. First, deregulated territory attracted domestic resources, talent, and investment from all over China. Chinese localities or enterprises, still operating under regulatory constraints, moved their resources into deregulated territory to increase global

2. Matthew Evangelista, "Stalin's Revenge: Institutional Barriers to Internationalization in the Soviet Union," in *Internationalization and Domestic Politics*, ed. Robert O. Keohane and Helen V. Milner (Cambridge, UK: Cambridge University Press, 1996), pp. 159–85.
3. Anthony Leeds, "Locality Power in Relation to Supralocal Power Institutions," in *Urban Anthropology: Cross-Cultural Studies of Urbanization*, ed. Aidan Southall (New York: Oxford University Press, 1973), pp. 15–41.
4. David Stark, "Path Dependence and Privatization Strategies in East Central Europe," *East European Politics and Society* 6 (1991): 17–54.
5. Lu and Tang see three types of "preferential policies": investor-oriented, region-oriented, and industry-oriented. I discuss here the impact of region-oriented preferential policies. See Ding Lu and Zhimin Tang, *State Intervention and Business in China: The Role of Preferential Policies* (Cheltenham, UK: Edward Elgar, 1997), pp. 10–12.

contacts and carry out business in a less constrained environment. In contrast to development theories that see internationalized communities as growth poles, radiating development in a fanlike manner to an expanding number of surrounding communities, deregulated territories in China initially functioned as magnets, attracting investment, resources, technology, and human capital from both inside and outside China.[6] Thus while capital did flow to areas of higher return as predicted by market explanations, the end point of those capital flows was also the result of political intervention.

Second, spatial deregulation pushed local entrepreneurial elites to engage in a multilayered and diverse game of internationalization whose goal was to gain deregulated or open status, preferential policies, and the rents and/or extra-normal profits that followed.[7] Because rigid institutional arrangements limited exchanges or kept transaction costs high elsewhere, a dual economy of open and closed spaces created enormous opportunities for extra-normal profits and rents. Administrators in deregulated territories could grant preferential policies to cities, producers, and end users from nonopen spaces if they invested in their locality. Similarly, open spaces attracted more FDI than localities without such privileges. As a result, local officials lobbied central leaders for preferential policies—discretionary power that could be translated into money, investment capital, and other resources. A common slogan of the times was "*bu yao qian, zhi yao chuan*" (I don't want money, just power).

Gaining open status brought other benefits, some of which are predicted by the neoliberal model and others that are not. Under a state policy favoring the buildup of infrastructure in export-oriented communities, deregulated localities were far more likely to receive capital investment for infrastructure projects than nonopen areas. But the calculations of urban leaders were also based on the administrative constraints within which they functioned. Open status was valued because it raised the community's position in the hierarchy of urban settlements,[8] thereby escaping the constraints of many supralocal authorities; it gave the community the right to

6. In Britain, analysts were also disappointed that newly opened science parks did not attract new foreign or domestic investment but instead attracted already established firms that simply relocated to the park. In fact, over two-thirds of the plants in science parks in England were simply transplants from outside the parks. See Doreen Massey, Paul Quiontas, and David Wield, *High-Tech Fantasies: Science Parks in Society, Science and Space* (London: Routledge, 1992).

7. Yang calls this contest for preferential policies "competitive liberalization," and although the dynamic is somewhat akin to spatial deregulation, in that localities liberalized in order to attract domestic and international capital, Yang sees liberalization more as the result of local decisions to liberalize in order to attract foreign investors, rather than local efforts to create the conditions that would persuade the center to bequeath preferential policies and a more liberal trade regime to them. See Dali Yang, *Beyond Beijing: Liberalization and the Regions in China* (New York: Routledge, 1997).

8. G. William Skinner, "Cities and the Hierarchy of Local Systems," in *The City in Late Imperial China*, ed. G. William Skinner (Stanford: Stanford University Press, 1977), pp. 275–351.

negotiate directly with higher-level territorial governments for capital allocations; it increased the locality's authority to allocate its own capital;[9] it simplified the process of land acquisitions; and it allowed the local governments or zones to grant access to China's domestic market to foreign investors on terms that were more liberal than the central government preferred.

In fact, gaining access to preferential policies was so critical to a locality's future that entrepreneurial governments all over China sought to establish various types of development zones because such zones might become deregulated territories whose lower transaction costs and rent-seeking opportunities could benefit the entire community.[10] Zones also were channels of global transaction that allowed urban and rural communities to link with the outside world, as well as evade many institutional constraints limiting global exchanges. Thus, one strategy discussed in more detail later involved building a development zone, attracting enough domestic enterprises to create a thriving economic environment, and then lobbying central officials for deregulated status and preferential policies.

Therefore, segmented deregulation, the process by which the center internationalized cities or regions in China, led to atomistic collective action,[11] where localities sharing common constraints and a common desire for deregulation lobbied for individual concessions rather than jointly demanding collective benefits. These separate acts became a powerful lobby for deregulation that, at times, turned into a feverish effort to build development zones and attract preferential policies, and pushed the state to deregulate its boundaries with the international system.

So, despite efforts to control global influences, spatial deregulation undermined the government's control over the opening and global transactions. Cities learned the game quickly; the deregulation of some cities during one phase of liberalization increased the number of cities that aggressively prepared for the next round of deregulation. Although the state was committed to controlling transnational exchanges, the number of

9. According to Jacobs, while a county only retains 3 percent of its fiscal revenues for local construction, the same county, once elevated to a county-level city, retains 8 percent. Bruce Jacobs, "Uneven Development: Prosperity and Poverty in Jiangsu," in *Politics beyond Beijing: Region, Identity and Cultural Construction*, ed. Hans Hendrischke and Chongyi Feng (New York: Routledge, 1999), pp. 113–50.

10. One measure of local government entrepreneurship is a government's ability to restructure its domestic resources and alter the domestic and political climate in the community. See Mark Schneider and Paul Teske, with Michael Mintrom, *Public Entrepreneurs: Agents for Change in American Government* (Princeton: Princeton University Press, 1995). According to Cooke, proactive leaders can be internally innovative or more aggressive in trying to restructure their community's relationship to upper level governments. See Philip Cooke, "The Local Question—Revival or Survival," in *Localities: The Changing Face of Britain*, ed. Philip Cooke (London: Unwin Hyman, 1989), pp. 297–98.

11. I share this perspective with Zhou Xueguang, "Unorganized Interests and Collective Action in Communist China," *American Sociological Review* 58 (February 1993): 54–73.

open spaces continued to grow, and, despite the absence of organized interests advocating deregulation, the level of internationalization increased.

In the 1990s, two phenomena of note emerged. First, some development zones became successful linkage channels facilitating global transactions. Of the fourteen open coastal cities (OCCs), the zones in Tianjin, Qingdao, and Dalian attracted a significant number of joint ventures (JVs) that used their deregulated space as export platforms. Pudong, in Shanghai, also came to life. But many zones contributed only slightly to China's level of internationalization. Second, spatial inequality resulting from segmented deregulation intensified as the 1990s progressed.[12] Efforts to ameliorate the inland-coastal gap seemed futile; challenges to preferential policies in 1995–96 did not end this policy strategy. Only in 2000 did Jiang Zemin announce a major new initiative, the Western Region Development Strategy (*Xibu kaifa zhanlue*), but whether it will be able to overcome twenty years of unbalanced development, and the coast's many natural advantages, remains to be seen.

OPENING THE COAST THROUGH SPATIAL DEREGULATION

After 1949, the central government controlled the flow of resources, capital, technology, and workers, and under spatial deregulation determined which regions of the country would flourish.[13] In 1978, China's elites rejected Mao's concerns for regional balance, under which China in the 1950s had expanded industries in inland cities,[14] and let comparative advantage and uneven development replace balanced development and regional redistribution as the strategies for nationwide growth. After thirty years of pro-inland policies, China, under an export-led growth strategy, tilted investment toward the coast.[15] Finally, because East Asia had used

12. Terry Cannon, "Regions: Spatial Inequality and Regional Policy," in *The Geography of Contemporary China: The Impact of Deng Xiaoping's Decade*, ed. Terry Cannon and Alan Jenkins (London: Routledge, 1990), pp. 28–60.
13. See Cannon, "Regions."
14. Mao Zedong, "On the Ten Great Relationships," in *Chairman Mao Talks to the People: Talks and Letters, 1956–1971*, ed. Stuart Schram (New York: Pantheon, 1975), p. 65; Charles R. Roll Jr. and K. C. Yeh, "Balance in Coastal and Inland Industrial Development," in *China: A Reassessment of the Economy*, ed. Joint Economic Committee of the United States Congress (Washington, D.C.: Government Printing Office, 1981), pp. 82–84.
15. "Tilted policies" (*qing xie shi zhengce*) under the Sixth and Seventh Five-Year Plans included (1) state appropriations, loans, and subsidies; (2) foreign exchange retention policies; (3) smaller revenue remittances; (4) price scissors between industrial (coastal) and primary (inland) products; (5) greater financial freedoms; and (6) higher incomes for residents of the open cities. See Xu Changming, "Guanyu 'qinxieshi quyu' jingji zhengce sikao" [Reflections on the tilted-style regional economic policy], *Jingji wenti tansuo* [Explorations in economic issues] 1 (1989): 21–25. I thank C. Cindy Fan, who sent me a copy of the article.

Table 2.1   Pattern of Spatial Exemptions, 1979–2000

Date	Policy
January 1979	4 SEZs
May 1980	Opening of Guangdong and Fujian Provinces
May 1984	14 OCCs with ETDZs
February 1985	Opening 3 river deltas
March 1988	Expanding open coastal economic area
April 1988	Hainan established as fifth SEZ
Fall 1988	Establishment of Haidian high-tech development zone as an experimental zone in Beijing
June 1990	Opening of Pudong (deepened in July 1992)
March 1991	Establishment of 21 SSTC new high-tech development zones
1992	Additional 18 State Council ETDZs established
June 1992	Opening of 28 harbor cities on Yangzi River
June 1992	Opening of 14 border cities
June 1992	11 State Council tourist vacation zones established
1992–1993	Opening of 13 bonded warehouses
March 1993	Establishment of another 27 SSTC NHTDZs
1994–1996	Inland regions receive greater authority in approving FDI
March 2000	Investors in Western China get special tax breaks under the Western China Development Strategy

Note: ETDZ, economic and technical development zone; FDI, foreign direct investment; NHTDZ, new high-technology development zone; OCCs, open coastal cities; SEZ, special economic zone; SSTC, State Science and Technology Commission.

international resources and markets in the 1960s and 1970s to grow rapidly, China decided to open up to foreign investment.[16] And because they were more accessible to world markets, were the ancestral home to millions of overseas Chinese whose capital and knowledge were critical for the success of the open policy, and were not home to many state-owned enterprises (SOEs) that could not compete globally, coastal areas in south China were deregulated first.

As table 2.1 shows, spatial deregulation followed a consistent wavelike process in which, despite subsequent retrenchments, the overall trend always spiraled outward.[17] Why? First, despite Deng's belief that China needed to open up if it were to survive, conservatives wanted to protect China's sovereignty and the prerogatives of the central administration, while bureaucrats, the implementers of reform, preferred administrative

16. According to Gu Mu, Deng Xiaoping had recognized the need for this policy change in 1975, but the Gang of Four had prevented him from pursuing this strategy. See Gu Mu, "Opening Up to the World—A Strategic Decision to Make China Strong and Prosperous," *Kaifang* 9 (8 September 1985): 2–8, reprinted in *Foreign Broadcast Information Service* (hereafter *FBIS*), no. 197 (10 October 1985): K1–10.

17. For an excellent chronology of China's opening, see Jude Howell, *China Opens Its Door: The Politics of Economic Transition* (Boulder: Lynne Reinner Publishers, 1993), pp. 44–124.

controls over market transactions.[18] Some reformers may have wanted to exchange transnational linkages for provincial political fealty.[19] Zhao Ziyang and Hu Yaobang probably believed that the benefits of global markets would generate support for the opening among closed or inward-looking localities, gradually undermining institutional resistance to globalization. Moreover, they preferred to test the waters before moving forward, creating what Zhao reportedly called "small environments" (*xiao huanjing*) of reform.[20] Second, because central leaders made new concessions, opening more localities than had been announced initially, or new promises that localities turned down this time would be granted exemptions in subsequent rounds of internationalization, the localities were encouraged to prepare themselves for subsequent phases of spatial deregulation. Third, organizations and interests created during an opening phase served as a bulwark against excessive retrenchment;[21] for example, while six thousand new local foreign trade companies (FTCs) emerged in 1987–88, the five thousand that survived the subsequent crackdown had strong interests in maintaining the newly established regulations on trade liberalization. And finally, reformers always resolved most unintended consequences of internationalization before they could trigger a major crackdown. As the neoliberal or global market hypothesis predicts, trade liberalization and investment in infrastructure such as harbors, roads, and zones lowered transaction costs, increased foreign investment and trade, and enriched bureaucrats in coastal regions. As a result, reformers could easily declare each phase of the opening a success. A brief historical outline of the major initiatives deregulating China's institutional constraints on global transactions follows.

DEREGULATING CHINA'S URBAN CENTERS

Despite a minor reference to opening to the outside world in the documents of the historic Third Plenum of December 1978, the first major deregulation occurred in July 1979, when the central government granted Guangdong and Fujian provinces special economic policies—in particular, tax breaks and special foreign trade privileges—and at the same time opened four SEZs. Although some analysts see this opening as the result of pressures by southern leaders in Guangdong Province, Yang Shangkun and

18. Robert Kleinberg, *China's "Opening" to the Outside World: The Experiment with Foreign Capitalism* (Boulder: Westview Press, 1990); David Bachman, "Differing Views of China's Post-Mao Economy: The Ideas of Chen Yun, Deng Xiaoping, and Zhao Ziyang," *Asian Survey* 26 (March 1986): 292–321; Joseph Fewsmith, *Dilemmas of Reform in China* (Armonk: M. E. Sharpe, 1994).
19. Susan L. Shirk, *The Political Logic of Economic Reform* (Berkeley: University of California Press, 1992).
20. Interview BXPL-92, 1992.
21. Howell, *China Opens Its Door.*

Xi Zhongxun, then vice-governors of Guangdong Province, were both close allies of Deng Xiaoping, who had been farmed out to the provinces during the Cultural Revolution.[22] Also during this period, Jiang Zemin and Zhu Rongji, who would manage the opening in the 1990s, went overseas on a study tour funded by the UNDP to visit export-processing zones in Ireland, Sri Lanka, and South Korea.

Although several new laws were introduced over the next few years, such as the joint venture law, the next major opening occurred in spring 1984. In summer 1983, Premier Zhao Ziyang had been alarmed by a report by his advisor Huan Xiang, outlining the enormous technological gap that was emerging between China and the West.[23] And although an attack on spiritual pollution from conservative forces in fall 1983 temporarily derailed his plans, Zhao used the failure of that campaign and a visit to the SEZs by Deng and several senior leaders in spring 1984 to pass the opening of fourteen coastal cities.[24] Twelve of the fourteen cities were granted economic and technical development zones (ETDZs) with more preferential policies than the OCCs nearby. Although the original plan was to open five cities, central leaders, under provincial pressures, increased the number to fourteen.[25] The following February, central policy directives opened the Yangzi River delta, the Min and Li Rivers in Fujian, and the entire Pearl River delta, allowing FDI into many parts of rural China.[26] Official discourse at that time reinforced the belief that future deregulation would follow; the announcement of the opening of these river deltas described this event as occurring under the "new conditions of further carrying out reform and opening" (*zai jinyibu shixing gaige yu kaifang de xin xingshi xia*). At that time leaders in the Liaodong and Shandong peninsulas, who had been promised and then denied foreign trade and investment exemptions, received assurances that in time their regions, too, would receive benefits similar to the three river deltas.[27]

In November–December 1987, Zhao Ziyang, the new general secretary of the Chinese Communist Party (CCP), detailed his Coastal Development

22. George Crane, *The Political Economy of China's Special Economic Zones* (Armonk: M. E. Sharpe, 1990).
23. Carol Lee Hamrin, *China and the Challenge of the Future* (Boulder: Westview Press, 1990).
24. Zeng Jianhui, "The Birth of an Important Decision: A New Step in Opening the Country to the World," *Liaowang* 24 (11 June 1984), as reported in *Nanfang ribao* [Nanfang daily], 11 June 1984, reprinted in *FBIS*, no. 118 (18 June 1984): K1–7.
25. Hamrin, *China and the Challenge*, p. 83.
26. "Notification about the Approval of the Minutes from the Meeting Concerning the Districts of the Yangzi River and Pearl River Delta and the Min and Li River Delta, February 18, 1985," in Legal Work Committee of the Standing Committee of the National People's Congress, ed. *Yanhai, yanjiang, yanbian kaifang falu fagui ji guifanxing wenjian huibian* [Compendium of documents concerning the laws, regulations, and standardization of the opening of the coastal, riverine, and border regions] (Beijing: Falu chubanshe, 1992) (hereafter Yanhai compendium), pp. 307–15.
27. Ibid., p. 309.

Strategy. This policy created thousands of foreign trade companies with the authority and financial incentives (based on a quota system) to increase the flow of goods and services in and out of China.[28] In 1988, the new province of Hainan was declared the fifth SEZ, and more cities and rural areas in Jiangsu, Shandong, Hebei, Fujian, and Zhejiang provinces; Tianjin Municipality; and border regions in Liaoning and Guizhou provinces received the same preferential policies as areas opened in 1985.[29] The result was a much closer link between coastal rural China and the international economy, both in exports and in JV formation.

Despite high tensions between China and the West after the June 4, 1989, crackdown, China's internationalization continued apace, and, in fact, even before Deng's famous southern trip of January 1992, China began to lay the foundation for a zone fever and a dramatic nationwide explosion in the number of export zones and high-tech development zones (HTDZs). In April 1990, to make amends for limiting Shanghai's level of internationalization in the previous decade, Pudong District in eastern Shanghai was declared a special open zone. Different than any other zone, the Pudong New District was to house financial, free trade, and HTDZs and become the focus of China's reform for the next decade. The central government promised to pour in 10 billion RMB. City officials all over China were aghast, fearful that Pudong would suck up all the new foreign and domestic capital. Suddenly many municipalities created Taiwan investment zones in response to the increased inflow of Taiwanese capital. This pro-Taiwan frenzy stalled when the State Council's Tax Bureau criticized this trend, but it reemerged in 1992.[30] Two years later, Pudong received even more important preferential policies to aid its role as the "dragon's head" for the entire Yangzi River, whose twenty-eight ports, running all the way upriver to Sichuan Province, were opened in June 1992.[31] Also thirteen border zones in interior provinces were established to attract investment from the rest of China.

In 1988, the State Science and Technology Commission (SSTC), hoping to expand its *guanxi* (relationships) and promote technological innovation,

28. Dali Yang, "China Adjusts to the World Economy: The Political Economy of China's Coastal Development Strategy," *Pacific Affairs* 64 (spring 1991): 42–64.
29. "Guowuyuan guanyu kuoda yanhai jingji kaifang qu fanwei de tongzhi" (State Council notification concerning expanding the sphere of the open coastal economic region) 18 March 1988, Yanhai compendium, pp. 316–18.
30. Zhang Jianxiu, "Zhongguo xin yilun kaifang qian zai shenme wenti" [What is the potential problem in China's next round of opening?], *Guang zhao jing* [Wide mirror—Hong Kong], in *Editor and Translator's Reference Journal* 1 (1991): 2–5.
31. See B. Michael Frolic, "China's Second Wave of Development: The Yangtze River Region," (paper prepared for the Canadian International Development Agency, January 1994); J. Bruce Jacobs and Lijian Hong, "Shanghai and the Lower Yangzi Valley," in *China Deconstructs: Politics, Trade and Regionalism*, ed. David S. G. Goodman and Gerald Segal (London: Routledge, 1994), pp. 224–52. The government policy is contained in Central Document No. 4, June 1992, cited in Yang, *Beyond Beijing*.

introduced new HTDZs (*xin gao jishu kaifaqu*), with tax breaks for imports, exports, and new products. By recognizing Beijing's Zhongguancun District as an official test point for these high-tech zones, the SSTC and the State Council declared a new form of spatial deregulation. Suddenly, ninety cities in China established local high-tech zones and began lobbying the SSTC to grant them national status. The SSTC lacked the authority to grant tax exemptions on foreign investment and imports; in March 1991, the State Council, which did, formally endowed twenty-seven high-tech zones with the same regulatory exemptions possessed by the ETDZs in the OCCs.[32] And although in 1991 the State Council's Special Economic Zone Office (SEZO) rejected the high-tech zones in twenty-five cities, in spring 1993 it granted another twenty-seven zones national status.[33]

Between 1990 and 1992, the center established thirteen bonded warehouses. Usually set up in ETDZs or in the harbors of OCCs, these zones allowed goods to be imported, reprocessed, and then reexported completely duty free.[34] In this same period, it also allowed eleven localities to set up State Council tourist vacation zones. The final breakdown of open areas and their regional distribution can be seen in table 2.2.

In 1994–96, a heated debate began over preferential policies.[35] According to Yang, by the late 1980s, the pro-coast regional strategy was "suspect—intellectually, morally and politically."[36] So as China's leaders debated the Ninth Five-Year Plan, inland regions began to demand a concrete redirection of the pro-coast policies. In 1994–95, proposals were floated for opening SEZs in western China. And although President Jiang tried to close down the debate, asserting that the center would not change its policies,[37] many economists criticized the favoritism shown to the coast. In particular, the outspoken economist Hu Angang argued that the preferential policies exacerbated regional inequality and created "privileged cliques and groups with vested interests" who opposed dismantling these preferential policies.[38] By fall 1995, after a heated defense of SEZ policy by political authorities in Shenzhen, the central government, in particular President Jiang Zemin, decided both to maintain SEZ privileges until at least 2000, but also to allow inland provinces much greater leeway in authorizing FDI. In the eyes of some analysts, however, the Ninth Five-Year

32. Erik Baark, "China's New High Technology Development Zones: The Politics of Commercializing Technology, 1982–1992," *Washington Journal of Modern China* 2 (spring–summer 1994): 83–102.
33. Wang Yong, "Hi-Tech Research Gets Sales Power," *China Daily*, 13 March 1993, p. 2.
34. Li Rongxia, "Free Trade Zones in China," *Beijing Review* (2–8 August 1993): 14–19.
35. The discussion here draws heavily on Yang, *Beyond Beijing*, pp. 117–20.
36. Ibid., p. 86.
37. See *People's Daily*, 23 June 1994, p. 1, cited ibid, p. 120.
38. Hu Angang, "Why I Am for 'No Preferential Treatment' for Special Economic Zones," *Ming bao*, 23 August 1995, reprinted in *FBIS*, no. 188 (28 September 1995): 39.

Table 2.2   State Council–Approved Open Zones, Cities, and Regions, 1995

Zones	Coastal	Central	Western	Total
Bonded free trade zones	13	0	0	13
SEZs	5	0	0	5
ETDZs	28	4	1	33
New HTDZs	29[a]	14	9	52
State Council tourist vacation zones	10	0	1	11
TOTAL	85	18	11	114

Cities and Regions	Coastal	Central	Western	Total
Open coastal cites	14	0	0	14
Open coastal areas (cities and counties)	260	0	0	260
Open river valley cities	0	5	1	6
Open border-region areas	2	5	6	13
Open provincial capitals	2	8	8	18
TOTAL	278	18	15	311

Source: Dali Yang, *Beyond Beijing: Liberalization and the Regions in China* (New York: Routledge, 1997), p. 31; Ding Lu and Zhimin Tang, *State Intervention and Business in China: The Role of Preferential Policies* (Cheltenham, UK: Edward Elgar, 1997), pp. 42–43.
Note: ETDZs, economic and technical development zones; HTDZs, high-technology development zones; SEZs, special economic zones.
[a] Includes Pudong New District, Taiwan Investment District in Xiamen, and Suzhou Industrial Park.

Plan promulgated in 1996 took significant benefits away from the coastal regions.[39]

    Finally, in summer 2000, Jiang Zemin travelled to Xian to unveil his Western Region Development Strategy. Aimed at resolving the vast inequalities created by two decades of tilted development, it gave preferential policies to coastal and foreign firms who invested in the inland regions. It promised to enhance the quality of infrastructure in the western and interior provinces. Whether these policies have begun to narrow the gap or speed up the pace of western development remains unclear. But at least the state finally decided to end the regulatory discrimination that had so complicated development away from the coast.

    Throughout this process, the central leaders always displayed a willingness to continue to expand the categories of deregulated areas and the number of localities eligible under each category. During his 1984 trip to the SEZs, Deng stressed that the guiding thought behind openness and the SEZs was not to "reign in" (*shou*) but was to "let things go" (*fang*).[40] Particularly when the political initiative shifted to advocates of radical reform,

39. Lu and Tang, *State Intervention and Business in China*, p. 52.
40. For an analysis of the open policy that focuses on *fang* and *shou*, see Richard Baum, *Burying Mao* (Princeton: Princeton University Press, 1994). The Deng Xiaoping quote is on page 165.

such as Zhao and Hu Yaobang, and as long as they could convince Deng that the benefits of moving forward were greater than the risks, these central leaders drove this process forward. Localities understood this policy dynamic and during periods of retrenchment drew up local plans, mobilized local resources, and prepared the groundwork for the subsequent round of deregulation. In fact, SEZO, the office responsible for recommending which localities were appropriate for internationalization, invested a great deal of time preparing closed areas for the openness all cities desired.[41] Following the strategy of "building nests to attract birds" (*zuo ying yin niao*), entrepreneurial officials at all levels of the system, instead of waiting for the "birds" (foreigners) to appear, created the "nests" (the conditions for openness within zones), and then lobbied the central government to grant them the preferential policies that went with it. The result was a policy dynamic that was centrally administered but was at the same time driven by strong local demand for the deregulation of China's global linkages.

Demand for Internationalization:
Constraints and Opportunities under Segmented Deregulation

Why were cities so interested in internationalization? Under China's Sixth, Seventh, and Eighth Five-Year Plans, which promoted export-oriented development, cities that could claim that their development promoted exports could also demand resources from the central and provincial governments. Internationalization increased the sale price of a key commodity and source of government revenue—land. Internationalization freed cities from administrative, political, and economic constraints that limited economic activities. Internationalized cities had greater flexibility over domestic labor, land, and raising domestic capital. Lower tax rates and lower transaction costs in managing foreign commerce attracted investments from other regions. In sum, while other areas functioned within the planned economy, those who could gain the preferential policies that came with internationalization were very well positioned to undergo rapid economic growth.

Urban officials faced enormous administrative constraints as they tried to promote economic development. Efforts at urban renewal, industrial restructuring, transnational linkages, and economic expansion needed the approval of supralocal authorities who had their own development plans.[42] Public ownership of land, rigid administrative boundaries among communities, and tight links between a locality's GNP and its cadre's political

---

41. Interview at SEZO in Beijing, 1992.
42. Leeds, "Locality Power."

status also restricted the redistricting needed for urbanization. Internationalization offered cities myriad ways to bypass these institutional constraints.

A locality's status (whether province, prefect/municipality, county-level city, or rural county and still part of the countryside) impinged directly on its economic development. Rigid guidelines determined the level of government with which local leaders could negotiate for resources, funds, projects, or policies, affecting what one Chinese observer called their *mendao* (gates and roads).[43] For example, county leaders could not directly petition provincial officials; requests went through municipal or prefectural officials, who had their own views about who should have access to provincial resources. Nor could provincial officials invest directly in counties; they had to give funds to the municipal government and hope that it would forward the funds to the target county. Thus a provincial official in Jiangsu Province responsible for technology transfer told me that he had been unable to establish any project in Zhangjiagang because the municipality in which Zhangjiagang was situated, Suzhou, redirected provincial funds to other counties under its domain with which it had closer ties.[44] But when internationalization raised Zhangjiagang's status, making it a county-level city and a line item in the provincial budget, direct exchanges between the province and Zhangjiagang could ensue. Similarly, after becoming OCCs in 1984, several cities were elevated in the urban hierarchy and became line items on the national budget, which allowed them to sidestep their provincial governments and lobby Beijing directly for investment funds.

Open cities often had access to higher quality and more talented personnel who could promote the city's development. Some OCCs, such as Dalian and Qingdao, were sent "high-flying" mayors, often the sons of high officials, who had better access to other high-ranking officials and investment capital.[45] Also, although by the mid-1980s, most cities could add few formal posts, the open cities, official zones, and new harbors received expanded establishments (*bianzhi*) and higher salaries for their staff, which attracted talented and entrepreneurial officials.

Whereas formal regional plans restricted urban leaders' economic strategies, internationalization offered new avenues for development. In the late 1970s, regional planners' designs influenced each city's development trajectory, affecting their projected population, territory, finances, energy and resource allocations, and influenced their developmental label. These plans limited the amount of agricultural land a city could requisition

---

43. Interview TJZWCAM, 1994.
44. Interview JSPPC, 1992.
45. Jae Ho Chung, "Preferential Policies, Muncipal Leadership, and Development Strategies: A Comparative Analysis of Qingdao and Dalian," in *Cities in China: Recipes for Economic Development in the Reform Era*, ed. Jae Ho Chung (London: Routledge, 1999), pp. 105–40.

for urban development; development labels, albeit informal, defined a city's industrial structure and the sectors in which it could get loans and government assistance. Thus urban officials always preferred labels that "increased their independence and made the upper levels give them more 'policies'—that is, raise their status."[46] In particular, cities preferred that some international aspect be incorporated into their label to help the city expand its territory, population, and industrial base and attract funds from other levels of government.

Acquiring public land and redrawing administrative boundaries had very high transaction costs. The number of officials and units needed to approve such transfers was problematic, and into the 1990s the lack of land markets meant that "good connections and practical political considerations" influenced which units could buy land.[47] Similarly, the administrative system demarcating communities complicated urban development. Each community's GNP determined its tax base, its leaders' relative political prestige, and its informal status, which in turn affected its access to other financial resources. Also, cities needed industry to create new jobs. Thus, any effort by community leaders at territorial redistricting confronted fierce resistance from neighboring communities or supralocal authorities who feared losing some of their GNP.

However, a jump in status put more land into a community's long-term plan and increased the probability that higher-level officials would approve land requisitions. When the Pukou district government that was to house Nanjing's HTDZ held out for a higher price per hectare, the Nanjing Land Administration Bureau told it to either sell the land to the HTDZ at a fair price or be denied the permit it needed to build new offices beside the zone.

Open cities or zones could more easily invest their own taxes in urban infrastructure. As previously mentioned, counties only retained 3 percent of their fiscal revenues for local construction, but county-level cities kept 8 percent.[48] Although, in general, cities could not float bonds to raise money from their citizens, they could do so if the funds went toward building a formal development zone.

Selling land or its use rights to foreigners for hard currency helped cities' infrastructure development. According to C. Y. Chang, SEZs used land "as a resource to attract capital for development expenses which could not be obtained from the central government."[49] In fact, much of the

---

46. Interview ZJGCXGHJS, 1991.
47. The World Bank, *China: Urban Land Management in an Emerging Market Economy* (Washington, D.C.: World Bank, 1993), p. 96, n. 3.
48. Jacobs, "Uneven Development."
49. C. Y. Chang, "Bureaucracy and Modernization: A Case Study of the Special Economic Zones in China," in *China's Special Economic Zones: Policies, Problems and Prospects*, ed. Y. C. Jao and C. K. Leung (Hong Kong: Oxford University Press, 1986), p. 115.

capital flowing into newly opened cities and SEZs targeted real estate, whose returns on investment far exceeded those in industry, commerce, and transport. Why? Because the potential of foreign interest in land increased the price of land in the domestic market as well.[50]

If a project might attract FDI, its priority rose and community leaders were motivated to make previously difficult decisions. For years, traffic jams had made crossing the Nanjing Bridge during rush hour hellish. Despite constant complaints, neither the city nor the province had earmarked funds for the project. But then Japanese businessmen from Sony and Fujitsu decided not to invest in the Pukou HTDZ because of the traffic problems. This decision "caused a big stir in the city," so "when the management committee met in September 1991 . . . a committee member responsible for urban transport said that the city had to solve the bridge [problem]. The committee decided on two strategies, improve the bridge's management and expand its size."[51] The management committee, with top officials from the city's bureaus, suddenly found 120–50 million RMB to build a new bridge, while a provincial vice-governor, also a member of the zone's leadership small group, committed provincial funds as well.

Instruments that eased transnational exchanges came to communities that were internationalized. Export licenses, import powers, export quotas, overseas travel, and international shipping lines, all distributed by government bureaus, were more available to deregulated cities, particularly second-level cities, which were usually allowed to establish independent import-export companies. These instruments became marketable commodities that could be sold for cash or bartered for goods or future considerations. Such instruments improved a community's comparative advantage in trade and investment, particularly when others did not possess them.

Firms in national ETDZs increased control over their own funds and paid less in taxes to their central ministries. In Nantong's ETDZ, domestic firms paid 15 percent, the same tax rate as foreign firms, far less than the 55 percent they would have paid outside the zone. In Qingdao's zone, industrial enterprises paid 30 percent of their original taxes (or 16.5 percent), while nonindustrial firms paid 60 percent of their original tax (or 33 percent). Enterprise managers were given the flexibility to keep money in their own hands by setting up legal *xiao jingku* (small coffers).[52] And although the precise definition of this flexibility was unclear, people tested

50. Profit rates in Shenzhen in 1983 for foreign-invested enterprises were 15.2, 16.1, and 18.3 percent in industry, commerce, and transport, respectively; real estate profits were 49 percent. C. H. Chai, "The Economic System of a Special Economic Zone in China," in *China's Special Economic Zones: Policies, Problems and Prospects*, ed. Y. C. Jao and C. K. Leung (Hong Kong: Oxford University Press, 1986), p. 145.
51. Interview ODPukou3, 1992.
52. Interview TJZWCAM, 1994.

its legal boundaries by spending money and then seeing if customs agents approved how it was used. According to a zone director:

> Within the cities, regulations limit how government officials use money on banquets, cars, or gifts. . . . But in zones we do that legally. . . . They call that "giving flexible power to do a lot of things." You need it to deal with foreign investors. We call that "international habit or custom" (*guoji guanli*) [*guan*, "custom"; *li*, "example"]. But it [an internal document] didn't say what kind of flexibility we had, so you can create that. At the beginning some inspection committees asked why I did that, so I explained, but gradually they took it for granted . . . that I would do it.[53]

The thirty ministries that set up shop in the Yantai zone reportedly could use their money more freely there than in Beijing, where they needed ministerial approval. In Tianjin, industrial bureaus simply registered some factories in the zone without moving them into the zone, thereby remitting less to their ministries.[54] Interestingly, domestic Chinese firms working in Xiamen's Huli zone were more efficient in that less constrained environment than the zone's JVs, which faced a bevy of regulatory constraints.[55]

Foreign trade companies (FTCs) that moved into ETDZs increased their foreign exchange intake because FTCs functioning outside of zones had foreign exchange quotas to turn over to the Ministry of Foreign Economic Relations and Trade (MOFERT), while FTCs in ETDZs did not. By swapping their extra foreign exchange on the black market for domestic currency they could earn even more renminbi despite exporting the same product as FTCs outside the zone. Thus, the relative value of the goods they exported was greater if exported through a zone.

Zones also afforded more flexible labor policies. The freedom to hire and fire staff attracted the director of a university-owned factory to Nanjing's HTDZ. Because many domestic factories brought their old workers into the new plants, the limitations on firing workers were still in effect, but SEZs often ignored such rules, pulling in talented workers from all over the country. Overall, therefore, firms could make more money and use their resources more efficiently if they gained access to deregulated space.

---

53. Interview TJZWCAM, 1994.
54. Ibid.
55. Li Shujuan, "Improving Infrastructure: A Cost-Benefit Analysis of the Huli Zone," *China Paper* 91/2, Economics Division, Research School of Pacific Studies, Australian National University, 1991.

Hypothesis Testing

In this section, we test the key hypotheses of the book. First, we test when cities and zones in coastal China became more internationalized, whether they received a larger share of domestic resources. Second, we assess the relative weights of administrative versus market forces in affecting the pattern of China's internationalization—whether linkage opportunities pushed central, regional, and local elites to invest in projects that abetted an export-oriented economy, whether administrative forces and path dependence undermined this shift, or whether government policy in the form of segmented deregulation, which combines market and administrative forces, determined investment decisions by local government agencies and the business community. Third, we test whether the potential beneficiaries of lower barriers to trade (as predicted by the neoliberal school of international political economy) acted as an interest group and lobbied the central government to decrease regulatory constraints, or whether they adapted to the authoritarian nature of the Chinese political system and followed strategies in line with segmented deregulation.

Our analysis takes place at both the macro- and microlevel. Microlevel data rely primarily on a series of interviews conducted in several communities in southern and northern Jiangsu Province, including Nanjing, Nantong, Zhangjiagang, and Kunshan (see map 2.1). The fieldwork for these studies was supplemented by a series of detailed interviews with some zone directors in other parts of China.

DID DOMESTIC CAPITAL FLOW TO OPEN SPACES?

Logically, Chinese localities receiving preferential policies should have attracted domestic capital and labor seeking higher returns on investments or easier access to the global marketplace. Also, China's export-led growth strategy should have increased investment in harbors, roads, and telecommunications—the stuff of a modern trading state. But did the state actually increase its investment in coastal areas? Did inland regions move funds to the coast to use the coastal region's policy exemptions? Or did normative concerns about equity, path dependence, vested interests in maintaining ongoing investment flows, and the power of supralocal authorities undermine market forces and limit capital flows to these high-yield advantaged areas?

Between 1978 and 1991, the flow of cargo through China's principal ports rose at an average annual rate of 7.3 percent, and, particularly after 1983, growth rates were above 10 percent a year (see table I.1). The resulting shortage of harbor facilities triggered a crisis in 1985, and between 1985 and 1994 the number of berths capable of handling ships of 10,000 tons more than doubled, from 178 to 373. By 1999, the number was 490.

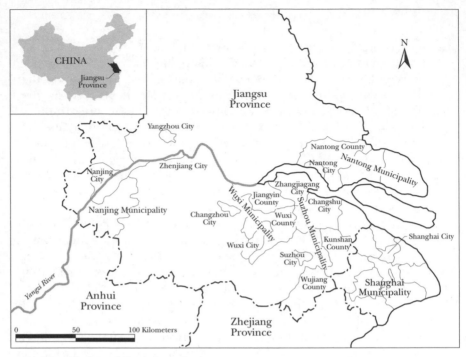

Map 2.1   Major Research Sites in Jiangsu Province

These pressures, as well as a change of policy favoring the coastal areas under the Sixth, Seventh, and Eighth Five-Year Plans led to a major shift in state investment. For example, the Sixth Five-Year Plan (1981–85), which focused on constructing harbors along the lower reaches of Yangzi,[56] allocated funds to harbors in Nantong and Zhangjiagang, in Jiangsu Province. More money poured into Jiangsu's harbors under the Seventh Five-Year Plan (1986–90) as part of a national key construction project, which included 260 million RMB for five new 10,000-ton berths at Zhangjiagang and 220 million RMB to upgrade one old berth and create three new ones at Nantong.

Thus, whereas total investment in fixed assets (TIFA) in the central and western regions during the Fifth Five-Year Plan (1976–80) was 54.2 percent of the national total, with investment in the coastal regions at only 45.8 percent (averaging only 40.6 percent between 1953 and 1980), TIFA on the coast in the first three years of the Sixth Five-Year Plan

56. Shen Wei-cheng, "Development and Problems of China's Ports," in *China's Spatial Economy*, ed. G. J. R. Linge and D. K. Forbes (Hong Kong: Oxford University Press, 1990), p. 97.

(1981–83) rose to 50.2 percent, and peaked at 55.5 percent in 1987.[57] In 1985, the ratio of TIFA to total population for coastal, central, and western China was 52:41, 31:36, and 16:23, respectively, showing that the coast received significantly more investment than its share of the population.[58] As table 2.3 shows, TIFA for the open coastal areas (the SEZs; OCCs; and open coastal provinces, OCPs) as a percent of national TIFA grew dramatically from 46.7 percent in 1983 to 56.6 percent by 1989, with the major jumps in 1984 and 1987–88, key years in the opening of coastal China.

Like vacuums, SEZs, which needed enormous infrastructure investments and were the first localities given preferential policies, sucked in domestic capital from all over China.[59] Between 1983 and 1985, TIFA for the four SEZs as a percentage of national TIFA doubled from 1.2 percent to 2.4 percent. In real terms, investment increased fourfold, jumping from 1.7 billion RMB to 6.13 billion RMB in three years. And although TIFA slumped in 1986, by 1988 it was up to 10.5 billion RMB or 2.35 percent of national TIFA. Similarly, Thomas Chan found that Shenzhen's capital construction relied "partly on the ability of the city government to solicit domestic capital, and partly on local accumulation," but not primarily on foreign investment.[60] As the largest zone with preferential policies, Shenzhen relied on domestic capital from China's interior for 89 percent of its loans.[61] If we look at annual growth rates in TIFA in 1980–85 for China's major cities, Shenzhen, Zhuhai and Xiamen—all SEZs—were in the top four, while the third, Haikou, capital of Hainan Province, another city built from nothing, was soon to become the center of China's fifth SEZ.[62] Similarly, if we look at the area of paved roads per capita in major cities in China for 1985 and 1988, Shenzhen and Zhuhai were far more built up than any other city in China, while Xiamen's growth in 1985–88 was the fastest among the ten most well-paved cities.[63]

57. Dali Yang, "Patterns of China's Regional Development Strategy," *China Quarterly* 122 (June 1990): 235; Dali Yang, "Reforms, Resources, and Regional Cleavages: The Political Economy of Coast-Interior Relations in Mainland China," *Issues and Studies* (September 1991): 53, table 4.
58. Cannon, "Regions," p. 41. I built the ratios from his table 2.1.
59. According to Li, the Xiamen-Huli zone was very overbuilt in terms of infrastructure. Li, "Improving Infrastructure." According to Crane, although SEZs were propelled by foreign investment, domestic sources formed the "second pillar" of the SEZ economy. Crane, *Political Economy*.
60. Thomas M. H. Chan, "Financing Shenzhen's Economic Development: A Preliminary Analysis of Sources of Capital Construction Investments, 1979–1984," *Asian Journal of Public Administration* 7 (December 1985): 170–97. Quotes are from p. 195.
61. Ibid.
62. Guojia tongjiju chengshi shehui jingji diaocha zong dui (The Urban Social and Economic Research Team of the State Statistical Bureau), ed., *Zhongguo chengshi sishi nian* [Forty years of China's cities] (Beijing: Zhongguo tongji ju xinxi zixun fuwu zhongxin, 1990), pp. 266–67.
63. Ibid., pp. 316–17.

The state also set great store in the fourteen OCCs, which under the Seventh Five Year Plan's three-tiered investment policy were to become "spearheads in a designated region of accelerated growth."[64] Because new technologies were to be developed there and then introduced into inland industries,[65] the center granted twelve of the fourteen OCCs the right to build ETDZs with tax-deferred status. It also loaned them over 2 billion RMB for infrastructure, as well as 5 million RMB per year per city for five years for industrial and technological upgrading.[66] OCCs also received low-interest long-term loans for capital construction.[67]

Provincial governments gave their OCCs extra funds.[68] Jiangsu Province gave Nantong and Lianyungang each 20 million RMB over four years (1986–89) and an interest-free loan of four million RMB in 1990–91. According to a Jiangsu provincial official: "No other cities in the province got this money. We had lots of places to spend money but we spent it here [Nantong and Lianyungang] because of the open policy."[69] OCCs such as Shanghai, Tianjin, and Dalian received foreign exchange loans of $300, $200, and $100 million, respectively, while other OCCs received less generous, but useful, allocations.[70]

By "borrowing ships to go out to sea," inland provinces invested heavily in coastal harbors to ensure access to berths, shipping lines, and favorable treatment for their products.[71] In 1988, Shanxi Province announced that it would invest 30 million RMB in Tianjin's port to promote its own coal exports, while Henan, Shaanxi, Gansu, and Anhui provinces constructed nine berths in Jiangsu Province's Lianyungang to guarantee berths for their exports.[72]

---

64. Yue-man Yeung and Xu-wei Hu, *China's Coastal Cities: Catalysts for Modernization* (Honolulu: University of Hawaii Press, 1992), p. 5.

65. Cannon, "Regions," p. 42.

66. Interviews at the SEZO of the Chinese State Council. According to Chen, between 1984 and 1987 the central government gave 2.33 billion RMB to the twelve ETDZs in the OCCs. See Chen Jian, "Wo guo jingji jishu kaifaqu jianshe de jige wenti," [Several problems in the construction of our country's economic and technical development zones], *Nankai xuebao: Zhixue ban* [Nankai University Journal: Philosophy], no. 4 (1989): 70–75, in *Renda ziliao: Tequ yu kaifang chengshi jingji* [People's University reference material: SEZs and open coastal cities' economies] 12 (1989): 33–38.

67. "Notes from a Meeting on Coastal Cities, 30 April 1984," in Yanhai compendium, pp. 295–306.

68. Interview TJZWCAM-1994. Liaoning Province gave Dalian 10 million RMB for its zone, while Guangdong government reportedly gave Guangzhou zone 150 million RMB.

69. Interview JIAOPPOL, 1991.

70. "Notes from a Meeting," p. 298.

71. The "four borrows" were "borrow ships to go out to sea; borrow borders to go out of the border; borrow stages to perform operas [promote business in other provinces]; and "borrow hens to lay eggs" [establish companies in SEZs]. Yang Rudai, "Several Issues on Opening up Hinterland Areas," *Renmin ribao* [People's daily], 23 August 1992, p. 2, reprinted in *FBIS*, no. 177 (11 September 1992): 60–62.

72. Chen Qu, "Inland Provinces Help Develop Ports," *China Daily*, 2 May 1988, p. 2; *Xinhua*, "Inland Provinces Invest in New Jiangsu Port," 21 September 1988, reprinted in *FBIS*, no. 185 (23 Sept. 1988): 55, respectively.

Table 2.3, however, does not show that these OCCs got larger amounts of TIFA. The most likely explanation is that although some coastal cities such as Qingdao, Dalian, and Guangzhou were quite successful, as of 1991, others such as Nantong, Beihai, and Lianyungang were not. But between 1985 and 1988, the share of TIFA in the OCPs including the fourteen cities, three river deltas, four peninsulas, and Hainan, rose 7 percent, an enormous jump in capital allocations. According to Y. Y. Kueh, their much higher rates of FDI compared to other regions "was in most cases accompanied by a remarkable implied expansion of domestic capital, compared with the average for China as a whole. The inference is that the substantial complementary domestic investment in infrastructure and other facilities needed to realize the potential available from overseas capital supplies has been forthcoming."[73]

These changes in resource allocations greatly affected regional growth rates, which explains why so many localities sought preferential policies. As table 2.4 shows, the share of gross value of industrial output (GVIO) of urban centers in the east, as a percentage of national GVIO, rose by 5.7 percent between 1984 and 1994, a remarkable shift in wealth. If we look only at the urban areas, the share of GVIO in the east grew by an astonishing 9.2 percent in just ten years. Also, the SEZ share of national GVIO grew from 0.9 to 2.4 percent for the entire municipal area and 0.9 to 2.8 percent for the urban area only. Once again, the fourteen OCCs did not meet expectations.

FDI followed the flow of regional openings under segmented deregulation. Initially FDI flooded the SEZs, but, as other parts of coastal China were opened, FDI shifted. The Yangzi River valley had only 4.9 percent of national FDI in 1991; its opening (and particularly the opening of Pudong) in 1992 redirected foreign investment. By 1994, it had become home to 29 percent of all FDI in China.[74] Similarly, the share of national FDI going into the SEZs began to drop in 1984, as other parts of the coast were opened. In 1984, it was 30 percent; by 1991, it was only 22 percent; and by 1995, it was only 11 percent.[75]

DOMESTIC STRUCTURE AND IMPEDIMENTS
TO MARKET FORCES

Macrolevel data confirm the argument that capital flowed to areas characterized by greater internationalization. Did bureaucratic forces, path dependence, and domestic structure limit or skew that flow? In the discus-

73. Y. Y. Kueh, "Foreign Investment and Economic Change in China," *China Quarterly* 131 (September 1992): 659.
74. Yang, *Beyond Beijing*, p. 91.
75. See Lu and Tang, *State Intervention and Business in China*, p. 49.

Table 2.3 Total Investment in Fixed Assets in Open Coastal Regions, 1979–1991

Year	National Total (100 million RMB)	SEZs		OCCs[a]		OCPs[a]		All Open Areas (%)
		Renminbi (100 million)	Percentage	Renminbi (100 million)	Percentage	Renminbi (100 million)	Percentage	
1979	n.a.	n.a.		—		—		
1980	910.85	n.a.		—		—		
1981	961.01	n.a.		—		—		
1982	1,230.40	n.a.		—		475.41	38.6	
1983	1,430.06	17.04	1.2	156.23	10.9	494.27	34.6	46.7
1984	1,832.87	29.27	1.6	191.45	10.4	680.57	37.1	49.2
1985	2,543.19	61.27	2.4	262.06	10.3	940.54	37.0	49.7
1986	3,019.62	51.33	1.7	303.84	10.1	1,167.77	38.7	50.4
1987	3,640.86	71.14	2.0	366.34	10.1	1,510.16	41.5	53.5
1988	4,496.54	105.47	2.3	507.51	11.3	1,907.25	42.4	56.0
1989	4,137.73	86.10	2.1	477.26	11.5	1,780.15	43.0	56.6
1990	4,449.29	92.77	2.1	463.34	10.4	1,911.52	43.0	55.5
1991	5,276.82	n.a.						

Source. Y. Y. Kueh, "Foreign Investment and Economic Change in China," *China Quarterly* 131 (September 1992): 684, table A3. Used with permission.
Note. n.a., not available; OCCs, open coastal cities; OCPs, open coastal provinces; SEZs, special economic zones.
[a] OCCs did not receive preferential policies before 1984, while the only provinces to receive special privileges before 1985 were Fujian and Guangdong provinces.

Table 2.4   Share of Gross Value of Industrial Output by Region, 1984–1994

A. Whole City (including rural areas)

Region	1984	1985	1988	1989	1990	1991	1994
East	64.1	64.0	65.0	65.3	65.7	66.7	69.8
14 OCCs	26.2	23.3	22.0	21.8	21.7	21.9	20.3
4 SEZs[a]	0.9	1.2	1.8	1.8	2.1	2.5	2.4
Central	24.8	24.2	24.3	24.1	23.6	22.9	20.9
West	11.1	11.9	10.7	10.6	10.7	10.5	9.3
TOTAL	100.0	100.0	100.0	100.0	100.0	100.0	100.0

B. Urban Areas Only

Region	1984	1985	1988	1989	1990	1991	1994
East	60.8	61.2	62.0	62.4	62.8	64.0	70.0
14 OCCs	25.0	24.6	19.7	19.1	18.7	18.5	14.5
4 SEZs[a]	0.9	1.1	1.7	1.8	2.1	2.5	2.8
Central	27.5	26.8	26.9	26.4	26.0	25.1	20.9
West	11.7	12.0	11.2	11.1	11.2	10.9	9.1
TOTAL	100.0	100.0	100.0	100.0	100.0	100.0	100.0

Source: Calculated from Chinese Statistical Bureau Research Team on Urban Society and Economy, *Statistical Yearbook of China's Cities* (Beijing: China Statistical Information Consulting and Service Center, 1985, 1990, 1995).
Note: SEZs, special economic zones; OCCs, open coastal cities.
[a] Hainan Province is not included as an SEZ in this data.

sion that follows, I address this issue from two perspectives. First, I look at the general conflicts between the emerging transnational linkage channels, such as zones and harbors, and the cities or supralocal powers above them in the urban hierarchy. Zones were a key transnational linkage channel for urban centers and could play a major role in internationalizing the city. Second, I detail the experiences of several cities in Jiangsu Province to assess the relative role of market, administration, and government policy in the process of internationalization.

Although the fourteen OCCs were able to deepen their level of internationalization through lower tax rates (24 percent) and the establishment of ETDZs (with 15 percent tax rates), powerful political and bureaucratic interests in 1984 limited their ability to maximize their interests. Most municipalities placed the zone far from the city core (table 2.5). Why did they do this? In 1984–85, at the beginning of the second wave of reform, concerns that pernicious foreign influences would pollute socialist China remained powerful. As one urban planner commented in discussing the Nantong zone, "our guiding thought was to build a separate area to cut off the influence of the foreigners and the capitalistic management systems that we expected to be used in the zone. Initially, we thought the zone

Table 2.5 Distances from Economic and Technical Development Zone to Mother Cities

Mother City	Distance to City (km)
Qinghuangdao	1
Tianjin	50
Yantai	6
Qingdao	4.2 by sea 110 by land
Lianyungang	22
Minhang (Shanghai)	30
Hongqiao (Shanghai)	6.5
Ningbo	18
Fuzhou	24
Guangzhou	35
Nantong	12

would be all foreigners. Keeping it separate would be good for management."[76] But the zone's location dramatically increased the costs of internationalization, for the city had to invest 150 million RMB on infrastructure, including 22 million RMB on the road to town and 10 million RMB on a power transformer substation. It had to borrow $40 million from the Austrian government for the water purification plant (the zone put in 20 million RMB of its own), and spend another 22 million RMB for a hotel in the zone, which nobody used. Similarly, Qingdao, which put its zone on an island, had to raise $400 million in 1993 to build a 16-kilometer bridge to link the zone to the city.[77] Thus, as of 1989, after ideological concerns had lessened, Chinese analysts called on cities to build their zones close to cut costs.[78]

City-Zone Relationship

A successful city-zone relationship needed just the right balance between autonomy and dependence. For city governments, zones were fraught with opportunity and risk. If city bureaucrats controlled the zone and the strength of the zone's property rights and corporate nature remained weak, a city could use its zone's preferential policies and linkage function to its own advantage. New jobs, higher salaries, foreign contacts, and tax breaks for new plants could strengthen the city's and its bureaus' interests. But if the zone was not given a certain degree of financial support and corporate autonomy and if the zone's internal environment was not

76. Interview, JIACGH, 1992.
77. "Shandong Using Foreign Funds for Construction," *Xinhua*, 23 October 1993, reprinted in *FBIS*, no. 205 (26 October 1993): 43.
78. Chen, "Wo guo jingji jishu kaifaqu."

more market-oriented than the nearby city, the zone would be unable to fulfill its intended function. The city would not be threatened, but neither would it benefit as much as it might have were the zone successful. But complex organizational structures, a developmental ethos, a cadre of like-minded officials, and internal and external networks could give zones their own corporate interests that could lead them to compete with the city and undermine the state's interest in controlling transnational boundaries.

Initially, most city governments dominated their development zone. The zone director was often a vice-mayor of the city and the original management committee was composed of urban officials holding co-appointments in the zone and the city government. Zones needed the city to get land from suburban governments, capital from banks, permits to float bonds, new roads, new enterprises, a labor force, and facilities such as bank branches and post offices. However, overlapping administration often translated into indecisiveness. In Nanjing's Pukou HTDZ, the management committee's general office running the zone lacked clearly demarcated authority, so no one raised funds for it.[79] Nanjing's Science and Technology Committee, functionally responsible for the zone, blocked investors whose level of scientific sophistication was too low, making it hard to raise capital.

Once up and running, the zone's level of autonomy could be a problem. Zone directors depended on urban officials for energy, water, capital, and human resources, much like SOEs. Each year the deputy director of the Tianjin zone negotiated with Tianjin's energy bureau for its energy allocation; when negotiations stalled or if a new large factory increased the zone's energy needs, the zone director had to renegotiate with the head of the economic commission or the city mayor.[80] In Nanjing, where the municipal government paid the interest on the zone's loans for infrastructure development, the new zone director advocated a continuing role for the municipality's "leadership small group for zone development."[81]

But some city officials preferred to build the technical (and export capacity) of enterprises in the city not in the zone. They channeled resources intended for the zone into older factories in the city that needed technical upgrading or capital infusion. Cities competed for new JVs, preferring to have the foreign linkage under their supervision.

The Nantong zone shows how domestic structure and path dependence undermined the development of one channel of global transaction. Under the neoliberal hypothesis, capital should flow to points of openness that

79. "Nanjing Pukou xingao jishu wai xiang xing kaifa qu jingji guihua yanjiu" [Research on the recent plan of the Nanjing Pukou high-tech externally oriented development zone], *Keji yu jingji* [Technology and economy] 3, special issue, (1991): 29–45.
80. Interview TJZWCAM, 1994.
81. Gong Zhisen, "Jia kuai Nanjing gao xin jishu kaifa qu jianshe buzhai de shixiang" [Some ideas on speeding up the pace of construction for Nanjing's new high tech zone], *Keji yu jingji* [Technology and economy] 3 (1991): 27–28, 45.

lower the costs of international business and facilitate exogenous easing.[82] However, Nantong's traditional industrial base was centered at Tang Za Town, in the city's northwest, over 30 kilometers from the ETDZ in the city's southeast corner. To reflect this spatial distribution of productive facilities, the city's development strategy under its urban plan of the 1980s was to build "a harbor city with two wings"—incorporating both the development zone in the southeast and Tang Za Town in the northwest.[83] But because the zone was composed of officials from city factories, not from the city's own bureaus, and because these zone officials sought greater autonomy from the city, municipal leaders saw the zone as a threat, not an ally or opportunity. So they neither used the zone to promote the city's development nor shifted domestic and foreign investment from the city and Tang Za Town to the ETDZ. Through the mid-1990s, the zone did not develop, nor was it promoted by the city that hosted it. Central funds allocated to Nantong for buying foreign technology and for developing JVs and new export products for the zone were used to subsidize old factories producing old products.[84] City leaders apparently felt that if the central government wanted to give money and policies to the zone, fine, but the city would not use its own funds to promote the zone.[85] SEZO officials agreed. "The city government didn't put enough emphasis on the zone, didn't get it investment, and the leadership of the zone was not very strong."[86] The city took 7 million RMB targeted for the zone to build its own Nantong Hotel, as well as another 9 million RMB for other projects. City leaders steered domestic factories and JVs to the city, not the zone, afraid that they would lose the tax base. The city failed to build a good road from the city to the zone for six years. The zone officials, confident of their comparative advantage in taxation, wanted foreigners to decide themselves where to set up shop. "Let them see our situation, only 15 percent tax, versus 24 percent tax in the city."[87]

If a development company, responsible for profits and losses and led by a strong manager, replaced the city's management committee, a relatively autonomous corporation emerged. Some urban officials preferred this, aware that government management created parasitic bureaucracies, reinforced dependence, and undermined zone entrepreneurship. Thus Yantai's ETDZ made its economic development bureau into an independent service center, turned its environmental protection bureau into a capital construction coordinating service center, and made two other public organizations into enterprises that were responsible for their own

82. Frieden and Rogowski, "Impact of the International Economy."
83. Interview with urban planning officials in Nanjing and Nantong, spring 1992.
84. Interview at SEZO, 1992.
85. Interviews with Nantong zone officials, April 1992.
86. Interview at SEZO, 1992.
87. Interview with Nantong Zone officials, 1992.

profits and losses.[88] On the other hand, until the Nanjing government turned the management committee of its Pukou zone into a nonregulatory public organization that was run on a profit incentive and empowered it to secure loans, the zone's thirty- to forty-member development committee played cards, waiting for central government largesse.[89]

Finally, the zone's status in the hierarchy of urban places affected its development. Zones that were only one-half level below the nearby city had greater freedom vis-à-vis district governments over land management, labor policy, and the approval of foreign investments than did zones that were constituted a full administrative level below the mother city. Thus Yantai's zone, ones-half level (*fu di ji*) below Yantai Municipality, was far more independent of its city government than Nantong's zone, which was a full bureaucratic level (*chu ji*) below the city.

Zhangjiagang's Harbor: Resistance to Internationalization

Zhangjiagang (originally Shazhou County), a county-level harbor city on the south side of the Yangze River whose harbor serves the cities of Wuxi and Changzhou, illustrates how domestic structure and local political and economic interests can undermine market forces and slow internationalization. Zhangjiagang's comparative advantage was its harbor. As southern Jiangsu (Sunan) developed rapidly, market opportunities based on the harbor's role as a transnational linkage channel generated an economic logic to ease the flow and lower the transaction costs of goods and services. However, supralocal powers, path dependence, and vested interests in Zhangjiagang slowed the harbor's growth and the flow of goods and services toward it.

Zhangjiagang's development was deeply affected by its status in Suzhou Municipality. Because Suzhou sent its goods out through Shanghai (see map 2.1) and the province often discussed moving Zhangjiagang under Wuxi's administration control, Suzhou had no incentive to spend a penny there. Why? With Zhangjiagang on board, Wuxi's gross national income (GNI) and its informal political status would surpass that of Suzhou.[90] So

---

88. See Yu Moying, "Jiehe zishen tedian, tansuo ziji de fazhan moshi" [Unite the independent characteristics, discuss one's own model of development], *Duiwai jingji maoyi* [Foreign Trade: Tianjin] 1 (1988): 31–33, in *Renda ziliao: Tequ yu kaifang chengshi jingji* [People's University Reference Material: SEZs and Open Cities Economies] 7 (1988): 51–53.

89. According to Yi-min Lin, *shiye danwei*, a legacy of the central planning era, used to refer to nonregulatory and nonprofit public institutions (such as hospitals, schools, newspapers, publishing houses, and opera troupes). Both rules have been broken in the reform era, making it an anachronism; only a relatively small number of them have taken on regulatory functions, whereas most have become profit-making entities and do not necessarily remain in the public sector. Personal communication, 27 April 2000.

90. Suzhou's 1990 GNI was 17.884 billion RMB, and Wuxi's GNI was 13.474 billion RMB. If Zhangjiagang, whose GNI in 1990 was 2.444 billion RMB shifted from Suzhou's administration to Wuxi's, Suzhou's GNI would drop to 15.440 billion RMB while Wuxi's would rise to 15.918 billion RMB. See Jiangsu Statistical Bureau, *Jiangsu tongji nianjian, 1991* (Nanjing: China Statistical Publishing House, 1991), p. 331.

Suzhou ignored Zhangjiagang and channeled funds, technology, and business opportunities to nearby Wu, Changshu, and Wujiang counties.

Provincial officials wanted to develop Zhangjiagang according to their interests. During a December 1984 visit, Zhao Ziyang called for a harbor city that could "attract external funds and make internal linkages (*wai yin nei lian*)" and become a major distribution center for import and export products for the lower reaches of the Yangzi River.[91] A national harbor would receive national funding and free the province from paying Shanghai for the use of its docks. So in 1985, a retired vice-governor suggested building a town of 300,000 at the harbor to serve as the "major doorway to the outside world for Suxichang" (Suzhou, Wuxi and Changzhou).[92]

But if Zhangjiagang's harbor became part of an independent city, Suzhou would lose more of its GNI. So, Suzhou wanted to keep Zhangjiagang and its harbor within its administrative boundaries, but did not want the harbor or Zhangjiagang to develop quickly. "After several reports we could see that they couldn't see the importance of the project, and that they had a much different viewpoint from the province. They simply didn't do a good job. They send all their export products through Shanghai, so they didn't need this harbor to be developed."[93] So the province's own planning group proposed a new second-level city and insisted that new industries be established in the town beside the harbor.

Leaders in Zhangjiagang opposed this plan because if the county government seat moved from Yangshe Town (the current county seat) to the new Harbor Town, government employees would have to move too, or travel 18 kilometers each day. Also if factories moved to Harbor Town, job creation in Yangshe Town would not keep pace with the expanding labor pool and county officials could have more difficulty getting their children factory jobs. Zhangjiagang had just spent 700 million RMB rebuilding Yangshe Town, another disincentive for moving all the buildings to the harbor. Townships in Zhangjiagang feared that a zone built at the harbor

91. For Zhao's comments see Wu Zhengxin, "Work Report to the Meeting Celebrating the 20th Anniversary of the Establishment of the Harbor," in *Jiaotongbu Zhangjiagang gangwu guanli ju, jian gang ershi zhounian zhuanluo* [Ministry of Transport, Zhangjiagang Harbor Management Bureau, special edition to celebrate the 20th anniversary of the establishment of the harbor], ed. Zhangjiagang gangwu guanli ju [Zhangjiagang's Harbor Management Bureau], May 1988, p. 12. Wu Zhengxin is director of the Zhangjiagang Harbor Management Bureau.

92. Interview JIACGH, 1992.

93. Ibid. For a criticism of Suzhou's 1985 report, see Lu Dazhuang, "Jiakuai jianshe, chongfen fahui Zhangjiagang gang de youshi he zuoyong" [Speed up construction and fully use Zhangjiagang harbor's advantages and utility], in *Jiaotongbu Zhangjiagang gangwu guanli ju, jian gang ershi zhounian zhuanluo* [Ministry of Transport, Zhangjiagang Harbor Management Bureau, special edition to celebrate the 20th anniversary of the establishment of the harbor], ed. Zhangjiagang gangwu guanli ju [Zhangjiagang's Harbor Management Bureau], May 1988, pp. 13–15.

would suck up all the factories and JVs. So Suzhou and Shazhou County officials asked provincial planners to delete the idea of creating a pro-vincial-level city from their proposal to the State Council.[94] The planners refused. Nevertheless, when the State Council elevated Shazhou County to Zhangjiagang City in 1986, the capital was not moved to the harbor as the provintial planners had recommended.

In a 1988 speech heralding the twentieth anniversary of the harbor, the deputy chair of the Zhangjiagang Harbor Commission suggested that Zhangjiagang officials were not giving the harbor the attention that higher-level authorities expected: "The whole city, from top to bottom, must clearly understand the leading ideas behind 'letting the harbor construct the city, and letting the city promote the harbor' (*yi gang jian shi, yi shi cu gang*), and they must focus most of their work on Zhangjiagang's harbor district, and put the task of constructing the harbor in an important position."[95] He called on Zhangjiagang officials to invest time, energy, and funds promoting the harbor and to set aside their local interests to promote the greater good—the harbor: "Whether in human effort, mate-rial, or financial strength, it must be incorporated into the plans of units and ministries, to manage the relationship between the city and the harbor, assertively serve harbor construction, end arguments over trifles, be of one mind, unify efforts, and speed up the installation of a complete system to meet the needs of the harbor development even more rapidly."[96] Yet, until 1992 when a new party secretary came to power in Zhangjiagang, leaders invested more time, energy, and funds in Yangshe Town than in Harbor Town.[97]

Nantong: Market Forces Increase after Deng's Southern Trip

Although domestic structure had slowed the process of international-ization, the political climate that emerged following Deng's southern trip lifted many of the administrative constraints, both institutionally and psy-chologically, that had limited the flow of resources to open spaces in the localities. Market forces and the need to increase the pace of economic development truly liberated the thinking of many local officials and led urban leaders to place greater emphasis on promoting their transnational linkage channels.

---

94. Interview ZJGCXGHJS, 1991.
95. Yang Shoukai, "Yi gang xing cheng, yi cheng cu gang: ba Zhangjiagang shi jiancheng xiandaihua de gangko chengshi" [Let the harbor develop the city and the city promote the harbor: Turning Zhangjiagang City into a modern port city], in *Jiaotongbu Zhangjiagang gangwu guanli ju, jian gang ershi zhounian zhuanluo* [Ministry of Transport, Zhangjiagang Harbor Management Bureau, special edition to celebrate the 20th anniversary of the estab-lishment of the harbor], ed. Zhangjiagang gangwu guanli ju [Zhangjiagang's Harbor Man-agement Bureau], May 1988, p. 24. (Author's translation.)
96. Ibid. (Author's translation.)
97. Interviews in Zhangjiagang, June 1997.

In Nantong, where leaders had hesitated to promote their zone, the economy picked up after the city redirected investment towards the river, the zone, and the harbor.[98] In June 1992, new city leaders revised the city's spatial development plan as "taking the harbor as the forward position and using the old city as the base."[99] They built a new road between the city and zone and created five development centers in the southeast part of the city to help develop the ETDZ. They also began plans for a bonded warehouse, although that lobbying effort failed. Many companies from around the province put in their own harbors, which brought new business to the city. Analysts had long argued that Nantong needed to use the harbor to promote industrial development;[100] and the boom created by Pudong and the 1992 opening of the Yangzi River finally increased opportunities for using the harbor and the city's riverine status to promote the city's growth.

Although Nantong's development pace remained average for China as a whole, it sped up dramatically after 1992 as did the rest of the country. As table 2.6 shows, GNP between 1978 and 1994 increased at an average annual rate of 12.6 percent per year, above the national average, and Nantong got its share of the contracted FDI boom that hit China after 1992, almost doubling between 1992 and 1993 and jumping again in 1994–95. Used FDI also grew at a steady pace, increasing almost sevenfold in 1992–96. As for exports, their dollar value increased 20.4 percent per year in 1988–94, but increased fourfold in 1992–96. Moreover, exports as a percentage of GDP jumped from 18.1 percent in 1993 to 32.4 percent in 1994, although it hovered around 25 percent in both 1995 and 1996.[101]

But despite its harbor and zone, Nantong's level of internationalization was shallow before 1992. Constraints, path dependence, and weak leadership limited Nantong from fully using the opportunities granted to it as one of China's fourteen OCCs. Its location on the north side of the Yangzi River, across from one of the fastest growing centers in China, created great competition for Nantong. Its harbor and airport were held back by supralocal authorities. Nor was its hinterland conducive to industrial restructuring.

98. See Shen Shuxin and Li Shaobing, "Jianshe xiandaihua xin chengqu: Nantong kaifa qu tiaozheng fazhan zhanlue liang nian shu yao" [Build a new modern urban district: The two-year results of Nantong zone's revised development strategy], *Waijing daobao* [Foreign Economic Report] (May 1995): 14–15.
99. Ibid.
100. Ceng Shougu, "Nantong gang de xingqi he Nantong shi de fazhan zhanlue" [The rise of Nantong harbor and the development strategy of Nantong city], *Jingji dili* [Economic geography] 8 (1988): 46–51.
101. Much of the local data remain suspect as local cadres face enormous pressure to inflate the numbers. See Yongshun Cai, "Between State and Peasant: Local Cadres and Statistical Reporting in Rural China," *China Quarterly* 163 (September 2000): 783–805. Overall trends are more reliable, although sudden leaps of 50 percent in output, exports, or sales are usually responses to the need of the upper levels to prove that a new policy is having positive results, rather than real events.

Table 2.6 Nantong Municipality Production, Trade, and Investment Data, 1978–1996

	GNP^a (100 million RMB)	GVIO^b (billion RMB)	Export^c Purchases (100 million RMB)	FDI (million \$)^d Contracted	FDI (million \$)^d Used	Foreign Trade (million \$)^e Exports	Foreign Trade (million \$)^e Imports
1978	27.85	5.04					
1984	53.50	10.93	7.2^f				
1985	64.66	13.63	7.41^g	61.86^g	12.95^g		
1988	115.48	22.83	17.16^h	78.75^i	26.52^i	260.28	42.5^i
1990	127.45	24.16	33.98^{e,k}	51.38	42.16	156^l	34.02
1992	180.48	35.15	85.38^m	306.28	60.39	398	55.87
1993	194.56	50.80	149.00^m	556.98^e	147.01^e	556	202
1994^n	216.22	75.70	193.95^o	509.92^e	323.40^{e,p}	954^q	256
1995	446.5	78.7	n.a.	1,530	413	1,366	322
1996	530.4	79.7	n.a.	834	834	1,689	524

Sources:

[1] Nantong shi tongji ju, *Lishi de zuo biao: Nantong shi, xian, shehui jingji yilan, 1949–92* (Nantong: Nantong Statistical Bureau, 1993).

[2] Editorial Board of the Almanac of China's Foreign Economic Relations and Trade, ed., *Almanac of China's Foreign Economic Relations and Trade, 1988–1996* (Hong Kong: China Resources Advertising Co., 1989–97).

[3] Zhongguo duiwai jingji maoyi nianjian bianweihui, *Zhongguo duiwai jingji maoyi nianjian,* for 1984, 1986, 1989, 1990, 1991, 1995–96 (Beijing: Zhongguo shehui chubanshe).

[4] Nantong shi tongji ju, *Nantong shi shehui jingji tongji nianjian,* for 1993, 1994 (Nantong: unpublished reference material, 1994, 1995).

Note: FDI, foreign direct investment; GVIO, gross value of industrial output; n.a., not available.

^{a} GNP for 1978–1992 is in 1990 renminbi. From [1]. 1993–1996 GNP is from [2].

^{b} In current renminbi, 1978–1992 GVIO from [1]. 1993– 1996 GVIO is from [2].

^{c} In current renminbi. 1978–1992 data are from [1].

^{d} 1985–1992 data from [1]. All other data from [2].

^{e} All foreign trade data unless indicated otherwise are from [2]. Local data, received in Nantong in 1992, reports 1990 export purchases as 2.016 billion, not 3.398 billion RMB. Similarly, local data for 1985 are 0.896 billion, not 0.741 billion as in [1].

^{f} From [3, *1984*], p. 198.

^{g} [3, *1986*], p. 228, reports 1985 export commodities procurement purchases as 896 million RMB, up 14.4% over 1984. It also reports contracted FDI for 1985 as \$32.41 and used FDI as \$7.53 million, much less than [1].

^{h} [3, *1990*] reports procurement export sales for 1988 at 1.651 billion RMB, less than [1].

^{i} [3, *1989*] lists 1988 contracted FDI as \$69.35 million, of which \$5.2 million was in government loans and used FDI as \$27.47 million.

^{j} From [3, *1989*], p. 213.

^{k} [4, 1993] pp. 13, 248, report total export procurement purchases for 1990 as 4.72 billion RMB, significantly more than [2].

^{l} [3, *1991*], reports total foreign trade for 1990 as \$385 million, but the following year's yearbook adjusts that figure to \$190 million, saying that \$195 million of this value had been earned by joint operation (*lian yin*).

^{m} From [4, *1993*], p. 248.

^{n} From [4, *1994*], p. 248.

^{o} Values reported in planned priced (*jihua jia*).

^{p} [4, 1994] reports used FDI in 1994 as 290.2 million RMB and 269.5 million RMB for 1993.

^{q} 1994–1996 data from [3, *1995–1996*], p. 269.

Still, when compared to successful OCCs,[102] Nantong's limitations were largely due to hesitant leaders who failed to use their opportunities to break out of institutional constraints and link tightly with external markets and capital.

POLITICS UNDER SEGMENTED DEREGULATION

Segmented deregulation made development zones a key way for cities to gain preferential policies, international exchanges, and economic advancement. It further explains why provinces and localities lobbied for preferential policies and the fever for development zones that emerged in the late 1980s and early 1990s.

Lobbying for Openness

Under the market hypothesis, potential beneficiaries of freer trade should collectively lobby for trade liberalization. But China's political authoritarian regime delegitimizes collective action and the pursuit of regional interests. Moreover, most analysts see central leaders determining the pace of the opening. But although regional actors rarely pursued collective interests, the incentives created by segmented deregulation, whereby the state gradually removed constraints on transnational exchanges for individual cities, zones, peninsulas, and regions over a decade and a half, led localities to lobby the center for preferential policies rather than request that all cities be deregulated.

In fact, each time the center deregulated some part of China, a plethora of supplicants pleaded that their locality or a part of it be included in this round of beneficiaries. The demand for preferential policies peaked between 1988 and 1993, resulting in a paroxysm of local zone creation that has been called China's zone fever. But uncoordinated demands became unorganized collective action that undermined China's boundaries with the outside world, significantly opening China's urban centers to global exchanges.

As the key level of government with the administrative status to negotiate directly with the State Council, provinces actively lobbied on behalf of their cities and regions. Usually they asked for preferential policies for their communities or they helped these localities build a development zone.

Provincial officials participated in the central meetings that heralded new stages in the opening. And although their pressure did not create new phases, they did increase the number of cities that were deregulated during

---

102. Qingdao, which had many more advantages than Nantong—it became a line item on the national budget—also failed to break out until after Deng's southern trip; then a new leader began to use the city's endowments, transformed the investment climate in the city, and pressed the central government for more preferential policies. See Chung, "Preferential Policies."

any particular phase. Deng originally planned to open five coastal cities in 1984, but provincial pressure led to the opening of fourteen cities, although the economies of Beihai, Nantong, Fuzhou, and Lianyungang did not warrant inclusion.[103] Provinces wrote proposals to SEZO, recommending that cities that had been excluded from an open region be included.[104] According to one SEZO official, "We get lots of requests. The province reports to the State Council which passes all documents requesting open policy privileges to us. We study the request and if it seems fair, we ask the opinions of the appropriate ministries and departments, including the State Planning Commission, the Ministry of Finance, MOFERT, and Customs. We assemble their views and tell the State Council whether we agree or not. The State Council corresponds with the province."[105]

Lobbying by Shandong Province in 1984 helped Weihai Municipality's harbor receive some preferential policies, and after Shandong petitioned the State Council in November 1989, Jinan, the provincial capital, was included in the open coastal economic region and granted all the benefits granted to the coastal areas opened in 1985.[106] Provinces also argued for the opening of entire regions within their boundaries. In early 1985, Gu Mu announced that four regions—the Pearl River delta, the Yangzi River delta, the Shandong peninsula, and the Liaodong peninsula—would be opened, but the official decision opened only the first two regions and the Xiamen-Quanzhou-Zhangzhou region of southern Fujian. Thereafter, Liaoning Province continued to push hard for the opening of the Liaodong peninsula.

Inland provinces pressured the center to expand the openings to inland regions. In fact, except for fall 1982 when a coalition of twelve inland provinces apparently criticized the open policy at the Twelfth Party Congress,[107] inland provinces favored more not fewer open areas, although critical of a policy that discriminated against them.[108] In May 1984, after the opening of the fourteen OCCs, governors in Shaanxi and Shanxi provinces

---

103. SEZO officials said that provincial pressure won out at this meeting. Interview at SEZO, June 1993.
104. Officials in Jiangsu's Open Policy Office (*kai fang ban*) constantly wrote reports to SEZO asking that closed cities be opened. Interview JIAOPPOL, 1992.
105. Interview with SEZO officials, summer 1992.
106. For Weihai, see "Guanyu Shandong sheng Weihai gang, Longkou gang dui wai kai fang de huiyi jiyao" (Summary of the Minutes from the Meeting on Opening Shandong Province's Weihai Harbor and Longko Harbor), and for Jinan, see "Guowuyuan guanyu jiang Jinan shi huaru yanhai jingji kaifang qu de fuhan (A Reply Letter from the State Council about Jinan Municipality being delineated within the open coastal economic region), in Yanhai compendium, pp. 1222–23, 457, respectively.
107. Susan Shirk, "The Domestic Political Dimensions of China's Foreign Economic Relations," in *China and the World*. ed. Samuel S. Kim (Boulder: Westview Press, 1984), pp. 57–81.
108. In 1985, Xian researchers known as the Western School (*Xibu xuepai*) criticized the inequities of the open policy and the favoritism afforded to the coastal regions. Yang, "Reforms, Resources, and Regional Cleavages," p. 64; interviews in Toronto, 1986.

asked for similar privileges for their provincial capitals. By August, pressure from the inland areas bore fruit; when the Bank of China announced special foreign exchange privileges to encourage FDI in thirty cities, twenty-four of them were inland cities.[109] At the March 1988 National People's Congress, Sichuan Province lobbied to become an SEZ, and some inland provinces that had complained about policy discrimination were allowed to set up small open zones. They even used foreign journalists to express concerns about regional favoritism.[110] In fall 1989, inland provinces did not use the post-Tiananmen climate to advocate closing China down; rather, they argued that their regions be opened.[111] Thus after Deng's southern trip, provincial officials from Qinghai Province reported that they were particularly nervous that the inland areas would be left even further behind, so the party secretary and the governor both lobbied the center for more liberal policies for their own areas.[112]

Despite Yang's reference to "organized expression of regional interests,"[113] there was no indication of any well-organized local effort to open China to the outside world. Localities pursued their own regional interests and lobbied the center to gain benefits for their own locality. Nevertheless, as Yang shows, regional interests did express those views through regional cooperation conferences, through direct advocacy to central leaders and central organizations, through delegates to the National People's Congress, and through academic journals.

"If You Build It, They Will Come!" – Zones as a Strategy for Segmented Deregulation

A second strategy for attracting preferential policies was to build a fully operational development zone and then lobby the central government to have it included in the subsequent round of deregulation. By "building nests to attract birds" (*zuo ying yin niao*), or what Baark calls the infrastructure model of development,[114] officials borrowed money wherever possible and poured it into zones in order to attract domestic and foreign investment and make it look competitive and thriving to the outside. Thus, under segmented deregulation, cities learned to first build zones and then

109. Madelyn C. Ross, "China's New and Old Investment Zones," *China Business Review* (November–December 1984): 14–18.
110. Nicholas Kristoff, "China's Frontier: The Search for Development," *New York Times*, 24 November 1989, p. A8.
111. Elizabeth McCoy Chen, "The Domestic Political Dimensions of China's Increasing International Economic Integration, 1978–1992" (unpublished paper, Harvard University, February 1993).
112. Interviews in Beijing, summer 1993.
113. Yang, *Beyond Beijing*, p. 132.
114. Erik Baark, "Technological Entrepreneurship and Commercialization of Research Results in the West and in China: Comparative Perspectives," *Technology Analysis and Strategic Management* 6, no. 2 (1994): 203–14.

lobby for national recognition and preferential policies. As in the case of Kunshan outlined next, early entrepreneurs responded to the ETDZs in the OCCs and began building zones in 1985–86. In 1988, ninety cities mimicked Haidian District in Beijing after it established an experimental HTDZ by building their own HTDZs and gambling that Haidian's success would lead the center to authorize more HTDZs.[115]

Provinces helped their cities build zones by exempting them from provincial taxes and land regulations, giving them special provincial status, liberalizing the rules for raising domestic capital, and lifting regulations in spheres outside their authority. In June 1988, Henan reportedly opened two zones for FDI despite higher-level disapproval,[116] and in 1990 so many cities established special zones for Taiwanese capital that the State Council's Tax Bureau criticized this frenzy publicly.

Kunshan Lobbies for Deregulation

Kunshan County, outside Shanghai, illustrates the strategy of building a zone, attracting domestic firms to defray costs, getting a few foreign firms, and then lobbying, lobbying, lobbying for national status and the deregulation that came with preferential policies. Planning for the zone began in late-1984 with construction underway by 1985, after Kunshan was included in the open coastal economic zone established in the Yangzi River delta in 1985. Officials had planned to build a simpler industrial park, but the region's opening offered Kunshan a chance to be a window linking inland areas with the outside world (*wai yin nei lian*). In late 1986, the Jiangsu Provincial People's Congress approved the establishment of a development zone and the provincial governor voiced public support for it. By 1987, urban planners from Nanjing had redrawn the county's plan, increasing the zone from 3.75 to 6.18 square kilometers.

Lacking preferential policies, county leaders had to keep costs down. By building the zone beside the city, rather than separating the zone and the town, they used the town's water, energy, and gas facilities and they also did not need much new housing. All this defrayed their costs. The zone gave domestic firms the same rights as township and village enterprises—more flexible labor policies, few welfare benefits for employees, and three years tax-free development—all particularly attractive to the SOEs that were their target audience. And they offered JVs access to the domestic market, stipulating that as long as they balanced their foreign exchange, they could sell 50 percent of their products domestically (30 percent was the legal limit)

115. Guangzhou began constructing the Tianhe HTDZ in June 1988, finishing its "technology road" in June 1989. "Qianjin zhong de Tianhe gaoxin jishu kaifaqu" [The Tianhe High and New Technology Development Zone is marching forward], *Guangzhou jingji* [Guangzhou's economy] 4 (1991): 22–23.
116. Willy Wo-Lap Lam, *The Era of Zhao Ziyang: Power Struggle in China, 1986–1988* (Hong Kong: A. B. Books, 1989), p. 249.

and still get the benefits of an export-oriented JV. Even firms that failed to export 50 percent of their produce were still exempted from national regulations as firms facing difficulties (*kunnan qiye*).

Kunshan officials, with provincial help, lobbied SEZO and the central government for a State Council ETDZ. Because southern Jiangsu, the province's industrial heartland, had no such zone, the provincial government exempted the county from provincial taxes for several years to give it initial investment capital and labeled Kunshan a key provincial development zone. Also Zhao Ziyang was brought to the zone in December 1987 during his coastal tour.

Fei Xiaotong, China's leading anthropologist, a native of nearby Wujiang County and a member of the Standing Committee of the National People's Congress, lobbied for the zone. In the 1980s, together with Jiang Zemin, then party secretary of Shanghai, he had called for a greater opening of southern Jiangsu Province. Fei's efforts helped the zone get its provincial status. Then in December 1989, after Jiang Zemin became general secretary of the CCP, Fei petitioned SEZO and the State Council to grant Kunshan the same policies as the ETDZs in the fourteen OCCs. County leaders, he argued, "didn't want any state funds, only these policies, (*bu yao guojia de qian, zhi yao zhexie zhengce*)," which would give foreign businessmen full confidence in the zone.[117]

To increase national support, the zone stressed communist norms, such as self-reliance, which suggested that granting Kunshan special status would not cost the center money. In July 1988, a *People's Daily* special report, "Self-Financed Development: Reporting on Kunshan's Economic and Technical Development Zone," and a "Commentary" lauded the county for self-reliance and "the spirit of bitter efforts with little money."[118] In response to these pressures, a team from SEZO visited the zone and deferred some taxes. But despite a positive report from SEZO, no formal document establishing an ETDZ ensued. According to the investigating SEZO officials, "We place great emphasis on Kunshan, but it is not completely in our power to decide. If other ministries oppose, we can't do anything. We worked hard to help their development zone reach national status. We gave them financial support. Most national-level zones get a five-year moratorium on taxes to the state, so we negotiated with the Ministry of Finance and got Kunshan a moratorium of 5 million RMB in taxes. Based on the experience of other zones, we advised them on what problems to avoid, and they have visited us as well."[119] But this request for special consideration was ill-timed. "Opposition arose first in 1989 because they put forward their request at the time

---

117. Fei Xiaotong, Letter to the National People's Congress, December 1989.
118. Wu Kequan, "Kunshan kaifa qu zou zifei jianshe zhi lu" [Kunshan Development Zone follows the road of self-financing] (unpublished document, April 1989).
119. Interviews, SEZO, summer 1992.

of the economic retrenchment, so the Ministry of Finance didn't want to cut their taxes further. Then came Pudong which has had a great impact on all aspects of the economy; it costs the centre lots of money. To make those payments [to Pudong] they need money from elsewhere. If the state cuts Kunshan's taxes, it has to make up that money elsewhere. But if the state cuts taxes nationwide, where will it get funds to make up for these cuts?"[120]

Nevertheless, the zone brought in a great deal of new investment. One-fourth of the funding came from loans and one-third from county finances; the rest was from firms in the zone.[121] By 1991, the zone produced 16.5 percent of the county's GVIO (and 7 percent of Gross Value of Industrial and Agricultural Output [GVIAO]), significantly more than zones in the fourteen OCCs, which produced only 2–3 percent of GVIO.[122] It also earned foreign exchange and paid state taxes. All the work paid off because after Deng's southern trip triggered another round of deregulation, Kunshan's zone became a national development zone in 1992.

Zhangjiagang Gets a Bonded Warehouse

The final form of deregulated space created by the central government was the bonded warehouse. In such a warehouse, which was like a fenced development zone with factories, goods brought in duty free were processed and then reexported. As long as the goods were used in the production process and reexported, no taxes were paid.

From the late 1980s, Zhangjiagang had been searching for a strategy by which it could gain preferential policies. In 1991, it received the right to approve FDI projects of $30 million, much higher than its status as a third-level city dictated. Thereafter, it needed only to send the decision to the provincial Foreign Investment Bureau in Nanjing for final approval.[123] This preferential treatment resulted from strong ties with provincial officials, in particular the vice-governor responsible for the external opening, Gao Dezhen, who had been party secretary in Zhangjiagang in the 1960s and in Suzhou in 1988 when the municipality turned outward. Also in 1992, the city was put in the national plan for foreign trade, giving it important import-export powers.

But beginning in 1992, a new leader in Zhangjiagang, Qin Zhenghua, increased the community's global integration by overcoming many of the remaining administrative constraints that had bound the hands (and minds) of the county's leaders. First he made developing the harbor a top priority, along with creating a modern, sparkling clean, new city that would

120. Ibid.
121. Wu Kequan, "Kunshan Development Zone."
122. Yang Wei, "Development Zones in China's Coastal Cities" (unpublished paper, Nanjing University, 1992).
123. Interview, Jiangsu Waimao, 1992.

be the envy of the entire country. Although developing the harbor and the town beside it had been the county's formal development strategy, Qin felt that "it was just a slogan. . . . They were not completing the work."[124] So, on his second day in office, Qin called a meeting at the harbor and "the slogan of 'using the harbor to build the city and using the city to develop the harbor' really took on meaning."[125] Qin empowered Harbor Town officials, gave them 500,000 RMB per year for urban management and keeping the town clean, got fourteen thousand of its citizens urban residence permits, built new roads, and made the town into a major center.

Qin aggressively pursued a bonded warehouse. Although the provincial government supported Zhangjiagang's candidacy for a bonded warehouse, Zhangjiagang was vying with other cities around the country for this preferential policy. Throughout China, the zone fever was whirling. In June, 1992, when Li Peng attended a conference in nearby Changzhou, Qin persuaded him to visit the harbor and write the characters for "bonded warehouse" (*bao shiu qu*). For three days, Qin mobilized the whole community to respond to Li's message, moving farmers off their land and fencing in a zone. Reportedly, he took Li's calligraphy to SEZO and persuaded its director, Hu Ping, to choose their community; after all, the prime minister had approved. In this way, Zhangjiagang became the only county-level city in China to gain a bonded warehouse.

After 1992 Zhangjiagang's global economic contacts exploded (table 2.7). Contracted FDI jumped very quickly in 1992 and stayed at about the same level through 1996, while used FDI, increased dramatically from 1992 through 1994. (Much of this money, however, could have been based on "round-tripping," where Zhangjiagang TVEs established companies in Hong Kong that became their joint venture partner.) Exports in dollars doubled more than twice between 1990 and 1994 and grew eight fold between 1990 and 1997 as Zhangjiagang officials used their export powers to buy up goods from all over China, which they then exported.

The role of the harbor, however, did not meet expectations because a harbor fever swept Jiangsu Province. Once everyone learned that harbors could attract investment, towns all along the Yangzi River began vying for funds to build harbors and berths. So some of Zhangjiagang's anticipated cargo went out through smaller cheaper ports.[126] According to provincial officials, funds for the bonded warehouse also dried up during the macro-economic tightening of 1994–95, although local officials denied this. Foreigners working in Zhangjiagang reported very little activity in the bonded zone and during a visit in summer 1997 I saw that much of the land was lying fallow.

124. Qin Zhenghua, interview, June 1997.
125. Interview, Urban Planning Office, Zhangjiagang, June 1997.
126. Interview, Geography Department, Nanjing University, June 1997.

Table 2.7   Zhangjiagang Production, Trade, and Investment Data, 1978–1999

Year	GNP (million RMB)	GVIO (million RMB)	FDI (million $) Contracted	FDI (million $) Used	Foreign Trade[a] (million $) Exports	Foreign Trade[a] (million $) Imports
1978	324.43	505.20	n.a.	n.a.	n.a.	n.a.
1984	890.02	2,339.30	n.a.	n.a.	n.a.	n.a.
1985	1,286.53	3,806.80	0.27	0.27	n.a.	n.a.
1988	2,262.28	7,312.10	21.59	8.75	n.a.	n.a.
1990	2,782.07	9,387.10	25.09	9.82	99.00	0.00
1992	6,317.02	22,008.00	994.27	198.42	187.00	23.00
1993	10,279.49[b]	35,207.10	1,114.95	359.10	291.00	94.00
1994	15,250.49[b]	49,079.40	1,201.17	579.69	470.00	300.00
1995	19,101.29[b]	57,237.50	1,010.55	599.80	560.00	450.00
1996	23,007.10	49,586.24	1,003.00	567.00	695.10	517.00
1997	23,020.10	49,721.84	632.20	455.40	800.20	662.70
1998	23,501.10	47,035.10	373.70	327.80	811.04	636.90
1999	24,510.20	49,494.00	307.49	300.22	831.16	667.03

Sources: Jiangsu Provincial Statistical Bureau, *Benxiang xiandaihua zhi licheng, 1949–1992* [The historical process of leaping toward modernization, 1949–1992] (Nanjing: Jiangsu Statistical Bureau, 1994), pp. 541, 553; Zhangjiagang COFERT, June 1997 (for 1996 data); Zhangjiagng Statistical Bureau, *Zhangjiagang Statistical Yearbook* (Zhangjiagang: Zhangjiagang Statistical Press, 1996–99).

Note: COFERT, Commission on Foreign Economic Relations and Trade; FDI, foreign direct investment; GVIO, gross value of industrial output; n.a., not available.

[a] Includes total value of imports and exports by local trade companies (*difang ziying jinchukou zong'e*). Data on exports in the Suzhou Statistical Bureau, ed., *Suzhou Statistical Yearbook* (Beijing: China Statistical Publisher, 1990–97) are: 1990, $12.5; 1993, $50.7; 1994, $120.3; 1995, $212.1; 1996, $285. Data for imports are: 1978–92, n.a.; 1993, $27.5; 1994, $57.9; 1995, $90; 1996, $145. These values are reported as total volume of self-managed imports and exports (*ziyin jin chukou zong'e*).

[b] Data reported are GDP figures, not GNP (which are no longer available) in current prices.

Undermining Transnational Boundaries

The regulations for establishing zones were unclear, maximizing the zone officials' power to determine which type of firms were allowed access.[127] Flexible ambiguity, combined with the need to expand the flow of goods and services passing through the zone in order to defray the costs of building it, afforded JVs easy access to the domestic market and domestic factories easy access to the zone's deregulated space. This situation mirrors what Ding Lu and Zhimin Tang call the "soft authority constraint," where legal constraints do not effectively bind bureaucratic behavior, so that the rules "can be 'stretched' at will by the officials who liberally interpret their own

127. David Wall, "Special Economic Zones in China: The Administrative and Regulatory Framework," *China Paper 91/7*, Economics Division—Research School of Pacific Studies, National Centre for Development Studies, Australian National University, 1991.

authorities."[128] Much of the corruption in China today is the result of this soft authority constraint. In this section, we discuss the incentives that zone officials had to ignore the state's rules and how these unclear rules facilitated the weakening of China's regulatory regime.

ATTRACTING DOMESTIC FIRMS

Spatial deregulation and preferential policies created incentives for urban leaders and particularly zone directors to attract domestic firms (*neilian qiye,* literally "domestically connected") into the zone, and many domestic firms sought the lower transaction costs and the greater ease of establishing global linkages that came with urban internationalization. Thus although preferential policies, which endowed zones with comparative advantage, targeted foreign investors, they also attracted domestic firms to coastal cities, increasing the regional gap. Many domestic firms speculated in land or engaged in the service sector, but domestic industrial firms interested in exporting had strong incentives to move to the zones. Because the data in table 2.8 show that exports by many domestic firms were not that high, the zone's low tax rates and the ease of doing business in its deregulated environment, more than its function as a global linkage, was probably the key attraction.[129]

Why did zone directors use preferential policies to attract domestic firms? Their investments deferred infrastructure costs in the zone, and more firms created the aura of a prosperous international business environment. According to one zone director, "if you don't have any domestic firms in the zone, it will look very empty, so foreigners will not come."[130] And while this director preferred to take bank loans to pay for the zone's development rather than accept domestic firms, the tightness of finance capital in 1984–85 when he built his city's zone caused him to swap his preferential policies with domestic firms that invested in the zone's infrastructure. In 1984, Shenzhen approved highly attractive policies geared at domestic (*neilian*) firms, including land leases that were 30 percent cheaper than those offered to foreign investors.[131] As a result, by mid-1986, twenty-seven ministries and twenty-seven provinces had established 2,300 cooperative enterprises in the Shenzhen SEZ. To attract third front factories, which had been established in 1964–71 in the isolated mountains of central China, Kunshan let these factories become rural enterprises, which had more flexible labor policies than SOEs and three years tax-free devel-

---

128. Lu and Tang, *State Intervention and Business in China,* pp. 87, 88. Their reference to a "soft authority constraint" is a play on Janos Kornai's "soft budget constraint."
129. As previously mentioned, domestic firms in Xiamen's Huli zone were more efficient than the joint ventures in the zone. Li, "Improving Infrastructure."
130. Interview TJZWCAM, 1994.
131. Yang, *Beyond Beijing,* p. 49.

Table 2.8 Domestic Firms in Economic and Technical Development Zones in Open Coastal Cities, 1996

City	Nantong	Qinhuangdao	Dalian	Tianjin	Yantai	Qingdao	Lianyungang	Caohejing	Hongqiao	Minhang	Ningbo	Fuzhou	Zhanjiang	Guangzhou
Domestic industrial firms														
total	337	198	570	760	175	—	253	391	—	—	118	254	55	—
operational	171	95	—	210	51	—	207	391	—	—	48	—	49	290
operational (%)[a]	59	45	—	11	22	—	57	76	—	—	17	—	35	55
Firms in tertiary sector														
domestic	1,506	563	6,198	6,121	—	—	933	—	3	—	3,356	222	88	112
foreign	62	35	265	597	—	—	81	—	83	—	73	149	16	6
total investment (100 million RMB)														
domestic	20.59	8.30	83.00	143.19	—	—	13.84	—	—	—	56.10	2.39	14.98	—
foreign	13.04	6.72	97.58	67.73	—	—	12.22	—	72.90	—	37.72	24.60	33.95	—
Joint ventures														
contracted	200	296	1,057	2,744	401	832	332	206	83	140	407	511	319	486
operational	120	115	460	1,785	181	388	154	126	61	118	239	196	93	233
Exports (million $):														
total	296.1	96.9	1,255.2	1,450.2	209.9	239.7	80.2	309.0	892.7	295.2	481.4	406.8	138.4	460.0
by joint ventures	178.3	82.3	1,205.2	1,440.7	99.1	210.3	55.1	305.6	892.7	295.2	160.7	246.9	106.9	322.0
by domestic firms	117.8	14.6	50.0	9.5	110.7	29.4	25.1	3.2	—	—	320.8	155.9	31.6	138.0
by domestic firms (%)	39.8	15.1	4.0	0.7	52.8	12.3	31.3	1.0	—	—	66.6	38.3	22.8	30.0
Total employees	14,565	15,090	96,833	140,150	35,030	44,579	19,140	43,316	10,876	—	40,352	51,451	26,994	42,089
in domestic firms (%)	35	25	39	29	57	62	64	61	21	—	50	46	72	31

Source: Economic Development Bureau, Nantong Economic and Technical Development Zone, ed., *Nantongshi jingji jishu kaifaqu, tongji gongbao, 1996* [Nantong Municipality economic and technical development zone statistical report] (Nantong: n.p., 1996), pp. 11–13.

[a] Total industrial firms include total number of operational joint ventures plus total number of operational domestic industrial firms.

opment. In Tianjin, the zone offered SOEs in the city core a 10 percent tax cut if they simply registered in the zone—they did not need to move—and the zone and the enterprise split the difference.[132]

Nantong Municipality passed official guidelines outlining special benefits that domestic firms entering their zone would receive.[133] But to limit conflicts with communities that were losing the enterprise and an important source of their tax revenues, Nantong promised to remit some taxes from neilian factories to the original community.[134] The most flexible strategy belonged to Changzhou Municipality in southern Jiangsu, which reportedly made the management company running its development zone a JV and invited all domestic enterprises entering the zone to establish a joint firm with this management company. In this way, all domestic firms entering the zone could gain JV status and a bevy of tax and import breaks.

In fact, initially, many enterprises in ETDZs in OCCs were neilian firms, making them critical for new zone development. In Yantai, I was told that seven hundred of eight hundred plants approved for the zone were domestic firms, while in Tianjin, approximately 45 percent of companies and factories were domestic firms seeking tax breaks, modern facilities, and personnel or labor policies.[135] In 1989, 68.8 percent of the funds for Guangzhou's ETDZ came from domestic firms, while in Nantong, the percentage of domestic firms was always more than 75 percent; after Deng's southern trip, the percentage peaked at over 90 percent (table 2.9).

As of 1996, domestic factories still played an important role in all State Council development zones. Table 2.8 shows the number of domestic industrial firms, rather than all the domestic firms, because these firms are a better indicator of the movements of capital and productive capacity from communities outside the zone and exclude land speculators or service companies. Thus in 1996, twelve years after these zones were established, the number of domestic industrial firms in some zones far surpassed the number of JVs, as did the level of their exports, whereas for others these firms simply played a very important role. Exports from domestic firms were critical in Ningbo (66.6 percent), Yantai (52.8 percent), Nantong (39.8 percent), Fuzhou (38.3 percent), Lianyungang (31.3 percent), and Guangzhou (30 percent). As mentioned previously, many plants moved to Yantai from Beijing to escape the control of the ministries under which

132. Interview TJZWCAM, 1994.
133. "Nantong shi renmin zhengfu guanyu Nantong shi jingji jishu kaifaqu de neilian qiye shixing youhui de zhanxing guiding" [Regulation of the Nantong City People's Government concerning favorable policies for domestic firms in the Nantong Development Zone], in Yanhai compendium, pp. 1801–3.
134. Ibid.
135. Interviews in Yantai, 1992, and Tianjin, 1993. Dalian was one of the few zones that truly had a large preponderance of foreign firms. What I was told in these cities differs somewhat from the 1996 data in table 2.8, but the situation probably changed significantly after 1992.

Table 2.9 Nantong Economic and Technical Development Zone, 1986–1996

	1986	1987	1988	1990	1991	1992	1993	1994	1995	1996
Firms at year end[a]	22 (4)	31 (9)	79 (10)	99 (18)	109 (25)[b]	663 (70)	1,151 (150)	1,783 (190)	1,729 (183)	2,036 (200)
Industrial output[c] (million RMB)	n.a.	2.27	30.15	175.08	209.61	556.00	1,901.77	3,005.00	3,635.21	4,006.00
Exports (million $)	1.13	0.10	3.89	18.11	35.61	68.63	123.05	181.05	290.32	296.09
Exports[d] (million RMB)	5.49	15.00	69.63	123.16	135.89	192.97	n.a.	n.a.	n.a.	n.a.
Tax on Profits (million RMB)	0.53	3.45	7.99	20.22	24.52	96.28	280.00	344.12	483.65	225.28
Used FDI (million $)	0.00	2.37	1.31	0.18	6.29	18.05	35.00	78.76	52.95	149.18

Sources: 1986–91 data from Nantong Economic Development Zone, June 1992; 1992 data from Editorial Board of the Almanac of China's Foreign Economic Relations and Trade, ed., *Almanac of China's Foreign Economic Relations and Trade 1993/94* (Hong Kong: China Resources Advertising Co., n.d.), p. 295; 1993 data from Editorial Board of the Almanac of China's Foreign Economic Relations and Trade, ed., *Almanac of China's Foreign Economic Relations and Trade 1994/95* (Hong Kong: China Resources Advertising Co., n.d.), pp. 335–36; 1994 data from Editorial Board of the Almanac of China's Foreign Economic Relations and Trade, ed., *Almanac of China's Foreign Economic Relations and Trade 1995/96* (Hong Kong; China Resources Advertising Co., n.d.), p. 325; 1995–96 data from Economic Development Bureau, Nantong Economic and Technical Development Zone, ed., *Nantong shi jingji jishu kaifaqu, tongji gongbao, 1996* [Nantong Municipality economic and technical devlopment zone statistical report] (Nantong: n.p., 1996), p. 10.

Note. FDI, foreign direct investment; n.a., not available.

[a] Number of joint ventures in parentheses. The other firms are domestic Chinese firms (*neilian*).

[b] Of 25 foreign firms in 1991, 16 were joint ventures, 1 was a cooperative firm, and 8 were wholly owned foreign enterprises.

[c] Reported as based on 1990 prices.

[d] Includes purchases from outside the zone sold through the zone's export firm. The original value of export sales given to me in 1991 is 251 million RMB. But the data are contradicted by a report I received in Nantong in 1997, which gives 1991 exports as 135.89 million. Because the 1992 value of 192.97 million is lower than the 251 million, I have accepted the data given to me in 1997. Unfortunately, after 1992 domestic purchases for exports was no longer used, only exports in dollars.

they functioned. Overall, I remain convinced that cities wanted zones and their preferential policies because these policies attracted domestic, not just foreign, investment.

GRANTING FOREIGNERS ACCESS
TO THE DOMESTIC MARKET

Although many foreign investors used China's cheap labor for offshore production, others targeted the domestic market with their highly competitive products. One of the strongest cards a zone director had to play to attract FDI was to facilitate access for the JV to the domestic market. Writing in the mid-1980s, C. K. Leung argues that because foreign investors are "essentially attracted by the potentially vast domestic market, a situation has developed whereby . . . SEZ cadres who are given incentives to promote foreign investment, vigorously compete on behalf of their 'clients' for higher and higher proportions of domestic sales."[136]

One zone director showed no remorse over allowing foreign firms access to the domestic economy, even if it forced mainland firms to close. His zone had received little central funding, so selling foreign investors land and charging them fees was an important way to build the zone. And if giving them access to the domestic market was necessary to attract them, so be it. For him, not letting JVs sell domestically and protecting backward (*luohou*) or unproductive firms harmed consumers who otherwise would not be able to get better prices or products. Also many zones were partners with JVs and together they could earn extra-normal profits or rents in the domestic economy. In this way, zones had strong incentives to serve as inward-oriented, rather than outward-oriented, windows and to become channels for foreigners to enter China's internal market.

UNDERMINING THE FOREIGN TRADE REGIME

Although development zones were established to help the state manage foreign investment and export-import affairs, the possession of export-import powers allowed zones to become entrepôts for the export of domestically produced goods, undermining the foreign trade system's monopoly on transnational exchanges.

Nantong's zone earned a great deal of money helping domestic firms export their products. According to interviews in the zone in 1992, approximately 40–50 percent of the goods that were exported from the zone had been manufactured outside the zone. This ratio varied considerably from

136. C. K. Leung, "Spatial Redeployment and the Special Economic Zones in China: An Overview," in *China's Special Economic Zones: Policies, Problems and Prospects*, ed. Y. C. Jao and C. K. Leung (Hong Kong: Oxford University Press, 1986), p. 10.

year to year, with export purchases in renminbi by the zone outpacing the zone's industrial output in 1987 and 1988 (table 2.9). One small workshop I visited simply sewed labels onto clothes produced outside the zone by a conglomerate of seventeen enterprises. But as long as the products' value increased 15 percent within the confines of the zone, this conglomerate's goods were treated as exports produced in the zone and therefore exempt from most of the state's production tax.

Nantong zone's companies shared their export power with enterprises that wanted to manage their own exports, increasing the number of firms with unofficial import-export authority. According to one firm, "We have no export power but Trade Bureau No. 1 in the zone lets us do our own exports—they simply stamp the paperwork. They have a rule that if you earn US\$ 2–3 million per yr., they will give you this export power. They still control the macroeconomic factors, keeping track of how much is exported, but they give us the power to do this."[137]

Bonded warehouses also became channels for circumventing state controls. Imported materials entered a bonded warehouse tax free if they were reexported. But according to sources in Hong Kong, communities such as Zhangjiagang often overstated the value of the goods that went into the exported item, presenting their production process as less efficient than it truly was. They then sold remnants of the imported goods domestically without paying import duties. Given this opportunity for corruption, it is no wonder there was enormous lobbying by local communities for the right to set up a bonded warehouse.[138] This way, too, foreign goods penetrated the domestic market without official approval.

Segmented Deregulation and the Outbreak of Zone Fever

Between Deng's southern trip in spring 1992 and summer 1993, zone fever (*kaifaqu rì*) swept China. The boundaries of existing zones ballooned by a factor of ten or twenty. Nantong and Yantai expanded their zones from 4 to 45 square kilometers in spring 1992; in 1993, Qingdao's zone grew from 15 to 152 square kilometers.[139] Jiangling County, along the Yangzi River in Hubei Province, designated 18 square kilometers as the site for a HTDZ, and isolated Neihuang County, in northern Henan Province, established six small industrial zones.[140] The types of zones proliferated. By summer 1993, Jinan, the capital of Shandong Province, had established six zones,

137. Interview in Nantong Zone, April 1992.
138. Both Nantong's development zone and Nanjing's Pukou high-tech zone reported lobbying SEZO for the right to set up a bonded warehouse. Both efforts failed.
139. Jae Ho Chung, personal communication, 1996.
140. "Industrial Park," *China Daily*, 8 June 1992, p. 2; "Industrial Zones," 9 May 1992, p. 2, respectively.

including a tourist zone, an agricultural high-tech zone, a regular development zone, and a new HTDZ.[141] The boundaries of zones became abstract; the nationally recognized new HTDZ in Chengdu, Sichuan Province, extended preferential policies to labs in suburban universities that did not move into the zone.

The frenzy was obvious. According to one mainland magazine, "the fever must have gone to peoples' heads," with zone development "betraying a certain blindness."[142] In spring 1992, a Jiangsu urban planner complained he was exhausted from drawing up zones for county seats across the province. "There is a 'development fever' in China these days; every city and town wants a development zone. Even cities closed to foreign investment want to build development zones."[143] In this fervor, provinces and localities ignored national laws and "approv[ed] on their own bids to set up various kinds of development zones."[144] By the end of 1992 every province in China, excluding Tibet, had sold use rights totaling 4,000 pieces of state land, equal to 25,000 hectares, and by June 1993 another 3,000 parcels of land totaling 22,000 hectares had been sold.

Land was being parcelled out for future development despite the fact that there was not enough investment capital in all of China to build these zones. According to Beijing television,[145] as of summer 1993 there were 8,000 development zones across China, covering 20,000 square kilometers. But international and domestic funds could develop only 20 percent of the land in these zones.[146] The gap between the planned area of development and capital available for investment was enormous. To develop all Hunan Province's 211 development zones needed 300 billion RMB; yet total investment in fixed capital in the entire province in 1988 was 14.2 billion RMB.[147] According to Chinese reports, only 30,700 hectares, or 2 percent, of the 1.5 million hectares planned for development—most of it good farmland around cities and towns—was being developed. The remainder was fallow and deteriorating.[148]

---

141. Personal observations during a visit to Jinan in summer 1993.
142. Li Yongzeng, "Woes and Weals for Economic Development Zones—Part 3 of the Year End Economic Commentary," *Liaowang* (overseas ed.) 51 (21 December 1992): 16–17, reprinted in *FBIS*, no. 11 (19 January 1993): 30–32.
143. Interview in Nanjing, spring 1992.
144. This was the report by Wang Xianjin, the director of the State Land Administration Bureau. See "With One-Third of Development Zones Suspended, Over 20 Million Mu of Land Has Been Recovered," *Ta Kung Pao*, 30 September 1993, p. 5, reprinted in *FBIS*, no. 193 (7 October 1993): 20.
145. On July 4, 1993, Beijing Television channel no. 1 broadcasted nationwide a heavily sarcastic and decidedly critical program that attacked land speculators in Beijing and Beihai, Guangxi Province, the poorest of the fourteen OCCs.
146. Li, "Woes and Weals."
147. See Guojia tongji ju, *Zhongguo tongji nianjin, 1989* (Beijing: Zhongguo tongji chuban she, 1990), p. 479.
148. Li, "Woes and Weals."

ROOTS OF ZONE FEVER

Zone fever was the logical result of the incentive structures created by segmented deregulation and the fear of being left behind when others were
using zones to get preferential policies. By giving some localities policies, as
the rest of the country remained constrained by regulations governing its
global interactions, segmented deregulation generated the frenzy that
peaked in 1992. As table 2.2 shows, the growth of development zones
accelerated between 1988 and 1992, so that by the end of that period
almost one hundred additional zones had been opened.

The idea that development zones could attract preferential policies
intensified in 1988 after Haidian District in northwest Beijing established a
test HTDZ. In that year, officials in Nanjing Municipality began searching
for land and capital for their HTDZ in Pukou across the Yangzi River from
the city. As previously mentioned, ninety localities nationwide drew up
plans for new zones in 1988, many with the help of their provincial governments. The SSTC contributed to this frenzy because it told cities that
approached it that if they could establish the necessary conditions (i.e.,
infrastructure and a scientific base nearby), they would be eligible for
special policies as new HTDZs as soon as the SSTC could persuade the State
Council to authorize this new form of zone. According to one SSTC official, "they came to see us, and we gave them nods that if they could meet
the necessary levels, if they could establish the necessary conditions, they
were likely to be approved."[149]

Following petitions from provincial governments and investigations by
the SSTC, the State Council in March 1991 formally endowed twenty-seven
HTDZs with preferential policies previously reserved for SEZs and ETDZs
in the fourteen open coastal cities. These policies included duty-free
imports of high technology, greater freedom to hire and fire workers, and
a 15 percent (not 55 percent) tax rate for high-tech domestic firms that
created new products in the zone. The decision in 1992 to recognize
another twenty-five HTDZs, leaving thirty-five to thirty-six unsuccessful peti-
tioners, sent a clear signal to local and provincial bureaucrats all over
China: build a zone, lobby, and your zone might be anointed with national
preferential policies in the subsequent round of approvals.

In 1990, the establishment of Pudong, with enormous preferential policies aimed at attracting domestic capital for infrastructure development
and the planned investment by Beijing of 10 billion RMB in the zone,
shocked local leaders, who feared it would suck in all foreign and domestic
investment.[150] What particularly frightened them was that scholars who had
previously argued that domestic capital should play no role in Pudong's

---

149. SSTC official, interview, Cambridge, Mass., 1995.
150. This and the following paragraph draw heavily on Zhang, "Zhongguo xin yilun
kaifang" [What is the potential problem].

development, now asserted that domestic funds had become absolutely necessary.[151] So provinces and localities lobbied intensely for their own locality to be deregulated. For example, Guangxi Province petitioned the central government in March 1990 for more export quotas and export licenses to Hong Kong, more trade organizations with direct export power, more international ports serving Guangxi-Hong Kong, and more direct transport links to Hong Kong.

The cyclical nature of spatial deregulation, with spirals of openings and closings, pushed officials to move quickly in 1992 once China had shifted into another upswing. During these openings, the state was more likely to distribute policies, loans, land, and new bureaucratic posts.[152] The previous wave of internationalization under the Coastal Development Strategy of 1987–88 had been soundly suppressed from late 1988 through early 1992. This lesson was clear: open phases could be short, so quickly create new organizations and take control of resources and policies while the liberalization phase lasts; and, even if your locality's zone is not granted preferential status, it is important to confiscate land, get capital for investment, and begin construction while the ethos of the system allows it. As more and more localities rushed to build zones, the frenzy intensified.

With gross value of industrial output (GVIO), not profits, the criterion for promotions for local cadres, going into debt to attract more enterprises into the locality was a wise strategy. Zones became indicators of a leader's ability to promote modern science and technology, as each locality had to prove that it too could build a bridge to the twenty-first century. A "you follow me, I'll pass you" mindset emerged, in which localities felt that "not going forward [with a zone] is going backward, and going forward slowly is in fact going backward."[153] For cities with few global linkages, renting land to foreign businessmen whose global networks might attract JV partners was smart, and in fact, during the 1992–93 zone fever, locations were accused of running policy auctions—selling land and policies, such as lower taxes, to attract new plants.[154] In some places, after foreigners invested funds for zone development, 70 percent was returned as working

151. See Zhang Chun, "Jingji zhuanjia xuezhe yanlun Pudong kaifa guandian zongshu" [Summary of views of economic scholars and experts' research on opening Pudong], in *Renda ziliao: Tequ yu kaifang chengshi jingji* [People's University Reference Materials; SEZs and Open City Economies], F14, 12 (1991): 53–58.
152. Howell, *China Opens Its Doors.*
153. In Chinese, "*bu jin zi tui, jin de man ye shi tui.*" See *Nanjing Pukou xingao jishu waixiangxing kaifa qu guan wei hui bangongshi* [Office of the management committee of the Nanjing City Pukou new high tech externally oriented zone], "Nanjing Pukou xin gao jishu waixiang xing kaifa qu jingji guihua yanjiu" [Research on the current plan of Nanjing's Pukou High-Tech Export-Oriented Development Zone], *Keji yu jingji* [Technology and economics] 3 (1991): 30.
154. Shi Jian, "Policy Auctions in Development Zones Viewed, *Zhongguo tongxun she,* 4 November 1992, in *FBIS,* no. 228 (25 November 1992): 28–29.

capital after the foreigners moved into the zone.[155] Zones let officials create new posts and companies for friends and allies, strengthening their networks. These proliferating real estate and land development companies each took a share of the transaction fees that were charged at each step of the land-transfer process. All this had a highly corrupted flavor.

ECONOMIC INSTITUTIONS:
SOFT PROPERTY RIGHTS AND LOANS

Government planning, soft property rights, and the local state's predatory strategy towards tax and resource accumulation formed the institutional bedrock of zone fever.

Socialist planning follows a pattern of permissive sequencing, in which enormous amounts of social overhead capital are spent in anticipation of directly productive activities.[156] This pattern contrasts with market economies, which follow a compulsive sequencing strategy in which the expansion of industrial enterprises determine the demand for social overhead capital. Therefore, in socialist planning localities first borrow money to build the spatial infrastructure, or "the nest to attract birds." Also, because state-led development follows Erik Baark's infrastructure model of technological entrepreneurship, which stresses creating the physical infrastructure for investors;[157] because zones and cities competed to attract domestic and foreign investors; and because cities had put expansive urban development plans designed in the 1987–88 liberal era in the drawer following the restrictive fiscal climate of 1988–1991, the emergence of a political and economic climate conducive to maximalist strategies led cities all over China to expand extant zones, ignore earlier zoning decisions by government planners, expropriate land, and take out bank loans that otherwise would not have been available.

Weak economic institutions allowed local officials access to domestic resources with little risk of penalty. First, property rights on land in China have always been soft, and with the land bureau under the horizontal control of territorial governments and party committees, the vertical authority structures of the central government were ill-equipped to monitor land transfers.[158] Villagers and district governments surrounding

---

155. An Weihong, "Garment City Offers Incentives to Investors," *China Daily*, 10–16 May 1992, p. III.
156. Reginald Y. W. Kwok, "Structure and Policies in Industrial Planning in the Shenzhen Special Economic Zone," in *China's Special Economic Zones: Policies, Problems and Prospects*, ed. Y. C. Jao and C. K. Leung (Hong Kong: Oxford University Press, 1986), pp. 39–64.
157. Baark, "Technological Entrepreneurship."
158. We can see this as a principal-agent problem or simply as what the Chinese see as a conflict of *tiao tiao* (vertical or ministerial) control versus *kuai kuai* (horizontal or territorial) control, with the latter winning out.

cities might demand better prices, but when municipal party officials who outranked suburban officials pressed the case, resistance was futile. And who could oppose preparing land for FDI in the development fever that followed Deng's trip south?

Second, soft property rights decreased any accountability if investments brought no returns, insuring the emergence of a great deal of bad debt, if not outright corruption. Who owned the zone, who was responsible if it failed, and who was responsible for the loans used to purchase the land if they were never repaid, remained unclear. Opaque property rights were particularly the norm in the early stages of zone development, before self-supporting development companies took over the zone.

The local state also expropriated land and subsidized government companies that developed it.[159] For example, the government of Qingdao established a local real estate company whose shareholders comprised the city government, surrounding villages, rural enterprises whose plants had been expropriated, and villagers; each was given shares based on the contribution to the company.[160] Rural residents and villages were compensated for the land, while the city government was given shares for the use rights that it transferred to the land management company. To facilitate development, however, the zone's management committee (composed of city administrators) helped the management company receive loans worth 70 percent of the value of the land. In essence, the government expropriated land, transferred it to a management company, and then arranged for banks to loan that company money to build the zone. Fortunately, in this case villagers were compensated; but in many cases they were forcibly moved to other locations. And although in this case the interest rate paid by the development company was 11.34 percent, in some cases city governments subsidized the interest payments, allowing the management company to have the money for free. Speculation was further fueled (but domestic funds raised) by leasing the land to domestic real estate investors at a rate that was 10 percent below that charged to foreigners, insuring a real estate company an instant 10 percent profit if it could find foreign investors. According to Beijing television, land speculators earned 500 percent profit at each stage of the land-sale process through a process the Chinese call "stir-frying land property (*chao di chan*)."[161] With so little serious financial liability, it is no wonder so many zones lay fallow.

In the end, an enormous amount of revenue was generated for government officials, bureaucrats, and semipublic companies with very little risk, and much of this funding probably lined the pockets of bureaucrats. Why? The ethos of the period justified their behavior; their political power and

159. Jane Duckett, *The Entrepreneurial State in China: Real Estate and Commerce Departments in Reform Era Tianjin* (London: Routledge, 1998).
160. Yang, "A Study on Chinese Economic Development Zones," p. 19.
161. Beijing Television channel no. 1, July 4, 1993.

monopoly on coercion prevented serious opposition; the widespread nature of the phenomenon prevented recriminations; soft property rights insured that hidden profits were easy to take; and the hope that this strategy might make the central government deregulate their locality—these legitimized this strategy and created an enormous problem for China's political economy.

STATE REACTION TO ZONE FEVER

Although conservative spokesman Yuan Mu criticized zone fever in fall 1992, it was only in 1993 that the central government clearly opposed zone proliferation because reformers in Beijing worried that any negative signals would dampen the local initiative generated by Deng's southern trip. But the widespread and corrupt nature of this phenomenon could not be ignored. In January 1993, then Vice Premier Zhu Rongji criticized zones covering 20–30 square kilometers as "fantasy."[162] In early February 1993, Benxi, a large city in Liaoning Province, closed two zones, and Anhui Province closed all township-level development zones, returning the land to farmers.[163] In July 1993, the Beijing Television exposé appeared, outlining the waste, corruption, and role of personal networks in this fever. The sharpness and openness of the attack suggests that it must have had top-level support. In summer 1993, the State Council SEZO, which was responsible for approving State Council ETDZs, investigated this policy aberration, and in August 1993, Hu Ping, its director, reported that only 10 percent of zones were beneficial, while 20 percent were awaiting funds to start projects. By summer's end, the coastal areas had closed over 75 percent of their zones, and seven counties had cut the area of their zones by 89 percent.[164] The fever was over.

Zones and Urban Internationalization

Segmented deregulation made zone construction a strategy by which urban leaders attracted domestic investment; however, did zone construction eventually become a force for urban internationalization? Using data from a series of reports from the Nantong Development Zone, we can assess the level of internationalization of the development zones using three measures: zone exports as a percentage of the zone's total GDP;

162. Ho Shui-yee, "Zhu Rongji Discusses Economic Development in Liuzhou, Calls for Cool Heads," *Ta kung pao*, 17 January 1993, p. 2, reprinted in *FBIS*, no. 11 (19 January 1993): 29.
163. "Establishment of Development Zones Slow," Xinhua (Beijing), 11 February 1993, reprinted in *FBIS*, no. 27 (11 February 1993): 21.
164. "Coastal Areas Close Several Economic Development Zones," *Xinhua* (Beijing), 11 August 1993, reprinted in *FBIS*, no. 154 (12 August 1993): 32.

Table 2.10   Economic and Technical Development Zone Exports as Share of Zone's Total GDP, 1993–1996

	1993	1994	1995	1996	Average
Tianjin	0.660	0.960	0.940	0.920	0.870
Qinhuangdao	n.a.	1.060	1.050	1.020	1.043
Dalian	0.860	1.306	1.368	1.183	1.179
Minhang	n.a.	n.a.	n.a.	0.196	
Caohejing	n.a.	n.a.	n.a.	0.257	
Lianyungang	n.a.	n.a.	1.709	0.810	1.260
Pudong	0.350	0.530	0.500	0.530	0.480
Nantong	1.075	1.463	1.322	1.288	1.287
Ningbo	1.225	1.724	1.524	1.000	1.368
Fuzhou	0.420	1.031	1.243	0.743	0.859
Qingdao	0.418	1.089	1.415	0.657	0.895
Yantai	0.400	0.656	0.663	0.868	0.647
Guangzhou	0.837	0.947	0.635	0.510	0.732
Zhanjiang	n.a.	0.904	0.955	0.206	0.688

Source: Economic Development Bureau, Nantong Economic and Technical Development Zone, ed., *Nantongshi jingji jishu kaifaqu, tongji gongbao* [Nantong Municipality ETDZ statistical report] (Nantong: n.p., various years).
Note: Values are percentages. n.a., not available. Because reported values for exports are in dollars but GDP is in renminbi, the ratio is computed based on the exchange rate for each year as reported in the *Almanac of China's Foreign Economics and Trade.*

output of industrial JVs in the zone as a percentage of the zone's total industrial output; and zone exports as a percentage of the neighboring (or mother) city's exports.

An important measure of internationalization is ETDZ exports as a share of GDP (table 2.10). For the fourteen OCCs, the exports as a share of the zone's GDP was quite high and in some years exports surpassed the zone's entire GDP. As previously explained, because zones were granted FTCs with import-export powers, they functioned as entrepôts, exporting many goods produced outside the zone. Similar to Singapore and Hong Kong, whose reexports make them the only two countries in the world whose exports surpass their GDP, ETDZs functioned as channels through which Chinese domestic goods reached international markets. Some FTCs shared their export power with industrial firms in the zone even if the firms exported through the zone goods bought in other regions. As we have discussed, some small workshops in the zone exported finished goods produced elsewhere, yet the value of the exports included the entire value of the good, not just the value-added created in the zone. Thus the ratio of exports to GDP in cities such as Nantong, Ningbo, Dalian, and Qinghuangdao was consistently above 1.00, while in cities such as Tianjin, Fuzhou, and Qingdao exports surpassed GDP in selected years. On the other hand, zones where this ratio was considerably below 1.00 were either deeply penetrated by domestic firms or had invested a great deal of money in

Table 2.11   Joint Venture Industrial Output as Share of Total Zone Industrial Output, 1991–1996

	1991	1992	1993	1994	1995	1996	Average
Tianjin	82.0	91.7	96.1	98.6	98.4	98.5	94.2
Qinhuangdao	37.9	53.2	63.8	86.7	86.5	87.3	69.2
Dalian	81.6	81.6	85.6	90.1	84.4	86.4	84.9
Minhang	100.0	100.0	100.0	100.0	100.0	100.0	100.0
Caohejing	13.4	24.2	30.3	36.5	49.0	55.0	34.7
Pudong	n.a.	n.a.	14.0	29.3	24.0	26.9	23.6
Lianyungang	18.3	18.1	42.8	48.7	47.3	50.2	37.6
Nantong	38.7	81.7	71.5	74.4	68.7	73.1	68.0
Ningbo	75.4	69.4	60.7	58.2	50.3	38.3	58.7
Fuzhou	87.0	70.9	71.5	74.7	73.2	71.7	74.8
Qingdao	30.5	33.1	30.1	40.2	46.1	43.9	37.3
Yantai	60.9	52.3	66.5	72.4	77.6	82.7	68.7
Guangzhou	93.8	91.5	91.1	95.9	96.5	96.0	94.1
Zhanjiang	21.7	17.6	18.3	19.1	32.1	34.7	23.9

Source: Economic Development Bureau, Nantong Economic and Technical Development Zone, ed., *Nantongshi jingji jishu kaifaqu, tongji gongbao* [Nantong Municipality ETDZ statistical report] (Nantong: n.p., various years).
Note: Values are percentages. n.a., not available.

infrastructure or housing in the zone, which enlarged the share of their GDP that was based on domestic investment (see table 2.10).

The second measure, the output of industrial JVs as a percentage of total industrial output, reflects both the outward orientation of the zones as well as the inward flow of international forces. Given the enormous amount of funds expended to attract JVs, did this strategy work or did zones attract primarily domestic factories? The data show a successful deepening of internationalization after 1991 in the fourteen OCCs (table 2.11). Except for Ningbo and Fuzhou, the output of industrial JVs as a share of total zone industrial output grew—and in many cases significantly—between 1991 and 1996. Zones had matured, and domestic firms, which played a critical role in early zone development, gave way to JVs, in terms of their contribution to industrial production. Domestic firms still dominated the service sector in the zones (see table 2.8), but for industrial goods, which represent the modernization of China's export economy, JVs became key, allowing zones to fulfil their original goal of attracting industrial capacity from overseas to help China compete globally in high-end sectors.

However, did zones also become channels though which foreign firms gained access to the domestic economy? ETDZs were to serve as locations where external and domestic forces could meet under the watchful eye of state agents, whose task was to protect the domestic economy from external penetration. But as a zone official from Tianjin told me, foreigners wanted access to the domestic market and the zone, needing investment

Table 2.12   Joint Venture Exports as Share of Total Zone Joint Venture Industrial Output, 1991–1996

	1991	1992	1993	1994	1995	1996	Average
Tianjin	35.5	22.8	23.3	31.5	28.4	32.8	29.1
Qinhuangdao	13.4	10.5	30.3	24.3	23.9	30.8	22.2
Dalian	n.a.	75.8	69.6	80.4	85.2	71.5	76.5
Minhang	39.4	38.8	27.6	31.5	23.4	19.6	30.0
Caohejing	21.3	11.7	n.a.	27.6	37.7	46.2	28.9
Pudong	n.a.	n.a.	13.0	9.6	11.2	13.1	11.7
Lianyungang	31.2	123.7	47.6	30.6	24.4	28.5	47.7
Nantong	67.5	37.3	56.4	73.2	83.4	71.7	64.9
Ningbo	43.9	43.2	33.4	48.7	80.9	37.0	47.9
Fuzhou	24.5	19.5	19.1	42.4	43.1	39.0	31.3
Qingdao	69.8	40.2	49.8	67.8	77.3	58.6	60.6
Yantai	35.2	31.2	13.6	21.0	19.9	22.1	23.8
Guangzhou	n.a.	31.9	22.2	22.4	16.1	15.7	18.1
Zhanjiang	34.5	35.3	20.3	31.8	24.3	41.1	31.2
Average	37.8	40.2	32.8	38.8	41.4	37.7	38.1

Source: Economic Development Bureau, Economic and Technical Development Zone, ed., *Nantongshi jingji jishu kaifaqu, tongji gongbao* [Nantong Municipality ETDZ statistical report] (Nantong: n.p., various years).
Note: Values are percentages. Because exports are in dollars but industrial output is in renminbi, the ratio is computed based on the exchange rate for each year as reported in the *Almanac of China's Foreign Economics and Trade*.

funds, willingly traded away China's domestic market in return for that capital.[165] How widespread was this phenomenon?

Although zones did not report domestic sales by JVs, we can measure these flows by looking at joint venture exports as a share of joint venture industrial production (because joint venture industrial production includes goods that could be exported or sold domestically). The data in table 2.12 suggest that most products manufactured by JVs in the ETDZs were not exported. Despite the national regulation that JVs must export 70 percent of their production to be eligible for many preferential policies, the average over six years for all fourteen OCCs is 38.1 percent and the yearly average was fairly constant from 1991 through 1996. For cities such as Dalian where Japanese and Koreans produced cheap goods for their own countries' domestic markets, the ratio of exports to production for JVs was over 70 percent. In Nantong, too, where many Japanese manufactured products for the home market, 65 percent of JV products were exported. Nevertheless, despite the mercantilist goal of using zones to prevent foreign access to the domestic market, the zones were apparently an inward channel for foreign investors.

165. Interview TJZWCAM, 1994.

Table 2.13   Economic and Technical Development Zone Exports as Share of the Mother City's Exports, 1989–1997

	1989	1990	1991	1992	1993	1994	1995	1996	1997	Average
Tianjin	1.8	3.6	6.8	9.1	14.2	22.7	30.1	35.8	39.9	18.2
Qinghuangdao	8.1	22.1	18.5	43.2	66.4	64.3	53.0	56.4	n.a.	41.5
Dalian	7.4	14.9	29.1	38.7	40.7	42.5	42.7	47.5	49.2	34.8
Shanghai										
Minhang	1.0	1.3	2.9	3.5	3.2	2.8	2.2	n.a.	n.a.	2.4
Caohejing	0.7	0.4	0.8	1.7	n.a.	1.3	1.9	2.2	2.5	1.4
Pudong	n.a.	n.a.	n.a.	n.a.	13.7	18.2	18.8	21.6	19.1	18.3
Lianyungang	n.a.	67.4	71.3	51.5	57.6	26.7	27.7	26.6	30.4	44.9
Nantong	4.3	5.2	13.7	17.2	22.1	19.0	21.4	17.5	17.1	15.3
Ningbo	11.7	14.2	16.7	17.4	17.2	16.0	4.3	9.1	7.6	12.7
Fuzhou	4.5	17.1	15.4	15.1	11.6	16.6	22.6	23.0	23.7	16.6
Qingdao	7.3	9.4	6.0	6.3	7.6	11.6	15.1	n.a.	14.8	9.8
Yantai	19.7	29.4	49.0	36.8	15.3	15.3	11.3	11.3	10.3	22.0
Guangzhou	9.3	7.7	10.8	9.2	7.4	6.4	6.7	7.1	6.7	7.9
Zhanjiang	18.3	25.2	26.3	21.5	21.3	21.2	29.4	31.4	23.6	24.3
Average[a]	8.5	18.2	22.3	22.6	24.9	23.7	23.9	26.3	22.3	21.4

Sources: Economic Development Bureau, Economic and Technical Development Zone, ed., *Nantongshi jingji jishu kaifaqu, tongji gongbao* [Nantong Municipality ETDZ statistical report] (Nantong: n.p., various years); Editorial Board of the Almanac of China's Foreign Economic Relations and Trade, ed., *Almanac of China's Foreign Economic Relations and Trade* (Hong Kong: China Resources Advertising Co., various years).
Note: Values are percentages. n.a., not available.
[a] Average calculated using Shanghai as a single entity.

Finally, did ETDZs contribute to the mother or neighboring city's internationalization? This is measured by zone exports as a percentage of the neighboring city's exports. As table 2.13 shows, between 1989 and 1997, the zones contributed significantly to the internationalization of most of the neighboring cities. The average share of zone exports to city exports rose from 8.5 percent in 1989 to a peak of 26.3 percent in 1996, with some backsliding to 22.3 percent in 1997. Interestingly, the major deepening occurred in 1990–91, before Deng's southern trip and before Pudong came online. This jump in exports may have resulted from the export push that followed global financial sanctions placed on China after the 1989 Tiananmen crackdown. There are important variations among the cities. Tianjin follows the expected pattern; although in 1989 the zone's exports represented only 1.8 percent of the city's exports, as the zone developed, its share of the city's exports grew to 39.9 percent, fulfilling the goals set for it by the reformers in 1984. Dalian and Qinghuangdao show a similar pattern, as do Nantong, Pudong, Fuzhou, and Qingdao, although in these six cases the zone's share of municipal exports was not as great. Dalian's zone, which received strong support from the city, played a greater role as the 1990s wore on due to the increased role of Korean firms following China–South Korea normalization. Although the zone's share of total exports in the city peaked in 1991, zone exports increased between 1991 and 1997 at an average annual rate of 24.6 percent; however, the zone could not keep pace with the dramatic annual growth in the city's exports of 61.7 percent for the same period, hence its declining share. Finally, Pudong quickly became an important export channel for Shanghai as it, like other state council zones, used its preferential policies and import-export powers to become an entrepôt for exports from other parts of the country.

Overall, therefore, the ETDZs in the fourteen OCCs deepened the level of urban internationalization, in some cases quite significantly. Despite my own cynicism, which perceives zone development primarily as a strategy for gaining preferential policies (a view supported by interview data and the pattern of local behavior), by 1996 ETDZs linked urban China to the world. Interestingly, despite the hoopla about Pudong, by 1996–97 the older zones contributed on average more to their cities' exports than Pudong contributed to Shanghai. But given the enormous quantity of Shanghai's exports, Pudong's role in linking China globally will certainly intensify.

Conclusion

What determined the pace and pattern of China's opening to international market forces: the power of the global markets themselves, domestic institutions, government policy, or local entrepreneurship? Clearly China's comparative advantage in foreign trade and the highly competitive prices of China's goods in global markets offered some local governments enormous opportunities if they pursued trade, investment, and other transnational linkages. Also, many domestic actors understood how global linkages could benefit their location's economic development.

But at the start of the reform era, powerful domestic institutions prevented urban centers from knowing their interests. As those interests were clarified, they still confronted a bevy of institutional constraints limiting their ability to carry on global exchanges. Restructuring the rigid administrative boundaries was necessary to carve out transnational spaces. Harbor development remained tightly constrained by central ministries. These and other controls had to be circumvented, abrogated by government fiat, or simply ignored if communities were to link with global markets in a competitive manner.

State policy, therefore, by deregulating certain territories and determining which communities could pursue global markets, created a comparative advantage for beneficiaries of state policy and imposed a comparative disadvantage on localities that were not deregulated.[166] Gaining preferential policies became a prime task for local governmental entrepreneurs in their competition for resources, growth, and political power forcing communities to adopt a strategy of pursuing policies as well as pursuing markets, in order to override the institutions that blocked global access and increased transaction costs.

But the search for global exchanges was not the only reason to pursue policies. In open or deregulated areas, Chinese firms cut their transaction costs and increased control over their own resources, so spatial deregulation endowed localities with a powerful attraction that pulled in domestic resources and enterprises. Their lower tax rates on new products, liberal hiring and salary policies, freedom to use their own capital for business activities, and the ability to create new posts also helped them improve the roads, bridges, harbors, buildings, and communication facilities in and around the urban setting. Policies, therefore, meant wealth and an inflow of resources to those who pursued them successfully. But even as it doled out policies, the central government also favored localities with real comparative advantage in foreign trade, lowering transaction costs and facilitating exogenous easing in areas that could promote China's export-led economic development.

Yet, while central and regional capital flowed to deregulated areas, the microlevel picture was more complex. Some territorial governments resisted redirecting capital into projects that could cut the transaction costs of foreign trade or expand global market opportunities if such investment threatened the community's tax base or GNP (and therefore their cadres' status) or if it challenged entrenched economic and political interests. Especially before Deng's 1992 southern trip, even leaders in many of the fourteen OCCs were risk averse and did not redirect significant amounts of resources toward projects that facilitated exogenous easing. They wanted state investment and preferential policies that both decreased their tax obligations to higher-level government and attracted new resources and productive facilities into their community. With their own funds they could respond to local political pressures.

But who drove deregulation? How can we explain the progressive weakening of the administrative boundaries between China's economy and the outside world? The desire of community leaders to gain open status, their incessant lobbying of the center, and central leaders who were predisposed to gradual internationalization—all determined the pace of spatial deregulation. And although localities did not act collectively or determine when the phases of spatial deregulation occurred, incessant unorganized

---

166. Dorothy J. Solinger, "Despite Decentralization: Disadvantages, Dependence and Ongoing Central Power in the Inland—the Case of Wuhan," *China Quarterly* 145 (March 1996): 1–34.

pressure from individual territorial governments pushed the center to expand China's internationalization. As the center established new opportunities or criteria for attaining deregulated status, communities carved out territories, organized capital, and competed furiously for central policy largesse. The result was a curious mix of externally oriented infrastructure projects, more globally integrated communities, and a large amount of wasted energy, land, and capital as local governments sought linkages to the global economy.

As the 1990s wore on, however, investments in the ETDZs bore fruit. Industrial production from JVs increased, as did their exports, even as the importance of domestic firms declined. Similarly, for some of the original fourteen OCCs, exports from the zones contributed significantly to their overall internationalization. Nevertheless, ETDZs also became channels through which foreigners gained access to China's domestic market because the incentive structure faced by zone directors led them to undermine the very state controls they were expected to uphold. Their interests in promoting their local economy and the zone's corporate interests, rather than in protecting national sovereignty, helped deepen China's urban internationalization.

3

Internationalizing Rural China: Exports, Foreign Direct Investment, and Developmental Communities

Beginning in the 1980s, China's reform leaders progressively internationalized the rural areas around major coastal cities, especially in the key delta regions. Township and village enterprises (TVEs) penetrated global markets, and by the mid-1990s, over 50 percent of all products purchased by China's foreign trade companies (FTCs) were manufactured by former peasants working in rural factories. Foreign direct investment (FDI) particularly from Hong Kong and Taiwan flowed into the countryside as finished products flowed out. But why did China open its rural areas to foreign trade and investment? Was this process elite-driven or due to pressure by a coalition of potential beneficiaries of expanded foreign trade? What channels of global transaction were established to control the flow of goods and services between rural China and the global market and how effectively did they fulfil that role? Do markets and comparative advantage best explain who responded most enthusiastically to internationalization or did government policy and regulatory constraints determine the behavior of rural actors? Did a linkage fever emerge in this sector as well? Finally, did some regions benefit more than others from transnational exchanges and, if so, did these actors seek greater global linkages and undermine China's transnational barriers and foster greater interdependence?

Assumptions and Findings

Contrary to the expectations of some of the international political economy literature,[1] changes in the relative price of labor in East Asia in

---

1. Jeffry A. Frieden and Ronald Rogowski, "The Impact of the International Economy on National Policies: An Analytical Overview," in *Internationalization and Domestic Politics*, ed. Robert O. Keohane and Helen V. Milner (Cambridge, UK: Cambridge University Press, 1996), pp. 25–47.

the 1970s and 1980s did not create a coalition of advocates of rural internationalization. Lobbying by advocates of rural interests, such as the Ministry of Agriculture, or national advisors on rural affairs does not explain
the decisions by Beijing to lower barriers to TVE exports in 1987–88. The
decision to open rural China to exports and FDI was made by central
reformers who learned about the role export-led growth had played
in modernizing East Asia. Aware of China's comparative advantage
in foreign trade based on the relative price of its labor, they saw the
lost opportunity costs of not participating in foreign trade. Earlier
efforts in 1984 to promote the exports of state-owned enterprises (SOEs)
had failed. Moreover, with tens of millions of rural laborers, unemployed
because of decollectivization, flooding the cities, a rural crisis loomed. So
central leaders hoped that rural exports would earn foreign exchange
to upgrade SOE technology and employ the countryside's surplus
labor.

Changing incentives created by both the global market and the state
taught rural elites the benefits of export-led growth. Particularly after
the state granted TVEs more control over the foreign exchange that they
earned and allowed them to import technology that could help them
compete with the SOEs, local governments jumped into the export sector.
To this extent, Frieden and Rogowski are correct. Changes in the relative
price of rural labor vis-à-vis Taiwan and Hong Kong gave TVEs a comparative advantage in exports and brought down existing barriers; however, the
state, not social demand, was the primary agent of change by dismantling
rules that had prevented TVEs from reacting to the change in their relative
prices. In fact, before 1987, domestic institutions were so powerful that
rural elites, denied information about international prices, did not know
they had a comparative advantage in foreign trade—in the words of Evangelista, institutional constraints prevented potential beneficiaries of a more
internationalized economy "from pursuing or even recognizing their interests."[2] And even if they had known their policy preferences, they lacked any
formal organization through which they could collectively pursue those
interests.[3]

As the state opened the countryside to foreign capital, it established
channels of global transaction—rural joint ventures (JVs)—that were to be
monitored by local foreign trade officials and local governments. But the

2. Matthew Evangelista, "Stalin's Revenge: Industrial Barriers to Internationalization in the
Soviet Union," in *Internationalization and Domestic Politics*, ed. Robert O. Keohane and Helen
V. Milner (Cambridge, UK: Cambridge University Press, 1996), pp. 159–85. Quotation is
from p. 177.
3. Thomas P. Bernstein, "Farmer Discontent and Regime Responses," in *The Paradox of
China's Post-Mao Reforms*, ed. Merle Goldman and Roderick MacFarquhar (Cambridge,
Mass.: Harvard University Press, 1999), pp. 197–219.

preferential trade and tax policies given to JVs and the local governments that were the foreigners' partners influenced domestic behavior significantly. As their interests clarified, TVEs, hungry for global linkages that circumvented institutional constraints imposed by the state and its foreign trade companies, flocked into the transnational sector, triggering a JV fever.

Contrary to expectations that internationalization would undermine the authority of the state, the opening of rural China to FDI and foreign trade strengthened local governments.[4] What we find is the emergence of communist party–dominated, export-oriented developmental communities[5] that used foreign trade and links with foreign investors to enrich their rural residents, strengthen their party authority, improve their industrial structure, and challenge the central state's control over China's external boundaries. Counterintuitively, therefore, the deeper the foreign penetration, the more stable the communist party system.

These rural communities undermined China's transnational boundaries. Under the pre-reform trade regime, the central state managed China's foreign exchange reserves, reaped enormous rents by underpaying domestic producers, kept foreign producers out of China's domestic market, and protected SOEs.[6] Rural JVs, however, offered local producers direct export channels to foreign vendors, squeezing out the middlemen— the state FTCs, their controls, and their fees. As did the development zones, community leaders served as linkage agents[7] for foreign investors who sought access to China's domestic market and to the rents available for those with better technology, efficiency, and products.

This chapter also highlights the role of network capital in China's internationalization. Multinational corporations were uninterested in rural

4. Skidmore sees foreign trade as strengthening authoritarian regimes, whereas Evans sees FDI playing this role. See Thomas E. Skidmore, "Politics and Economic Policy Making in Authoritarian Brazil, 1937–1971," in *Authoritarian Brazil: Origins, Policies, and Future*, ed. Alfred Stepan (New Haven: Yale University Press, 1973), pp. 24–25; Peter B. Evans, "Transnational Linkages and the Economic Role of the State: An Analysis of Developing and Industrialized Nations in the Post-World War II Period," in *Bringing the State Back In*, ed. Peter B. Evans, Dietrich Rueschemeyer, and Theda Skocpol (Cambridge, UK: Cambridge University Press, 1985), pp. 192–226.
5. Johnson characterizes Japan as a "developmental state." See Chalmers Johnson, *MITI and the Japanese Miracle* (Stanford: Stanford University Press, 1982), p. 10.
6. Nicholas R. Lardy, *Foreign Trade and Economic Reform in China, 1978–1990* (Cambridge, UK: Cambridge University Press, 1992).
7. The classic study on the modes of linkage between the external and internal world is Karl Deutsch, "External Influences on the Internal Behavior of States," in *Approaches to Comparative and International Politics*, ed. Barry R. Farrell (Evanston: Northwestern University Press, 1966), pp. 5–26. For a more contemporary analysis, see Barbara Stallings, "International Influences on Economic Policy: Debt, Stabilization, and Structural Reform," in *The Politics of Economic Adjustment*, ed. Stephan Haggard and Robert R. Kaufman (Princeton: Princeton University Press, 1992), pp. 41–88.

China and its TVEs; without the willingness of overseas Chinese to invest in this sector and channel TVE exports into the worldwide markets that they controlled and without the encouragement and preferential policies of the central government, which wanted to attract Taiwanese investment for political reasons, rural internationalization could not have occurred. TVEs were perfectly compatible with the small-scale export-processing firms in Taiwan. No doubt rural China's comparative advantage in labor—the result of rising labor costs in Taiwan and Hong Kong—attracted FDI and foreign interest; but cultural compatibility and the willingness of the overseas Chinese to link with local governments and participate in strategies that circumvented the institutional constraints imposed by the Chinese government helped enormously to bring down the barriers to rural internationalization.[8] Unlike the multinational corporations and the United States government, which publicly pushed for China to open its domestic market, network capital undermined China's transnational boundaries in a much more subtle yet effective manner.

Central Policy toward Rural Exports: The Early Days

Community development depends on national strategies whose laws and regimes constrain local economic activity or offer incentives and opportunities for growth. They may affect the particular mix of ownership rights, sectoral investment, and marketing opportunities, as well as policy instruments available to local actors to promote their own economic development.[9] In China, how rural areas interact with the global community depended greatly on the central leaders' development strategy. Before the late-1980s, the state tightly constrained all interaction between rural areas and the outside world. Only after the decentralization of foreign trade, the growth of JVs, and new incentives for TVEs to export did rural areas escape the cordon that had slowed their export development.

After 1949, China's leaders adopted the Soviet strategy of centrally planned foreign trade, in which imports merely supplemented insufficient domestic production. China exported only to earn the foreign exchange to buy needed inputs. Specialized FTCs under the Ministry of Foreign Trade monopolized all trade. To insure that domestic allocations followed the plan and were not diverted by market scarcity, export prices were planned

8. You-tien Hsing, *Making Capitalism in China: The Taiwan Connection* (London: Oxford University Press, 1998); David Zweig, "Developmental Communities on China's Rural Coast: The Impact of Trade, Investment and Transnational Alliances," *Comparative Politics* 27 (April 1995): 253–74.
9. Stephan Haggard, *Pathways from the Periphery: The Politics of Growth in the Newly Industrializing Countries* (Ithaca: Cornell University Press, 1990).

and often divorced from world prices. China's export mix also ignored China's comparative advantage.[10]

China's open policy involved a shift from central planning to export-led growth, combined with import substitution industrialization. While China decentralized control to an increasing number of local FTCs, it introduced and expanded a system of export-import licensing to control the volume and composition of trade.[11] Export prices began to reflect international prices, but most firms still could not trade directly with foreigners. Numerous policies promoted exports, including giving exporters preferred access to foreign exchange, foreign technology, domestic energy and resources, and bonuses for earning foreign exchange. China repeatedly devalued its currency to make exports more competitive and improve the climate for FDI, hoping to gain access to foreign technology, management skills, and capital.

Post-1978 liberalization led to a partially reformed foreign trade regime (see table 3.1). Many new goods and resources entered and left China, not through free and open markets but through bureaucratically controlled channels. And although by 1988 the number of FTCs increased to approximately six thousand, the state also forced all localities to turn over a fixed sum of foreign exchange. The result was a state that promoted export activity by stimulating local initiative, but which attempted to maintain institutional constraints on the boundaries between the countryside and the international system.

Nevertheless, under the contract managerial responsibility system, export-producing firms were allowed to contact different FTCs, generating competition among FTCs, which were still expected to help provinces meet assigned export quotas. According to Madelyn Ross, "this system begins to shift the FTCs' source of livelihood from MOFERT—which used to control and subsidize their activities—to the enterprises themselves."[12] State agents were pressured to facilitate transnational flows, not just control them. The reforms also strengthened local governments who controlled most of MOFERT's local trading companies and its bureau-level offices.[13]

The introduction of the foreign exchange contract system (*waihui baogan*) put great pressure on local governments to meet relatively fixed quotas. But it also gave them great incentives to increase their foreign exchange earnings because they had use rights to 80 percent of the above-quota foreign exchange earnings. The surplus could be sold at prices

10. For a detailed discussion of the pre-reform foreign trade systems, see Lardy, *Foreign Trade*, chap. 2.

11. For this discussion of foreign trade reforms I draw on ibid., p. 44.

12. Madelyn C. Ross, "Changing the Foreign Trade System," *China Business Review* (May–June, 1988): 34.

13. Thelen, Marrin, Johnson and Bridges, *China Business: Current Regulations and Practice* (law firm newsletter), May 1988, p. 13.

Table 3.1   Key Events in Rural Internationalization, 1978–1998

1978–79	Opening of four counties in the Pearl River delta
1985	Emphasis placed on growing crops to meet foreign demand under slogan "*mao, gong, nong*" (trade, industry, agriculture) introduction of foreign trade responsibility system opening of rural areas around three river deltas—Yangzi River (Suzhou, Wuxi, Changzhou), Li and Min rivers in Fujian, and Pearl River delta, including rural areas around the SEZs
1987–88	Coastal Development Strategy Opening to FDI of entire Liaodong and Shandong peninsulas, rural areas around 14 OCCs, Hangzhou, all of western Jiangsu Province, and the rural coastline of Jiangsu. Major reform of foreign trade system TVEs given same rights as SOEs to use foreign exchange to import technology Major campaign in summer 1988 to push rural areas to enter export market
October 1989	39 Points curtail TVE's competition with SOEs in domestic market
February 1990	8 Point Program to encourage TVE exports
1991	TVEs receive same rights as SOEs: loans for technology imports, import licenses, and right to present tenders to supply parts for electrical machinery exports
1992–93	Joint venture fever in southern Jiangsu and northern Zhejiang
1993	First group of TVE conglomerates get import-export powers
1997	East Asian financial crisis
1998	First major contraction in TVE sector East Asian crisis leads to first slowdown in TVE exports

Note: FDI, foreign direct investment; OCCs, open coastal cities; SEZs, special economic zones; SOEs, state-owned enterprises; TVEs, township and village enterprises.

higher than the official exchange rate to other governments, factories, or firms with export licenses through the new foreign currency exchange markets (*wai hui tiaoji zhongxin*) also called SWAP shops, established in 1988 in many cities and provinces. But rural factories still had to ask permission to use these funds from the local planning commission and report their actions to the Foreign Exchange Management Bureau.

Export-Led Growth in Rural China: The Role of National Policy

Pressure from the central government, the countryside's industrial structure, and comparative advantage in foreign trade made rural coastal China a key beneficiary of the open policy. Many of those benefits were difficult to attain before 1978, but by the late 1980s all of our key variables were at work. The relative price of rural labor and lower transaction costs in coastal rural China stimulated central interest in TVE exports. State policy, however, first had to liberate rural China from its institutional constraints (and generate incentives) before local elites could respond to the benefits of foreign trade and FDI.

But until the mid-1980s, the central leaders' plans for internationalization ignored much of rural China (except for Guangdong and Fujian provinces) as China opened only the coastal cities and various zones to foreign trade. Rural exports were controlled by county and provincial foreign trade departments and FTCs, who bought all agricultural products through the procurement system at fixed prices that were often below world prices. This helped the state extract wealth from farmers. Some prices paid by FTCs for exportable goods were even below the domestic price (e.g., in 1987, MOFERT's purchase price for prawns was 30 percent below the domestic market price) leading to devastating outcomes for rural producers.[14] These low procurement prices forced many enterprises to grit their teeth and use the domestic sales of other products to supplement the sale of export goods; but, because they had lost so much money trying to earn the foreign exchange demanded by their quotas, they resisted getting deeply involved in the export market.[15] Rural elites could not import technology even with the foreign exchange their TVEs had earned.[16] Moreover, until 1988, FTCs limited all direct contact between villages or export-oriented TVEs and foreign importers. Also, export licences were unavailable to organizations outside the foreign trade system forcing rural leaders to spend time building relations with FTCs rather than foreign importers.[17]

As table 3.2 shows, MOFERT maintained a relative monopsony over TVE exports in most provinces, and, although levels of control varied among provinces for the years for which data are available, the foreign trade bureaucracy had immense control over this growing segment of China's exports. Excluding Guangdong Province, control was greater in the major exporting provinces and cities such as Jiangsu, Shandong, Zhejiang, and Shanghai, whose percentage of direct exports not through MOFERT (Other Direct Exports) was lower than the national average.

The foreign trade responsibility system weakened MOFERT's controls over foreign trade. With the end of compulsory sales of many crops in 1985, prices, not administrative power, became an important factor affect-

14. "Diaodong qi fazhan chuanhui nongye de jijixing" (Mobilize enthusiasm for developing foreign exchange earning agriculture), *Nongmin ribao* [Farmer's daily], 8 July 1987, p. 1.
15. Letter to the editor, "The Ministry of Foreign Trade Must Find an Urgent Solution for the Stripping and Slicing of Contract Contradictions," ibid., 11 August 1988.
16. Even exporting TVEs could not allocate the foreign exchange they earned. As of the late 1980s, most of the 12.5 percent of the foreign exchange earned by a TVE, which by law was its to use freely, remained in the hands of the local planning commission, which allocated the funds according to its local plan. Interviews in Wuxi County, Jiangsu Province, January 1989.
17. Interview DRCRWW, Beijing, April 1989.

Table 3.2   MOFERT Control over Township and Village Enterprise Exports by Province, 1987 (thousand RMB)

Location	Total Exports	Direct Exports	Direct Exports through MOFERT	Other Direct Exports		Indirect Exports
				Absolute	Percentage	
Total	16,195,770	11,902,670	10,204,530	1,698,140	14.27	4,293,100
Beijing	496,860	330,590	317,490	13,100	3.96	166,270
Tianjin	789,630	789,630	736,430	53,200	6.73	—
Hebei	770,620	352,240	339,630	12,610	3.58	418,380
Shanxi	120,980	86,830	83,170	3,660	4.22	34,150
Inner Mongolia	24,050	16,150	16,150	—	—	7,900
Liaoning	600,020	442,920	434,440	8,570	1.93	157,050
Jilin	46,400	39,260	34,400	4,860	12.38	7,140
Heilongjiang	74,620	53,840	52,220	1,620	3.00	20,780
Shanghai	2,190,510	1,526,630	1,526,630	—	—	663,880
Jiangsu	3,253,220	2,296,370	2,150,990	145,380	6.33	956,850
Zhejiang	1,647,990	1,019,460	912,230	107,130	10.52	628,530
Anhui	102,710	67,580	64,710	2,870	4.25	35,310
Fujian	652,190	561,870	440,310	119,560	21.28	90,320
Jiangxi	158,660	95,140	87,690	7,450	7.83	63,520
Shandong	1,090,320	910,010	910,010	—	—	180,310
Henan	225,800	157,710	138,270	19,440	12.33	98,090
Hubei	278,220	211,370	203,370	8,000	3.78	66,850
Hunan	371,980	251,470	186,240	65,230	25.94	120,510
Guangdong	2,489,500	2,112,960	1,022,240	1,090,720	51.62	376,540
Guangxi	161,460	129,030	123,530	5,500	4.26	32,430
Sichuan	412,590	297,230	282,570	14,660	4.93	115,360
Guizhou	47,180	39,680	33,950	5,730	14.44	7,500
Yunnan	60,210	35,670	34,780	890	2.50	24,540
Tibet	—	—	—	—	—	—
Shaanxi	36,750	30,080	24,720	5,360	17.82	6,670
Gansu	30,090	21,550	20,800	750	3.48	8,540
Qinghai	9,320	9,030	9,030	10	—	290
Ningxia	15,530	12,520	11,320	1,200	9.58	3,010
Xinjiang	8,360	5,800	5,250	550	9.48	2,560

Source: *Township and Village Enterprises Yearbook, 1978–1987* (Beijing: Agricultural Publishing House, 1989), pp. 616–17.
Note: MOFERT, Ministry of Foreign Economic Relations and Trade.

ing where farmers sold their crops. Also the institution of quotas allowed FTCs, local governments, and TVEs to keep more of the surplus foreign exchange they earned, which they could swap at a profit, barter for shortages, or use to buy foreign products unavailable to most Chinese. Expanding domestic markets and the new opportunities for farmers to sell to merchants other than FTCs increased the value of exportable goods, so farmers and TVEs sought to extricate themselves from contractual arrangements, especially when the FTCs tried to enforce excessively low purchasing prices.

The result was bad blood. In a survey in 1988 in Weifang, Shandong Province, by the Research Center on Rural Development in Beijing, 40 percent of three hundred rural entrepreneurs reported "problems with export procurement prices" as the main obstacle to expanding agricultural exports.[18] Over 28 percent reported major disagreements or only "acceptable" relations with FTCs. Problems between MOFERT and local entrepreneurs were the subject of a meeting convened in summer 1988 by the Ministry of Agriculture and MOFERT, where some of the one hundred exporting TVEs complained that MOFERT had constrained their access to international resources and opportunities in four ways: MOFERT paid them for their goods at least a year after the initial sale (no doubt MOFERT waited until it was paid by the foreign buyer first); MOFERT had cut the foreign exchange retention level in Sichuan Province by 4 percent; MOFERT had compelled Jiangsu Province to buy foreign exchange with local currency at a high price to meet its foreign exchange quota; and the price MOFERT paid for finished goods had not changed in almost ten years even though the price of inputs had gone up by 150–200 percent since 1979.[19]

MOFERT lost more authority after 1992. As table 3.3 shows, the formerly all-powerful provincial specialized FTCs under MOFERT had been losing their monopoly since the late-1980s. Their influence decreased most dramatically in 1991–92 as the share of exports handled by municipal FTCs and joint ventures rose from 30 to 50 percent. By 1993, these two exporting sectors were responsible for over 62 percent of all provincial exports and, by 1995, 74 percent of all goods shipped out of the province. Interestingly, in 1995 local FTCs took back control of over 5 percent of provincial exports that had been shipped out by JVs the previous year.

MOBILIZING TOWN AND VILLAGE ENTERPRISE EXPORTS

Although the state in many less-developed countries marginalizes the countryside, China's export-led growth incorporated China's rural coastal communities into the regime's endeavors. Beginning in 1985, the central government pushed parts of rural China, and particularly TVEs, to export. As they opened the three delta regions of the Pearl River, the Yangzi River,

---

18. Lai Yitai, "Fazhan nongcun chuanhui jingji qianjing leguan" [An optimistic perspective on developing a foreign exchange earning rural economy], *Nongmin ribao* [Farmer's daily], 26 August 1988, p. 1.

19. Sun Weihui, "Wei xiangzhen qiye chukou chuanzao tiaojian," [Create favorable conditions for township and village enterprises to export], ibid., 19 July 1988, p. 1.

Table 3.3   Decentralization of Foreign Trade in Jiangsu Province, 1985–1997 (thousand $)

Exporting Unit	1985	1989	1991	1992	1993	1995	1997
Centrally and provincially controlled FTCs[a]	155,851 (100)	213,227 (87.35)	241,302 (69.73)	238,336 (51.03)	224,618 (37.70)	299,877 (25.43)	320,494 (21.06)
Municipal-level FTCs	0 (0)	22,022 (9.02)	59,336 (17.14)	98,120 (24.01)	144,393 (24.23)	471,548 (39.99)	543,156 (35.69)
Joint ventures	0 (0)	8,862 (3.96)	45,415 (13.12)	130,639 (27.94)	226,850 (38.07)	407,793 (34.58)	658,160 (43.25)
TOTAL	155,851 (100)	244,111 (100)	346,053 (100)	467,095 (100)	595,861 (100)	1,179,218 (100)	1,521,810 (100)

Source: Jiangsu tongji nianjian, 1994, 1996, 1997 and 1998 (Jiangsu statistical yearbook, 1994, 1996, 1997, and 1998).
Notes: Numbers in parentheses are percentages. FTCs, foreign trade companies.
[a] Because data from 1995 onward combine exports by provincial specialized foreign trade companies (which are arms of the Ministry of Foreign Trade and Economic Cooperation in Beijing) with provincial local trade companies and central industrial foreign trade companies, I have combined these three categories with exports by provincially owned industrial companies to create one category: centrally and provincially controlled FTCs. Note the shift of control to municipalities and joint ventures and away from centrally controlled FTCs.

and the southern section of Fujian (the Min and Li river basins), central leaders called on rural elites to make their decisions about crop production based on global demand and to produce crops that could be processed into exportable commodities. The earlier slogan, "*nong, gong, mao*" (agriculture, industry, exports), implied that surplus agricultural and industrial products could be exported if markets (and products) were acceptable; the new slogan raised in 1985, "*mao, gong, nong*" (trade, industry, agriculture), directed farmers to study global market demand and respond to it.[20]

And that is precisely what rural China did. Exports of processed agricultural products increased dramatically after 1985. Such exports doubled from $3.4 billion in 1978 to $6.97 billion in 1985, at an annual rate of 9.3 percent; by 1989 exports reached $13.5 billion, an annual rate for 1985–89 of 14.2 percent. Nevertheless, top leaders in the agricultural sector, including Zhao Ziyang's key rural advisor, Du Runsheng, had not forcefully promoted rural exports to Zhao.[21] Also, the central government offered local governments few incentives, such as access to technology or foreign exchange, to engage in foreign trade.

20. Guowuyuan guanyu pizhuan "Changjiang, Zhujiang sanjiaozhou he Minnan xiazhangchuan san jiao diqu zuotanhui jiyao de tongzhi" [Notification of the passing down by the State Council of the "Summary of the Minutes of the Conference on the Yangzi River, the Pearl River Delta and the Triangular District in Southern Fujian of Xiamen, Zhangzhou and Quanzhou"], 18 February 1985, in *Yanhai, yanjiang, yanbian kaifang falu fagui ji guifanxing wenjian huibian* [Compendium of documents concerning the laws, regulations, and standardization of the opening of the coastal, riverine, and border regions] (Beijing: Falu chubanshe, 1992), pp. 307–8.
21. Interview with a member of the Research Centre on Rural Development who had put forward this policy suggestion to Du.

Only in 1987, did Zhao create a new policy framework to stimulate TVE exports through his Coastal Development Strategy. Key agencies, such as the CCP's Rural Work Department, the State Economic Commission, the SSTC, and MOFERT were all involved.[22] Zhao, other leaders, and economists recognized that this was China's last chance to join the rising tide of export-led growth in East Asia. Also, Zhao's inability since 1984 to make SOEs more flexible highlighted the responsiveness of TVEs to global markets.[23] He also understood the concept of relative prices and rural China's comparative advantage in export promotion.[24] His years at the grassroots in Guangdong and Sichuan provinces taught him to trust the power of material incentives in the rural areas. Perhaps most important was the fear of an impending rural labor crisis. Decollectivization had caused millions of rural laborers to be unemployed; SOEs could not soak up the exploding surplus labor. So, Wang Jian, a researcher in the State Planning Commission proposed the concept of the great circle (*da xunhuan*), through which TVEs would import foreign resources, process them for export, and thereby employ the surplus labor.[25] Foreign exchange would upgrade China's SOEs. Thus central planners, not rural or provincial elites, proposed expanding rural exports in order to solve rural China's surplus labor problem.

Beginning in 1988, reformers allowed counties around the fourteen OCCs, as well as rural areas around cities near the coast such as Nanjing and Hangzhou, to accept FDI.[26] New state regulations promised exporting TVEs the right to use their retained foreign exchange to import technology, equipment, and raw materials on the same terms as SOEs and admonished bureaucrats not to interfere with TVE technology imports.[27] Analysts

22. Tian Zhun-Mei, "Zhongguo dalu xiangzhen qiye yu xiang cun jingji fazhan" [Mainland China's township and village enterprises and rural economic development] (paper presented at the Conference on Problems in Rural Development, Columbia University, 1995).
23. According to Zhao Ming of the State Planning Commission, China's heavy industry had failed to enter the international market. See "Seize the Opportunity to Head for the World," *Renmin ribao* [People's Daily], 5 February 1988, p. 2, in *Foreign Broadcast Information Service* (hereafter *FBIS*), no. 33, 19 February 1988, pp. 17–20.
24. "Zhao on the Coastal Area's Development Strategy," *Beijing Review*, 8–14 February 1988, p. 18.
25. Wang Jian, "The Correct Strategy for Long-Term Economic Development—Concept of the Development Strategy of Joining the 'Great International Cycle,'" in *China's Coastal Development* ed., Joseph Fewsmith and Gary Zou, special issue, *Chinese Economic Studies* 25 (fall 1991), pp. 7–16.
26. Yanhai compendium, "Guowuyuan guanyu kuoda yanhai jingji kaifangqu fanwei de tongzhi" [State Council notification on expanding the sphere of the open coastal economic region], 18 March 1988, pp. 316–18.
27. "Yinfa 'guanyu tuidong xiangzhen qiye chukou chuanhui rougan zhengce de guiding' de tongzhi" [Notification about the rules on some policies to promote township and village enterprises to export and earn foreign exchange], in Zhongguo xiang zhen qiye nianjian bianluo weiyuanhui [Editorial Board of the Chinese TVE Yearbook], ed., *Xiangzhen qiye nianjian, 1989* [Township and village enterprises yearbook, 1989] (Beijing: Nongye chuban she, 1989), pp. 140–41.

Table 3.4   Foreign Exchange Earnings from Township and Village Enterprises, 1984–1998 (billion $)

Year	TVE Export Earnings	Total Export Earnings[a]	TVEs (% of total export earnings)
1984–85	2.4[b]	52.1	4.6
1986	4.5[c]	31.4	14.3
1987	5.1[d]	39.5	12.9
1988	8.0[e]	47.6	16.9
1989	10.1	52.9	19.1
1990	12.5[f]	64.5	19.4
1991	17.0[g]	71.9	23.6
1992	20.0	85.5	23.4
1993[h]	38.1	91.6	41.6
1994[h]	37.3	121.0	30.8
1995[i]	53.0	148.0	35.8
1996[j]	72.3	151.1	47.8
1997[j]	83.8	182.8	45.8
1998[j]	82.7	183.8	45.0
1999[k]	93.3	195.0	47.8

Sources:
[a] 1984–85 figure is from International Monetary Fund, *Direction of Trade Statistics Yearbook, 1991* (Washington, D.C.: International Monetary Fund, 1991); 1992 and 1993 data are from International Monetary Fund, *Direction of Trade Statistics Yearbook, 1994* (Washington, D.C.: International Monetary Fund, 1994), p. 151. All other data are from International Monetary Fund, *Direction of Trade Statistics Yearbook, 1999* (Washington, D.C.: International Monetary Fund, 1999). All figures are Direction of Trade Statistics World Total.
[b] Based on *Foreign Broadcast Information Service*, 13 April 1990, which reported that 1984–89 TVE exports totaled $35 billion.
[c] *China Daily*, 15 December 1987, p. 1.
[d] Interview REBDZ-4/89, 1989.
[e] *China Daily*, 25 September 1989, p. 1.
[f] *Beijing Review*, 24 (1991): 29.
[g] *Xinhua General News Service*, 4 October 1992.
[h] The number has been converted from renminbi to dollars, because in 1994, the average rate of renminbi to dollars changed from 5.76 to 8.62.
[i] These data are drawn from Zhang Xiaohe, "Rural Industrialization and International Trade," in *China in Transition: Issues and Policies*, ed. David C. B. Teather and Herbert S. Yee (New York: St. Martin's Press, 1999), p. 158.
[j] From 1996 on, the value of TVE Export Earnings was converted from renminbi to dollars by using average exchange rate of renminbi to dollars for the year.
[k] Zhao Huanxin, "Official Urges Support Policy for Companies," *China Daily*, 17 July 2000.

in Jiangsu Province saw this as a critical opportunity for TVEs to participate in the outward-oriented economy.[28]

Although table 3.4 shows that TVE exports increased significantly between 1985 and 1986, leaders in most industrialized rural communities preferred relational contracting, that is, dealing with people that they knew in the domestic market, to the risky venture of foreign trade and global

28. Zhang Bolin and Tao Pengde, "Fazhan waixiangxing qiye de jige wenti" [Several questions on developing outward-oriented TVEs], *Zhongguo xiangzhen qiye lilun yu shijian* [Theory and practice in China's TVEs] 1–2 (1990): 30.

markets.[29] TVEs had established their businesses based on close links to SOEs that had been searching for new production facilities.[30] Township leaders also feared turning their TVEs into JVs because as JVs they paid no taxes for three years and half taxes for two more years, weakening local budgets and undermining official efforts to meet their tax obligations under the fiscal responsibility system.[31]

Faced with this hesitancy but committed to its new strategy, the state resorted to policy instruments borrowed from Maoist political campaigns.[32] Test points, which received favorable but secret preferential treatment, and models to be emulated were promoted in the press.[33] Export promotion became a political obligation as foreign exchange and export quotas were passed down, level by level.[34] The result was a government-produced export fever. Although many localities that otherwise might have never moved into the export sector did make a successful transition, others that should never have been involved in export production tried and failed. Propagating false models and rags-to-riches stories created false expectations and frustration for localities that were eventually unsuccessful. The negative results proliferated; to meet their quotas, many localities bought foreign exchange, pushing up its domestic price. Nevertheless, given the state's incentives[35] and the ease with which TVEs could respond to global markets due to their low level of capitalization, labor-intensive TVEs and their communities quickly marched into the maelstrom of the international market.[36]

29. Oliver E. Williamson, *The Economic Institutions of Capitalism: Firms, Markets, Relational Contracting* (New York: Free Press, 1985). For TVE resistance to producing for export, see Luo Xiaopeng, "Ownership and Status Stratification," in *China's Rural Industry: Structure, Development, and Reform*, ed. William A. Byrd and Lin Qingsong (New York: Oxford University Press, 1990), pp. 134–71.

30. Dwight H. Perkins, "The Influence of Economic Reforms on China's Urbanization," in *Chinese Urban Reforms: What Model Now?* ed. R. Yin-Wang Kwok, William L. Parish, and Anthony Gar-On Yeh (Armonk: M. E. Sharpe, 1990), pp. 78–108.

31. A township party secretary in Nantong County, Jiangsu Province, expressed those concerns. Interview, June 1992.

32. Under Deng, campaign-like mobilization remained a key method for obtaining economic policy compliance. See Tyrene White, "Postrevolutionary Mobilization in China: The One-Child Policy Reconsidered," *World Politics* 43 (October 1990): 53–76.

33. *Nongmin ribao* [Farmer's Daily] summer 1988 was replete with reports of how individual entrepreneurs and entrepreneurial communities had suddenly grown rich through exports.

34. Jiangsu Province introduced the "double-line contract system," in which export quotas were passed down to enterprises while export purchase quotas were passed down to local FTCs. Samuel P. S. Ho, *Rural China in Transition: Non-agricultural Development in Rural Jiangsu, 1978–1990* (Oxford: Clarendon Press, 1994), pp. 72–73.

35. In 1988, TVEs in Jiangsu were given subsidies to cover any losses incurred by selling to FTCs instead of on the domestic market. Ibid. p. 73.

36. According to Shafer's schema, TVEs are a "low/low" sector, with low economies of scale, low factor inflexibility, and low capital intensity that allow them to restructure relatively easily and follow "market conforming strategies." See D. Michael Shafer, *Winners and Losers: How Sectors Shape the Developmental Prospects of States* (Ithaca: Cornell University Press, 1994), pp. 10–13.

Ironically, the domestic political and economic retrenchment of 1988–89, which overtook Zhao's Coastal Development initiative, further pushed TVEs into export markets. Conservatives in Beijing, such as Yao Yilin and Li Peng, blamed TVEs for stealing SOE markets and inflating their input costs, thereby cutting SOE profits. On June 9, 1989, in his speech to the martial-law troops who controlled Beijing after the June 4 Tiananmen crackdown, Deng himself said that "concerning certain TVEs which waste electricity and raw materials, we must close a batch (*guan yi pi*)."[37] In fall 1989, the Thirty-nine Points called on TVEs to return to earlier activities, such as processing agricultural products and local raw materials, and to remain adjuncts to the major industries "instead of scrambling with large enterprises for raw materials and energy."[38] Handicraft and labor-intensive exports were in, but the growing electronics sector belonged to the SOEs. TVEs were now ineligible for loans unless they were involved in exports, energy production, or agricultural processing, and, according to Li Peng, their development was to remain in line with "the actual requirements of state industrial policies" (i.e., the state plan).[39]

Yet a looming debt burden, due to the post-Tiananmen freeze on foreign loans by all international lenders, led China to increase incentives for exporting firms, including an eight-point program to encourage TVE exports.[40] TVE exporters could now repay technical transformation loans with pretax income. In 1991, new policies gave TVEs the same rights as SOEs in terms of loans for technical innovation, tax breaks for technology imports, and import licenses for material, parts, or other components used for increasing exports. And although they were not to compete with SOEs for domestic market share, they could compete on the same terms as SOEs when the state sought tenders to supply exports for light industry, electrical machinery, and agricultural produce.[41]

INDICATORS OF TOWN AND VILLAGE ENTERPRISE INTERNATIONALIZATION

Beginning in the late 1980s and into the mid-1990s, the rural areas became closely linked to the international market through export promo-

37. Quoted in "Dashiji" [Important events], *Xiangzhen qiye nianjian, 1990* [Township and village enterprises yearbook, 1990], p. 359.
38. See "Decision on Further Improving the Economic Environment, Straightening out the Economic Order and Deepening the Reform," *Beijing Review* 33 (12 February 1990): ix. Point 19 focuses specifically on TVEs.
39. "Li Peng's Government Work Report," 20 March 1990, in *FBIS*, no. 67 (6 April 1990), p. 24.
40. See Li Erkuan, "Central Authorities Formulate Eight Preferential Policies to Encourage Township and Town Enterprises to Develop Export-Oriented Economy," *Wen wei po*, 26 February 1990, reprinted in *FBIS*, no. 39 (27 February 1990), pp. 32–33.
41. See "State Council Promotes TVEs to Participate in International Competition," *Jiangsu xiangzhen qiye* [Jiangsu township and village enterprises] 3 (1991): 7.

Table 3.5 Purchases of Export Commodities from Township and Village Enterprises, 1985–1999

Year	Purchases of TVE Export Commodities (million RMB)	Total Purchases of Export Commodities (million RMB)[a]	Purchases of TVE Export Commodities (% of purchases of total export commodities)
1985	3,900	81,200	4.8
1988	26,900	140,700	19.1
1989	37,100	169,300	29.9
1990	48,600	199,300	24.4
1991	67,000	225,900	29.7
1992	119,200	281,300	42.4
1993	235,100	436,800	53.8
1994	339,830	n.a.	n.a.
1995	539,454	n.a.	33.7[b]
1996	600,790	n.a.	35.7[b]
1997	682,648	n.a.	n.a.
1998	685,360	n.a.	n.a.
1999	720,000	n.a.	n.a.

Sources: Zhongguo xiangzhen qiye nianjian [Township and village enterprise yearbook] (Beijing: Nongye chubanshe, 1994), p. 203; 1996–97, p. 122; 1997–99, p. 136; and Zhongguo nongcun tongji nianjian, 1995 [Chinese rural statistical yearbook] (Beijing: Nongye chubanshe, 1995), p. 41. Data on export percentages in 1995–96 and purchases of export commodities for 1996 come from interviews with officials from the Chinese State Council. Data for 1999 come from BBC, Survey of World Broadcasts, FEW/0624, FEW/0643.
Note: n.a., not available.
[a] In 1994, China stopped calculating the total value of its purchases of export commodities; thereafter it only reported exports shipped out of the country in dollars.
[b] The drop in the percentage of total exports from 1993 to 1995 may be due to the fact that many exporting TVEs became joint ventures after 1993.

tion and FDI. Making up only 5 percent of China's export earnings in dollars in 1984–85 (table 3.4), TVE export earnings increased dramatically between 1990 and 1991, jumping again after 1992. By 1993, TVEs earned 32.7 percent of all of China's foreign exchange. Of the total value of commodities purchased by FTCs for export,[42] TVEs made up only 4.8 percent in 1985. By 1991 they made up almost 30 percent of all export purchases, and by 1993 over half (53.8 percent) of all purchases of export commodities by state FTCs were produced in TVEs (table 3.5).[43] In 1994 this figure increased 35 percent over 1993, showing that the enormous upswing in the role of TVE exports was continuing.

42. The value of TVE products the state bought in renminbi for exports did not equal the value of foreign exchange the state earned for selling those products. TVEs produced low-value goods that the state sold cheaply on the international market; therefore, these goods made up a smaller percent of China's foreign currency earnings.
43. We must be concerned about the validity of these numbers given the fact that China now admits that local TVE figures were inflated, particularly after Deng's 1992 trip.

Table 3.6   Export Value of Rural Enterprises, 1990–1997 (billion RMB)

	1990	1991	1992	1993	1994	1995	1996	1997
Garments	6.38	9.80	18.64	36.34	54.92	83.85	96.68	113.45
Artwork and handicrafts	6.14	8.17	13.23	21.53	34.83	48.82	55.00	60.18
Light industrial manufactures	6.35	10.17	18.60	44.62	60.71	105.29	120.64	146.23
Chemical products	2.47	3.24	6.69	10.96	17.70	28.84	32.99	36.61
Silk products	2.91	3.39	5.84	8.31	11.06	17.17	13.06	11.12
Textile products	8.09	10.71	18.63	28.85	50.42	69.98	68.05	75.60
Machinery products	2.64	3.79	7.28	14.56	24.71	36.05	42.81	50.65

Source: Zhongguo xiangzhen qiye nianjian [China township and village enterprise yearbook] (Beijing: Nongye chubanshe, 1991–98).

Table 3.7   Township and Village Enterprise Exports as Share of TVE Production, 1990–1997

	1990	1991	1992	1993	1994	1995	1996	1997
Garments	27.84	32.46	37.46	43.22	45.57	48.85	55.38	59.71
Artwork and handicrafts	55.31	57.29	63.22	64.22	n.a.	n.a.	n.a.	n.a.
Light industrial manufactures	1.21	1.56	3.56	5.16	4.70	5.70	6.51	7.53
Chemical products	8.79	8.75	11.83	12.94	13.83	16.68	17.90	19.76
Textile products	11.50	12.62	15.40	15.60	18.42	20.10	23.69	25.91
Machinery products	5.33	6.03	7.67	n.a.	6.01	6.72	7.84	8.81

Source: Zhongguo xiangzhen qiye nianjian [China township and village enterprise yearbook] (Beijing: Nongye chubanshe, 1991–98).
Note: Percentage of total township and village enterprise production in that sector. n.a., not available.

According to the Ministry of Agriculture, exports had become the engine of growth for TVE development.[44] The data in the tables 3.6 and 3.7 demonstrate the greater involvement of rural industry in the global economy. Table 3.6 shows the remarkable growth in exports from 1990 to 1997 in seven industrial sectors. Although China clearly has comparative advantage in labor-intensive sectors, it also increased exports in more technical sectors, such as machinery products, where the annual growth rate in exports grew by 44.7 percent in 1990–97. Table 3.7 shows the progressive internationalization of these seven sectors by presenting TVE exports as a share of TVE production in each sector. By 1997, almost 60 percent of all garments produced in TVEs nationwide were shipped overseas.

Particularly in the early 1990s, rural internationalization was critical for China's overall economy. TVEs, along with JVs, were the engine driving China's overall export performance during this key period of export-led

44. See "Nongcun jingji yunxing qingkuang fenxi baogao" [Report on the analysis of the current situation of the 1994 rural economy], Ministry of Agriculture, Rural Research Centre, Group on Current Trends, Beijing, February 1995.

Table 3.8 Township and Village Enterprise Exports as a Share of Total Exports, 1988–1992

	1988	1989	1990	1991	1992
Garments	49.6	65.2	72.0	77.5	89.7
Artwork and handicrafts	39.0	43.1	45.0	52.0	63.7
Light industrial manufactures	19.3	22.8	28.5	38.7	53.9
Chemical products	23.6	36.3	27.3	31.5	53.2
Silk products	21.4	25.1	24.3	33.7	54.0
Textile products	16.4	19.2	21.9	25.0	n.a.
Machinery products	16.2	19.6	21.8	23.8	n.a.

Source: Zhongguo xiangzhen qiye nianjian [China rural enterprise yearbook], cited in Yan Shanping, "Export-Oriented Rural Enterprises," *JETRO China Newsletter* 118 (September–October 1995): 11.
Note: Values are percentages of total nationwide exports in that sector. Exports of rural enterprises are totals of renminbi-based direct and indirect exports and revenues from consignment processing. n.a., not available.

growth.[45] The increase in overall exports in dollars between 1986 and 1990 was $33.1 billion; in that same period, TVE exports grew $8 billion, contributing 24 percent of that growth. But in 1990–93, when China's exports jumped $26 billion, TVE exports increased $17.5 billion, 67 percent of export growth in that same period.

Several economic sectors relied heavily on TVEs to develop their export markets (table 3.8). In 1990 TVEs produced nearly 75 percent of all of China's exported garments, and by 1992 they produced 89.7 percent of all clothing exports. In 1992 TVEs made up an even greater proportion of exports in chemicals (53.2 percent), light industry (53.9 percent), silk (54 percent), and handicrafts (63.7 percent).[46] These ratios show that parts of rural China were far more internationalized than the urban SOEs.

Finally, TVEs attracted FDI to coastal China, giving foreign firms access to China's cheap labor and domestic market. By the end of 1990, foreign investors had established over 7,000 rural joint ventures and rural wholly owned foreign enterprises (WOFEs), comprising 24.1 percent of the total number of joint venture and foreign investment contracts, with a total investment of $3.4 billion.[47] After the 1992 opening, rural JVs and

45. For support that TVE exports were critical to China's overall export performance see Zhang Xiaohe, "Rural Industrialization and International Trade," in *China in Transition: Issues and Policies*, ed. David C. B. Teather and Herbert S. Yee (New York: St. Martin's Press, 1999), pp. 158–70.
46. See Zhou Handa, "Xiangzhen qiye waixiangxing jingji qude xin tupo" [Township and village enterprise export-oriented economy achieved a new breakthrough], in *Xiangzhen qiye nianjian, 1993* [China township and village enterprise yearbook, 1993] (Beijing: Nongye chubanshe, 1993), pp. 272–73.
47. Xinhua News Service, "Ma Zhongcheng Addresses Forum on Joint Ventures," 14 May 1991, reprinted in *FBIS*, no. 94 (15 May 1991): 33. Chinese statistics included wholly foreign owned enterprises among the number of rural joint ventures until 1997 (see table 3.9). But outside Guangdong and perhaps Fujian provinces, this category of enterprise was not that large. Still, they must have made up a not insignificant part of the total amount of foreign direct investment in rural China.

rural WOFEs jumped to 15,000, still about 16.5 percent of the national total,[48] and, by 1995, 35,000 rural JVs and rural WOFEs were actually using $5.68 billion.[49]

CHANGING GLOBAL CONTEXT: TVE
INTERNATIONALIZATION DURING THE EAST ASIAN
FINANCIAL CRISIS

In 1998, the East Asian financial crisis washed over the TVE sector, demonstrating that global markets were critical to rural internationalization. Foreign exchange earnings and exports remained flat, showing no improvement over 1997. A significant number of exporting TVEs and rural JVs were forced to close as their markets disappeared. As table 3.9 shows, the number of rural JVs dropped 25 percent from 1996 to 1997 and continued to drop in 1998. Similarly, FDI was deeply affected by the economic calamity that overtook network capital in Southeast Asia; from 1996 to 1998, the yearly inflow of FDI into rural China dropped by 24 percent, in dollars. The price of labor had been the comparative advantage for TVEs; the nose dive in the value of currencies in Southeast Asia and Korea, even as the Chinese renminbi was kept stable, allowed enterprises in Southeast Asia to steal away Chinese markets in the United States and Europe.[50] Interviews in Anhui and Jiangsu provinces in early 2001 suggested that most TVEs were helpless to respond to the crisis in the short term, although some did shift their markets and upgrade the value of the products.[51] The disruption, however, was temporary; by 1999 the sector had recovered somewhat as export purchases from TVEs rose 5.1 percent (see table 3.5).

Local Incentives for Rural Internationalization

By the beginning of the 1990s, many domestic incentives pushed rural officials into the international market. First, after the 1988–90 retrenchment hit TVEs hard, rural officials needed a foot in both the domestic and inter-

---

48. Perhaps 50 percent of rural JVs were linked with domestic firms that had set up shop in Hong Kong (called "round tripping") in order to get tax free policies and the right to buy two foreign cars. Interview with researchers in Ministry of Agriculture, December 1991.

49. "Dalu xiangzhen qiye wu yue chukou 1,146 yi yuan" [In the previous five months, mainland TVEs exported 114.6 billion yuan], *Shijie ribao* [World daily], 5 July 1995, p. A18.

50. Hua Jiayi, "Sunan xiangzhen qiye ruhe miandui Yazhou jinrong weiji?" [How can township and village enterprises in southern Jiangsu deal with the East Asian financial crisis?], *Sunan xiangzhen qiye* [Southern Jiangsu's TVEs] 8 (1998): 4–5, 9.

51. These interviews were carried out by a team of Chinese graduate students in five counties in February 2001.

Table 3.9   Foreign Direct Investment in Rural China, 1989–1998

Year	Foreign Direct Investment[a] (million RMB)	Number of Firms with Foreign Investment[b]
1989	788.19	2,915
1990	2,234.64	6,987
1991	1,611.09	8,500
1992	6,400.58	15,000
1993	18,034.81	27,506
1994	22,959.10	29,371
1995	30,603.22	38,743
1996	32,250.92	39,508
1997	31,815.41	29,779
1998	26,584.11	27,658

Source: FDI in renminbi from *Zhongguo xiangzhen qiye nianjian* [China township and village enterprise yearbook], 1990–99. Firms with foreign investment from selected newspaper reports and State Council documents.

Note: n.a., not available.

[a] FDI in RMB could include foreign currency loans from the Bank of China, but it was unlikely to make many such loans to TVEs. Also, it may include foreign government loans, gifts by international organizations, overseas Chinese and funds from the Hong Kong Monetary Authority. The amount of these funds going into the rural areas is likely to be very small. In any case, it is the trend in investment that is most important. Thanks to Carsten Holz for his help on this.

[b] Data here could include wholly owned foreign enterprises (WOFEs) which were established in the townships and villages. The sharp decrease after 1996 may result in part because WOFEs were excluded from this data source in 1997, when only true joint ventures were included. Previously, the number of WOFEs in Guangdong could have been significant. But, the decline may also have resulted from the East Asian financial crisis.

national markets. Second, there was the "power of attraction of things foreign." Export markets enhanced the reputation of an enterprise's products; if foreigners bought them, they were clearly superior. Third, imported technology raised a firm's domestic competitiveness.[52] Foreign exchange earned from exports allowed local officials to buy critical resources that were in short supply in the domestic market. For example, Wujiang County in Suzhou Municipality, a leading silk exporter, purchased Japanese fertilizer in the mid-1980s when domestic supplies were short, stabilizing agriculture and relations between the local state and the farmers.[53]

Another major incentive for rural internationalization was the opportunity to establish rural JVs. Turning TVEs into JVs created global linkages for

52. In Shunde City, Guangdong Province, one bicycle-light plant that imported a production line controlled 25 percent of the domestic market. See Chen Jiyuan, ed., *Xiangzhen qiye moshi yanjiu* [Research on township and village enterprises models] (Beijing: Chinese Academy of Social Sciences Publishers, 1989), pp. 176–77.

53. Interview in Wujiang County, 1988.

an otherwise isolated countryside, helping TVEs import technology at low tariff rates. JVs brought money to a capital-deprived TVE sector; allowed rural officials to import cars duty free, although in July 1994 new regulations denied TVEs the right to import cars until the JV was capitalized; created new and relatively secure export markets because the foreign partner usually supplied the global market channels; and allowed rural entrepreneurs to bypass the FTCs, which constrained business relationships. According to one TVE manager who had established two JVs, "the Chinese government doesn't allow us to do business directly with the outside world, so we must find foreign partners. I must have the right to send people out of China for business."[54] Rural JVs also provided opportunities for foreign travel and access to foreign exchange; some rural JVs received permits to export a variety of products including goods bought from domestic factories in local currency.

Symbolic and political factors were also at work. JVs became status symbols for local cadres, signs that they were progressive, that foreigners appreciated their management skills. Finally, many township and village cadres were given quotas for establishing JVs, which they needed to fulfill as part of their year-end evaluation. The pressure came from above to find foreign partners and led, no doubt, to a significant amount of false reporting and fictional rural JVs.

External Pressures for Rural Internationalization

While domestic interests promoted rural internationalization, the enormous demand of overseas Chinese network capital for access to cheap rural labor and domestic markets was equally important. With the dramatic increase in labor costs in Taiwan and Hong Kong in the 1980s, network capital knocked loudly on the doors of rural China.[55] Whereas the large multinational corporations preferred working in the cities, the overseas Chinese felt quite comfortable in the more personalized, face-to-face world of rural China; here ethnic or familial ties, as well as linguistic and cultural compatibility, explain the depth of the transnational economic links.[56] One study in Panyu and Nanhai counties in Guangdong Province and in Suzhou Municipality in Jiangsu Province found only four nonethnic-Chinese investors in the 113 rural JVs they studied in Guangdong, although they found twenty Japanese investors among forty-one investors in Suzhou.[57]

54. Interview BBXG/1992.
55. Hsing, *Making Capitalism in China.*
56. Constance Lever-Tracy, David Ip and Noel Tracy, *The Chinese Diaspora and Mainland China* (New York: Macmillan, 1996).
57. Constance Lever-Tracy, David Ip, and Noel Tracy, "Rural Partnership and Global Markets: Partnership Ventures in Guangdong and Jiangsu," *Regional Development Studies* 3 (winter 1996–97): 67.

Among twenty rural JVs in Nantong County and Zhangjiagang that I studied in 1991–92, 77.5 percent were investors from Hong Kong or Taiwan, and the 15 percent from the United States appeared to be owned by U.S.–based Taiwanese firms.[58]

Network capital undermined central controls through these informal relations with rural governments. Taiwanese investors were particularly interested in the enormous rents in China's domestic economy.[59] A study cited by Hsing found that the most common reason for 40.9 percent of Taiwanese investing in China was access to the domestic market. Low production costs (27.1 percent) and an abundant supply of labor (24.9 percent) were the second- and third-ranking reasons.[60] Some rural governments helped their partners access the domestic market. Because most rural JVs were capitalized at less than $500,000, local governments had legal authority to approve them with little oversight by supralocal authorities. And once word spread in Taiwan of these profitable opportunities, the swarming nature of Taiwanese investment[61] (many investors quickly following the lead of a successful investor) brought a multitude of foreign investors into rural China.

Regional and Provincial Context of Rural Internationalization

A rural locality's incentives and opportunities to link with the international system were strongly affected by its province's or region's level of internationalization, its location, the views of its elites, and the central government's decisions about which regions were opened to transnational exchanges and the policies governing these interactions. Here again we see a mix of central policy, local economic conditions, and the nature of external linkages—proximity to ethnic Chinese, Korean, or Japanese markets—affecting internationalization.[62]

The regions that were deregulated earlier generally established stronger transnational linkages. Four Guangdong counties, classified in the late

58. David Zweig, "Reaping Rural Rewards: China's Town and Village Enterprises Can Make Good Investment Partners," *China Business Review* (November–December 1992): 12–17.
59. Interviews in Zhangjiagang with investment brokers for Taiwanese investors, November 1991.
60. Hsing, *Making Capitalism in China*, p. 209.
61. Gary G. Hamilton, "Organization and Market Processes in Taiwan's Capitalist Economy," in *The Economic Organization of East Asian Capitalism*, ed. Marco Orru, Nicole Woolsey Biggart, and Gary G. Hamilton (Thousands Oaks: Sage Publications, 1997), pp. 237–93.
62. Graham E. Johnson, "Open for Business, Open to the World: Consequences of Global Incorporation in Guangdong and the Pearl River Delta," in *The Economic Transformation of South China*, ed. Thomas P. Lyons and Victor Nee (Ithaca: Cornell East Asia Program, 1994), pp. 55–88.

1970s as export bases for supplying Hong Kong, established powerful
FTCs; through the mid-1980s, these "small dragons" bought up exportable
products from all over China and shipped them out through their own
county's FTCs, earning large rents.[63] In the coastal countryside, some rural
areas around the fourteen OCCs were opened to FDI in 1985, while other
parts of the countryside had to wait until March 1988 (see table 3.1). As of
1999, some parts of rural China still remained closed.

Physical proximity to external trading partners created what Brantly
Womack and Guanzhi Zhao call the "grand trade advantages" of being a
coastal province.[64] My own data on the regional distribution of TVE exports
show the following ratios for coastal to western to central regions:

	coastal	western	central
1987	84.0	0.89	14.0
1992	89.9	0.55	9.5
1998	90.8	0.40	8.5

As these data show, these advantages, which already existed in 1987,
expanded by 1992, deepening the links between TVEs on the coast and the
outside world, compared to the rest of rural China.

The attitude of provincial or municipal officials toward rural internationalization influenced the scale of TVE exports and FDI in the countryside. Jiangsu provincial leaders were quite suspicious of foreign investors,
and in the late 1980s criticized rural areas that established too many JVs.[65]
Also, concerns that FDI would increase inequalities between northern and
southern Jiangsu contributed to the lukewarm provincial response to
foreign capital. Yet as more open-minded provincial leaders took over the
provincial reins of power, Jiangsu's stress on export-led growth increased.

Hypothesis Testing: Rural Industrialization and Internationalization

A key domestic market force affecting rural internationalization was the
level of TVE development in a locality. Products from rural industry, rather
than agricultural or cash crop production, became the major exports from
rural China because overseas Chinese were looking for workshops with
cheap labor to keep their own manufacturing competitive. I hypothesize
that the stronger a region's TVE sector, the deeper its level of internationalization, both in terms of exports and FDI, because provinces with strong
TVE sectors, including adept management, skilled workers, economies of
scale, and networks linking the countryside to FTCs and foreign markets,
were more competitive globally than those regions with few enterprises.
Second, and conversely, I hypothesize that the greater the role of agriculture in a region, the less its level of internationalization.

The potential role of politics or institutional constraints leads to a third group of hypotheses focusing on the relationship between SOEs and TVEs. In Nantong, I was told that because the municipality relied more on SOEs than TVEs, urban administrators had channeled prospective foreign investors to SOEs and away from TVEs. In such regions, FTCs might also favor SOEs over TVEs when seeking exportable products. In fact, I was told that FTCs in Nantong turned to TVE exports only after 1992 when more and more SOEs received direct export powers, allowing them to bypass FTCs entirely. Also, many provinces were unable to open their rural areas to FDI before 1988; in fact, many rural areas remained closed through the 1990s. Therefore, I hypothesize that in provinces with significant SOE sectors, administrators channeled economic activity away from TVEs. To test this hypothesis, I have created a variable TVE/SOE—where TVE reflects the gross value of industrial output (GVIO) of TVEs in a province and SOEs reflect the GVIO of SOEs in that province. A negative correlation will support my hypothesis.[66]

A fourth hypothesis to test concerns the independent role of location on TVE exports and FDI. Based on the arguments of Womack and Zhao, I anticipate that a province's being on the coast should correlate with higher levels of TVE exports because coastal provinces had the "grand advantages" of trade. Similarly, because coastal regions were closer to foreign markets and were opened to FDI earlier, these areas should attract more FDI. So I have created a dummy variable, TVECOAST, which measures the impact of a province's being on the coast versus not being on the coast.

Using a provincial-level data set on TVEs from 1987 to 1993, I have developed a model to test these hypotheses.[67] I employ two dependent vari-

63. John Kamm, "Reforming Foreign Trade," in Ezra Vogel, *One Step Ahead in China: Guangdong under Reform* (Cambridge, Mass.: Harvard University Press, 1990).

64. The "grand" advantage of a coastal province is juxtaposed to the "petty" advantage of being a border province; the latter has only one close trading partner rather than access to the whole international system. Brantly Womack and Guanzhi Zhao, "The Many Worlds of China's Provinces: Foreign Trade and Diversification," in *China Deconstructs: Politics, Trade and Regionalism*, ed. David S. G. Goodman and Gerald Segal (London: Routledge, 1994), pp. 148–149.

65. Interview in Nanjing with provincial officials, April 1992.

66. An alternative explanation is that TVEs were more developed in coastal provinces, which generally had weaker SOE sectors, and that SOEs were strongest in inland provinces where TVEs were not developed. For the argument in China that there is a negative relationship between the strength of a province's SOE sector and its level of FDI, see Francois Gipouloux, "Integration or Disintegration: The Spatial Effects of Foreign Direct Investment in China," *China Perspectives* 17 (May–June 1998): 8.

67. My deepest thanks go to Wu Changqi and Leonard Cheng of the economics department at the Hong Kong University of Science and Technology who so generously shared this database with me. Wu Changqi also gave me excellent advice on the data. Chung Siu Fung analyzed the data and also gave me excellent advice.

ables: total exports by TVEs in each province (TVPEXP)[68] and FDI in the
TVE sector per province (TVPFDI).[69] My independent variables are coastal
versus noncoastal (TVPCOAST); the number of people with high school
education (EDUHIGH), which taps differences in human capital endowments; government subsidies to TVEs (GSF); the size of the TVE labor
force (TVPLAB); the value of agricultural output in the province (GVAO);
and the gross value of TVE industrial output per province (TVEGVIO). I
also include a variable (TVE/SOE), which is the ratio of TVE GVIO to SOE
GVIO in the province.

Considering TVE exports first, this model explains most of the variation
in the levels of internationalization in China's provinces, particularly their
level of TVE exports ($R = .899$) (table 3.10). Three of the variables—TVE
labor, TVE industrial output, and level of government subsidies—are very
significant ($p < .000$), but a province's location on the coast is not significant in explaining export activity. Therefore, although the bivariate relationship between TVEEXP and TVPCOAST is significant ($p < .004$) and the
data on the regional breakdown of TVE exports show that coastal TVEs
dominated TVE exports, I cannot confirm Womack and Zhao's argument
about the "grand advantages" of coastal provinces for TVE exports when all
other factors, particularly TVE industrial output, are included in the
model.

Therefore, an important market force, the level of rural industrialization, was the key factor here (not simply being on the coast). Agricultural
output (GVAO) is significant and negatively correlated, suggesting that
provinces that relied more on agriculture had fewer TVEs and therefore
fewer TVE exports. The ratio of TVE GVIO to SOE GVIO (TVE/SOE) is
not significant, so I cannot argue that bureaucrats in provinces with strong
SOE sectors limited the role of TVE exports. The size of the TVE labor pool
is significant and negatively correlated with TVE exports, suggesting that
smaller, more efficient firms might have been the more important
exporters. Finally, the level of high school education is not significant,
which probably reflects the low level of education of most TVE workers.

The model is slightly less powerful in explaining the levels of FDI
in TVEs in China's provinces ($R = .792$). Five of the variables—TVP
labor (TVPLAB), TVP industrial output (TVPGVIO), agricultural output

---

68. I included all forms of TVEs—cooperative, private, and collective—so as to avoid penal-
izing any province that relied more on private than collective firms. Therefore, the variable
is called TVP, not TVE.

69. According to Wu Changqi, there is a double accounting problem in this data: exports
from TVEs that had already been transformed into JVs count twice. If we add the reported
exports by TVEs, rural JVs and SOEs, the sum is larger than the total exports of the nation.
The impact on the GVIO of TVEs may not be a problem, but this biases the impact on
exports because provinces with more TVEs—Jiangsu and Guangdong provinces—have more
exports and more JVs.

Table 3.10 Factors Affecting Township and Village Enterprise Exports, 1987–1993

| | Unstandardized Coefficient | | | |
	B	Standard Error	t	Significance
(Constant)	42,287.204	47,485.500	0.891	.374
GVAO	−253.612	112.743	−2.249	.026**
GSF	20.614	5.151	4.002	.000***
EDU_HIGH	−210,322.800	279,189.180	−0.753	.452
TVPCOAST	56,168.433	34,180.698	1.643	.102
TVPLAB	−8.08E-02	0.017	−4.814	.000***
TVPGVIO	7.86E-02	0.007	11.739	.000***
TVP/SOE	−13,890.074	68,411.073	−0.203	.839
FK	−0.443	0.428	−1.035	.300

$R = .899$; $R^2 = .807$

Dependent variable: Exports from TVEs
Independent variables: GVAO, gross value of agricultural output; GSF, government subsidies to TVEs; EDU_HIGH, number of people in province with high school education; TVPCOAST, whether province is on the coast; TVPLAB, size of TVP labor force; TVPGVIO, gross value of TVP industrial output; TVP/SOE, GVIO of TVPs/GVIO of SOEs; FK, FDI in TVPs.

Note. **, significant; ***, highly significant; FDI, foreign direct investment; GVIO, gross value of industrial output; SOEs, state-owned enterprises; TVEs, township and village enterprises; TVPs, township, village, and private enterprises.

(GVAO), TVP/SOE, and government subsidies (GSF)—are significant at the .001 level (table 3.11).[70] The role of agriculture is significant and positively correlated, suggesting either that agricultural processing by TVEs attracted FDI to these regions or that foreigners were investing in certain types of commercialized agriculture. Regional factors have some influence on the level of FDI ($t = 1.750$, with $p < .08$), but, again, TVE industrial output is probably too important a factor in the level of FDI for location on the coast to play an important explanatory role, even though it too shows a highly significant bivariate relationship ($p < .004$).

My hypothesis that in provinces with strong SOEs, bureaucrats kept foreign investors away from TVEs cannot be refuted because the value of TVP/SOE is significant (it produces a strong $t = -3.363$ that was negatively

70. Because TVE/SOE and GVAO were both not significant in the first model, I ran the second regression which explained rural FDI two times, once without them, and then with them. The R value for the entire equation increased from .756 to .792 when I added TVE/SOE and GVAO to the original model.

Table 3.11   Factors Affecting Foreign Direct Investment in Township and Village Enterprises, 1987–1993

| | Unstandardized Coefficient | | | |
	B	Standard Error	t	Significance
(Constant)	−3,156.813	8,402.604	−.376	.708
GVAO	62.567	19.635	3.186	.002***
GSF	4.753	.880	5.403	.000***
EDU_HIGH	−36,163.013	49,314.783	−.733	.464
TVPCOAST	10,555.815	6,030.822	1.750	.082*
TVPLAB	−1.358E-02	.003	−4.554	.000***
TVPGIOV	8.610E-03	.001	5.966	.000***
TVP/SOE	−39,383.505	11,709.600	−3.363	.001***
TVPEXT	−1.381E-02	.013	−1.035	.302

$R = .793; R^2 = .629$

Dependent variable: FDI
Independent variables: GVAO, gross value of agricultural output; GSF, government subsidies to TVEs; EDU_HIGH, number of people in province with high school education; TVPCOAST, whether province is on the coast; TVPLAB, size of TVP labor force; TVPGVIO, gross value of TVP industrial output; TVP/SOE, GVIO of TVPs/GVIO of SOEs; TVPEXT, exports from TVPs

Note. *, somewhat significant; ***, highly significant; FDI, foreign direct investment; GVIO, gross value of industrial output; SOEs, state-owned enterprises; TVEs, township and village enterprises; TVPs, township, village, and private enterprises.

correlated, as predicted.) Thus in provinces with large SOE sectors, bureaucrats might have channeled FDI away from TVEs. Alternatively, this finding may derive from the fact that TVPs were more developed in coastal provinces, where there were fewer SOEs and more FDI, while SOEs were stronger in inland provinces, where there were weak TVP sectors and lower levels of FDI. In this case, the key factor was that provinces with strong SOEs sectors did not attract FDI, which we know to be partly true.

Finally, with this data I can also test whether external or internal forces better explain rural internationalization. After testing the original model—which shows that internal factors explain much of the variation in both rural exports and rural FDI—I introduce an external variable into each model (see tables 3.10 and 3.11). In the model testing TVE exports (TVPEXT), I include another independent variable, rural FDI (FK). Similarly, in the model testing FDI in TVEs, I include the independent variable TVE exports (TVPEXT). In both cases the inclusion of these external variables has no impact on the model, and the specific variables are not significant. Therefore, the level of TVE exports in a province did not play a significant role in attracting foreign investment, a somewhat surprising finding. Nor did the level of FDI promote exports. Perhaps the fact that the data set runs only through 1993 explains this limited relationship. Nevertheless, at this early stage of rural internationalization, internal variables, particularly the level of TVE industrial output, were more significant than external ones in explaining which provinces responded to global forces.

RURAL INTERNATIONALIZATION IN JIANGSU PROVINCE

Subprovincial data for 1993, 1994, and 1995 from the *Jiangsu Statistical Yearbook* show that for rural Jiangsu, TVE output, a county's location, and when it was deregulated best explain the level of FDI.[71] Areas that relied primarily on agriculture were less likely to be targets of FDI, although they might still have been involved in exports of rural commodities.[72]

Several variables were highly correlated, particularly regional factors and the level of industrialization. Jiangsu Province has a highly regional economy. Its southern section, Sunan—comprising the municipalities of Suzhou, Wuxi, and Changzhou—has a far more industrialized countryside than the rest of the province. The northern and inland sections in the Huabei plain (Subei) are far poorer than the rest of the province and possess much less industry. In the central section, we can differentiate between the western part of the province, including rural Nanjing, Zhenjiang, and Yangzhou, and the coastal parts, in particular the counties around Nantong and Yancheng (Suzhong). Dividing the province into these four regions, and excluding the suburbs, I find a very high correlation between region and total industrial production ($R^2 = .68$) for 1994; if I combine the two middle-level areas and divide the province into three regions, which reflects the historical stages of the opening of the province, the correlation between the date a county was opened and its industrial production is $R^2 = .73$. As we can see from map 3.1, TVE production was also highly regionalized, with the south having a far more industrialized countryside. FDI was also highly regionalized, with the majority going to Suzhou and Wuxi, as well as to Changzhou and Nanjing (map 3.2).

Visually, there is a close relationship between TVE output and the level of internationalization. But how strong is this relationship statistically? The

71. I employ two dependent variables, the dollar value of FDI in each county or suburban district and the number of JV contracts. And there are eight independent variables: GNP, GVIO, GVAO, township industrial production, village industrial production, region, date opened (i.e., the date when the locality was opened for foreign investment, 1985, 1988, or not opened yet), and whether it was a suburb. Because there are only seventy-six cases, it is harder to explain FDI in dollars than the number of contracts because a few very large contracts skewed the results.
72. I do not have data on county-level exports in Jiangsu Province, so I could not use it as a dependent variable.

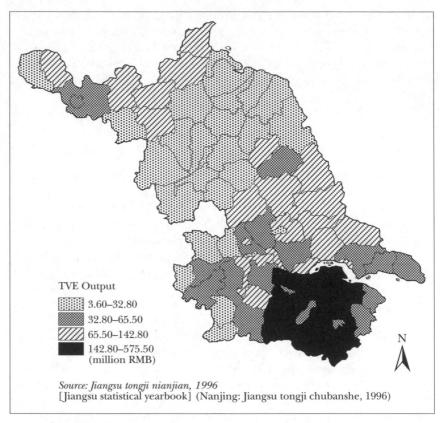

TVE Output

3.60–32.80

32.80–65.50

65.50–142.80

142.80–575.50
(million RMB)

N

Source: Jiangsu tongji nianjian, 1996
[Jiangsu statistical yearbook] (Nanjing: Jiangsu tongji chubanshe, 1996)

Map 3.1   Gross Value of Township and Village Enterprise Output, Jiangsu Province, 1995

data suggest that we must differentiate between suburban districts of cities, which had significant amounts of rural industry (but also many enterprises owned by the city government) and purely rural areas, which had very little industry owned by governments higher than the rural township or village.[73] Thus when we include suburban districts, which had a significant amount of state-owned industry (SOEs), we find three important patterns. First, when we analyze the impact of township industry, village industry, agricultural output, and date of opening on the number of FDI contracts, $R^2 = .46$. This value, however, is much lower than $R^2 = .88$ generated by the impact of GVIO (which includes both TVE and SOEs) on the NUMBER OF CONTRACTS signed in 1993. Therefore, in suburban districts a great deal of FDI went into industrial enterprises owned by the county or district gov-

73. The Jiangsu provincial yearbooks included data for sixty-five rural counties, as well as data from the suburbs of Jiangsu's municipalities.

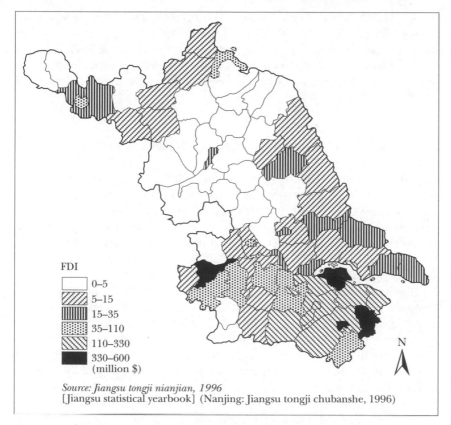

FDI

☐	0–5
▨	5–15
‖‖‖	15–35
▥	35–110
▧	110–330
■	330–600
	(million $)

Source: Jiangsu tongji nianjian, 1996
[Jiangsu statistical yearbook] (Nanjing: Jiangsu tongji chubanshe, 1996)

Map 3.2   Actual Foreign Direct Investment in Jiangsu Province, 1995

ernments, and not just into TVEs. In fact, when we look at the correlation between GNP (which includes both TVEs and SOEs) and FDI in dollars in 1993, 1994, and 1995, we find stronger correlations (.70, .68, and .68, respectively) than those between TVE output and FDI (.66, .61, and .54, respectively) for the same years.

However, when we take out the suburban districts, leaving only sixty-five rural counties, the correlation of township and village production, plus date of opening with FDI, is $R^2 = .86$, showing that TVE industrial production was again the key factor explaining rural internationalization in non-suburban areas. In these rural counties, because GVIO (which includes county-owned SOEs) plus date of opening yields a slightly weaker relationship ($R^2 = .81$) with the number of contracts than TVE output plus date of opening, we infer that FDI in the rural areas targeted TVEs more than county-owned SOEs. Thus, in rural counties foreign investors targeted TVEs (first, township enterprises and, then, village enterprises) more than county-owned SOEs, which are less flexible than TVEs, but in suburban areas FDI went to both SOEs and TVEs. In any case, the provincial-level data analysis presented previously and the subprovincial-level data for Jiangsu Province both confirm that a domestic factor, TVE industrial production, is the best predictor of the level of internationalization for a rural region.

Developmental Communities and the Role of Local Entrepreneurship

Despite a relatively uniform national policy encouraging export-led growth, rural localities responded to the opportunities inherent in internationalization with different degrees of intensity. The discussion that follows suggests that in addition to state policy—which opened some areas earlier than others—local factors, including an area's industrial structure, property rights, local elite entrepreneurship, and location, led communities to adopt different levels of transnational activity.

The most aggressive, far-sighted, and opportunistic developmental communities offered foreigners access to the domestic market or helped domestic actors gain access to global markets by becoming transfer points on China's global boundaries. In this way, they increased transnational exchanges and weakened the state's regulatory regime. The benefits they received for facilitating such access—domestic or foreign capital, foreign technology, management information or training—advanced their community's prosperity; foreign technology also improved their competitiveness in both international and domestic markets.

Although no single locality possessed all the qualities that might be incorporated under this concept, making it more a Weberian ideal type, certain attributes define a developmental community.[74] Local leaders possess a vision of community development that sees the benefits of interdependence as outweighing the risks of dependency, so they fight to harness domestic and international forces—both planned and market—to advance community interests. Drawing on their control over TVEs and the taxes derived from them to establish local corporate authority,[75] as well as the organizational and coercive power inherent in their roles as Communist Party officials, the leaders of developmental communities reorganize the community's norms and ethos; create new organizations; alter the

---

74. Wade and White see developmental states taming domestic and international market forces and harnessing them to national economic interest. Gordon White and Robert Wade, "Developmental States and Markets in East Asia: An Introduction," in *Developmental States in East Asia*, ed. Gordon White (London: Macmillan, 1988).
75. See Jean C. Oi, "Fiscal Reform and the Economic Foundations of Local State Corporatism in China," *World Politics* 45 (October 1992): 99–126.

industrial structure to build comparative advantage;[76] and mobilize factory workers, local officials, and members of the local bureaucratic elite for a massive shift into export-led growth.[77]

In a perfect world, such a community would demonstrate "corporate cohesiveness," with enough autonomy from society to suppress social demand yet enough responsiveness to social interests to avoid becoming predatory.[78] It would have a specific foreign trade plan, based on local rather than national interests. Community leaders would push TVEs owned by the local state and even by private firms to expand exports vigorously through subsidies, bank loans, bonuses to factory managers, or allocation of foreign exchange to local export-oriented firms. Enterprises in this community would rely on rather tight management regimens that reward productive workers and sanction laggards. At a minimum, perhaps 25 percent or more of GVIO would be involved in foreign trade, which may be handled by an expanding foreign trade bureaucracy that is closely allied to the local government and scours the country for export opportunities.

Development communities in the Chinese countryside rely on TVEs, with their cheap disciplined labor and low welfare benefits, which give rural China a comparative advantage in international trade. Compared to SOEs, which are tightly administered by industrial bureaus at different levels of the administrative hierarchy, TVEs are freer to restructure their product lines as export opportunities emerge. Also, as we have previously seen, the concentration of TVEs versus SOEs within a community can affect whether the community attracts FDI, which offers it export markets.

Developmental communities are located strategically on a river or the coast, which decreases the transaction costs of exports, or they control harbors that channel goods inland or overseas—all of this increases the impact of export-led growth on a community. The open policy's stress on global linkages should redirect significant proportions of state infrastructure investment into areas directly related to the export economy.

Such localities possess insiders and outsiders, with benefits restricted primarily to community members only. Internal migrants from China's hinterland, who perform menial work, remain outsiders under law unless they acquire local residence permits and, therefore, have limited access to welfare benefits, salaries, and public goods (such as schools) in the

---

76. Peter Evans, *Embedded Autonomy: States and Industrial Transformation* (Princeton: Princeton University Press, 1995), p. 9.
77. Other studies that assert the role of local leadership include Alan P. L. Liu, "The 'Wenzhou Model' of Development and China's Modernization," *Asian Survey* 32 (August 1992); Liu Yia-ling, "Reform from Below: The Private Economy and Local Politics in the Rural Industrialization of Wenzhou," *China Quarterly* 130 (June 1992): 293–316.
78. See Peter Evans, "The State as Problem and Solution: Predation, Embedded Autonomy, and Structural Change," in *The Politics of Economic Adjustment*, ed. Stephen Haggard and Robert R. Kaufman (Princeton: Princeton University Press, 1992), p. 163.

community. These communities may actively restrict goods from other areas, creating "market localism."[79] Building on the honeycomb nature of Chinese society, which emerged under Maoism,[80] developmental communities remain relatively impenetrable to outside authorities in a way that reflects international boundaries more than domestic regions, suggesting that we can apply characteristics previously ascribed to states to these rural communities.

Community flexibility is maximized by autonomy both from society, which allows elites to train workers and farmers to perform tasks that may not appear to be in their own interests, and from higher-level administrators, who would try to control the community's development trajectory. Whichever level controls the influx of FDI, authorizes JVs, and facilitates foreign trade; whichever level controls a significant source of revenue and owns or controls productive enterprises; and, whichever level controls personnel allocations—there we find the capacity for creating a developmental community. This may be the lowest level of the state hierarchy, the township. If it adopts an export-led growth strategy, it could actively promote JVs and shift capital into exporting enterprises. Yet townships function more like the branch companies of larger corporations headquartered at the county, where public services, such as building roads and schools, and authority over transnational relations are tightly controlled by county administrators,[81] who also make key decisions on personnel.

Thus, one administrative level well suited to implementing this strategy is the third-level or county-level city. County-level cities have no administrative level between the city government officials who make the key decisions and the township leaders who administer the rural community and own many TVEs. This situation differs structurally from second-level cities, which are separated from the township by two levels of administration—the district (*qu*) and the county—affecting promotions, political loyalties, and information flow. This difference is significant because under the rules, officials one level up decide which local party officials are chosen and approved. In second-level cities, then, more administrative levels weaken the link between the township directors and city officials, while in third-level cities those links are face-to-face and personal. Thus whereas second level cities might use documentary pronouncements to promote export-led growth, the key networks necessary for mobilization, monitoring, and information exchange, as well as the property rights incentives, are maximized through the county-township nexus of third-level cites.

79. Womack and Zhao, "Many Worlds of China's Provinces," p. 144.
80. Vivienne Shue, *The Reach of the State* (Stanford: Stanford University Press, 1988).
81. Andrew G. Walder, "Local Governments as Industrial Firms: An Organizational Analysis of China's Transitional Economy," *American Journal of Sociology* 101 (September 1995): 263–301.

Still, given the thickness of local bureaucratic networks in China, mayors of second-level cities, in particular the fourteen OCCs, might be able to mobilize their community to implement such a strategy. Because cities manage and control many factories under China's amorphous property rights system, a highly motivated, outward-looking mayor with a plethora of preferential policies, might construct a strong team of like-minded bureaucrats who for the community and their own interests shift into an export-led growth strategy.[82]

In China, developmental communities became a key corporate entity for rapid rural development. Through unified leadership, high rates of capital formation, suppressed wages, a capacity to manufacture exports and a marketing network reaching other provinces and the state administration, political ties to the state bureaucracy that helped circumvent domestic constraints, and transnational linkages to overseas markets, supplies, and technology, developmental communities could absorb the high costs of penetrating new markets while at the same time earning the extra-normal profits and rents that accompany successful innovation.

The data presented in maps 3.1 and 3.2 of Jiangsu Province also support the argument that local entrepreneurship played a role in internationalizing the countryside. Analyzing the provincial share of GNP per county and the share of FDI they received, I find that some areas received more FDI than their share of the province's GNP predicts, while other areas received less. If the share of FDI in each locality had matched its share of GNP, map 3.3 would have little or no variation. But parts of Suzhou—Zhangjiagang, Kunshan, Yixing and Wu counties—received much more FDI than their share of the province's GNP predict. Most other counties in Suzhou, Wuxi, Yangzhou, as well as Jiangpu County west of Nanjing, which was rather poor, received a healthy dose of FDI. Both Nantong and Lianyungang (in northern Jiangsu), the two OCCs in the province, also received more FDI than their levels of industrialization predict. In these cities, where the role of TVEs in the overall GNP was limited, the preferential policies of the OCCs probably explain this added dose of FDI. Overall, however, in the aforementioned counties, other factors were at work—the likely candidates being location, preferential policies, and the aggressiveness with which local leaders sought FDI.

Thus map 3.3 presents entrepreneurship as an explanation for internationalization. In counties where the share of provincial FDI to share of provincial GNP is greater than 1, some added factor drew in the foreigners. Location was important, but local leadership (i.e., the aggressive pursuit of

82. See Jae Ho Chung, "Preferential Policies, Municipal Leadership, and Development Strategies: A Comparative Analysis of Qingdao and Dalian," in *Agents of Development: Sub-Provincial Cities in Post-Mao China*, ed. Jae Ho Chung (London: Routledge, 1999), pp. 105–40.

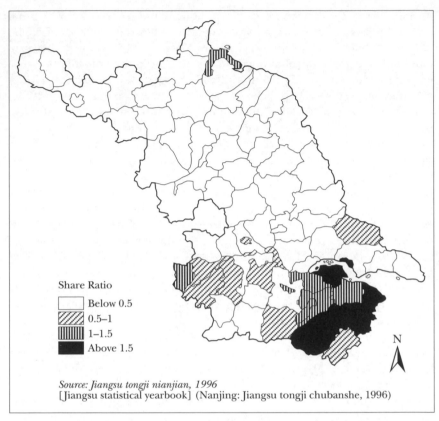

Source: *Jiangsu tongji nianjian, 1996*
[Jiangsu statistical yearbook] (Nanjing: Jiangsu tongji chubanshe, 1996)

Map 3.3   Share of Provincial Foreign Direct Investment as a Share of Provincial GNP, Jiangsu Province, 1993–95

FDI) and overseas Chinese relationships (another aspect of entrepreneurship in rural China) were also important.

Case Studies

The following studies present detailed information on two localities and
their supralocal environment in order to explore why one responded more
rapidly than the other to the opportunities for export-led growth that
emerged in the rural areas from the mid-1980s on. The two localities are
both in Jiangsu Province, allowing me to control for the provincial factor
in development. However, Zhangjiagang is located in Suzhou Municipality,
the more dynamic southern sector of the province where TVEs were
already an important pillar of the economy in the early 1980s; Nantong
County, the second community, was under the less flexible city of Nantong

in the central part of the province where TVEs were only a developing phenomenon.

ZHANGJIAGANG AND THE MAKING OF A
DEVELOPMENTAL COMMUNITY

Zhangjiagang, on the south shore of the Yangzi River, was particularly qualified to respond to the state's call for export-led growth and become a developmental community because of its leadership, its status as a county-level city, its location, its harbor, and its industrial structure.

Zhangjiagang has a tightly knit elite that based on its unity of purpose manifests the corporate coherence necessary for successful development. Surrounded by other counties in southern Jiangsu that began to industrialize in the mid-1970s, farmers and leaders in Zhangjiagang took many risks beginning in the early 1980s to enrich their locality. As map 3.3 shows, Zhangjiagang received more FDI than its GDP predicts, and based on field research I attribute this to local government entrepreneurship. Zhangjiagang officials are known throughout southern Jiangsu as being very tough, if not corrupt, businessmen. In the early 1980s, one thousand community members who had left in the 1960s during hard times returned annually, but after 1986 Zhangjiagang limited returnees to managers, engineers, skilled workers, and other talented people, as well as the spouses of urban residents, strengthening the meritocratic nature of its bureaucracy. These returnees, who were somewhat sheltered from local community pressures, possessed a degree of autonomy that was conducive to economic development.

Zhangjiagang's administrative qualities made it an exemplary linkage community. Formerly Shazhou County, under Suzhou Municipality, it became a county-level city in 1986, due to the internationalization of its harbor. Because it had been a county, only one administrative level separated the city government and township leaders who directly administered the rural community and owned its TVEs. Even before 1986, all township officials had been directly appointed by the county organizational bureau, which in 2001 was Zhangjiagang City's organizational bureau; so township officials owed their loyalty directly to the city leaders. Moreover, city officials often rotated posts with leaders in township and even in administrative villages, strengthening links between city leaders and the local community, making it easier for city leaders to mobilize the populace for export-led growth.

Zhangjiagang's economy depended heavily on TVEs, giving it incentives and opportunities to restructure its enterprises to enter the global market. In 1991, almost 60 percent of the total labor force (including officials and bureaucrats) worked in TVEs, and TVEs made up 87 percent of industrial firms in the locality. From 1974 to 1986, over two-thirds of the rural labor force left agriculture, and 80 percent of them moved into TVEs. With TVEs not part of the formal economic plan, provincial direction over production has been minimal. Because it is located closer to Wuxi than the city of Suzhou, officials there feared that the county would be transferred to Wuxi. As a result, not one factory owned by Suzhou Municipality established a branch plant in this area, furthering Zhangjiagang's autonomy from supralocal administrative interference. But when the economic retrenchment of 1988–89 dropped local GNP growth from 25 percent per year to only 5.5 percent, and dropped industrial employment by 7.6 percent, the local government vigorously grabbed the new opportunities emerging in export promotion and JV development. From 1990 to 1991, industrial employment increased by 19.8 percent due primarily to growth in exports.

The regional policy environment was conducive to export-led growth. After Guangdong Province, Jiangsu led the nation in exports from TVEs and was one of the earliest regions to be open to FDI in China. As part of Suzhou Municipality, Zhangjiagang was opened to foreign investment in 1985 along with the rest of the lower Yangzi River delta. Suzhou Municipality responded more rapidly to the Coastal Development Strategy than any part of Jiangsu Province. In 1988, when rural internationalization took off in Jiangsu, Suzhou signed 40.5 percent of the FDI contracts and received over 47 percent of the used FDI in the province (table 3.12). In 1993 and 1995, it received 50.3 percent and 48.7 percent of used FDI in the province, although its share dropped thereafter. Table 3.13 shows that Suzhou's level of FDI far surpassed all the other major cities, including Nanjing, the provincial capital.

Zhangjiagang had excellent ties to the provincial leadership. The provincial vice-governor responsible for external economic relations in 1992, Gao Dezhen, had been party secretary of Suzhou in 1988 and party boss of Zhangjiagang in the 1960s. Although provincial officials criticized Zhangjiagang for too many JVs in 1988, Gao made it a provincial model. In 1991, Zhangjiagang became the first of seventeen third-level cities in Jiangsu to become a line item in the provincial plan for foreign investment, which gave it the right to approve its own projects; under this agreement,

Table 3.12   Suzhou Municipality, Share of Foreign Direct Investment in Jiangsu Province, 1988–1998

	1988	1990	1993	1995	1996	1997	1998
Contracted FDI (%)	40.5	33.2	25.3	22.2	26.4	29.0	25.4
Used FDI (%)	47.4	23.9	50.3	48.7	44.5	42.2	41.6

Sources: 1988 data from Richard Pomfret, *Equity Joint Ventures in Jiangsu Province* (Hong Kong: Longman Professional Intelligence Reports, 1989), p. 11. Other years from Jiangsu sheng tongji ju, ed., *Jiangsu tongji nianjian* [Jiangsu statistical yearbook] (Beijing: Zhongguo tongji chubanshe), 1991–99.

Table 3.13 Foreign Direct Investment in Jiangsu Province, 1988–1998

City	Number of FDI Contracts						Used FDI (million $)					
	1988ᵃ	1990	1993	1995	1997	1998ᵇ	1998ᵃ	1990	1993	1995	1997	1998
Nanjing	29	47	1,340	663	374	371	173.00ᶜ	59.28	316.98	402.76	494.22	748.45
Suzhou	100	130	2,532	898	648	518	65.80	33.71	1,508.74	2,327.47	2,447.23	2,841.80
Wuxi	22	52	1,301	451	200	205	18.60	9.21	476.31	857.37	872.41	911.46
Nantong	21	33	1,151	498	146	122	18.40	10.24	140.74	307.63	608.07	377.92
Changzhou	26	40	810	292	145	265	9.10	4.39	119.91	261.70	410.32	506.28
Lianyungang	9	7	386	279	182	117	4.00	1.40	64.88	69.88	106.13	103.08
Huaiyin	1	3	219	80	17	53	0.40	2.84	21.44	38.70	41.00	56.35
Yancheng	6	22	508	228	93	95	2.30	1.82	28.29	60.47	109.79	141.84
Yangzhou	13	23	731	275	54	43	5.80	14.92	152.08	158.67	73.71	68.29
Xuzhou	8	6	421	159	51	83	4.70	1.10	37.28	104.32	89.29	228.16
Zhenjiang	12	27	560	207	140	100	7.90	2.19	133.60	164.84	441.76	746.55
Jiangsu Provinceᵈ	0	2	73	26	12	n.a.	n.a.	0.00	1.60	26.77	2.19	n.a.
Taizhouᵉ	n.a.	n.a.	n.a.	n.a.	25	54	n.a.	n.a.	n.a.	n.a.	96.39	98.14
Suqian	n.a.	n.a.	n.a.	n.a.	1	17	n.a.	n.a.	n.a.	n.a.	0.00	5.01
TOTAL	247	392	10,032	4,056	2,088	2,043	137.00	141.10	3,001.85	4,780.58	5,792.51	6,833.33ᶠ

Sources: 1988 data from Richard Pomfret, *Equity Joint Ventures in Jiangsu Province* (Hong Kong: Longman Professional Intelligence Reports, 1989), p. 11. Other years from Jiangsu sheng tongji ju, ed., *Jiangsu tongji nianjian* [Jiangsu statistical yearbook] (Beijing: Zhongguo tongji chubanshe, 1991–99).

Note: n.a., not available.

ᵃ Pomfret's data are for contracted FDI.

ᵇ The 1999 *Jiangsu Statistical Yearbook* reports only the number of agreements for "Foreign Capital Utilization." That number, 2,043, is higher than the number of FDI contracts, which is 1,818, because it includes loans to the province and municipalities. For that reason, I could not calculate the number of contracts signed by the provincial government.

ᶜ The figure for Nanjing FDI probably still includes foreign loans that I have excluded from all my data.

ᵈ Data for 1990 on are derived by subtracting the sum of the cities from the total.

ᵉ Starting in 1996, the provincial structure was changed, with several counties moving from one municipality to another, while two new municipalities, Taizhou and Suqian, were created.

ᶠ The total value of FDI in 1998 according to *Jiangsu tongji nianjian, 1999* is $6,652 billion, but when the values in this column (based on the individual listing for each city) are totalled, the total FDI is $230 million more. I cannot explain this discrepancy, but it is only a 3% difference.

Zhangjiagang's Foreign Trade Bureau needed only to notify the province for final approval.

Finally, Zhangjiagang's location on the south side of the lower reaches of the Yangzi River improved its comparative advantage in export production and eased the transaction costs of foreign trade. The city received support from Beijing to expand its harbor beginning in the mid-1980s, and in 1992 a new major highway linked the harbor to Suzhou city. As of 1991 it possessed the seventh busiest container harbor port in China, a strong invitation for foreign investors.

Incentives for Export-led Growth in Zhangjiagang

Trade was unimportant to Zhangjiagang's development until the mid-1980s (table 3.14). All exports passed through Jiangsu Province's FTCs, or those in Shanghai or Suzhou, making Zhangjiagang dependent on FTCs for information about export markets.

In summer 1988 things changed.[83] Party meetings in Suzhou called for a jump in exports and empowered localities to approve foreign investment projects under $15 million without higher-level approval, transforming Zhangjiagang's policy agenda. Previously, Zhangjiagang's first economic meeting each year focused on agriculture; after 1988, the main goal of the January meeting was to promote exports and JVs. Between 1989 and 1991, this meeting distributed approximately 200 thousand RMB to TVEs that earned the most foreign exchange. In 1990, Zhangjiagang's foreign trade bureau gave industrial enterprises earning over $10 million from exports a subsidy of 2 million RMB for electricity, and supplied cotton and silk at a low planned price. In 1989, township leaders who met their quotas for exports and JVs were personally awarded 1,500 to 2,000 RMB, six to seven times the salary of an average TVE worker,[84] while those who failed to meet these quotas were to be passed over for promotions.

Zhangjiagang responded dramatically to the incentives. With only 2 rural JVs in 1987, it established 29 in 1988, 19 in 1989, 16 in 1990, 48 through October 1991, and 572 in 1992, more than any other county in China.[85] According to one source, Zhangjiagang had established 1,372 foreign-funded companies by the end of 1994, but in June 1997

---

83. Information in this paragraph is based on interviews in November 1991 with officials in Zhangjiagang.

84. The guidelines stipulated that in townships that exported 50 million RMB of goods, increased exports by 30 percent, had one JV, and had per capita exports of 4,500 RMB, the township head and the person making the contribution would receive a bonus of 2 thousand RMB. Interviews in Zhangjiagang, November 1991.

85. Data through October 1991 are based on field research. Data on 1992 are from *Suzhou tongji nianjian, 1993* [Suzhou statistical yearbook, 1993] (Suzhou: Suzhou City Statistical Bureau, 1993), p. 240. I thank Bruce Jacobs, who shared his copy of this statistical yearbook with me.

Table 3.14   Role of Exports in Zhangjiagang, 1978–1999

Year	Export Purchases (million RMB)	GNP (million RMB)[a]	Exports (% of GDP)	TVE Industrial Labor Force (in 1000s)
1978	18.12	324.43	5.50	94.40
1980	35.22	432.43	8.10	106.30
1982	49.41	517.66	9.50	123.20
1984	59.98	890.02	6.70	168.40
1985	71.79	1,281.46	5.60	187.20
1986	125.18	1,436.75	8.70	189.10
1987	283.92	1,770.18	16.00	189.40
1988	504.70[b]	2,262.28	22.30	183.70
1989	637.43[c]	2,385.60	26.70	169.80
1990	920.63[d]	2,782.07	33.10	167.60
1991	1,181.20[e]	3,200.10	34.90	200.60
1992	3,705.00	6,317.02	58.70	n.a.
1993	n.a.[f]	10,279.49[g]	n.a.[f]	n.a.
1994[h]	4,050.79	15,250.49	26.56	207.60
1995	4,687.24	19,101.29	24.50	192.51
1996	5,778.75	23,007.11	25.12	185.80
1997	6,637.75	23,020.07	28.82	177.85
1998	6,714.68	23,501.09	28.57	172.38
1999	6,881.67	24,510.15	28.08	n.a.

Source: Data for 1994–99 from Zhangjiagang tongji ju, ed. Zhangjiagang tongji nianjian [Zhangjiagang statistical yearbook] (Zhangjiagang: Zhangjiagang tongji ju, 1994–99). Data for 1992 from Suzhou tongji nianjian, 1993 [Suzhou statistical yearbook, 1993] (Beijing: Zhongguo tongji chubanshe, 1993), pp. 47 and 238. Data for 1978–91 supplied by Zhangjiagang Statistical Bureau in 1991 and 1992. Data on 1993 exports provided by Zhangjiagang officials in 1997.

Notes: n.a., not available; TVE, township and village enterprise.

[a] Data in various provincial (Jiangsu) and municipal yearbooks presents GNP in current renminbi.

[b] According to the Suzhou tongji nianjian, 1989, Zhangjiagang's export sales in 1988 in planned prices (jihua jia) was 479.42 million RMB, although its reported GNP matches the data supplied locally. If we use the 1989 yearbook data, exports as a percentage of GNP for 1988 is 21.2 percent.

[c] The Suzhou tongji nianjian, 1990 reported export sales in Zhangjiagang for 1989 as 709.86 million RMB, which makes exports as a percentage of GNP for 1989 29.7 percent.

[d] The Jiangsu tongji nianjian, 1991 [Jiangsu statistical yearbook, 1991], p. 445, reports 1990 exports as 796.28 million RMB, 14 percent less than reported by the local Statistical Bureau in October 1991. Using that figure, exports as a percent of GNP actually dropped in 1990 to 24.7 percent. Given other data I received in Zhangjiagang and the push in 1990 to promote exports, I have trouble accepting the Jiangsu tongji nianjian data. In fact, the Suzhou tongji nianjian, 1991, p. 229, reports Zhangjiagang export commodity purchases as 1,005.11 million RMB.

[e] The Suzhou tongji nianjian, 1993 reports Zhangjiagang's export purchases in 1991 as 1,049.6 million RMB, or 11.2 percent lower. Using this data, exports as a percent of GNP is 32.8 percent.

[f] In 1997 Zhangjiagang foreign trade officials gave me approximate values for export purchases for 1993 and 1994. These values now seem grossly inflated. But although I could get exports in dollars for 1994, which could then be converted into renminbi, these data were unavailable for 1993.

[g] For 1993 and 1994, data are for GDP (guonei shengchan zongzhi), not GNP (guoming shengchan zong zhi), so they may differ slightly from previous years. GDP for 1993 and 1994 come from Suzhou tongji nianjian, 1994, p. 41, and Suzhou tongji nianjian, 1995, p. 33, respectively.

[h] From 1994 to 1999, the data are reported in dollars and have been converted into renminbi by using the average exchange rate of renminbi to dollars (middle rate) for this year.

trade officials in Zhangjiagang reported having approximately 1,300 rural JVs.[86]

Zhangjiagang's links to the outside world deepened and exports became the engine of growth; however, the data available to substantiate this point are somewhat problematic. Local data that I was given during my two visits are at variance with those reported in Suzhou's and Jiangsu's statistical yearbooks (table 3.14). In particular, data I received on export purchases for 1992–94—which put export purchases at 3.7 billion RMB in 1992, 7 billion RMB in 1993, and 9 billion RMB in 1994—seem highly inflated; it seems doubtful that exports doubled from 1991 to 1993 and then jumped again in 1993. I also question whether exports as a share of GNP could have jumped from 35 percent in 1991 to 68 percent in 1993. On the other hand, the data in table 3.14 are also suspect. Because China stopped reporting domestic export purchases in renminbi in 1993, thereafter reporting exports in dollars, the export purchases data in table 3.14 for 1995–98 have been calculated by converting the value of exports in dollars into renminbi based on the renminbi-dollar exchange rate in that year. This method could deflate the renminbi value of exports relative to the earlier years, hence the large drop in exports as a share of GNP from 1994 to 1995.

Nevertheless several points are worth making. First, the nonstatistical data show that elites in this community mobilized the entire population to engage in export-led growth, which was the key strategy for economic development in the 1990s. Second, the fact that Zhangjiagang inflated its export data shows that it wanted to be seen as making exports central to their growth. Finally, the trend in the late 1980s to early 1990s is clear; even using more reliable data from statistical yearbooks rather than verbally reported data, by 1990 over 33 percent of GNP was based on exports, and given the great emphasis on export-led growth of Qin Zhenghua, the party secretary who took over in 1992, the share of exports at least remained around 35 percent if not increasing somewhat. In fact, trade officials in 1997 in Zhangjiagang argued that exports in 1997 were expected to make up over 30 percent of GNP.[87]

Export-led growth strengthened local state capacity. The city's FTC, an agent of the provincial Commission on Foreign Economic Relations and Trade, was set up in 1987 with seventy-four employees. It purchased goods in Zhangjiagang for provincial FTCs, which must meet the provincial foreign trade plan. In 1989, it began to seek aggressively unfilled export contracts allocated to other provinces. As a result, the number of sales agents in the city company doubled to 144 (table 3.15). By 1997, the

86. Xinhua News Service, "Port City of Zhangjiagang Attracts Foreign Investors," reprinted in *FBIS*, no. 63 (3 April 1995): 55–56; interviews in Zhangjiagang, June 1997.
87. Interviews with foreign trade officials in Zhangjigang, June 1997.

Table 3.15 Growth of Foreign Affairs and Trade Bureaucracy in Zhangjiagang, 1985–1997

Department	1985	1986	1987	1988	1989	1990	1991	1997[a]
China International Travel Service	—	—	est. 17	17	17	17	17	n.a.
Foreign Affairs Office	est.	3–4	4	4	7	7	7	n.a.
City FTC	—	—	74 est.	[91]	[108]	[125]	144	344[b]
Foreign Economic Relations Department	—	est.	[7]	[14]	21	27	32	33[c]
Local FTC	—	—	—	est. 22	41	53	64	n.a.
TOTAL			81	127	170	205	240	n.a.
Percentage Increase				37%	26%	17%	15%	

Source: Interviews in Zhangjiagang, 1991, 1997.
Note: [] signifies a best guess of the number of positions based on perfectly average annual percentage increases; est., year established; FTC, foreign trade company; n.a., not available.
[a] In 1997, I was not able to get data on the other organizations.
[b] In 1997, I was told that the Foreign Trade Conglomerate Company had added approximately 40 employees per year since 1991.
[c] In 1997, I was told that there were only 25 positions on the official establishment and 8 part-time employees. The data I received in 1991 may also have included part-time employees, but I was not told that at that time.

number of officials in the foreign trade sector had grown to five hundred bureaucrats (as well as over one thousand employees in stores, factories, and restaurants owned by the foreign trade bureau).

Other institutional innovations followed. In 1988, a local FTC under the city government opened with twenty-two employees. Its main purpose was to visit cities across China, including Dalian, Wuhan, and Hefei in Anhui Province, looking for unused export quota, particularly in textiles. In 1988 it purchased 22 million RMB of exportable commodities, in 1989 it bought 36 million RMB, in 1990 89 million RMB, and the projection for 1991 was 150 million RMB. Other local bureaus began to engage in trade and FDI. Under the leadership of the former director of the TVE Bureau, the Foreign Affairs Office sought foreign investments aggressively, as did the Taiwan Office. The local China Travel Service branch became a trade promotion organization as well.

Foreign trade and FDI helped Zhangjiagang's factories increase their level of technology. In 1991, a local meeting advocated improving the role of science and technology in the community. One township, whose exports reportedly grew from 1.38 million RMB in 1987 to over 137 million RMB by 1990, imported 30–40 million RMB of equipment in both 1989 and 1990, and 64 million RMB in 1991. Zhangjiagang imported equipment for a small steel plant and received an export quota for steel in 1991 worth $8 million, a major accomplishment for a rural community. Moreover, throughout the locality, JVs were using medium-level foreign technology to produce new goods for which there was little domestic competition, thereby earning large profits.

Attitudes toward export-led growth varied according to people's positions in the division of labor, but overall most local bureaucrats favored greater internationalization.[88] The sales director for a JV knew that strict management and better products strengthened his enterprise's market position; and because he worked on commission, increased sales put more money in his pocket. He also supported domestic sales by JVs—a policy that threatened SOEs and undermined the state's control over its boundaries—because the foreign manager promised him a new motorcycle if his sales department reached its quota. A technician in another factory reported that under the old system his factory could not produce high-quality goods, leaving salaries unstable; clear lines of authority under the new management system eased his work. In 1991, managers of successful export factories and JVs earned over 1 thousand RMB a month, a hefty incentive. However, one Chinese co-manager of a JV complained that the Chinese Communist Party was his real boss because the local party committee expropriated most of his salary.

Workers' views varied. Although a worker in an export factory admitted that it had taken him two years to adjust to stricter management, he applauded these innovations for ensuring factory jobs for him and his wife; before that, his wife had worked in the fields. Now each of their monthly salaries had increased from 70–80 RMB in 1988 to almost 300 RMB in 1991. On the other hand, in one village where the party secretary planned to turn all four of its TVEs into JVs, workers who feared the stricter regimen were not allowed to change jobs. A dissatisfied worker admitted that although his salary had been cut, all jobs in the village were controlled by the party secretary and he could not work elsewhere.

Initially, in 1987, when foreign trade first expanded, 90 percent of Zhangjiagang officials feared the international market.[89] Several TVEs had bought second-hand machinery at new-machinery prices from Hong Kong businessmen, and in 1988, after many firms began to produce latex gloves for the AIDs-conscious U.S. market, a sudden shift away from Chinese

---

88. Due to the tightness of the political climate in fall 1991, I was able to interview only two factory workers in private; one supported JVs and one opposed them. I also interviewed sales representatives and several factory managers.

89. Interview with the Zhangjiagang Foreign Economic Relations and Trade Bureau, June 1997. Still, Zhangjiagang was the most aggressive exporting county in Suzhou Municipality, overfulfilling its planned export purchases in 1987 by 84 percent, more than any other county. See *Suzhou tongji nianjian, 1988* [Suzhou statistical yearbook, 1988] (Suzhou: Suzhou renmin chubanshe, 1990), p. 521.

sources by U.S. purchasers caught Zhangjiagang with containers full of unmarketable products. The lesson they learned, however, was to diversify, give foreign partners less control over imported equipment, and investigate projects well before accepting FDI.[90] By 1991, only 10 percent of local officials questioned the utility of establishing JVs.

Zhangjiagang officials believed that higher value-added products would accelerate prosperity, so they helped export firms and townships import foreign technology. As TVEs move up the technology ladder and their need for labor decreases, officials looked forward to the day when they could expel the guest workers who build roads, perform menial labor, and expand exports.[91] With outsiders gone, only insiders would share the spoils of economic development. In the words of one Zhangjiagang official: "We want to be the Second World; internal China can be the Third World."[92]

NANTONG AND EXPORT PROMOTION

Nantong Municipality and its key rural community, Nantong County (renamed Tongzhou County in 1993), lie on the northern shore of the Yangzi River. Ten times larger than Zhangjiagang in population and area, Nantong Municipality has six counties under its jurisdiction. In 1984, Nantong became one of fourteen OCCs and received special grants from the provincial and central governments, an ETDZ, and several import-export companies. With its tradition of textile production, good links with Japan, its harbor, and status as the trade outlet for northern Jiangsu, it was well placed to expand exports.

Yet Zhangjiagang's development outpaced Nantong. Between 1978 and 1991, per capita GNP in Nantong increased fourfold at an annual rate of 13.3 percent; in the same period, per capita GNP in Zhangjiagang reportedly increased almost nine times at an average annual rate of over 19 percent. So, in 1978 Zhangjiagang's per capita GNP was 18.8 percent higher than Nantong's, by 1985 it was 100 percent greater, and by 1991 it was over 150 percent higher, as shown in figure 3.1. Figure 3.1 also shows that the gap between the two regions jumped in 1984, when the national policy on TVEs was liberalized.

Both communities also had different levels of involvement in the global economy. Although both cities increased exports from 1984–92,

---

90. Zhangjiagang officials claimed that such investigations have cut prices by 20 percent and saved $100 thousand. See Zhangjiagang City, Xizhang Town Economic Committee, "Ban hao hezi qiye, gao hao waixiangxing jingji" [Run joint ventures well, develop the foreign-oriented economy], *Jiangsu xiangzhen qiye* [Jiangsu's TVEs] 3 (1991): 43–44.
91. As of March 1989, there were over 800,000 guest workers in Jiangsu Province, with over 200,000 of them working in TVEs in Wuxi County. See Gu Chengwen, "Jiangsu to Shut Down Poorly Run Rural Firms," *China Daily*, 25 March 1989, p. 1.
92. Interview with officials from Yangshe Township, November 1991.

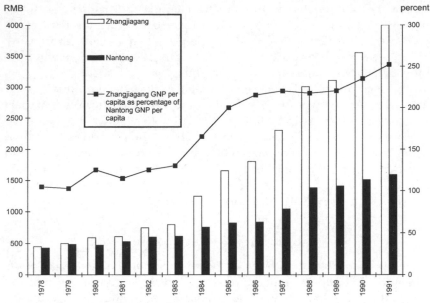

Figure 3.1   Zhangjiagang and Nantong GNP per Capita, 1978–1991

Source. Interviews in Zhangjiagang and Nantong, 1991–92

Zhangjiagang's efforts appear to have greatly outpaced Nantong. Even after becoming an OCC in 1984, Nantong's exports as a percentage of GNP remained fixed at approximately 15 percent; only in 1991 did this figure reportedly increase to 21 percent, although national data place it still at 13 percent.[93] Nantong's exports and GNP increased each year, but exports were not helping to expand the overall GNP; they merely kept pace with overall economic growth.

Explaining the Differences

Nantong officials attributed the different rates of internationalization to location, leadership, and industrial structure. The dominance of SOEs in

93. This figure is based on data supplied by the Nantong Statistical Bureau in 1992. But according to the Ministry of Foreign Economic Relations and Trade, export purchases as a percentage of GNP in Nantong in 1991 was 13.3 percent and in 1993 13.7 percent. See Editorial Board of the Almanac of China's Foreign Economic Relations and Trade, ed., *Almanac of China's Foreign Economic Relations and Trade, 1993/94* (Hong Kong: China Resources Advertising Co., 1994), p. 293; Editorial Board of the Almanac of China's Foreign Economic Relations and Trade, ed., *Almanac of China's Foreign Economic Relations and Trade, 1994/95*, (Hong Kong: China Resources Advertising Co. 1996), p. 363. In 1994, it reached 25.06 percent. See Editorial Board of the Almanac of China's Foreign Economic Relations and Trade, ed., *Almanac of China's Foreign Economic Relations and Trade, 1995–96* (Hong Kong: China Resources Advertising Co., 1997), p. 322.

Nantong, as compared to the leading role of TVEs in Zhangjiagang, explains much of the variation in internationalization. State-owned textile and electrical machinery industries in Nantong Municipality could not compete with growing TVE exports up and down the coast. As we have seen, TVEs totally dominated garment exports and became more serious competitors in both textile and machinery exports (see table 3.7). Without restructuring its exports from textiles to electronics, Nantong found it difficult to increase them.[94] Nantong used funds provided by the central government for industrial restructuring to prop up bankrupt SOEs rather than for technological innovation. In fact, in 1988–90, Nantong officials who favored SOEs over TVEs used the national criticism of TVEs to push Nantong County to close down many rural enterprises.[95] Also SOEs were less flexible than TVEs in responding to global market demands. As one older trade official complained, foreign insistence on "small quantities, high quality, and all in a short period of time," were too much for Nantong's state firms.[96]

Favoring SOEs over TVEs is quite rational. According to Geoffrey Garrett and Peter Lange, governments are much more likely to prop up wages in the nontradable sector during hard times than they are in the tradable sector that must compete globally.[97] Zhangjiagang avoided such pressures, and in 1992 it was better positioned to benefit from further trade deregulation. The reliance on SOEs also made state bureaucrats less flexible in negotiating with foreign investors. Although many multinational corporations visited Nantong in 1984–86 after it became an OCC, few signed deals. Its overcharging for land apparently chased the foreigners away. After 1992, when it finally tried to rectify this situation, it was too late—southern Jiangsu had established its reputation as a more hospitable place for foreigners to do business.

Comparing Nantong County and Zhangjiagang

The pace of internationalization in Nantong County was constrained by national policy that kept it closed to FDI until 1988, three years after Zhangjiagang was opened, and by municipal officials who steered foreign investors away from TVEs. Institutionally, export-led growth affected Nantong County, but at a much slower pace than Zhangjiagang. In 1986,

94. See Zhang Chi, "Nantong shi jingji jiegou de tedian yu tiaozheng zhengce" [Characteristics and strategy for adjusting Nantong city's economic structure], *Jiangsu jingji taolun* [Jiangsu economic debates] 3 (1990): 8–12.
95. See Susan Whiting, *Power and Wealth in Rural China: The Political Economy of Institutional Change* (New York: Cambridge University Press, 2001).
96. Interview, Nantong Foreign Trade Bureau, April 1992.
97. Geoffrey Garrett and Peter Lange, "Internationalization, Institutions, and Political Change," in *Internationalization and Domestic Politics*, ed. Robert O. Keohane and Helen V. Milner (Cambridge, UK: Cambridge University Press, 1996), pp. 48–75.

two years before the county was opened to the outside, the county government set up a two-person foreign trade section in the local planning commission. In 1987, the county established its own foreign trade bureau with four people. In 1989, a year after the rural areas of Nantong Municipality were opened to FDI and export promotion, the foreign trade bureau expanded to nine people; as of 1992 it had fifteen people. But unlike Zhangjiagang, Nantong County did not have its own local FTC that sold products outside the province. Similarly, while Nantong County had four people in its foreign trade bureau in 1987, Zhangjiagang's foreign trade bureau had many more people and that year Zhangjiagang also established a local FTC with seventy-four people.

Despite the birth of a foreign trade bureaucracy in 1986, trade, which first jumped in 1984, did not boom again until 1988, when the county was opened to FDI. While the annual growth in exports in Nantong County from 1984 to 1991 was 24.6 percent, in the same period, the annual growth in exports in Zhangjiagang was 45.1 percent. Still, once Nantong County was opened to international forces in 1988, its export activity increased rapidly, showing that national policy, which determined which rural regions opened first, was a critical constraint. In fact, between 1988 and 1991, export procurements from Nantong County grew more rapidly (28.9 percent) than in Zhangjiagang (23.7 percent). On the other hand, more and more exports from Zhangjiagang's TVEs were going out directly through JVs, and these values do not show up under export procurements. After 1992, however, as more and more SOEs received import-export power, FTCs in Nantong depended more on purchases of exportable goods from TVEs to meet their export contracts. Otherwise, they might have had foreign clients but no goods to sell to them.

Explaining China's Joint Venture Fever

JVs were one of the main institutions through which central leaders hoped to control the interactions between Chinese and foreign firms. But as more and more domestic actors—firms and local governments—and foreign investors saw the potential benefits of global linkages, the demand for administrative approvals for JVs increased, overburdening central bureaucrats. Foreign investors are an impatient lot; if the time required for approval is too slow, they move elsewhere. Local governments, competing with their neighbors for FDI, were hungry for the power to establish JVs as quickly as possible. So, as with the foreign trade regime, great pressure was placed on the Chinese government to decentralize the decision-making authority over JVs. As a result, most open rural counties were able to approve FDI projects of under $5 million.

But decentralization weakened the government's capacity to monitor compliance with its foreign investment regime. In rural coastal China, where JVs often involved a capital investment of less than $1 million, hundreds of projects could be approved by county officials. But these local governments, who owned production and FTCs, and their agents in the foreign trade bureaucracy, had strong material and political incentives to liberalize the norms governing JVs. This could involve not enforcing the rule that JVs must export over 70 percent of their products to receive special tax privileges. Or, as I outline later, this could involve setting up false JVs that allowed them to circumvent FTCs and the constraints imposed by the state. In this way, JVs became a core institution through which domestic and foreign firms, pursuing their own self-interests, undermined state controls.

After Deng's southern trip, JV fever swept rural areas in southern Jiangsu.[98] By 1994, one-third of all TVEs in Suzhou Municipality were JVs,[99] and most counties in south and central Jiangsu were establishing 200–300 new JVs each year. This local fever mirrored national trends. Nationwide the number of JV contracts increased fourfold between 1991 and 1993 (doubling again a year later), and the level of contracted FDI increased almost fivefold in 1992, doubling again in 1993 (table 3.16). Also, FDI in rural China ballooned from $446 million in 1992 to $3.1 billion in 1993. Although it dipped in 1994 (as it did for FDI in general), it rose again in 1995 and 1996. No doubt, a significant amount of this jump in investment was round tripping (in which domestic firms move funds offshore and then establish a JV with themselves).

With global exchanges so critical for community development, officials in Zhangjiagang sold out the national interest and became a transnational linkage point through which foreigners accessed China's domestic market on more favorable terms than the central state preferred. Despite national rules stipulating that JVs must export 70 percent of their production to get special tax privileges (three years tax free, two years half taxes), five of eleven JVs I visited in Zhangjiagang in 1991 offered foreign partners the chance to sell 50 percent or more of their products domestically.

In return for this access, the rural community received foreign capital, equipment, or access to international markets that otherwise would have been closed to their exports. Although exports from JVs were only 3 percent of Jiangsu's exports in 1989, by 1993 they made up over 38 percent of all provincial exports, and by 1997, 43.3 percent. And although many JVs in Jiangsu Province were not with TVEs, a significant number of

98. Taicang County in Suzhou had approximately seventy-five JVs by early 1992, but established seventy-six more in a two-month period in 1992. Kunshan City, also in Suzhou, had 107 JVs by the end of 1991, but established another twenty-six by the middle of April 1992.
99. Xinhua, "Overseas Investment Pours Into Suzhou's Rural Industry," reprinted in *FBIS*, no. 167 (29 August 1994): 65.

Table 3.16   Foreign Direct Investment in China, 1979–1999

	Number of Contracts	Amount Contracted (million $)	Amount Used (million $)
1979–82	922	4,608	1,771
1983	470	1,731	916
1984	1,856	2,650	1,419
1985	3,073	5,931	1,956
1986	1,498	2,834	2,245
1987	2,233	3,709	2,647
1988	5,945	5,297	3,740
1989	5,779	5,600	3,774
1990	7,273	6,596	3,410
1991	12,978	11,980	4,366
1992	48,764	58,122	11,008
1993	83,437	111,436	27,515
1994	47,490	81,406	33,787
1995	37,011	91,282	37,521
1996	24,556	73,276	41,726
1997	21,001	51,004	45,257
1998	19,799	52,102	45,463
1999	16,918	41,223	40,319
TOTAL	341,003	610,787	308,840

Sources: China Business Review (May–June 1995): 32; State Statistical Bureau, *China Statistical Yearbook* (Hong Kong: Economic Information and Agency, 1997), p. 605; 1998, pp. 638–9; 1999, p. 595; 2000, p. 605.

them were, making rural Jiangsu's alliance with foreign capital a critical channel through which its TVEs marketed their products globally (see table 3.3). JVs offered TVEs new product lines that gave rural communities extra-normal profits in the domestic market. In fact, when challenged that the JV law prohibited them from giving tax benefits to foreign investors who sold most of their product domestically, some JV managers in Zhangjiagang and Nantong in 1991–92 told me they would circumvent these rules and give foreigners tax breaks and access to the domestic market. If they did not, while other localities did, the JV would move elsewhere. Similarly, in 1997 foreign trade officials in Zhangjiagang admitted that in 1991–92, when competition for FDI had been so intense, they had ignored the regulations governing JVs to beat their neighbors.[100]

100. Interview with foreign trade officials, Zhangjiagang, June 1997. This process reflects Yang's concept of competitive liberalization. See Dali Yang, *Beyond Beijing: Liberalization and the Regions in China* (New York: Routledge, 1997); David Zweig, "Export-Led Growth, Local Autonomy, and U.S.–China Relations," *In Depth* 3 (fall 1993): 19–36.

Rural officials were chasing two types of rents. The first was the rent that the provincial FTC earned through its monopsony on foreign trade. The second involved selling goods produced by JVs that were in high demand in the domestic economy, but whose imports were restricted by various barriers. Producers of these goods earned large profits in the domestic economy because limited competition, due to import constraints, inflated the prices of these goods in the domestic market. Rural officials were also seeking extra-normal profits in the domestic market that existed due to the limited production of goods needed for manufacturing industrial or producer goods that were in high demand. But because market shortages rather than import barriers were generating these high prices, economists do not classify these as rents but instead as extra-normal profits that erode as production increases.

RENT-SEEKING IN THE EXPORT SECTOR

Despite the decentralization of controls over foreign trade, most areas still exported through FTCs which, until the early 1990s, kept TVEs in the dark as to the international price of their products. So, FTCs earned rents based on the difference between the domestic purchase price, which they were able to force down, and the international selling price to which only they had access, due to the limited number of export licenses.[101]

Rural elites in Zhangjiagang decided to bypass the FTCs by establishing direct export channels through JVs; and where they could not find real partners, they linked with friends and relatives in Hong Kong or with anyone else they could find. Many firms were JVs in name only. For example, one overseas Chinese from the United States was merely a front for the JV, for which he received a salary; but JV status allowed the Zhangjiagang partner to export through his own contacts.[102] My own wife, while visiting Zhangjiagang in 1992, was invited to form a JV with a table-cloth factory, which believed that the FTC had inflated its markup. Similarly, a Canadian businesswoman living in Nanjing became the legal front for a JV in a coastal province.[103] By June 1994, all the five hundred major exporting TVEs in Jiangsu Province had become JVs.[104]

101. According to David Dapice, normal trade companies charge competitive margins of 2–4 percent; anything more is rent. Personal communication, Medford, Mass., 1994. However, in China, FTCs are supposed to charge only 1–1.5 percent.
102. Interview in Zhangjiagang, 1991.
103. Interview in Nanjing, 1992.
104. Xinhua News Service "Jiangsu's Township Enterprises Make More Profits," August 5, 1994, reprinted in FBIS, no. 151 (5 August 1994): 35. These five hundreds firms still supplied 18.8 percent of the export commodities sold to specialized export companies in the province. Thus, not all their production went out through their JV channels.

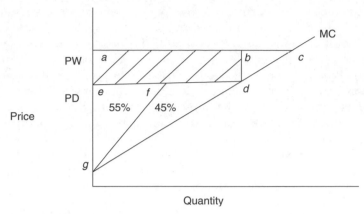

MC = Marginal cost
PD = Domestic price
PW = World price
abde = Profits collected by the FTC when the TVE produces at *d*; profits transferred to a JV when the TVE forms a JV. In worst case, all could be transferred to foreign partner.
bcd = Loss to society because the TVE does not produce at *c* when the FTC takes *abde*.
gef = Tax taken by state from the TVE; this can be recaptured by the TVE by forming a JV.

Figure 3.2   Rent-Capturing Opportunities in the Chinese Foreign Trade System

Copyright Edward Tower and David Zweig

   To illustrate, in figure 3.2[105] the rent earned by the FTC is represented by the rectangle *abde*. The enterprise produces at point *d* rather than *c* because the domestic price PD is below the world price PW. By taking the rent, the FTC leads to the creation of less social welfare, the triangle *bdc*. The state also takes 55 percent of the profits as tax, *efg*. We can see the advantages to the TVE of forming the JV and the loss incurred by the central state. First, because it now receives the world price PW, the TVE produces at *c* on the marginal cost curve and shares *acde* with its JV partner. Also, because of the tax break given to the JV, the TVE, which previously only received *dfg*, also keeps the tax triangle *efg* that it previously gave to the central state. In the short term, the enterprise and the foreign partner share whatever rent the FTC was taking; but the central state loses the foreign exchange the FTC would have earned and because of the tax break, the 55 percent tax owed to it. Thus the opportunity created by the Chinese state to circumvent those controls, by allowing JVs, undermined its own tax base. Depending on the division of profits, the foreigner might get 50 percent of *acg*, but before the JV was established more than half of the factory's production (*edg*) went to various bureaus in the Chinese state administration.

105. Figure 3.2 and some of the analysis on rent seeking were the result of detailed discussions between the author and Edward Tower of Duke University in 1992.

Beginning in 1992, the central government began granting import-export powers to TVEs, undercutting their need for JVs as a mechanism to circumvent the foreign trade system. And while the state jealously guards this opportunity—by August 1994, only 192 rural industrial conglomerates had import-export power—the number of large TVEs with these rights has grown throughout the 1990s.

RENT-SEEKING IN THE DOMESTIC MARKET

A second form of rent-seeking occurs because of the mixed market or planned nature of the foreign trade system. Under partial reform, the Chinese state imposed tariffs or import quotas on the importation of producer goods and machinery parts, products that are in high demand as China tries to export quality machinery. For example, in 1993, China established the National Office for the Control of the Import and Export of Machinery and Electronic Products, which placed quotas on these goods. Thereafter, importing any product on its list involved enormous bureaucratic effort and increased transaction costs. Local agents were empowered to prevent imports if they threatened or damaged domestic producers.[106] The resulting market scarcity made the domestic price higher than the international price so that anyone producing that good earned monopoly prices.

FDI created channels for foreigners and TVEs to access these rents. Employing foreign technology and foreign management improved the quality of products from rural JVs. But even if production costs were too high for the international market, import restrictions made the quality and price of these goods so competitive in the domestic market that some Chinese believed that even if they exported 70 percent of their production at a loss, they could still profit from selling 30 percent of their product domestically.[107]

This type of rent seeking was part of Zhangjiagang's development strategy. According to the Chinese manager in a JV: "Next year we will begin to sell about 20–30 percent of our product domestically. The foreign partner raised this and we agreed. If we sell domestically, Chinese factories will know that their domestic costs are too high. When we began this business, we saw from our own firm's perspective there was a domestic market, so we decided to import for the domestic market. The state 'gets burned' but it is good for our firm."[108] According to Evans, all developing states seeking FDI confront this dilemma: "it was the state's opposition to foreign entry

---

106. See "Provisional Regulations on the Control of the Import of Machinery and Electronic Products," Decree No. 1, State Economic and Trade Commission and the Ministry of Foreign Trade and Economic Cooperation, 7 October 1993, in Editorial Board of the Almanac of China's Foreign Economic Relations and Trade, ed., *Almanac of China's Foreign Economic Relations and Trade, 1994/95* (Hong Kong: China Resources Advertising Co., 1995), pp. 173–75.
107. Egypt's JV law allowed foreigners to establish import substitution firms, which earned high profits in a highly protected domestic market. See John Waterbury, "The 'Soft State' and the Open Door: Egypt's Experience with Economic Liberalization, 1974–1984," *Comparative Politics* 18 (October 1985): 76.
108. Interview in Zhangjiagang, November 1991.

that gave local capital its trump card in negotiating the initial alliances, but once alliances had been negotiated, relations between firms and states changed again. The state's leverage was undercut. Firms had, in effect, traded the rents associated with state protection of the local market for those associated with their transnational corporate allies' proprietary technology and global market power."[109]

Pro-rural officials in Beijing were unconcerned about weakened state controls over the domestic market because they believed that only these incentives would bring new capital and equipment into the Chinese countryside.[110] Also, they recognized that JVs strengthen the local economy and the local Communist Party organization.

Conclusion

The neo-liberal model suggests that foreign trade, with its diverse impact on industrial sectors, generates collective action among domestic coalitions who lobby for policy outcomes supporting their collective interests. Under this assumption, we expect elites in rural coastal China who controlled factors of production favorable to foreign trade (e.g., cheap labor) to have lobbied intensely for trade expansion and the opening of the countryside, and we expect this action to have begun in the mid-1980s, as the increasing costs of labor in Taiwan and Hong Kong improved rural China's comparative advantage in foreign trade. According to the regulatory controls model, we expect SOEs and their bureaucratic benefactors to have lobbied against opening rural China.

But such collective action did not occur. In fact, central leaders had to mobilize the rural areas to participate in the export economy, even though their labor surplus gave them a comparative advantage in foreign trade. Why? First, after decollectivization, individual householders became the major producers of agricultural products—when markets comprise many small producers, the private costs are too high for individuals to lobby for their interests.[111] And there was no powerful body to lobby successfully for the farmers' interests; farmers are represented in Beijing only by the weak Ministry of Agriculture, which confronts dozens of well-placed functional and line ministries protecting urban and industrial interests.[112] Nor could farmers legally organize on their own under China's nonparticipatory, authoritarian political system because the CCP maintains its monopoly on

109. Evans, *Embedded Autonomy*, p. 16.
110. Interview, Research Centre for the Rural Economy, Ministry of Agriculture, Beijing, December 1991.
111. Robert H. Bates, "Macropolitical Economy in the Field of Development," in *Perspectives on Positive Political Economy*, ed. James E. Alt and Kenneth Shepsle (New York: Cambridge University Press, 1990), pp. 41–43.
112. Bernstein, "Farmer Discontent and Regime Responses."

representing the farmers' interests. Similarly, managers of TVEs and village and township governments had no organization, such as a chamber of commerce, that could press Beijing on their behalf.

Second, in the mid-1980s, farmers, TVE managers, and rural elites lacked incentives to enter the export fray. The foreign trade administration controlled all external interactions and was the financial beneficiary of rural exports; it prevented rural leaders and provinces from knowing their interests. Before 1988, even if local elites and farmers had earned foreign exchange, they could not have used it to improve their income or competitiveness by importing foreign technology. Especially for the strong TVEs (who eventually became the bulwark of the rural export economy) relational contracting in the domestic market had been the key to their success; they were not about to shift markets and products if there were many risks with few rewards.

In fact, it was state leaders such as Zhao Ziyang who, beginning in 1987, started to lift the tight constraints that had been imposed on rural China. Although rural Guangdong Province and rural export production zones had been actively involved in export activities since the late 1970s, it was only in 1985 that Zhao called on more parts of rural China to produce crops with export markets in mind. Ironically, in 1989, to prevent TVEs from competing with the SOEs in the domestic economy, conservative party leaders made export-led growth the major strategy for the countryside's continued industrial expansion.

Once Zhao changed the countryside's incentives, allowing direct access to foreign exchange, technology, information, and global markets, rural leaders with manufacturing facilities displayed a powerful capacity for microlevel, community-based collective action, forming an alliance with foreign capital that promoted the locality's interests. Perhaps the competition for rents and the high costs of market entry galvanized this collective behavior.[113] Only if the county government centralized control over its FTCs—which had to find foreign investors, export quotas, domestic markets, and foreign technology—and helped township officials suppress worker demand and accumulate capital, could communities manage the risks of entering the unchartered international waters and generate the products, relationships, administrative protection, and information necessary to access the rents and successfully implement local export-led growth.

Whereas the development communities mobilized their constituents to act collectively, intercommunity behavior was characterized by internal competition. These communities did not collectively press Beijing to liberalize its foreign trade and foreign investment rules. Instead, as each county

113. Whereas I see the search for rents as the reason for the emergence of corporate communities in the foreign trade sector, Andrew Walder suggests that the high entry costs to new markets for TVEs may have contributed to this local collective action. Personal communication, 1995.

or township pursued its own global linkages, this unorganized collective action undermined the central state's regulatory regime.

How do we explain this strong demand for global linkages? First and foremost, rural industries' comparative advantage in labor and the low cost of TVE products helped win rural China new export markets.[114] Competitive labor costs attracted network capital that brought rural China new export markets and better-quality products and, as a result, deepened the level of internationalization of rural China. Local elites, who understood how these opportunities would advance their individual and their collective interests, became entrepreneurs who promoted foreign trade and sought FDI. Also, supporters of SOEs did not block TVEs from entering the export sector; in fact, their policies in 1989 diverted TVE competition from the domestic to the international market.

Second, China's partially reformed trade and FDI regime, including the rules governing JVs, created enormous opportunities for rent-seeking in both the domestic and international markets. The JV fever that resulted expanded the number of transnational channels and increased the level of internationalization.

Finally, state institutions established to monitor and control transnational exchanges failed to fulfill that function. By using a number of channels of global transaction—such as JVs, local FTCs, or other regions' FTCs—rural leaders and developmental communities used the state's own institutions to undermine the foreign trade administration's control and establish more direct ties with foreign markets. In particular, the decentralization of decision-making authority to approve JVs created thousands of horizontal channels for exchanges through which local governments swapped access to China's domestic markets in return for international capital and access to international markets. JVs thus became a mechanism for undermining, not maintaining, China's state authority over its borders.

114. Changqi Wu and Leonard K. Cheng, "The Determinants of Export Performance of China's Township-Village Enterprises" (unpublished paper, Hong Kong University of Science and Technology, March 1999).

4

Dollars, Scholars, and Fevers: The Political Economy of Educational Internationalization

After decades of isolation from the West, the People's Republic of China gradually reestablished scholarly exchanges with the West under its open policy in education.[1] But while tight central controls were maintained through the mid-1980s, China's universities and the science and technology sector became one of the most internationalized arenas in Chinese society. Academic and scientific exchanges and overseas education became the channel through which China's intellectuals and educational administrators could sojourn overseas, and the enormous demand for such opportunities has triggered a brain drain that rivaled most developing countries.[2] Academic exchanges brought western technology, innovative scientific methodologies, and new teaching materials into China. Multilateral donors such as the World Bank, numerous bilateral aid agencies such as the Canadian International Development Agency, and the overseas Chinese have poured millions of dollars into China's universities and colleges to improve their intellectual and physical facilities.[3]

But what was the driving force behind the opening—the central government leaders or societal demand? Again I hypothesize that the central government instigated the initial opening. But once the opening began, did market forces and relative prices on either side of the Chinese border expand it by mobilizing domestic beneficiaries to act in a concerted way to bring down the barriers? Or was the opening controlled by bureaucrats whose actions influenced access to the international realm and the domestic response to internationalization? Here I hypothesize that, given the

1. See David M. Lampton, ed., *A Relationship Restored: Trends in U.S.–China Educational Exchanges, 1978–1984* (Washington, D.C.: National Academy Press, 1986).
2. David Zweig and Chen Changgui, *China's Brain Drain to the United States: The Views of Overseas Students and Scholars in the 1990s* (Berkeley: Institute for East Asian Studies, 1995). See also Leo A. Orleans, "Perspectives on China's Brain Drain," in *China's Economic Dilemmas in the 1990s: The Problems of Reforms, Modernization, and Interdependence*, ed. Joint Economic Committee, U.S. Congress (Washington, D.C.: U.S. Government Printing Office, 1991), pp. 629–43.
3. Ruth Hayhoe, *China's Universities and the Open Door* (Armonk: M. E. Sharpe, 1989).

enormous variation in the returns to human capital between China and the West, and the clarification of the potential benefits of global linkages by the decentralization of the controls over exchange channels to provinces, cities, and lower levels of the administrative hierarchy, domestic demand grew dramatically.

Conceptualizing China's Open Policy in Education

Like water to a man dying of thirst, global resources offered China's universities and intellectuals resuscitation, rejuvenation, and even a source of life for new organizations. Cut off for twenty years, China's scholars hungered for transnational linkages, while their schools, starved in a similar manner, developed voracious appetites for international goods and services. Moreover, the relative poverty of China's educational system,[4] low faculty wages, collapsing infrastructure, and backward educational and resource skills created enormous differences between the relative values of goods and services and the potential return to human capital on either side of the border.

The value of these global resources gave enormous opportunities to those who could capture them. The fact that facilitators of exchanges, their children, and the children of high-ranking officials stood to benefit directly from the chance to go overseas created strong disincentives for the bureaucrats to restrict severely the transnational flows of students and scholars. Imported equipment gave research labs an economic advantage over those lacking global ties; foreign students became a money-making opportunity for a few key schools; new skills or knowledge brought back by returnee scholars earned extra-normal profits for their practitioners and the institutions that hired them; and working overseas brought higher salaries, easier access to valuable commodities, and higher status for those who returned and a better life for many who chose not to return. Permits to go overseas, visas, the right to use foreign funds to import equipment, and the foreign exchange needed by international sojourners remained the allocative privileges of China's educational and foreign affairs bureaucracy, creating opportunities for charging fees and earning rents. As the flow of goods expanded, so did the bureaucratic machinery that competed to control these channels. This commodification of educational exchanges created incentives for bureaucrats to maintain the flow of internationalization, if not accelerate the process. Entrepreneurs who could connect domestic and

---

4. China's investment per student in higher education is lower than average for countries on a similar economic level. Gu Qingyang, "Our Country's Higher Education Finances in International Comparative Perspective," *Gaodeng jiaoyu yanjiu* [Research on higher education] 3 (1989): 40–46.

foreign networks created exchange industries that earned income by facilitating the flow. These new institutions challenged existing monopolies in
the education system, creating a more pluralistic, marketized linkage
system. With universities as the training ground for local nationals seeking employment in an expanding transnational or multinational sector,
China's educational system underwent its own structural readjustment.
Schools and programs focusing on foreign trade, international economics,
business, and law suddenly attracted domestic and international funds, new
linkages overseas, and China's best and brightest students. All these trends
combined to form an export-led growth educational system.

This sector differs from the others I have discussed in several ways.
Although collective property rights dominated the educational system
and most people earned rewards through collectivities (universities,
research labs, research groups, and training centers), individual or familial
betterment based on increasing the relative value of individual human
capital drove people overseas as much as organizational interests. Moreover, by rewarding returnees with preferential policies, the state, which
usually denigrated individual interest as selfish and unpatriotic, legitimized
private activity in the educational realm before it did so in the industrial,
trade, or financial sectors. It created a catch-22 in which people could
advance more quickly in China if they went overseas, but, having done so,
were less likely to return and work for the state or their home organization.
The result was a fever to go abroad and a brain drain of enormous proportions, which demonstrated the loss of state control. These twin forces of
organizational and individual interests may explain the enormity of the
demand for internationalization in this sector.

National Policy, Global Pressures, and Mass Interests

Internationalization of the education sector was driven by both internal
and external forces, by elite policy predilections, domestic marketization,
and demands for global linkages by organizations and citizens who found
personal benefits in expanded overseas exchanges. Deng Xiaoping initiated the opening soon after returning to power in 1977, and extremely
positive external responses from foreign governments and multilateral
agencies facilitated many bilateral and multilateral exchanges and educational opportunities. Prominent Chinese scientists, both at home and overseas, encouraged government leaders to train students abroad. Overseas
Chinese, who wanted to help their relatives study abroad, propelled the
self-study program.[5] Increased opportunities for overseas links, however,

5. Paul Englesberg, "Reversing China's Brain Drain: The Study Abroad Policy, 1978–1993,"
in *Great Policies: Strategic Innovations in Asia and the Pacific Basin*, ed. John D. Montgomery and
Dennis A. Rondinelli (Westport: Praeger, 1995), pp. 99–122.

only clarified people's interests and intensified demand, even as the emergence of a market in the educational and the science and technology sector increased the value of exchanges, global resources, and returnees. Although individuals could not lobby directly, students and scholars, by their actions and demands to go overseas, forced organizations to expand transnational channels, undermining bureaucratic controls. So, when the state in 1985 responded to this pent-up demand for exchanges by decentralizing control, horizontal school-to-school as well as private channels proliferated, generating a fever to go abroad that was very difficult for the state to control.

The next sections tell the story of the internationalization of the educational and science and technology sectors, weaving in the critical changes in the domestic political economy that intensified economic interactions between internal and external forces. Elite policy prescriptions, the enormous value of international opportunities, domestic reforms, and individual and collective behavior influenced the pattern, pace, and depth of internationalization. Yet, despite greater internationalization, bureaucratic constraints remained a powerful influence on the nature of transnational exchanges and the way in which Chinese linked with the world.

PRE-REFORM ERA

Internationalization emerged within an educational sector highlighted by tightly constrained institutional arrangements. Universities relied completely on grants from the Ministry of Education (MOE) for all administrative expenses, giving MOE bureaucrats enormous leverage. This soft-budget constraint for universities, departments, and university bureaucrats left them little incentive to innovate or seek profits. Collective property rights over academic and scientific creations submerged all individual contributions and individual efforts; academic salaries were extremely low and there was no opportunity for generating private income. Within universities, department heads wielded enormous power, while faculty, lacking job mobility, had little negotiating leverage. Beginning in 1976, universities became responsible for their retirees, a burden that grew larger and larger. Yet state investment in education in China, at 2.3 percent of GNP, was among the lowest per capita in the entire world, leaving universities with enormous financial needs.[6]

6. United Nations Development Program, *World Development Report, 1994* (New York: Oxford University Press, 1994), pp. 158–59. The world average was 4.8; the average for sub-Saharan Africa, at 2.4 percent, was still higher than China.

INTERNATIONALIZATION BEGINS, 1978–1979

Internationalization of China's education and science and technology systems began in spring 1978 when Deng Xiaoping, concerned about the scientific gap between China and the world, affirmed the importance of learning from other countries in transforming China "into a powerful socialist country" at the National Conference on Education in 1978 (table 4.1). At the National Conference on Science in May 1978 he took his campaign for scientific engagement one step further when he argued that "backwardness must be recognized before it can be changed. One must learn from those who are most advanced before one can catch up with and surpass them." On June 23, 1978, Deng stressed the impor-

Table 4.1   Periodization of the Open Door in Education, 1978–1994

1978–79	Initial opening
March 1978	National Conference on Education
April–May	National Conference on Science
June	China decides to send people abroad to study subjects other than language
August	MOE notice, "Concerning the Increase of Students Study Abroad and Their Selection"
October	"Understanding on Educational Exchanges with the United States"
January 1979	Chinese-American Agreement on "Cooperation in Science and Technology"
	China joins the World Bank and begins to negotiate educational exchanges
1984–86	Second phase of reform
November 1984	Second National Work Conference on Study Abroad
December	State Council Regulations on People Who Study Abroad at Their Own Expense
March 1985	"CC-CCP Reform of Science and Technology Management System"; leads to major changes in the political economy of S&T and the commercialization of scientific results
May	"CC-CCP Reform of the Educational System" expands powers of universities, cuts financial support to most schools, but tightens controls over 36 key universities
July	U.S.-Chinese "Protocol for Cooperation in Educational Exchanges"
May 1986	"National Conference on Study Abroad" expands the authority of provinces and cities to send people abroad at their own expense
Fall 1986–87	Student protests trigger first round of tightening
December 1986	Major student protests over elections within universities lead to fall of General Secretary Hu Yaobang in January 1987
December 1987	"Certain Interim Provisions of the SEDC on the Work of Sending Personnel Abroad" (published in 1987)
Fall 1988	Another round of tightening
	Drop in number of returnees after spring 1987 Antibourgeois Liberalization Campaign triggers policy debate
	Zhao Ziyang supports "storing brainpower overseas"
October 1988	*Ming Pao* reports number of students to the United States to be cut from 6,000 to 500; never put into effect
	Increased number of university lecturers with M.A.s who go overseas on J-1 rather than F-1 visas

Table 4.1   (*cont.*)

Fall 1989–Spring 1992	Post-Tiananmen policies: external softening, internal tightening
	Class conflict applied to struggle between some overseas students and SEDC
	State initially suggests it will send fewer students and more visiting scholars overseas, but in October announces that level of government-sponsored students to be maintained
	Number of privately sponsored students increased significantly after Tiananmen
	TOEFL takers jump from 36,000 in 1989 to 60,000 in 1990
January 25, 1990	"Supplement Provisions for Personages with University Graduate and Postgraduate Qualifications Study Abroad at Own Expense"
	College graduates going abroad to study on their own must first pay back costs of their education
April 1990	U.S. Chinese Student Protection Act vetoed, but replaced by President George Bush's Executive Order allowing all Chinese in United States as of April 1990 to apply for permanent residence and all J-1 visa holders to shift to F-1 visas
Summer 1990	New regulation that graduates need 5 years work experience before going abroad
	Right of approval transferred from the work units to the provincial education commission
May 1991	"Decision to Send More Technical Workers Abroad" expands program for training managers and technical specialists abroad in countries with "good political and economic relations with China" (not United States or Canada)
Post-1992	Liberalization in the wake of Deng's southern journey
August 1992	Government circular offers incentives to return, especially better living and working conditions, grants for research, freedom to go out again (*lai qu zi you*), and right to import autos and computers duty free
	Intercity competition to lure back returnees through preferential policies
April 1993	"Conference on the Work of Sending Personnel to Study Abroad" relaxes standards for studying abroad
June 1993	"Joint Circular on the Placement of Returned Students" makes key point that "if some students want to move to work in other units, personnel departments should try to meet their requests"
	Returnees can apply for work in all areas of the economy or set up their own companies
January 1994	SEDC announces plans to expand China's education through foreign cooperation

Note: CC, Central Committe; CCP, Chinese Communist Party; MOE, Ministry of Education; S&T, Science and Technology; SEDC, State Education Commission; TOEFL, Test of English as a Foreign Language.

tance of increasing the number of overseas students, particularly in the natural sciences, called on the MOE to set up a special group to manage overseas study, and criticized the previous policy on overseas students as "too inflexible" (*bu neng name si*). And even as he stressed the importance of China's own creativity, independence, and self reliance—after all, many bureaucrats and officials feared relying on the outside world—he remarked that "independence does not mean shutting the door on the world, nor does self-reliance mean blind opposition to everything foreign."[7] Thus, argues Shiqi Huang, "Deng Xiaoping's personnel intervention in policy matters concerning education and science in 1977 [and 1978] were of crucial importance in the shaping of later policies."[8]

Deng began to create a positive environment for the concrete policies that would follow, including the decision to send students abroad to study subjects other than languages, the signing of major educational and scientific exchanges with the United States and other developed countries, and the establishment of many sister-school relationships. Apparently, in August 1979, Deng proposed that each year China send ten thousand students abroad, but due to MOE concerns the official quota was set at three thousand per year for five years.[9] In December 1979, Fang Yi, the reformers' leading spokesman on science and technology, convened the First National Work Conference on Study Abroad, which announced that overseas study was not a short-term policy but one that must be followed "for a long time to come."[10] Moreover, instead of sending only mid-career scholars, graduate students could also go abroad. All these discussions reflected the ongoing debate over the Sixth Five-Year Plan, which a year later announced China's plans to send a total of fifteen thousand students and scholars abroad over the next five years.

China received remarkably strong support for its overseas study program from all the developed countries. According to Mary Bullock, although political and economic interests established the original parameters of Chinese-western academic relations, "intellectual and cultural relations, driven by public enthusiasm, quickly became the cutting edge."[11] Unlike its tightly controlled exchange programs with the Soviet Union, the U.S. government decided not to limit the number of Chinese and gave out as many visas as the Chinese wanted. Also, after the U.S. government decided to involve American universities in exchanges, Chinese students quickly gained access to a motherlode of university fellowships that transformed the demand-supply equilibrium and accelerated the number of Chinese students going overseas once the Chinese government loosened its controls.[12]

7. Quoted in Jiao Guozheng, "Pengbo fazhan de chuguo liuxue gongzuo" [Flourishing development of the work of sending out overseas students], *Zhongguo gaodeng jiaoyu* [Higher education in China] (Beijing) 12 (1998): 6–8, in *Higher Education in China: Research Materials from People's University* 2 (1999): 72–74.
8. Shiqi Huang, "Contemporary Educational Relations with the Industrialized World: A Chinese View," in *China's Education and the Industrialized World: Studies in Cultural Transfer*, ed. Ruth Hayhoe and Marianne Bastid (Armonk: M. E. Sharpe, 1987), pp. 227–28.
9. Englesberg, "Reversing China's Brain Drain," p. 102.
10. Ibid.
11. Mary B. Bullock, "The Effects of Tiananmen on China's International Scientific and Educational Cooperation," in *China's Economic Dilemmas in the 1990s: The Problems of Reforms, Modernization, and Interdependence*, ed. Joint Economic Committee, U.S. Congress (Washington, D.C.: U.S. Government Printing Office, 1991), pp. 611–28.
12. Interview with Glen Schive, 15 June 1999, Hong Kong.

Before 1981, all students and scholars who went abroad were approved and funded by the MOE. But in 1980 pressures began building to allow people who could pay their own way (self-paying, *zi fei*) to go abroad.[13] According to Paul Englesberg, part of the pressure to introduce this category came from overseas Chinese who wanted to bring their relatives out for study. Children of high-ranking cadres also wanted to expand this channel. Yet, although the state agreed to let high school and college graduates with proper support go on their own, the visas for all university teachers, scientists, technicians, and other important individuals still had to be approved by the MOE, which incorporated them into the national plan even if they made their own arrangements; also, the regulations governing their sojourn were the same as those that applied to government-funded students. By 1982, however, the growing number of self-paying students, in particular the many children of high-ranking cadres who were using this category to go overseas, led the Central Committee of the CCP to issue a directive to restrict the self-paying category.[14]

New organizations emerged to manage the flow. In May 1981, the MOE created its own China International Examinations Coordination Bureau (CIECB) to administer the Graduate Record Exam (GRE) and the Test of English as a Foreign Language (TOEFL).[15] The CIECB also administered pretests to screen students nominated by institutes and universities, creating another layer of bureaucratic control. Within the universities, the bureaucracies controlling exchanges expanded. World Bank loan offices coordinated the purchase of World Bank–funded equipment and the flow of scholars overseas, while various administrative departments, such as personnel, foreign affairs, teacher quality, and research, established new bureaus to assert their right to control the growing flow of people, equipment, and money.

DECENTRALIZATION AND THE PROLIFERATION OF AUTONOMOUS CHANNELS, 1984–1985

Following the second wave of reform in spring 1984, the demand for expanding the number of channels intensified. With the number of sojourners taxing the state's bureaucracy, universities wanted a more decentralized expeditious process. After the Third Plenum of the Twelfth Party Congress called for major reforms of SOEs in fall 1984, the reformers were well positioned to propose new educational reforms. A drafting

13. "Request for Instructions Regarding People Applying to Study Abroad at Their Own Expense," *Guofa* 13 (14 January 1981), in *Chinese Law and Government* 19 (winter 1986–87): 30–33.
14. Englesberg, "Reversing China's Brain Drain," p. 108.
15. "TOEFL and GRE to Be Administered in China," *China Exchange News* 9 (September 1981): 13.

committee for an educational reform document was set up under Hu Yaobang and Zhao Ziyang.[16]

In November 1984, at the Second National Conference on Study Abroad, concerns were raised about how China could best use the fourteen thousand students and scholars who had already returned and about the emerging problem of the brain drain.[17] Many returnees apparently felt that their skills were being poorly used. But rather than create an intellectual labor market, the government readjusted the job-assignment system and any improper job assignments that had occurred. Centers were established for returned postdoctoral scholars, where they could work before being assigned to new and suitable units, and schools, such as Beijing Languages Institute, which taught foreigners Chinese and Chinese foreign languages, established a consulting center for Chinese thinking about studying abroad.[18] After this conference, a new State Council regulation allowed anyone (except current graduate students) who could get foreign financial support to study overseas. These self-paying students no longer needed MOE permission to leave, only the approval of their local Public Security Bureau.[19]

The growth of foreign funds expanded the outward flow of human talent. Although the number of Chinese students going to the United States stagnated between 1980 and 1983 at approximately 4,300 a year, it jumped to 6,097 in 1984, 9,913 in 1985, and 12,711 in 1986, tripling in three years.[20] Interest in studying abroad ballooned as well. The number of people taking the TOEFL increased tenfold in three years, from 1,427 in 1982, to 2,395 in 1983, 4,449 in 1984, and 16,483 in 1985.[21] According to Leo Orleans, in 1985 more new TOEFL centers opened in China, offering access channels to the United States.[22]

Reforms in science and technology and in education in spring 1985 significantly altered the context of educational and scientific exchanges.[23] Three Central Committee (CC) decisions involved significant policy innovation. According to *Liaowang*, these reforms were advocated by Hu

16. Yang Ruiming, "Pointing the Way to Reforming the Education System," *Liaowang* 23 (10 June 1985): 9–12, reprinted in *Foreign Broadcast Information Service* (hereafter *FBIS*) (26 June 1985): K11–17.

17. Leo A. Orleans, *Chinese Students in America: Policies, Issues, and Numbers* (Washington, DC: National Academy Press, 1988), p. 26.

18. "New Rules Help Students Go Abroad," *China Daily*, 14 January 1985, p. 3.

19. Englesberg, "Reversing China's Brain Drain," p. 109.

20. Orleans, *Chinese Students in America*, p. 88.

21. Huang, "Contemporary Educational Relations," p. 230.

22. Orleans, *Chinese Students in America*, p. 28.

23. Decision of the CC of the CCP on the Reform of the Science and Technology Management System, 13 March 1985," *Beijing Review* 14 (8 April 1985): 19; "Decision of the CC-CCP on Reform of the Educational System, 27 May 1985," reprinted in *FBIS* (30 May 1985): K1–K11.

Yaobang and Zhao Ziyang with strong support from Wan Li and Hu Qili and occurred in the context of an upswing in a reform cycle.[24]

Authority over finances, exchanges, curriculum, student enrollment, and capital construction was decentralized, and science and technology research was commercialized. A new national Natural Science Foundation became a main source of competitive funding for scientific research and a major source of support for returning students. Universities, laboratories, and scientific organizations were given huge incentives to pursue business and educational opportunities because profits could be used to improve the schools, increase exchanges, and raise faculty living standards. The MOE, soon to change into the more comprehensive State Education Commission (SEDC), jettisoned control over most universities under its aegis, many of which had been a financial burden. Yet although their autonomy increased, these schools lost financial support from the central government.

On the other hand, the new SEDC tightened its control over the top thirty-six universities in the country, allowing it to distribute resources and exchange opportunities to a small group of very elite key schools. A bifurcated or two-tiered educational system, with richer and poorer schools, emerged. SEDC schools and schools under some ministries remained relatively well-funded, albeit under relatively tighter regulatory controls, while schools under poorer ministries and provincial or municipal controls were left to their own resources.[25]

Efforts to enhance professionalism and establish criteria for promotion coincided with internationalization, altering the strategies of faculty and graduate students. By 1984, after decades without promotions, full and associate professors still made up only 10 percent of academic positions.[26] Promotion based on academic contributions made overseas study a critical career step. First, the enormous competition for graduate slots in China meant that it was easier to enter graduate programs overseas (table 4.2 on p. 176); and, second, the high value that accrued to foreign degrees, training, and experience placed a premium on going overseas for a period of time during an individual's academic training.

Nevertheless, the 1985 reforms left universities scrambling for funds. Allocations from the central government covered only two-thirds of the operating expenses of most key universities.[27] In open areas along the

24. Yang, "Pointing the Way."
25. Stanley Rosen, "Recentralization, Decentralization, and Rationalization: Deng Xiaoping's Bifurcated Educational Policy," *Modern China* 11 (July 1985): 301–46.
26. As of 1978, of 206,000 full-time faculty in higher education, 1.3 percent were full professors and 2.7 percent associate professors. Ministry of Education, *Achievement of Education in China, 1949–1983* (Beijing: People's Education Press, 1985), pp. 112–13.
27. Todd M. Johnson, "The Economics of Higher Education Reform in China," *China Exchange News* 17 (1989): 3–7.

south coast, personnel costs, travel costs, and subsidies were approximately 20 percent higher than for most other universities. Xiamen University could not fund over 3.6 million RMB in subsidies that it had to grant its faculty because of the high costs of living in an SEZ.[28] Inflation in 1987–89 was particularly problematic for schools in SEZs, which had to seek a variety of supplements to support their often meager grants from the SEDC. In fact, schools such as Beijing University, Beijing Normal University, and Tongji University in Shanghai generated 50 percent of their incomes by supplementary activities.[29]

Decentralization of financing, the emergence of tuition-paying students at Chinese universities, the growth of university factories, the commercialization of research at universities and research institutions, and access to international funds and exchange programs—all created alternative sources for funding that weakened the SEDC's influence. Universities no longer had to turn over to the SEDC any funds remaining at the end of the fiscal year, and they could now expand their physical plant without permission from higher-level bureaucrats, which simplified fund raising from overseas Chinese.

The commercialization of science and technology affected the political economy of universities and research institutes.[30] A competitive grants system based on peer review and a new technology market encouraged research institutes and universities to commercialize their research, establish partnerships with enterprises, or become independent economic entities. Instead of direct grants to schools, contracts from the state and enterprises became the chief means of gaining research funds. The result was an emerging culture of scientific competition over Natural Science Foundation funding among universities and research institutes in the Academy of Sciences. Similarly, line ministries and the new State Science and Technology Commission (SSTC) created "key" projects over which organizations would compete. Organizations also competed to have the State Planning Commission—with the SSTC as the advising organization—label their ongoing projects "key national-level" laboratories because the official title meant a steady flow of state support. And, although the funds went directly to the lab, the university took 5–10 percent as overhead. These national labs also paid rent to the school and salaries to the faculty. M.A.- and Ph.D.-training centers emerged under a similarly competitive

---

28. Cai Duiqiao and Li Xixiong, "Funds Shortages of Special Economic Zone Institutions of Higher Education under Ministry and Commission: Jurisdiction and Remedies," *Xiamen daxue xuebao: Zhexue shihui kexue ban* [Journal of Xiamen University: Philosophy and social sciences edition] 1 (January 1990): 57–61, 67, reprinted in *Joint Publication Research Service* (hereafter *JPRS*), no. 37 (14 May 1990): 85–91.
29. Ruiqing Du, *Chinese Higher Education: A Decade of Reform and Development, 1978–1988* (New York: St. Martin's Press, 1992), p. 24.
30. "Decision of the CC," pp. 19–21.

program and funding went only to schools awarded such training programs and status.

Although labs, research groups, and faculties had specific tasks to perform, letting them keep some of the residuals gave them incentives to pursue income-generating endeavors. Of the extra funds earned by labs and departments through cooperative research, universities took 30 percent, the department or lab got back 30 percent, and the smaller research group received 40 percent, which was divided directly among team members.[31] Computer centers on campus were allowed to charge outsiders a user's fee; although most of these funds went to the central administration, 20 percent of their earnings went to the lab and its employees. Also, although the university took 40 percent of a professor's outside consulting fee, the individual professor kept 50 percent, leaving the department with 10 percent. All these policies increased the value of people with international experience who could compete successfully for grants, be certified as a Ph.D.-granting institution, or establish global ties.

A PHASE OF CONSTRICTION, 1987–1991

The student protests of December 1986 tightened the reins on overseas study.[32] Also, by mid-1987, it had become apparent that most students sent abroad for Ph.D.s after 1983 were not returning, despite the state's intention to use them in national construction. In mid-1987, He Dongchang, vice-chairman of the SEDC, led a delegation to the United States that revealed plans to send more advanced academics—those with M.A.s and Ph.D.s, and senior scholars—as short-term visiting scholars. Under these new guidelines, the ratio of government-sponsored visiting scholars, research students, and undergraduates was set at 70:25:5. This Chinese delegation also insinuated U.S. complicity in China's brain drain because in late 1987 the SEDC discovered that unit-sent, publicly sponsored (*dan wei gong pai*) students who needed foreign financing and who were not under SEDC control were flooding into the United States. A report addressing this issue expressed grave concerns that so many students were going to the United States, where anti-China forces were so strong. So, in December 1987 Deng insisted that fewer students go to the United States, and this speech, which became Central Document No. 11 (1987) and SEDC Document No. 749, was disseminated throughout China. Its main purpose was to cut dramatically the number flowing to the United States, and to pressure students in the United States to return.[33]

31. Interview, Chinese university finance official, Cambridge, Mass., 1993.
32. Kimberley Silver's research assistance was essential for this historical review.
33. Interview with a former official in the SEDC, Cambridge, Mass., 1989.

To fulfill the first goal, the SEDC instituted two versions of form JW-102 for unit-sent publicly supported sojourners: one for applying to the United States and the other for all other countries. It also created one version of each for Visiting Scholars and another for graduate students. Then the SEDC severely cut the number of forms available in China for applying to the United States and the number of overseas applications available for graduate students. Conflict then erupted between the SEDC and the SSTC. In the SSTC's view, the JW-102 strategy severely restricted scientific exchanges with the United States. The SSTC insisted that the form be withdrawn or it would institute its own form. This dispute reached the desk of Li Peng, and in the end, the SEDC agreed that the form would not apply to scholars sponsored by the SSTC.

Document 107 targeted applicants for overseas Ph.D.s and stated that anyone, including those with overseas sponsorship, above the rank of lecturer had to use formal government channels to go overseas.[34] It also restricted visits by students' spouses, and it stated that government-funded students in the United States had only five years to complete their degree and would be required to sign a contract that subjected them and their families to fines if they did not return.[35] To insure that students did not stay abroad much longer than five years, the SEDC decided that those already abroad for five years would be allowed only a one-year extension on their passports; they then had to return or lose their passports.

Chinese students already in the United States delivered a protest letter to the Chinese Communist Party, challenging the five-year limit.[36] Those wanting to go to the United States applied first to go to other countries and then transferred to the United States or applied as Visiting Scholars and shifted to graduate school once in the United States. Thus, many people circumvented the Chinese authority's new barriers. The plan to shift students away from the United States was never implemented "because American universities, foundations and private individuals provide about US$100 million a year in scholarship aid to the Chinese students, with the Chinese Government paying only a fraction of this amount."[37] Here again the power of foreign funds undermined China's institutions.

In 1988, the SEDC forced university lecturers in universities (many with M.A.s) to shift from private to public passports, making them eligible for the more restrictive J-1 student visas, rather than the highly flexible F-1 visas.[38] They became self-paying, publicly sponsored (*zi fei gong pai*) stu-

34. Interview with a former official in the SEDC, Cambridge, Mass., 1989.
35. Dennis Harvest, "China Policy Shift on Study Overseas," *New York Times*, 4 April 1988, p. 5.
36. Interview with a former official in the SEDC, Cambridge, Mass., 1989.
37. Fox Butterfield, "China Plans to Let Fewer Students Go Abroad, Especially to the U.S.," *New York Times*, 24 March 1988, p. 1.
38. Interview with a Wuhan education official, 1994.

dents, and the U.S, government acceded to this request. According to U.S. law, people on J-1 visas must return to their country of origin after graduation (and were not eligible for H-1 employment visas); F-1 visas could be extended almost indefinitely. Also, J-1 visas were processed by a university's foreign affairs office and needed SEDC approval, while F-1 visas were processed by a university's personnel department and needed only the municipal public security bureau's approval. However, as an incentive for students to accept these new restrictions, the jobs, apartments, and salaries of J-1 visa holders were to be kept for them until they returned, while all links were cut with those going out on F-1 visas. Many accepted the SEDC's offer because it allowed their spouses and children to live in relative comfort in China. The Ministry of Personnel also tried to entice these younger teachers to return by announcing in October 1989 that younger returnees and junior academic personnel would be given preference in job assignments and initially on returning would be allocated to service centers located primarily at scientific and technological research institutions and at large- and medium-size enterprises.[39]

In September 1988, the Standing Committee of the Politburo convened a historic meeting to discuss how to respond to the brain drain. The SEDC reportedly insisted that all students return, while the SSTC recognized that only if people stayed abroad longer could they get access to U.S. high-tech facilities, which would benefit China's science and technology sector. Similarly, the Overseas Affairs Commission of the State Council hoped that some students could become U.S. citizens to increase China's influence in the overseas Chinese communities. Finally, the Personnel Ministry, which was having difficulty assigning returnees good jobs, saw too many returnees as a problem.[40] Summing up these views, Zhao Ziyang put a positive spin on the brain drain calling it "storing talent (or brain power) abroad."[41] Nevertheless, Chinese education officials in the Washington embassy rejected this interpretation, and in March–April 1989 embassies overseas circulated a more critical speech on overseas policy, ending the more lenient policy initiated by Zhao.

June 4 complicated the issue as self-funded applications jumped, the number of people taking the TOEFL rose from 36,000 in 1989 to 60,000 in 1990, and the number of government-funded students staying abroad was deemed to be a serious problem.[42] The response was a wide array of new controls. Older scholars were favored over younger students, more Visiting Scholars were funded for short-term sojourns, fewer degree candidates were permitted to study abroad and only those in fields where

39. "Personnel Ministry to Step up Guidance for Returned Students," *Xinhua*, 4 October 1989, reprinted in *BBC Summary of World Broadcasts*, 6 October 1989, FE/0580/B2/1.
40. Lecture by Xu Lin, Fairbank Center, Harvard University, December 1989.
41. Ibid., p. 12.
42. Jiao, "Pengbo fazhan" [Flourishing development].

China's own training capabilities were weak. Hotbeds, such as the United States, were to be avoided. Furthermore, new graduates had to work for five years before going abroad. However, this policy gave many college graduates who had already worked for five years or more after graduation "a clearer path to the exits. . . . College students five years out of [school] can now go to their *danwei* with state regulations in hand and say more convincingly that they should be allowed to leave for overseas study."[43] But if a student did not return, either the employer or family might have to pay a fine or reimburse the government. Limits were also set on the number of people studying social sciences and humanities.[44] Finally, the right of approval was transferred from the work units to the provincial education commission. The result was a 13 percent drop in 1990–91 from 1989–90 in the number of self-paying students going abroad.[45] And, as table 4.2 shows, the number of students going abroad continued to drop from 1989 through 1992, while the number of returnees almost halved between 1988 and 1989 and dropped again in 1990.

A high tide of leftism affected official attitudes toward exchanges and overseas students. A secret document sent to Chinese embassies worldwide declared that "PRC [People's Republic of China] policy on overseas students must be raised to the high plane of international struggle and competition for our talented personnel. . . . The personnel stationed abroad on the front lines are now engaged in a very hard struggle that will affect our destiny."[46] No doubt this hard line was due in part to President George Bush's Executive Order of April 1990 that allowed all Chinese in the United States at that time to apply for permanent residence and all J-1 visa holders to shift to F-1 visas. Similar policies in Canada and Australia meant that close to 100,000 Chinese students did not need to return to China, leading China to accuse the world of stealing Chinese brains.

INTERNATIONALIZATION RESUMES, POST-1992

The renewed emphasis on economic modernization following Deng's 1992 southern trip led central leaders to devise positive incentives to attract people back. Thus, people's refusal to return from overseas pressured the government to adjust its policy. External pressure also came from the United States, which under the 1992 Chinese Student Protection Act allowed the over fifty thousand Chinese students in the United States to

43. Glen Shive, "Where Has the Dust Settled on U.S.–China Educational Exchange?" *Institute of International Education*, 5 March 1991, p. 4.
44. Sheryl WuDunn, "China Weighs New Restrictions on Study Abroad," *New York Times*, 19 October 1989, p. 13.
45. Liang Chao, "More Approved to Go Abroad," *China Daily*, 20 February 1991, p. 3.
46. "Internal Document on Overseas Student Policy," *Pai Hsing* (Hong Kong), 16 May 1990, pp. 21–23, reprinted in *JPRS*, no. 67 (31 August 1990): 17–23.

Table 4.2 Graduate Students Studying Abroad and Rates of Return, 1952–1999

| | Graduate Students in China | | | Students Going Abroad[a] | | | Returnee Students | |
Year	Current Enrollment	New Enrollment	Degree-receiving Students	Number by Year	Percentage of New Students[b]	Total Number Who Have Studied Abroad	Number by Year	Percentage of Total Graduates[c]
1952	2,763	1,785	627	231	11.5	231	—	n.a.
1957	3,178	334	1,723	529	61.3	760	347	16.8
1962	6,130	1,287	1,019	114	8.1	874	980	49.0
1965	4,546	1,456	1,665	454	23.7	1,328	199	10.7
1975[d]	—	—	—	245	n.a.	1,573	186	n.a.
1978	10,934	10,708	9	860	7.4	2,433	248	n.a.
1980	21,604	3,616	476	2,124	37.0	4,557	162	25.4
1985	87,331	46,871	17,004	4,888	7.0	9,445	1,424	7.7
1986	110,371	41,310	16,950	4,676	10.2	14,121	1,388	7.6
1987	120,191	39,017	27,603	4,703	10.8	18,824	1,605	5.5
1988	112,776	35,645	40,838	3,786	9.6	22,610	3,000	6.8
1989	101,339	28,569	37,232	3,329	10.4	25,939	1,753	4.5
1990	93,018	29,649	35,440	2,950	9.0	28,889	1,593	4.3

Year							
1991	88,128	29,679	32,537	8.9	2,900	31,789	2,069	6.0
1992	94,164	33,439	25,692	16.4	6,540	38,329	3,611	12.3
1993	106,771	42,145	28,214	20.3	10,742	49,071	5,128	15.4
1994	127,935	50,864	28,047	27.3	19,071	68,142	4,230	13.1
1995	145,443	51,053	31,877	28.5	20,381	88,523	5,750	18.0
1996	163,322	59,398	39,652	26.0	20,905	109,428	6,570	14.2
1997	176,353	63,749	46,539	26.0	22,410	131,838	7,130	13.5
1998	198,885	72,508	47,077	19.6	17,622	149,460	7,379	13.6
1999	233,513	92,225	54,670	20.5	23,749	173,209	7,748	12.4

Sources: National Bureau of Statistics, *China Statistical Yearbook, 2000* (Beijing: China Statistical Press, 2000), p. 652.

Note: n.a., not available.

a This column in the original table is labeled "*Ge lei chuguo liu xue ren yuan*" (various types of people who went overseas to study). Because of the word "study," this does not include Visiting Scholars; it could include undergraduates, although their numbers have been limited. That this number reflects graduate students and not Visiting Scholars is corroborated by table 4.5, which shows that as of 1997 the total number of students and scholars who went overseas since 1978 was 293,000, significantly more than 131,838, as listed here.

b For this column, I have added the Students Going Abroad, Number by Year to the Graduate Students in China, New Enrollment to obtain the total number of new graduate students. I am assuming that those going overseas are not enrolled in China that year, so there is no overlap. I then divided the Students Going Abroad, Number by Year, by the total number of new graduate students that year to determine Students Going Abroad as Percentage of New Students.

c For this column, I have added the Returnee Students, Number by Year, to the number of degree-receiving students and then divided the Returnee Students, Number by Year, by that total. Here I am treating all returnees as degree-receiving students, which most were, and the resulting percentage really reflects the share of returnees among the total number of graduate students who had received degrees and who were looking for jobs that year in China.

d There were no new graduate students that year and no ongoing graduate students.

apply for permanent residence status. To compete with the United States for this pool of human talent, China had to liberalize its policies dramatically.

Deng himself tried to overcome the impact of Tiananmen by warmly welcoming all returnees, regardless of their previous overseas activities, as long as they forsook antigovernment action. During his southern trip, Deng said: "We hope that all people who have gone overseas to study will come back. It doesn't matter what their previous political attitude was, they can all come back, and after they return things will be well arranged. This policy cannot be changed."[47] Deng also said that "if people want to make a contribution, it is better to return."[48] Deng reportedly had tried to improve the climate for returnees in 1991, but strong opposition at that time prevented him from instituting a new policy.[49]

In March 1992, the Ministry of Personnel announced a strategy to entice students to return under the slogan "improving services for returnee students." The new policy included:

1. Job introduction centers for returnee students in Shenzhen, Shanghai, and Fujian (although five cities had established their own centers in previous years).
2. Preferential policies, including giving returnees more living space and more chances to receive higher professional titles, giving family members the freedom to move to new cities where the returnees had found jobs, and permitting students who had signed two- or three-year contracts with their research centers to either remain or switch jobs when their agreements expired.
3. Assisting in the founding of a national association of returned students.
4. Providing greater support for scientific research.[50]

Funds provided by the SEDC averaged 30,000 RMB ($5,127) for each beneficiary who held a foreign doctorate. The highest grant was 400,000 RMB ($69,000). On August 14, 1992, a State Council notification addressed many concerns of overseas students, liberalizing policy on an array of issues including the extension of passports, visits by relatives, travel permits for scholars in China, and, most important, allowing returnee scholars to decide where they wanted to work.[51] This was the first break in

47. Quoted in Jiao, "Pengbo fazhan" [Flourishing development], p. 72.
48. Ibid.
49. Englesberg, "Reversing China's Brain Drain," p. 117.
50. "China to Improve Service for Returned Students," *Xinhua General News Service*, 13 March 1992, on Lexis-Nexis, item no. 0313167. Later reports indicated that the policy was working. See He Jun, "Returning Students Find Jobs at Home," *China Daily*, 22 May 1993, p. 1.
51. "Guanyu zaiwai liuxue renyuan youguan wenti de tongzhi" [Notification on related questions concerning scholars overseas], cited in Jiao, "Pengbo fazhan" [Flourishing development], p. 73.

the previously rigid intellectual labor market. Central and provincial governments also resorted to bribery, offering returnees the option of purchasing domestic cars at preferential prices, permitting them to import computers and equipment, and giving them houses.[52]

Cities and provinces competed to attract returnees, outlining preferential policies in wages, housing, and job selection. In June 1992, Shanghai enacted twelve measures to attract returnees and encourage them to transfer their technical knowledge to local enterprises by permitting them to "retain up to six percent of the profits of local products they help to sell overseas. Their income may (also) be used to buy foreign currency."[53] At the Fourteenth Party Congress in 1992, General Secretary Jiang Zemin stated that China "warmly welcomed people who are studying overseas to use various ways to express concern, support and to participate in the motherland's modernization."[54] Still, by the end of 1992, dissent and feelings of resentment among locally trained scholars led to a call for more equal treatment in the recruitment of personnel based on ability and contribution, not educational origins.[55]

In April 1993, the Conference on the Work of Sending Personnel to Study Abroad admitted that policies since 1989 had been "too political."[56] New rules relaxed standards for study abroad, permitted the schools and units to establish their own standards for approval of candidates for study abroad, and required higher levels of foreign language capability before permission was granted to study abroad. The Third Plenum of the Fourteenth Party Congress put out a twelve-character slogan to direct overseas study: "Support overseas study, encourage people to return, and give people the freedom to come and go (*lai qu ziyou*)."[57] This twelve-character slogan continues to guide policy in 2002 and the freedom to come and go is seen as one of the most important aspects of deregulation in this sector.

In January 1994, to entice students to remain in China for graduate and postgraduate courses, the SEDC announced plans to expand China's education through foreign cooperation.[58] This form of study abroad within

---

52. "Returned Students Take Advantage of Preferential Car Policy," *Xinhua*, 28 December 1992, reprinted in British Broadcasting Corporation, *Summary of World Broadcasts*, FE/1580/B2, 7 January 1993; "Government Attempts to Lure Back Chinese Students Abroad," United Press International, 8 December 1992, on Lexis-Nexis.
53. "Shanghai Welcomes Students Studying Abroad," *Xinhua General News Service*, 13 August 1992, p. 1, on Lexis-Nexis.
54. Quoted in Jiao, "Pengbo fazhan" [Flourishing development], p. 72.
55. Kent Chen, "China: US Urged to Lift Computer Sales Ban," *South China Morning Post*, 11 December 1992, p. 13.
56. "SEC Holds Work Conference, Decides to Relax Policies for Overseas Study," *Xinwen ziyou daobao* [Press freedom guardian], 16 April 1993, p. 1.
57. Jiao, "Pengbo fazhan" [Flourishing development], p. 72.
58. He Jun, "State Looks Overseas to Boost Universities," *China Daily*, 11 January 1994, p. 1.

China would enable Chinese students to take western-style courses without leaving the country. Moreover, the benefits from these programs were immediately applicable in China. In February, the study abroad program was expanded to include accounting, auditing, banking, law, and management. The SEDC also announced that "as reform and opening develops further . . . China will send more students abroad."[59]

The fever to go abroad, however, remained strong. Although interest in overseas study reportedly declined in 1994,[60] demand picked up in 1996 when over 72 percent of high school students in a SEDC survey indicated a strong interest to go abroad.[61] Also, the limits on domestic funding for education pushed Chinese scholars to seek international collaboration. With state funding even for key universities declining, research centers must pay a part of their own personnel costs from grants.

Following Jiang Zemin's new call in 1996 for people to pay more attention to politics, rules on academic exchanges and overseas studies tightened. A new policy introduced in 1996 simplified applications but tightened bureaucratic control. Those going abroad on government scholarships were obliged to sign contracts with the new China National Scholarship Council for International Studies and deposit 50,000 RMB. This money plus interest was to be refunded if the student returned on time; otherwise, the deposit was to be forfeited and the student was also to be fired.[62] In late 1996, concerns over foreign infiltration led the Public Security Bureau and the Politburo of the Chinese Communist Party to promulgate new guidelines that dramatically increased the transaction costs of collaborative research. Chinese scholars now had to seek approval from their foreign affairs office three times—before beginning the research project, before approving questionnaires, and before handing over data. Despite almost twenty years of the open policy in education, ambivalence remained.[63]

Nevertheless, after 1995, the number of returnees picked up (see table 4.2). Higher salaries for Chinese academics at selected universities—with some salaries reaching 100,000 RMB—and the preferential policies given to returnees were having an effect. New programs, such as the Changjiang Scholars Scholarship program, funded by Li Ka-shing of Hong Kong, or the Chinese Academy of Sciences "One Hundred Talent Program" (*bai ren jihua*), begun in 1994, targeted mostly top young mainlanders overseas in

59. "New Push on Studies Overseas," *China Daily*, 3 February 1994, p. 1.

60. Zhongguo Xinwen She (China News Service), "Fever in Beijing to Go Abroad to Study at Own Expense," reprinted in *FBIS*, no. 37 (24 February 1994): 39.

61. Xiao Yu, "Students Aim for Overseas," *South China Morning Post*, 31 December 1996, p. 8.

62. "China in Transition," *Far Eastern Economic Review*, 7 March 1996, p. 29.

63. Willy Lam, "Cultural Invasion Feared," *South China Morning Post*, 23 November 1996, p. 8.

the natural sciences.[64] Leading universities, such as Qinghua, promised that returnees' children could automatically gain admission to the university's own prestigious primary and middle schools.[65] Also the state's more positive attitude toward the private sector outlined in 1999 generated greater interest among overseas scholars who wanted to start their own businesses.[66] Finally, in 2001 the Chinese government unveiled a new policy to protect the intellectual property rights of mainland scholars who remain overseas and to reward them financially so as to encourage them to contribute to China's development.[67]

Transnational Resources and the Educational System

Transnational linkages and resources, such as information, capital, books, technologies, management skills, and teaching methods, energized universities and became an important source of market-oriented competition among faculty, among departments and bureaus in the universities, and among the universities themselves. Foreigners became valuable resources because of the international and domestic capital they could attract. Similarly, returnee scholars, beneficiaries of what I call transnational capital, were a highly sought-after commodity.

Living overseas helped people enhance their incomes and standards of living in ways few other opportunities could match. The difference in pay between teaching in China and teaching overseas was enormous. Whereas a professor in China might have earned 5–6,000 RMB (or $1,500) a year in 1991, he or she could earn $40,000 for teaching the same courses in the United States, a staggering difference. Although private incomes in China

64. For the Changjiang Scholars Fellowships see "Introduction to the Li Ka-shing Fund," *Ta kung pao* (Hong Kong), 15 March 2001, p. A13, and Cong Cao and Richard Suttmeier, "China Faces the New Industrial Revolution: Research and Innovation Strategies for the 21st Century," *Asian Perspective* 24, 3 (1999): 153–200. For the "Hundred Talent Program" (*bai ren jihua*) see Wang Liping, "Year-end Check of the One-Hundred Talent Program," *The China Press—The Chinese Science Weekly* (New York), 17 December 2000, p. C8, and Wang Liping, "Investing One Billion Yuan to Recruit 500 Talented Young Scientists in Five Years," *The China Press—The Chinese Science Weekly* (New York), 29 April 2001, pp. C1 and C2. For the program in Shanghai, see He Zu, "Hu qu yanjiusuo yin cai hui guo de tansuo" ("Some thoughts on how research institutes in Shanghai region can attract human talent to return home"), *Xingzheng yu renshi* (Administration and Personnel) 136 (April 1997): 22–24. My thanks to Cong Cao for his assistance.
65. Interview LWSR, Hong Kong, August 2001.
66. Mark O'Neill, "Brain Drain Shifts Into Reverse," *South China Morning Post*, 30 September 2001, Focus Section, p. 2.
67. The government document is entitled, "Decision on Encouraging Students Overseas to Serve the Motherland in Various Forms," and was composed by the ministries of Personnel, Education, Science and Technology, Public Security, and Finance. See "China Encourages Students Overseas To Serve in Various Ways," Xinhuanet, 19 August 2001, *China News Digest*, global edition, http://www.cnd.org/Global/01/08/20/010820-9.html.

increased significantly after 1992, before that Chinese intellectuals who worked or traveled overseas came home with savings and consumer goods that would have taken decades to accumulate in China. According to one Chinese official, "a teacher who works overseas can earn the equivalent of thirty years of his teaching salary in a very short period of time."[68] In fact, through the mid-1980s, the greatest source of inequality in standard of living among Chinese academics was whether they had sojourned.

People who went abroad for a year or more could buy the eight big items (*ba da jian*)—color television, washing machine, dryer, stereo, refrigerator, VCR, camera, and air conditioner—tax free, while short trips allowed people to buy one big and one small item (*yi da yi xiao*) tax free. Frequent travelers to conferences slowly accumulated these high-status belongings. Or sojourners could sell the permit to buy these appliances at a handsome profit to people who could not get overseas. One official explained:

> People who went overseas get a permit to buy the "eight big items" when they re-enter China. If they can show that they have enough U.S. dollars to buy the goods, they can register to buy them. The goods are then bought from special stores where prices are pretty low. . . . But many people never buy the products; instead they sell the product—without having bought it—and the permit. For example, if I hadn't bought this stereo, people would pay me $600 for it, plus 2,000 RMB for the permit to buy it. . . . Many people borrowed the money to buy the permit as they entered the country and sold them once home.[69]

Although the total cost of purchasing the eight items was about $3,000, "the eight large pieces are worth about 25,000 RMB which is impossible for most of us ever to consider being able to save in our lifetime. . . . One couple at *Beida* worked in Washington for several years and now has $100,000. So while our salaries are very low, we have most of the modern equipment."[70] Little wonder the president of one Chinese university told his faculty in 1992 that if intellectuals wanted to make money, they had to go overseas to study or work.

People who went overseas even for six months were seen to have "painted on a little gold" (*du jing*), increasing their social status. That improved cultural capital had concrete ramifications when scholars returned.[71] According to a study in Shanghai, 65 percent of those who went

68. Interview XDJBGK, July 1990.
69. Ibid.
70. Ibid.
71. "Chinese society seems to attribute a form of cultural capital to intellectuals with an experience abroad." Michael Brzezinski, *Migration and Opportunity: A Qualitative Understanding of the Chinese Student Brain Drain Phenomenon*, NAFSA working paper 41 (Washington, D.C.: NAFSA, 1994), p. 17.

overseas in the late-1970s and early 1980s—the middle-aged scholars who were 40–55 at that time—to do research for one to two years had been promoted at least one level on returning.[72] No doubt, these people were among the best in their cohort and perhaps might have been promoted even if they had not gone overseas, but this seems to be a worldwide phenomenon.[73] Thus Ruth Hayhoe and Sun Yilin argue that foreign degree holders and scholars who studied abroad benefited from a "symbolic recognition" on return, "leading to ease of advancement that may at times be irrespective of proven quality of work."[74]

Because graduate degrees were particularly scarce in the mid-1980s, those who possessed foreign degrees had an enormous comparative advantage. As of 1984, only 1,203 (0.38 percent) college teachers had Ph.D.s, and only 9,865 (3.13 percent) had M.A. degrees, so that only 3.51 percent of all tertiary school educators had graduate degrees.[75] By 1990, the number of Ph.D.s remained infinitesimal, 3,382 (0.98 percent) university teachers, while the number of M.A.s had jumped to 60,105 (15.2 percent).[76] Yet as degree programs expanded in China, foreign degrees still improved an individual's competitive edge. It is not surprising that of the 70 people we interviewed in the United States in 1993 who had entered on a program of two years or less, 25.4 percent had intended to switch into a graduate program even before they left China.[77]

Returnee scholars benefited from preferential policies, such as special access to research grants, better housing, and better research conditions at newly established postdoctoral research stations, inflating the value of the foreign degree and deflating the value of a domestic one. Whereas the foreign degree holders were called *yang boshi* (foreign Ph.D.s), domestic degree holders were called *tu boshi*, which can be translated as "local" but also as "earthy," and therefore of less value. However, those with domestic Ph.D.s and middle-aged faculty members resented the high value granted to foreign Ph.D.s.[78] So, when a central Chinese university thought to attract

---

72. Ruth Hayhoe and Sun Yilin, "China's Scholars Returned from Abroad: A View From Shanghai, Parts One and Two," *China Exchange News* 17 (September–December 1989), p. 8.
73. In Israel, for example, a foreign degree holder's occupational attainment was also greater than that of people who had studied only in the home country. Abraham Yogev, "The Other Side of the Brain Drain: Foreign Diplomas and Socio-Economic Attainment of Israeli Professionals," *International Sociology* 7 (December 1992): 433–48.
74. Hayhoe and Sun, "China's Scholars Returned from Abroad."
75. See Wang Wenyou, "A Brief Discussion of the Three Basic Requirements for Developing Regular Higher Education," *Jiaoyu yanjiu* [Education research] 3 (March 1986): 10–19.
76. Calculated from *Zhongguo jiaoyu tongji nianjian, 1990* [China education statistical yearbook] (Beijing: People's Education Press, 1991), p. 32.
77. Zweig and Chen, *China's Brain Drain.*
78. For a detailed discussion of these incentives and the backlash against them in China see Leo A. Orleans, "China's Changing Attitude toward the Brain Drain and Policy toward Returning Students," *China Exchange News* 17 (June 1989): 3–4.

more Ph.D.s by building a special housing facility for foreign Ph.D.s (*boshi lou*), the faculty voted it down.

Technical knowledge gained overseas could be parleyed into income on an individual's return. In the early years, when China's domestic market was weak and foreign imports were few, imported technologies easily translated into extra-normal profits.[79] As mentioned above, many recent returnees sought to establish themselves in the emerging internet economy,[80] while one Chinese Ph.D. from the U.S. in biochemistry returned to China to market his own cancer drug.

Foreign aid, in particular the 1983 World Bank education loan valued at $805 million, helped many universities buy technical equipment and train people abroad. Just one loan, University I, sent over 2,470 faculty from twenty-eight universities abroad for research and study, consisting of 1,565 Visiting Scholars and 906 degree candidates. The Provincial Universities Project included 8,700 fellowship years abroad, while the Agricultural Education I and II made 691 faculty fellowships available.[81]

We need only compare two schools—the Wuhan University of Surveying and Mapping (WUSM), which received a World Bank loan, and the Wuhan Institute of Technology (WIT), which did not—to see the impact of foreign capital. As of 1980, both universities were directly affiliated with ministry-level government organizations and were of similar scale in terms of faculty, student body, and academic status (table 4.3). However, WIT did not file its World Bank application on time and did not receive a loan, whereas WUSM received $5 million from the World Bank, which doubled its capital equipment at that time.

The schools since that time followed different trajectories. WUSM sent out many more scholars; returnees under the World Bank program at WUSM roughly equal the total number of returnee scholars at WIT from all its exchange programs. At WUSM in 1992, 18 percent of all faculty had gone abroad and 11 percent of its current faculty were returnee scholars. At WIT, only 6 percent of the faculty had gone abroad and only 4 percent were returnee scholars. WUSM had ten returnee Ph.D.s, whereas WIT had only two, both of whom complained of being overworked becaused colleagues who are making grant applications need a returnee Ph.D. on the project to improve its competitiveness. WUSM has numerous modern labs, and its computer center, which is open to students, is in a temperature-controlled glassed-in center. WIT's students worked in far less comfortable

79. Denis Fred Simon, personal communication, 23 August 1995.
80. Frank Langfitt, "A Force for Change in China," *The Baltimore Sun*, 23 April 2000, p. 16A; Grace Fan, "The Net Is Calling Them Home, but Many More Are Needed," *The New York Times On Line*, 7 June 2000, section H, p. 30; Kathy Wilhelm and Dan Biers, "China Returnees: No Place Like Home," *Far Eastern Economic Review*, 15 June 2000, p. 72; Brook Larmer, "Home at Last," *Newsweek*, 23 July 2000, p. 32.
81. Hayhoe, *China's Universities and the Open Door*, pp. 179–181.

Table 4.3 Comparison of Two Universities in Wuhan, 1992

	Wuhan Institute of Technology	Wuhan University of Surveying and Mapping
University affiliation	Only affiliated college of the China General Automobile Co.	Only affiliated university of the National Surveying and Mapping Bureau
Number of students	3,850	4,210
Number of faculty	821	879
Value of World Bank loan	no loan	$5 million
Number of scholars going overseas after 1978	49	160 (28 supported by the World Bank loan)
Number of returnee scholars	31	100 (25 of 28 supported under World Bank loan)
Returnee Ph.D.s	2	10
National Research Laboratory	none	1
Fixed assets of equipment	43 million RMB	82 million RMB (50% of assets from World Bank loan)
Scientific Research Budget during Seventh Five-Year Plan	20 million RMB	50 million RMB
Number of National Level Specialists	1	5

Sources: Interview in Wuhan by Chen Changgui and David Zweig, January 1992.

surroundings. WUSM's government research budget of 50 million RMB during the Seventh Five-Year Plan helped establish a National Research Lab with five National Level Specialists and two National Academic Committee members. Because WIT was without such equipment, research projects were often rejected in national competitions, and its returnees could not continue projects begun overseas, so what they had learned abroad became useless. As of 1992, WUSM had built a major research center with Belgian money, including an international center with housing for foreign experts and meeting rooms for foreign guests. WIT had an apartment building for foreign teachers but no international center.

We should not attribute all differences between the schools to the loan. Leaders at WIT had made other bad choices, such as building a 4 million RMB gymnasium with an expensive wooden floor that is rarely used because they cannot afford to repair it. This misallocation of funding left WIT with inferior housing, so good faculty moved to other schools in Wuhan. Nevertheless, the impact of the loans and other development assistance on teaching, research, and faculty morale is clear. It is no wonder universities fought vigorously for foreign assistance projects.

Foreign students became valuable commodities in China's highly commercialized educational environment. At Nanjing University, the Foreign Student Department received no financial support from the university; instead, it aggressively marketed short-term teaching courses for exchange students, which in 1987–91 supplied 31 percent of its budget. The UN paid WUSM for each Third World student it accepted as well as for the educational materials the faculty wrote for the training programs.[82] Foreign student dorms built with SEDC funding became conference centers for domestic and international meetings and important money-making organizations. In return for housing two thousand SEDC-sponsored foreign students at discount prices, Beijing University received funds to build Shao Yuan, one of the largest foreign student and scholar complexes in China. Student exchange programs also helped Chinese faculty go abroad to teach. According to one returned administrator, "if a school can't recruit foreign students, it can't send out its own people."[83]

Foreign experts or teachers enhanced a school's financial and academic capacities. Cribbed lecture notes could be sold as teaching materials, and some of their research improved the scientific capabilities of new programs. Schools that could not promise a coterie of foreign teachers could not attract the best Chinese students. Universities used foreign teachers to bump up their tuition. Also, the pending arrival of foreign teachers could pry loose local funds for new housing. Between 1991 and 1995, six hundred institutions, mostly universities, were officially authorized to employ foreign teachers, but the number actually doubled, forcing the SEDC to limit foreign teachers and insist on cumbersome hiring procedures.[84]

Most educational exchanges needed foreign exchange for which "the demand greatly exceeded the supply."[85] For example, Huazhong University of Science and Technology in Wuhan, then the seventh-ranked university in China, earned less than $100,000 in 1991 through entrepreneurial activity. Otherwise, it relied on the SEDC for its foreign exchange allocation. In the mid-1980s, Nanjing University spent one-third of the budget assigned to teacher training to prepare young teachers for the TOEFL and then borrowed over $2,600 in foreign exchange to pay for the exam for approximately one hundred young teachers.[86] Why? "The returnees were great, had become department chairs very quickly, had new ideas, and could help our research. It was clear that sending people overseas was an

82. Interview EDWUCEFA, 1992.
83. Interview EDSABNND, 1991.
84. "Clampdown on Foreigners," *Times Higher Education Supplement*, 20 September 1996, p. 8.
85. Interview EDFOREX1, 1991 (interview with an official responsible for foreign exchange in a major university's finance department).
86. Interview EDSABNND, 1991.

excellent way to cut the gap between foreigners and Chinese. . . . There was a crisis—older professors had developed when China was closed, they were already quite old and had old ideas. China needed to educate a younger generation."[87] However, despite receiving this valued currency, few recipients returned.

The administrative procedures controlling such funds were extremely cumbersome and restrictive. Every university wrote a request at the beginning of the year for a set allocation of foreign exchange. And even if a school had funds to send scholars overseas, it had to submit a detailed outline of all planned expenditures on behalf of each scholar to the SEDC's International Cooperation and Exchange Department (*Guoji hezuo jiaoliu si*). It also had to get approval from the provincial Education, Finance, and Foreign Exchange Management bureaus. In fact, before 1990, universities were encouraged to pass up on their own initiative a set percentage—at one school 20 percent—of the foreign exchange they earned. Within universities, the vice-president for foreign affairs made all foreign exchange allocations.

Under internationalization, the knowledge of foreign languages, particularly Japanese and English, became a valuable commodity, with demand five to ten times greater than supply.[88] Organizations fought furiously for these people, helping those with good skills to gain access to the transnational sector, better jobs (often in the coastal urban centers), higher incomes, and better lives overall. For example, one urban youth sent to the countryside in the 1960s began studying English after hearing about the pending Nixon visit.[89] After graduating in 1976 from the Shanghai Foreign Language Institute in a class of four, he and his colleagues and their language skills became the target of a heated battle. The MOE wanted them for teachers, but the Ministry of Petroleum needed translators for its pending U.S. oil deals. The battle was resolved by the State Planning Commission in Beijing: a deal was struck whereby two people went to work for the MOE and two for the State Planning Commission, which seconded them to the Petroleum Ministry. In another example, Zhu Jiusi, president of Huazhong University of Science and Technology, recognizing the importance of English to his faculty and university, in 1977 used funds from the school's extra-budgetary account to establish a six-month English program for all faculty.

Those with good language skills were often able to get overseas first. Tour guides or interpreters in the early to mid-1980s established personal contacts with foreign visitors who helped them leave China. According to interviews in Chengdu and Wuhan, some sojourners in 1978–79 were not

87. Ibid.
88. "College Graduate Shortage Eased," *China Daily*, 17 October 1987, p. 3.
89. Interview in Medford, Mass., 1991.

the best researchers, but because they could pass the application's foreign language component they went first. Within one or two years, however, those with better technical skills, often those who had studied Russian in the 1950s, improved their English skills and began to go out more frequently.

This comparative advantage in the English language was compounded by the rigid nature of the educational system. Before the mid-1980s, joint majors were unheard of and students could not take courses outside their own majors. So, students with technical skills usually lacked the language skills to participate in transnational exchanges,[90] while English majors had no functional skills. But when the latter group graduated, many were automatically sent to a company's foreign affairs office to handle incoming "barbarians." As a result, foreigners frequently found translators in companies and organizations with limited technical knowledge but excellent English. Trapped in deadend positions, with little chance for promotion, English majors flooded out of China, becoming some of the first Chinese graduate students in the United States.

VALUE OF RETURNEES

Returnees brought great value to a school's political economy, graduate education, and prestige, and, despite concerns in the 1980s and early 1990s about their political loyalty, they played an important role in school administration. They were channels for technological transfers and other exchanges. They also were better researchers and fundraisers than people who had not gone overseas.

This section draws on interviews that I carried out with Chen Changgui in 1991–92 and a survey carried out by Chen in 1997.[91] I have divided the respondents to these surveys into two categories; short-term sojourners (STS) and long-term sojourners (LTS). Most of the STS, who stayed overseas for less than three years, were Visiting Scholars (82.7 percent) and probably stayed for less than two years. Only 10.5 percent of STS went abroad for degrees. On the other hand, 60 percent of LTS went abroad for a Ph.D. or M.A. and stayed over three years. Thus, although the surveys had no control group (people who had not gone overseas), we can differentiate these two groups and, as we see next, the differences between them are significant. To this I add Michele Shoresman's comparison of Visiting

90. Du, *Chinese Higher Education*, p. 46.
91. The data come primarily from interviews Chen Changgui of Zhongshan University and I carried out from December 1991 through April 1992. I also carried out many interviews on my own. I also draw on a survey of 472 returnee scholars, designed by Chen, Stan Rosen, and me and conducted in 1997 by Chen and his team.

Scholars at the University of Illinois, Urbana-Champagne, with a control group in China who had not gone abroad.[92]

Let us look first at research grants. In the 1980s, returnees established many new areas of research based on projects begun abroad, thereby "planting foreign seeds in Chinese soil."[93] Some became national-level research labs, insuring national-level funding.[94] One scholar reported that the president of her university had asked her to look for such a project when he sent her abroad.

Returnee scholars competed effectively for research grants against those who had never gone overseas. At the Electronics University of Science and Technology in Chengdu, the 143 returnee scholars, who composed 15 percent of the faculty, completed 41 percent of the total research projects under the school's Seventh Five-Year Plan. As of 1991, they had received 30 percent of the national-, provincial- or ministry-level projects awarded to the university.[95] Data from Southeast Medical University, also in Chengdu, show the major role that returnees played in the Natural Science Foundation grants and the national- and provincial-level awards received by the university. Although returnees only received 33 percent of Natural Science Foundation grants in 1984, they received 62 percent (13/21) in 1986 and 52 percent in 1991 (10/19). Their share of the national and provincial awards received by the faculty totalled almost 70 percent in 1991.[96] Similarly, Shoresman found that 39.1 percent of her returnees had received three or more grants, and 23.4 percent had four or more grants. Among nonsojourners, the numbers were 8.9 percent and 2.2 percent, respectively.[97] The forty-six returnees Chen and I interviewed in 1991–92 had received 176 projects, an average of 3.8 grants per person.

The cohort interviewed in 1997 reveals similar results (table 4.4). Of LTS, 56 percent had received national-level projects since returning, compared to 34 percent of STS. Similarly, 61.7 percent of LTS got provincial grants, compared to 46.0 percent of STS.[98] LTS were also more likely to have been awarded an international collaborative project, but the statistical

92. Michele Shoresman, "Promotions for Returned Visiting Scholars" (Ph.D. diss., University of Illinois, 1989); Michele Shoresman, "Returns to Education: The US/PRC Visiting Scholars Programme, 1978–88," in *Higher Education in Post-Mao China*, ed. Michael Agelasto and Bob Adamson (Hong Kong: Hong Kong University Press, 1998), pp. 79–98.
93. Leo A. Orleans, "Chinese Students and Technology Transfer," *Journal of Northeast Asian Studies* 4 (winter 1985): 3–25.
94. Field research in China, 1991–92.
95. Lan Xingzhi and Wang Yongkang, "Gao hao chu guo liu xue gongzuo, jiaqiang shizi duiwu jianshe" [Do the work of sending people overseas to study well, strengthen the construction of the quality of the faculty], *Jiaoyu yanjiu* [Education research] 3 (1991): 14–23.
96. Data supplied by the Southwest University of Medical Sciences, Chengdu, 1992.
97. Shoresman, "Promotions for Returned Visiting Scholars."
98. Both findings were statistically significant at the .005 level.

Table 4.4   Long-Term versus Short-Term Sojourners, 1997

	Long-Term Sojourners ($n = 115$)	Short-Term Sojourners ($n = 352$)
Those receiving after returning		
provincial-level research project	61.7	46.0
national-level research project	56.5	34.1
international research project	16.5	9.7
Those using the fruits of the international exchange in their teaching	80.0	59.2
Those teaching new graduate courses		
required courses	54.8	36.1
elective courses	33.0	22.2
Those receiving national teaching awards	7.0	2.6
Those presenting papers at international conferences	64.3	48.6
Those maintaining strong international contacts	31.9	20.3
Those arranging for foreign scholars to lecture in China	54.8	40.0
Those helping others go overseas	49.6	38.9
Those establishing international collaborative projects	43.5	24.1
Those translating foreign materials	42.6	29.5
Those helping to import foreign capital and technology	18.3	8.2
Those very satisfied with their current housing	14.3	5.5
Those believing they have received more research money than schoolmates who had not gone overseas	65.0	42.3
Those believing they were promoted faster than schoolmates who had not gone overseas	47.7	27.4
Those believing they got better housing on returning than schoolmates who had not gone overseas	33.3	15.6

Source: Chen Changgui, unpublished survey conducted in 1997. I am grateful to him for sharing his data.

Note: All values are percentages. Longer-term sojourners were abroad for over three years; shorter-term sojourners were abroad for under three years. Figures are significant at .01 or .05. Missing data = 4 cases.

results for this question were not so strong because only 16.5 percent of LTS had received such awards. Also, 55 percent of LTS believed that they had received more research funding than those who had not gone overseas at all, while 42 percent of STS had similar beliefs.

People who returned to China did so in part because they believed that they could attain higher status in China than in the United States. In fact, among the people Chen and I interviewed in the United States in 1993, the most common reason for returning to China was "higher social status in China" (26.7 percent).[99] Various data corroborate these beliefs. Returnees received important leadership posts, becoming department heads, lab

99. Zweig and Chen, *China's Brain Drain*, p. 122.

directors, and even university vice-presidents and presidents. As of 1988, almost one-third of all members of the Academic Board of the Chinese Academy of Sciences were returnee scholars.[100] In Shoresman's group, 38 percent of those with overseas experience reported having administrative duties, compared to only 10.2 percent of the control group,[101] while of the forty-six scholars Chen and I interviewed in China in 1991–92, 19 (41 percent) were bureau or department heads and another seven directed research labs or sections within departments. Similarly in 1992 at the Electronics University of Science and Technology, 91 percent of departments had a chairman or deputy chairman who was a returnee. According to the director of the Higher Education Office of the Provincial Education Commission of Hubei Province, 25 percent of the top positions at key point universities in the province were held by returnee scholars, and more than half the department chairships and directorships of teaching and research offices were also held by returnee scholars.[102] In terms of academic rank, Shoresman found that the Illinois group experienced little change in academic rank immediately after returning to China, but that by 1989 they had significantly more promotions than their peers without overseas experience.[103]

Returnees also link China to the outside world. University presidents, deans, directors of research offices, and twenty-four department chairs interviewed in 1991–92 felt that returnees had the following transnational skills: a better understanding of foreign science and research, broader research agendas due to familiarity with foreign research methods, a greater facility with foreign equipment, better foreign language skills, a stronger ability to adopt new research directions, and a greater ability to develop international cooperation.

The findings from the 1997 survey corroborate the idea that returnees perform important transnational functions. In terms of teaching, LTS were more likely to teach new graduate classes (54.8 percent) than were STS (36 percent). Of LTS, 80 percent were more likely to use "a lot" or "a comparatively large amount" of the "fruits of international exchanges" in their classes, compared to 59 percent of STS. LTS transferred more resources or personnel into China. Whereas only 8.2 percent of STS had imported capital or technology, 18.3 percent of LTS had done so. Similarly, the LTS group was more likely to have helped colleagues and friends go overseas to study (49.6 percent vs. 38.9 percent), and, despite having been out of China longer, they were more likely to have arranged for a foreign scholar

100. "Effort Contmues 'To Woo Back' Students," *Hong Kong Standard*, 8 December 1989, p. 1, reprinted in *FBIS*, no. 235 (8 December 1989): 18.
101. Shoresman, "Promotions for Returned Visiting Scholars," p. 94.
102. Interviews by Ruth Hayhoe and Chen Changgui, spring 1992.
103. Shoresman, "Promotions for Returned Visiting Scholars," p. 193.

to lecture in China (54.3 percent vs. 44.0 percent).[104] In this way, they were stronger bridges between China and the world.

Administrative Responses and Strategies under Internationalization

Bureaucrats and their organizations benefited from internationalization by charging informal fees (in reality, bribes) for facilitating exchanges. According to one source, "Once you have the power to decide who can go overseas. . . . many people come to find you to ask for favors. They can bother you all night."[105] Gifts became an important medium of exchange. According to one informant, although the "section for managing people going overseas" (*chuguo renyuan guanli ke*) did not really have the authority to decide who went out, they controled funds for new clothes, foreign exchange, and they processed all visa extensions. So, "you have to give them gifts or they will not make the necessary arrangements for your trip overseas. You must 'report' back to them when you return, which means that you have to give every person in their office a gift. If you don't give them a gift after you come back, it will be very difficult to get them to help if you try to go overseas again."[106] One scholar faced serious problems with his province's foreign affairs office because initially he refused to give a gift to the official issuing exit visas. But when this official told him that due to problems with his papers he could receive his visa only in Beijing, a 200 RMB gift convinced the official otherwise.

Some units forced overseas sojourners to remit some of their foreign stipend. According to one foreign affairs officer, it was necessary to "use exchanges to support exchanges (*yong jiaoliu yang jiaoliu*)," because universities lacked the funds to host foreign scholars. "If the other side wants to send people [to China], we try to get that school to give our scholars extra money which they remit to us to pay for the people that the foreign school sends to China. . . . Scholarly aspects, not money making, is the most important part of exchanges, but we must be concerned about economic aspects if we want to continue to send people out."[107] But Western universities complained about this process. "This year we got a letter from the director of X complaining that one of our scholars had to send home some of the money they gave him. We had not asked for money from people who went there before, because in the past the foreign side did not send anyone to us. But this year they did, so we asked this scholar for $600. The foreign side said they would cut his stipend if we did this, even though they gave him over $10,000."[108]

104. All findings were statistically significant at the .05 level.
105. Interview EDCWH, June 1992.
106. Interview EDCWH, December 1991.
107. Interview EDSABNND, 1991.
108. Ibid.

Overall, however, less rent-seeking occurred in the academic sphere than in the business world. When the SEDC and MOFERT imported equipment for the universities, they could not make large profits on imports because donors, like the World Bank, insisted that schools determine competitive prices and obtain approvals before ordering equipment. This procedure limited their ability to overpay in return for kickbacks, a common activity among state-owned FTCs in China. At each university, purchases were monitored by a World Bank office whose staff appeared to be relatively conscientious, with some followup supervision by Bank teams.

MARKET-ORIENTATION AND THE EMERGENCE OF EXCHANGE INDUSTRIES

As more and more people moved in and out of China, exchange industries emerged. Those planning to go abroad needed better English skills, so TOEFL preparation became a growth industry, as did reception centers for returnees who had trouble re-acclimatizing to China. As of 2001, there were 150 official reception centers throughout China. In particular, language training centers became substantial components of universities, bringing in equipment, foreign teachers, and state funding for buildings.

One beneficiary of internationalization was the Centre for International Education at Chengdu University of Science and Technology. One of eleven SEDC-supported training centers in 1992, it opened in 1979 with five students and one teacher in a training class under the university's Education Bureau. In 1983, they had one room and eighty students. According to their entrepreneurial director, they began to market their center aggressively that year. In response to her letters, SEDC sent a team to see their center; she even brought a vice–foreign minister to visit. After receiving a grant of 1.4 million RMB from the SEDC and a loan of 1 million RMB, she expanded the program enormously, building a clean, modern, three-storey, multimedia language center. The equipment from the SEDC was worth over 600,000 RMB.

In 1992, the center had over forty-five Chinese teachers and staff, ten to fourteen foreign teachers, and five hundred students a year—three hundred sent by the SEDC and another two hundred recruited directly from other units. Because the SEDC sends students, it pays the salaries of a number of teachers, and in 1992 gave the school 370,000 RMB to support foreign teachers. Charging 1,000 RMB for a training session, the center can turn over 50–60,000 RMB in profits to the university, still keeping 60 percent of its profits, which pays for bonuses and overseas travel for its staff. Center faculty also do translation work for the World Bank office in the university, as well as for other departments. Finally, the center is a major channel for going overseas; as of 1992, 25 percent of its staff were working or studying overseas. With its strong record, good bonuses, and high overseas flow, many people wanted to work in the center.

COMPETING FOR RETURNEES

As mentioned in the discussion of policy, cities recognized the value of returnees and began to compete for them, offering them preferential policies unavailable to those who had not gone overseas. According to Shenzhen's 1989 regulations, returnees could come directly to the SEZ, legally change their own residence and that of their family, keep any foreign exchange they earned in Shenzhen even if they left the SEZ, buy a new house at near cost, establish private enterprises, and "enjoy precedence over ordinary people with similar conditions and qualifications in the use of scientific and technological development funds."[109] As of 1995, over two hundred returnee scholars worked there.[110] In the early 1990s, other cities and provinces began sending delegations to the United States, Japan, Canada, and Australia to attract overseas scholars. Shanghai's municipal government built four Centers for Returned Scholars in the city's four development zones, a strategy that by 1994 had attracted over one hundred returnee Ph.D.s to the Zhangjiang HTDZ.[111] In 1999, Beijing built a high-tech park especially for returnee businessmen.[112] Even Yunnan Province sent a delegation in 1993 to Australia to attract returnees.[113]

MAINTAINING ADMINISTRATIVE CONTROLS OVER
TRANSNATIONAL CHANNELS

Beginning in the early 1980s, central administrative control over transnational exchanges decreased, even though bureaucrats struggled to maintain some authority. Before 1985, MOE (renamed SEDC in 1985), the Chinese Academy of Sciences, and the Chinese Academy of Social Sciences monopolized transnational educational channels. Based on negotiations with the key ministries—Personnel, State Economic Commission, and State Planning Commission—MOE set quotas for graduate students and research scholars going abroad based on the labor needs of the central Five-Year Plan. Key schools were favored, but to enhance geographic distribution administrators also chose people from nonkey institutions.[114]

109. "Shenzhen Announces Detailed Regulations on Students Returning to Work in the Country," *Zhongguo xinwen she*, 15 August 1989, reprinted in *FBIS*, no. 157 (16 August 1989): 47–48.
110. "Zhujiang sanjiazhou de liuxuesheng huigui re" [The fever to return among overseas students in the Pearl River Delta], *Shenzhou xueren* [China scholars abroad] 12 (1995): 13. I thank Lai Ho Sze for her research assistance on this issue.
111. "News Briefs," *China Exchange News* 22 no. 1 (spring 1994): 14.
112. Agence France-Presse, "Returning Students Offered Tax and Rent Lures at Hi-Tech Park," *South China Morning Press*, 19 December 1999, p. 6.
113. *China Education Yearbook, 1994* (Beijing: People's Publishing House, 1995), p. 743.
114. Ruth Hayhoe, ed., *Contemporary Chinese Education* (Armonk: M. E. Sharpe, 1984), p. 208.

But to what extent did decentralization in 1985 and decisions thereafter shift influence from the hands of central administrators into the hands of regional bureaucrats, universities, or other organizations that could increase the pace or ease of transnational exchanges? Could individuals circumvent administrative controls? In 1988 central bureaucrats tried to reassert some controls by introducing the category of self-paying, public sent (*zifei gongpai*) or publicly sent by their unit (*danwei gongpai*) scholars. As previously mentioned, people who made their own arrangements but were working in state organizations were pressured to leave on J-1 visas, under which they had to get the permission from their school's foreign affairs office and the SEDC in Beijing, rather than from just their municipality's personnel department, which was all that self-paying scholars were required to do. Central officials also created new exchange programs that they could control. One program that trained managers and technical specialists abroad on three- to eighteen-month stints was jointly sponsored by the SSTC, the SEDC and Chinese factories. Because these sojourners were not allowed to enroll in degree programs after completing their training, 98 percent of the 7,500 people sent abroad returned by 1991. In May 1991, the program was expanded to 3,000 technicians and managers each year under the Eighth Five-Year Plan.[115]

The diffusion of authority over overseas sojourners is best understood by the intersection of two continua. In the first, influence shifts from central to regional administrators in provincial educational commissions; in the second, a market-oriented continuum, authority moves from the educational bureaucracy to the universities, who establish horizontal linkages with overseas agencies, to a privatized position where individuals make their own connections with foreign universities. An additional third dimension characterized universities as having two options: either one office controls all exchanges, reinforcing administrative control, or there is competition among organizations in the school, generating a more open system. Where do the data fall on these intersecting continua?

Decentralization and privatization increased the number of people who went overseas. As table 4.5 shows, 16 percent of those who went overseas between 1978 and the end of 1997 went as state-sponsored scholars and 31.4 percent went as unit-sponsored, which often meant that scholars had made their own arrangements but accepted J-1 visa status in order to keep ties with their home unit. In other cases, the university or unit may have established the exchange opportunity. But the largest category of people who went abroad were self-paying, 52.6 percent. Private market forces were clearly at work here.

Also, the more decentralized and market-oriented the transnational channel, the less control the central state could exert. Data on returnees by

115. Yuan Zhou, "Overseas training plan to be expanded," *China Daily*, 23 May 1991, p. 2.

Table 4.5   Sojourners and Returnees by Category of Students and Scholars, 1978–1997

	State-Sponsored	Unit-Sponsored	Self-Paying	Total
Number gone overseas	47,000	92,000	154,000	293,000
Ratio to total overseas	16.0%	31.4%	52.6%	100%
Number of returnees	39,000	52,000	6,000	97,000
Return rate	83.0%	56.5%	3.9%	32.0%

Source: Jiao Guozheng, "Pengbo fazhan de chuguo liuxue gongzuo" [Flourishing development of the work of sending out overseas students], *Zhongguo gaodeng jiaoyu* [Higher education in China] 12 (1998): 6–8, in *Higher Education in China: Research Materials from People's University* 2 (1999): 72–74.

different categories of students and scholars show this effect. As table 4.5 shows, as of the end of 1997, the return rate among state-sponsored students and scholars was 83 percent, while those who went out with the official sanction of their unit—*danwei gong pai*—returned at a rate of 56.5 percent. Where market forces were really at work, under the self-paying category, the state was almost powerless to bring people back (3.9 percent).

Another way to evaluate the relative influence of central versus local forces is to look at the number of J-1 Visiting Scholar visas to see if significantly more people on J-1 visas went abroad from Beijing than from other cities. If so, central administrators might have maintained control over the official exchange channels. We can also see if the number of F-1 visas, which localities and universities could give out more readily and which to a certain extent reflect the influence of private or market forces, were distributed more evenly across the country. If so, then decentralization, market forces, and international opportunities weakened central control.

Data collected by Orleans for 1983–85 are useful for testing these hypotheses because before 1985, the SEDC determined almost all exchange opportunities, particularly exchanges that sent out J-1 visa Visiting Scholars. Table 4.6 shows Beijing's dominance over J-1 visas (34.2 percent). Shanghai received only 15.3 percent of J-1 visas, while the "All Other Provinces" category received 35.5 percent, which suggests that the central government was both keeping these opportunities to go abroad in its own hands and trying to insure a greater regional distribution. However, in the less official, more decentralized (and more marketized) category of F-1 visas, Shanghai sent out almost as many students (1,486 or 29.0 percent) as Beijing (1,535 or 30.0 percent), and therefore had a much larger percentage of F-1 visas than J-1 visas. Similarly, Guangdong, whose students had many overseas Chinese relatives, also had more F-1 visas (14.3 percent) than official J-1 visas (5.2 percent). Clearly under this more market-oriented visa category, where foreign funding played a key role, coastal areas

Table 4.6   Student and Scholar Visas to the United States, by Place of Residence in China, 1983–1985

Place of Residence	F-1 Visa		J-1 Visa		Total	
	Number	Percentage	Number	Percentage	Number	Percentage
Beijing	1,535	30.0	4,200	34.2	5,815	33.0
Shanghai	1,486	29.0	1,911	15.3	3,397	19.3
Guangdong	733	14.3	651	5.2	1,384	7.8
Jiangsu	163	3.2	691	5.5	854	4.8
Hubei	102	2.0	564	4.5	666	3.8
All other provinces	1,098	21.5	4,409	35.3	5,507	31.3
TOTAL	5,117	100.0	12,426	100.0	17,623	100.0

Source: Adapted with permission from Leo Orleans, *Chinese Students in America*, p. 93. Copyright 1989 by the National Academy of Sciences. Courtesy of the National Academy Press, Washington, D.C.

Table 4.7   Student and Scholar Visas to the United States, by Place of Residence in China, 1993

Place of Residence	F-1 Visa		J-1 Visa		J-1 Student Visa		Total	
	Number	Percentage	Number	Percentage	Number	Percentage	Number	Percentage
Beijing	40	37.7	22	42.3	23	54.8	91	43.5
Shanghai	27	25.5	8	15.4	3	7.1	38	18.2
Canton	5	4.7	1	1.9	0	0.0	7	3.3
Wuhan	3	2.8	3	5.8	4	9.5	11	5.3
Nanjing	7	6.6	3	5.8	3	7.1	13	6.2
Dalian	2	1.9	0	0.0	2	4.8	5	2.4
Sichuan	2	1.9	2	3.8	0	0.0	4	1.9
Inland	9	8.5	7	13.5	5	11.9	21	10.0
Other coastal cities	10	9.4	3	5.8	1	2.4	14	6.7
Near the coast	1	0.9	3	5.8	1	2.4	5	2.4
TOTAL	106	100.0	52	100.0	42	100.0	209	100.0

Source: Data from David Zweig and Chen Changgui, *China's Brain Drain to the U.S.* (Berkeley: Institute of East Asian Studies, 1995).

such as Shanghai and Guangdong Province with their global networks and overseas Chinese contacts were far more competitive.

By 1993, outbound trends had changed little, despite further decentralization and the expansion of the number of channels for overseas study, work, and research. Using data collected in 1993 in the United States (table 4.7), we find that even more J-1 Visiting Scholar visas were given to schools in Beijing, showing that the bureaucracy in Beijing still influenced

J-1 visa exchanges.[116] In table 4.7, Beijing's universities received over 42 percent of J-1 visas, far more than any other city in our survey group. Similarly, of the forty-two J-1 student visas in our survey group given to young university lecturers who went overseas after 1987, more than half were Beijing-based lecturers. Inland cities also got a larger share of the J-1 Visiting Scholar and J-1 student visas than F-1 student visas—although the variations are less stark—again suggesting that the central government allocated opportunities it controlled in a planned way and that the more marketized visas or exchange opportunities did not flow inland. Shanghai and Guangzhou again were able to use unofficial channels more than official ones; the same is also true for the "Other Coastal Cities" category. Statistically our data show a significant relationship between the city of origin of people in our sample and the type of visa received.[117]

For the second continuum, if bureaucratic controls were significant, we would expect to see a close relationship between a university's official status and the percentage of faculty going overseas. According to Du, "The higher an institution's line of authority was, the more visible it became, and with the visibility came the privileges—appropriations, capital investment, research projects and funds, priority for nationwide student selection and opportunities for government sponsored international exchange programs."[118] And although the higher-status schools were better schools, were the target of foreign universities seeking exchanges, and therefore could have sent more people overseas independent of administrative power, the absence of a relationship between status and outflow would allow us to reject the hypothesis of administrative control.

Table 4.8 shows that the opportunities to go abroad for faculty at the SEDC's key point schools were far greater than for those at other schools. In 1992, the percentage of scholars at SEDC schools who had gone abroad for at least six months was 44 percent,[119] while for State Council universities—schools affiliated with national ministries or commissions—the percentage of scholars going abroad was only 18.75 percent. Provincial and local universities sent out even fewer faculty, suggesting that under decentralization they lost out in the marketplace of exchanges to the more powerful key and State Council universities, who had a comparative advantage

116. Our sample of 273 people collected in 1993 is not representative in any scientific way. However, we did choose our informants from different types of cities and schools all over the United States, and, whenever we were able to build lists of students at schools, we chose from those lists randomly.
117. The Pearson chi-square was significant at the .001 level.
118. Du, *Chinese Higher Education*, p. 30.
119. Some administrators at SEDC schools felt that such data were extremely sensitive and that giving it to us might get them in trouble. Data for Nanjing University were obtained informally, through neither the Foreign Affairs Office nor its Higher Education Research Institute.

Table 4.8   Returnee Scholars by Type of University, 1992

Type of University	Faculty Going Abroad	Returnees to Total Faculty	Return Rate
Key point universities under the SEDC	44.0	39.0	64.0
Universities under State Council	18.8	10.4	55.6
Provincial universities	7.5	3.3	44.0
Local universities[a]	6.6	4.7	72.0

Source: Interviews at 26 schools by Chen Changgui, Ruth Hayhoe, and David Zweig.
Note: All values are percentages. SEDC, State Education Commission.
[a] Local universities refer to those under the "special district" (*zhuan qu*).

in attracting exchange opportunities. Finally, if we compare the "Returnees to Total Faculty" column, which reflects the ability of a school to send people abroad and attract these valued resources back, SEDC schools have a much richer faculty profile than the State Council or lower-level schools, with 39 percent of their faculty returnees, while the percentage for State Council schools was 10.4 percent. Returnees in provincial and local schools are almost nonexistent. Because returnees become important channels for subsequent exchanges, this becomes a self-reinforcing process.

Data on financial support for J-1 students and scholars (table 4.9), however, demonstrate the declining role of China's government in the exchanges and suggest that foreign universities used grants and fellowships to extract many of China's best and brightest. Although in 1979 the Chinese government supplied 54 percent of the financial support for J-1 visa holders, this share dropped dramatically to 25 percent by 1984, even before the major decentralization of 1985, which lowered the government share to only 17 percent. But in this case, the SEDC and Chinese universities consciously abdicated control over overseas sojourners by giving most government-sponsored students in graduate programs money for only one year. Forced to fend for themselves soon after arriving in the host country, even government-sponsored students sought fellowships wherever possible and established the types of relationships that encouraged them to stay abroad. In an undated policy paper aimed at Chinese officials, the U.S. government expressed concern that the consistent under-funding of officially sponsored Chinese students was forcing them to seek financial assistance elsewhere, rather than continue as PRC government funded students, and therefore may have been contributing to the development of ties which encouraged them to remain abroad.[120] Although the Chinese government's assumption that qualified Chinese students could get foreign funds was probably correct, less government control, fewer links between

120. "Student Funding," issue paper, Washington, D.C., May 1987. This paper was probably prepared for the visit of He Dongchang in 1987.

Table 4.9 Financial Support for Chinese J-1 Students and Scholars, by Source of Funding, 1979–1985 (thousand $)

Total Funding

Source	1979	1980	1981	1982	1983	1984	1985
Chinese government	3,968	7,729	15,011	16,980	21,211	27,623	22,280
personnel	187	789	1,982	2,521	5,353	8,832	12,031
U.S. government	550	1,490	2,586	3,297	4,499	5,000	5,295
U.S. university	1,354	6,487	17,117	24,944	38,584	53,621	76,423
U.S. foundation	263	814	1,003	1,113	1,800	2,314	3,151
U.S. corporation	17	32	557	602	506	343	758
International organization	70	203	606	636	1,233	1,161	1,140
Other	983	1,725	2,951	4,565	6,285	9,436	12,220
TOTAL	7,392	19,269	41,813	54,568	84,227	108,330	133,280

Percentage

Source	1979	1980	1981	1982	1983	1984	1985
Chinese government	54	40	36	31	31	25	17
personnel	3	4	5	5	6	8	9
U.S. government	7	8	6	6	5	5	4
U.S. university	18	34	41	46	46	49	57
U.S. foundation	4	4	2	2	2	2	2
U.S. corporation	—	—	1	1	1	—	1
International organization	1	1	1	1	1	1	1
Other	13	9	7	8	7	9	9

Source: Data for 1979–82 from M. David Lampton, *A Relationship Restored: Trends in U.S.-China Educational Exchange, 1978–1984* (Washington, D.C.: National Academy Press, 1986), pp. 48–49. Data for 1983–85 from Leo Orleans, *Chinese Students in America: Policies, Issues, and Numbers* (Washington D.C.: National Academy Press, 1988), p. 91.

these sojourners and China, and an emergent sense of self-confidence triggered an enormous brain drain.

Postdoctoral fellowships from U.S. universities kept graduates from returning to China. Of 16,500 Chinese citizens who received Ph.D.s in science and engineering between 1988 and 1996, 85 percent planned to stay in the United States, approximately 22 percent more than the percentage of all foreign science and engineering doctoral recipients. And of the 85 percent planning to stay, 48 percent had firm offers, with 65 percent (31 percent of 48 percent) holding post-doctoral fellowships, and only 35 percent (17 percent of 48 percent) with offers of employment.[121]

121. Of the 17 percent with firm job offers, 5 percent were in universities; so 36 percent of 48 percent, or 75 percent, had firm offers from U.S. academia. Clearly, funding from U.S. academic institutions was deeply involved in China's brain drain. See National Science Foundation, *Science and Engineering Indicators, 1999* (Washington, D.C.: National Science Foundation, 1999). I thank Pete Suttmeier for showing me this book.

This is not to say that Chinese schools did not have some leverage, particularly when an individual's spouse was still in China. In our 1993 North American sample, 20 of 39 people with spouses still in China had tried and failed to get them out. Sometimes the U.S. government refused the visa; in other cases, the Chinese unit would not let them go. A school in Wuhan that is aggressive about getting its faculty home pressured two professors to return. One, who had gone to a meeting in Canada and then found a job, succumbed to the school's constant cables and pressure; the other chose not to study for a Ph.D. in England because the school refused to let his wife out. Other universities simply charged large sums of money to let relatives out. The wife of a Chinese Academy of Sciences Ph.D. who was offered a job at the University of Toronto was denied the right to leave, but when confronted with Document No. 44—the policy of freely coming and going—the school decided instead to charge him 20,000 RMB and let his wife go.

The internationalization of the curriculum also undercut the monopolies over academic programs with global components. Before the early 1980s, MOFERT had monopolized education in foreign trade and job placements in that sector through its own universities. But as demand for trade specialists increased in the mid-1980s, schools, colleges, and departments related to international economics, finance, and trade boomed and more and more organizations demanded the right to train foreign trade personnel. Both the Shanghai Foreign Languages Institute and the Shanghai Finance and Economics University challenged the Shanghai Foreign Trade Institute's monopoly on programs in foreign economic relations and trade.[122] In 1985, Shanghai's Jiaotong University began an Institute of International Trade that farmed out foreign trade programs to technical universities in provinces all over the country.[123] By the early 1990s, comprehensive universities established foreign trade specializations within economics departments or created foreign trade departments in business schools.

The opportunities available in foreign trade—travel overseas and regular interaction with foreign businessmen—helped these departments Attract the best students in China. At Nanjing University, the GPA of students entering the School of International Business was reportedly higher than any other school in the university, and its foreign trade department was enrolling the top students in the business school. Students entering the University of International Business and Economics—a new and not very stellar school, but the official university of MOFERT—apparently had the best GPAs in the entire country.

---

122. Shen Benliang and Zhang Chengjun, "Ben shi gaoxiao zengshi yi pi shewai zhuanye" [Our city's institutes of higher education has added a number of foreign affairs specializations], *Wenhui bao* [Wenhui daily], 16 January 1986, p. 1, in *Chinese Education* 21 (spring 1988): 110–11.
123. Interview CUSTFA2, 1992. From 1987 on, a technical university in Sichuan ran such a program under the auspices of Shanghai Jiaotong University.

Officials and teachers in industrial schools under various ministries wanted to break MOFERT's monopoly over training foreign trade experts and expand their own enrollments and transnational channels. So they formed an association that lobbied MOFERT and the SEDC to open a new foreign trade specialization for industrial universities run by national ministries or national corporations (such as the General Automobile Company, the spin off of the former Ministry of Automotives). According to the head of the Industrial Exports Department at Wuhan Institute of Technology, a leader in this movement, you can teach foreign trade to people with technical skills more easily than you can impart technical knowledge to foreign trade specialists.[124] But, as of 1992, MOFERT had successfully resisted granting these new specializations official status because this would have undermined their ability to channel people into foreign trade corporations.

Within universities, the number of bureaus involved in transnational exchanges increased as well. Before 1985, MOE allocated its exchange opportunities only to the foreign affairs offices in the universities. But after the 1985 decentralization, competition over these valued channels increased and new offices or bureaus sought to create new exchange channels or control people going out through old ones. In the mid-1980s, as more faculty from Nanjing University went overseas, the Research Department (*keyan chu*) set up a section for sending people out (*paichu ke*) to conferences and seminars, or to participate in cooperative research that was outside the control of the foreign affairs office. The Research Department also created its own international exchange section (*guoji jiaoliu ke*), responsible for establishing international exchanges so that it "could promote its own people [to go overseas]."[125] Similarly, the Personnel Office argued that their teacher quality section (*shi zi ke*) should be responsible for academic exchanges under degree programs. In response, the Foreign Affairs Office set up its own international exchange section and began promoting more school-to-school exchanges. It also sent representatives to Beijing to lobby for more positions for its university on national-level exchanges. In 1987, when the university tried to recentralize responsibility for exchanges, none of these sections would give up control over its own transnational channel.

Another way channels proliferated was through the establishment of foreign student offices or departments outside the foreign affairs office. In larger universities that were authorized by the SEDC as foreign student centers, foreign student offices became departments or colleges with relatively high status, replete with their own teachers and exchange programs, through which they sent their own faculty overseas to teach and make

124. Interview WITIED, 1992.
125. Interviews at Nanjing University, summer 1992.

money. They also could obtain SEDC loans (or even foreign donations) to build housing or dormitories for the foreign students. For example, at Xiamen University, the original Foreign Students Section (*liu xuesheng ke*) under the Foreign Affairs Office became an international education center (*guoji jiaoyu zhongxin*) in 1984. In 1991 it combined with the Correspondence College to become an independent College of Overseas Education (*haiwai jiaoyu xueyuan*), whose programs, such as traditional Chinese medicine, were targeted at overseas Chinese and were administered both on campus and through correspondence courses. The college had an administrative status one-half level above a department, which allowed their director to create and supervise several departments. Although originally built in 1983–85 with SEDC funds, a new housing and program center was under construction in 1992 with $5 million from overseas Chinese.

Domestic and External Pressure to Lower Barriers

An enormous demand existed in China to go overseas. A 1990 survey found that almost 53 percent of Shanghai teachers under 35 years of age intended to go abroad. Among 36- to 45-year-olds, China's missing generation in science and technology, over 40 percent planned to go overseas. Moreover, many people under 45 might not have reported their intentions in a survey, suggesting that the share at key point universities may actually reach 70 percent.[126] As previously mentioned, even in 1996, 72 percent of high school students taking a SEDC survey indicated a strong interest in going abroad.[127] These pressures forced universities to increase the number of transnational exchange opportunities because the best students would come to their school only if they had a good chance of going overseas to study. According to officials at Nanjing University, to compete with Shanghai Foreign Language University for the region's best students its Foreign Language Department had to ensure that its students had a 20–30 percent probability of getting overseas.[128] So school officials spend a great deal of time establishing transnational channels, in part by lobbying the SEDC to give their school more overseas slots.[129] Also, the exchange industries that had emerged in response to the demand to go overseas created their own channels, as well as insisting that the state help them in their efforts. Finally, students throughout China invested enormous amounts of

126. Sun Changli, "Daxue sheng chu guo yixiang de diaocha yu fenxi" [Research and analysis of the intentions of university students to go overseas], *Gaodeng jiaoyu yanjiu* [Research on higher education] 1 (1991): 85.
127. Xiao Yu, "Students aim for overseas," *South China Morning Post*, 31 December 1996, p. 8.
128. Interview EDSABNND, 1992.
129. Inteview OEDZSMNJD, 1991.

time and money preparing for overseas study, which was one major reason for establishing the more liberal self-paying category.

Fevers to go abroad also developed whenever the government eased administrative constraints on overseas exchanges because of well-founded concerns that each opening might be quickly followed by a new round of retrenchment. This peripatetic policy pattern, detailed in the earlier historical review, meant that the mass swarming that occurred was not irrational; we have seen similar fevers in our two previous cases. Thus, after the decentralization of 1984–85, the number of Chinese going to the United States more than doubled, while the number of people taking the TOEFL quadrupled. With demand exceeding supply, students stampeded through the transnational channels when restrictions eased, panicking others who feared that they might miss this opportunity if they hesitated. The result was what one Chinese scholar calls "the wave to study abroad."[130]

International economic forces pulled people out of China and undermined the state's control over its population and boundaries. Just as China decentralized its controls over global exchanges in 1984–85, proliferating independent outbound channels, U.S. universities were granted the right to organize Chinese exchanges. Their large reservoir of fellowships and grants attracted China's best and brightest, especially those Chinese interested in graduate programs, which were just beginning in China.

Once they were out of China, individuals were compelled, in part by market forces, to stay out, which in turn created enormous pressure on the state to deregulate its rigid controls on the flow of human talent. Our findings in 1993 confirm that concerns about political instability weighed heavily on the minds of at least 30 percent of our respondents; however, economic and administrative concerns were also highly salient and were issues to which the government could respond (tables 4.10 and 4.11).[131] Table 4.10 shows that for people without children, how their overall economic situation now is compared to that in China is a highly significant explanation for not returning.[132] The bivariate relationship between household income and people's views about returning is statistically significant, although in our logistic regression model this relationship is not significant for people with children (table 4.11). Also, for people with children, the relative condition of their housing in the West as compared to China is salient, no doubt in part due to the desire of people with children for greater privacy.

Unorganized collective action by sojourners forced down administrative barriers restricting the flow of human capital out of China. China wanted

130. Su Qinfu et al., eds. *Wu ci lang chao* [The five waves] (Beijing: Zhongguo renmin daxue chubanshe, 1989).
131. Zweig and Chen, *China's Brain Drain.*
132. It would be preferable to have data on why people are going out rather than on why they are not returning, but such data are not available.

Table 4.10   Factors Explaining Views about Returning to China: People with No Children, 1993

Variable	Parameter Estimate	Standard Error of the Estimate	Probability Chi-Square	Standardized Estimate
Gender	0.8236	0.5709	0.1491	0.215566
Years worked before leaving China	0.1348	0.0630	0.0322**	0.399826
Original intentions about staying in United States before leaving China	−0.5619	0.3487	0.1071	−0.270171
Current visa status	1.8844	0.7688	0.0142**	0.410988
How U.S. housing is compared to housing in China	−0.3584	0.3549	0.3125	−0.213499
Household income	−0.3676	0.1358	0.0068**	−0.499966
How overall economic situation now is compared to that in China	0.6713	0.3314	0.0428**	0.354070
Trust of new policy of freedom to come and go	−0.6099	0.3604	0.0906*	−0.257547
Arrival before or after April 1990	−0.4735	0.7484	0.5270	−0.115853
Combined political variable	−0.1895	0.1184	0.1093	−0.254662

Source: David Zweig and Chen Changgui, *China's Brain Drain to the U.S.* (Berkeley: Institute of East Asian Studies, 1995), p. 126. Used with permission.
Notes: Criterion, − LOG L. Chi-square for covariates: 30.650 with 13 df ($p = .0038$); score: 24.738 with 13 df ($p = .0250$). *, significant relationship; **, highly significant relationship.

Table 4.11   Factors Explaining Views about Returning to China: People with Children, 1993

Variable	Parameter Estimate	Standard Error of the Estimate	Probability Chi-Square	Standardized Estimate
Gender	1.3051	0.5785	0.0241**	0.329188
Years worked before leaving China	−0.0583	0.0497	0.2407	−0.237538
Original intentions about staying in United States before leaving China	−1.2821	0.3151	0.0001**	−0.699179
Current visa status	−1.2647	0.4923	0.0102**	−0.475395
How U.S. housing is compared to housing in China	1.0295	0.3184	0.0012**	0.769709
Household income	−0.0491	0.1208	0.6847	−0.071369
How overall economic situation now is compared to that in China	0.1852	0.3109	0.5515	0.102882
Trust of new policy on freedom to come and go	−0.6754	0.3021	0.0253**	−0.386327
Arrival before or after April 1990	−1.3445	0.7059	0.0568*	−0.366649
Combined political variable	0.1928	0.1095	0.0783*	0.267561

Source: David Zweig and Chen Changgui, *China's Brain Drain to the U.S.* (Berkeley: Institute of East Asian Studies, 1995), p. 125. Used with permission.
Notes: Criterion: −2 LOG L. Chi-square for covariates: 101.480 with 13 df ($p = .0001$); score: 65.979 with 13 df ($p = .0001$). *, significant relationship; **, highly significant relationship.

western technology and skills and these people had them; by withholding those resources and petitioning the Chinese government to change its policy, overseas Chinese students combined Albert Hirschman's exit and voice options and forced the state to weaken administrative controls over students and scholars.[133]

First, by refusing to return, they compelled the central state and Chinese cities to offer them preferential policies unavailable to domestic intellectuals. Suddenly the path to success in China involved a study tour overseas, increasing the domestic demand for opportunities to go abroad, including postdoctoral fellowship for domestic Ph.D.s. Second, an important concern stopping people from returning was the difficulty of getting out the first time and the fear they would be unable to get out again.[134] In our sample, 5.8 percent of people chose these two concerns as their first reason for not returning, and many more chose it as their third choice. So, in 1993, the state introduced the freedom to come and go policy (*lai qu ziyou*), which allowed returnees to go abroad a second time more easily. Third, many who did not return were concerned about the lack of job mobility in China. In the mid-1980s, the administrative irrational allocation of returnees caused many to feel that their talents were being wasted.[135] In our 1993 survey, 16.1 percent of respondents chose either "lack of opportunity to change jobs in China" or "lack of opportunity for career advancement in China" as reasons for not returning. When selecting "positive things about the United States," 29.1 percent chose "lots of job choices or opportunity" or "job mobility." So, in 1993, the state decided that rather than force returnees back to their home unit, it would allow them to move to the city of their choice and the job of their choice. Suddenly enormous market competition emerged among cities, vying directly for overseas scholars who had not originated from their locality. But domestic scholars also began to demand and receive similar rights, so that by the mid- to late 1990s, a full-fledged academic market had emerged in China.

Level of Internationalization

At the end of this era, China's degree of internationalization in the education sector was quite significant. However, the depth clearly varied across

---

133. Albert O. Hirschman, *Exit, Voice, and Loyalty: Responses to Declines in Firms, Organizations, and States* (Cambridge, Mass.: Harvard University Press, 1970).
134. The survey data referred to in this paragraph are from Zweig and Chen, *China's Brain Drain to the United States.*
135. Julia Leung, "M. B. A. Elite in China Disillusioned," *Asian Wall Street Journal,* 26 May 1988, p. 1 and Wen Jia, "U.S. Trained Managers 'Misused'," *China Daily,* December 4, 1987, p. 1.

regions and types of school, and also intensified after 1992 when popular pressure for liberalization of the rules governing overseas travel increased.

Table 4.12 presents 1992 data on the percentage of faculty in universities who had gone abroad and those who returned as a share of the total faculty body. For category 1 universities—the thirty-nine key universities directly under the SEDC—the share of faculty who had gone abroad was impressive, particularly for schools on the coast. At Nanjing University over half the faculty had gone overseas for six months! Many category 2 schools, such as Huazhong Agricultural University in Wuhan, had sent over 25 percent of their faculty abroad. However, this data may reflect a brain drain more than the degree of internationalization because the "Returnees As Percent of Total Faculty" column shows that as of 1992 many faculty members had not returned, so the number of faculty members with overseas experience actually working in the universities was often 15 percent or less.[136]

Let us look again at data on the number of graduate students studying abroad in table 4.2. An important measure of internationalization is the students going abroad as a percentage of new students column. This value reflects the proportion of Chinese students entering graduate school overseas as a share of all new Chinese graduate students worldwide (i.e., new graduate student enrollment in China plus number of students going abroad, for the year). Between 1985 and 1991, this ratio averaged 9.4 percent a year. In 1992 graduate students going overseas, as a share of new Chinese graduate students worldwide, doubled to 16.4 percent, rising to 20.3 percent in 1993, and then peaking at 28.5 percent in 1995. Between 1992 and 1997 the yearly average was 24.1 percent, showing that approximately one of every four Chinese students to enter a graduate program worldwide in this period entered a program overseas. Since 1997, the percentage has decreased largely because Chinese universities have significantly increased their intake of graduate students.

Also, although the total number of returnee students does not appear to be high, these numbers also reflect a significant level of internationalization. If we assume that all returnee students have a graduate degree, then a meaningful measure of the depth of internationalization is the number of returnee students by year as a share of all Chinese graduate students who are in the job market in China (i.e., graduate students in China, degree-receiving students, plus returnee students, number by year). This ratio tells us what proportion of the total number of graduate students looking for jobs in China in any one year had an overseas graduate education. We find the same pattern as before. Although the "returnee students, percentage of

---

136. Unfortunately, Nanjing University, Xiamen University, and Chengdu University of Science and Technology were unwilling to share with us the number of returnees, probably because they were concerned about low return rates.

Table 4.12 Sojourning and Returnee Scholars by University, 1992

	Total Faculty	Sojourners		Returnees		Return Rate (%)
		Number	Percentage of Total Faculty	Number	Percentage of Total Faculty	
1. Key Point Universities under SEDC						
Chengdu University of Science and Technology	1,680	297	18	n.a.	n.a.	n.a.
Guangzhou Foreign Language College	340	300	88	240	71	80
Huazhong University of Science and Technology	2,311	810	25	370	16	46
Nanjing University	2,420	1,241	51	n.a.	n.a.	n.a.
Xiamen University	1,890	529	28	n.a.	n.a.	n.a.
Zhongshan University	1,799	800	35	536	30	67
2. Universities under Other Ministries or Commissions						
Electronic University of Science and Technology	1,025	306	30	149	15	49
Huazhong Agricultural University	693	189	27	105	15	56
Hunan University	1,218	200	16	120	10	60
Southwest Medical University	2,266	447	20	273	12	61
Wuhan Steel and Iron College	800	53	7	28	3.5	53
Wuhan Technical College	821	49	6	31	4	63
Wuhan University of Surveying and Mapping	879	160	18	100	11	63.5
Zhongshan Medicial University	1,500	400	26	200	13	50
3. Provincial Key Point Universities						
Zhengzhou University	1,132	60	5	41	3.6	68
Henan University	1,420	75	5	25	1.8	33
Hunan Agricultural College	961	124	13	42	4.4	34
Hunan Normal University	552	40	7	18	3.3	45
4. Provincial and District Universities						
Changsha Vocational University	320	37	12	20	6	54
Henyang Normal College	238	4	2	4	2	100
Huiyang Normal College	223	6	3	6	3	100
Jianghan University	500	47	9	30	6	64
Linglin Normal College	178	2	1	1	1	50
Shenzhen University	400	n.a.	n.a.	n.a.	n.a.	n.a.
Wuhan Radio and Television University	130	22	17	17	13	77
Xiaogan Normal College	250	5	2	5	2	100

Source: Data collected by Chen Changgui, Ruth Hayhoe, and David Zweig, 1992.
Notes: We include as returnees only those people who stayed abroad longer than six months. n.a., not available; SEDC, State Education Commission.

total graduates" column averages 6.1 percent between 1985 and 1991, the ratio between 1992 and 1999 is 14.1 percent per year, with a peak again in 1995 of 18.0 percent, which means that in that year, almost one out of every five new graduate students looking for jobs in China had a foreign graduate degree. Here, again, the drop-off since 1995 is due to the 72 percent increase in the number of degree-receiving graduate students in China between 1995 and 1999.

Conclusion

China's educational organizations and the channels of global transaction had only partial control over the personnel flows between China and the world outside. Decentralization of linkage-making authority to universities after 1985 proliferated the channels and opportunities for overseas exchanges, as many bureaus within schools competed to establish new channels that they could control. Pressed as well by demands to go abroad from talented students whom they wanted to recruit, universities across China sought new horizontal linkages with foreign universities or pressed the SEDC to give them more exchange opportunities. Schools also understood the rich resource of human capital encapsulated in returnees, so they pushed more of their own faculty to go abroad and then competed to attract them back.

Once the state deregulated its administrative controls over the allocation of returnees, the result of a 1992 policy decision, domestic market forces and the high value attributed to returnees because of their international experience, networks, and knowledge further undermined central government controls. Returnees could now negotiate their own deals with entrepreneurial cities, such as Shenzhen or Shanghai, that offered them preferential policies. A real market in intellectual labor began to emerge, which had serious implications for China's overall domestic labor market.

Letting individuals go overseas on private exchanges dramatically increased the outward flow as well as increasing the percentage of nonreturnees. More than any other group, self-paying students did not return.[137] But domestic pressures, the need for foreign technology, and the interests of bureaucrats in facilitating exchanges made even the channels for officially sponsored students and scholars relatively porous. Lacking money, the government let many of its own J-1 visa sojourners fund their own studies once they were overseas, binding them more closely to overseas

---

137. At one university in Nanjing, no self-paying student returned between 1985 and 1989. Ma Jibo, "We Should Take Note of the Fault in the Teaching Troops of Higher Learning Institutes," *Qunyan* (Public tribune), no. 5 (May 1990): 12–13, reprinted in *JPRS*, no. 60 (6 August 1990): 62–63.

organizations and decreasing the likelihood that they would return. Most important, whenever educational administrators threatened to constrain outward flows, pressures by Chinese students and scholars both within and outside of China and interagency competition in Beijing prevented them from carrying through on their threats.

Nevertheless, the Chinese state neither lowered all barriers nor lost all controls. Students and scholars still needed passports from the Public Security Bureau, which could be withheld. As of 1996, those going out on official exchanges had to leave a 50,000 RMB deposit to insure that they returned on time; if they failed to do so, they forfeited these funds. Quotas on the total number of students and scholars sent by the government, schools, and other units remained in place; only by quitting his or her job and getting foreign funding could an individual escape the state's controls. Even the allocation of foreign teachers and advisors, a key resource, and foreign aid to the education sector remained under tight administrative control.

Yet the system that dominated at the end of the Maoist era had undergone an enormous level of deregulation. The value of international work opportunities, the value ascribed to returnees and their accumulated knowledge, the higher living standards in foreign countries, and the wealth of fellowships provided by foreign universities—all weakened the administrative system controlling global transactions in the educational realm. In the end, students and scholars themselves, by withholding their services to China, forced the state to alter its regulatory regime in dramatic ways, undermining its own controls, resulting in a much more porous system than that which existed at the end of the Maoist era.

5

Controlling the Opening: The Struggle over Overseas Development Assistance

One of the great fears of developing states is that reliance on foreign aid will undermine national sovereignty and create dependence on the institutions of the world capitalist system. China, a socialist and neomercantilist state led by an elite that espoused an anti-imperialist, anti-colonialist ideology, was particularly sensitive about this issue. As in the other sectors addressed in this book, China established a coterie of institutional arrangements to try to shelter itself from foreign influences that might use overseas development assistance (ODA) to advance their national interests to the detriment of China's chosen development strategy. Yet, under the open policy, China received more and more foreign aid, accepting the risks that came with increased flows of foreign capital and development assistance programs.

Did China maintain control over this process? Some critics of ODA see donors as almost omnipotent, basing their power on a class of policy makers who undermine national autonomy on behalf of outside interests.[1] Others stress how the IMF uses structural adjustment loans to force developing states with serious balance-of-payments problems to adjust their developmental strategies.[2] Some China analysts fear that the need to supply counterpart funding for aid projects could force central and local elites to spend funds in ways that are not coterminous with China's domestic investment priorities,[3] or that reliance on ODA could allow foreign scientists to set the agenda for China's scientific development.[4] Alastair Iain Johnston, too, finds that once China joined international organizations, the pressure

---

1. Robin Broad, *Unequal Alliance: The World Bank, the International Monetary Fund, and the Philippines* (Berkeley: University of California Press, 1988); Cheryl Payer, *The World Bank: A Critical Analysis* (London: Monthly Review Press, 1982).
2. Miles Kahler, "External Influence, Conditionality, and the Politics of Adjustment," in *The Politics of Economic Adjustment*, ed. Stephan Haggard and Robert Kaufmann (Princeton: Princeton University Press, 1992), pp. 89–138.
3. For a critical view of foreign aid in China, see Ruth Hayhoe, *China's Universities and the Open Door* (Armonk: M. E. Sharpe, 1989).
4. Ruth Hayhoe, "Penetration or Mutuality? China's Educational Cooperation with Europe, Japan and North America," *Comparative Education Review* 31, 4 (1986): 532–59.

not to lose face, which he calls "image costs," made China sensitive to global norms.[5]

Yet other studies show China to be more capable than most Third World states of protecting its national interests. Harold Jacobson and Michel Oksenberg find that Chinese officials working in key multilateral organizations reflected China's views, not those of the international organization where they worked.[6] Similarly, Samuel Kim finds that participating in the United Nations (UN) has not seriously altered China's free-rider, self-interested behavior.[7] And even though Ruth Hayhoe fears that the World Bank could undermine China's sovereignty, her own data show that China, not the World Bank, determined the structure of the World Bank's educational aid projects.[8]

This chapter looks at China's opening to foreign aid and the efforts of the Chinese government to control that process. Again, I ask many of the same questions as in the previous cases. Was the opening to ODA elite or society driven? Did the channels of global transaction help the state control aid flows or did they eventually become channels through which domestic and foreign interests collaborated to undermine state controls? What was the relative value of the resources transferred by donor agencies and how large was demand for them? What role did external pressures play in undermining state controls over aid? And, finally, did state agents and potential aid beneficiaries, once they understood their interests, push for freer transnational exchanges and undermine the state's control over its boundaries?

Conceptualizing Internationalization of the Overseas Development Assistance Sector

To conceptualize internationalization in this sector and evaluate the role of foreign aid in China's development, we need to employ empirical measures. In terms of direct expenditures by multilateral agencies in China, we can see that since 1979 the scale of ODA has been enormous, making China one of the world's largest recipients of foreign aid. As of 2000, China was the largest beneficiary of United Nations Development

5. Alastair Iain Johnston, "China and International Environmental Institutions: A Decision Rule Analysis," in *Energizing China: Reconciling Environmental Protection and Economic Growth*, ed. Michael B. McElroy, Chris P. Nielsen, and Peter Lydon (Cambridge, Mass.: Harvard University Press, 1998), pp. 555–99.
6. See Harold K. Jacobson and Michel Oksenberg, *China's Participation in the IMF, the World Bank, and GATT* (Ann Arbor: University of Michigan Press, 1990).
7. Samuel Kim, "China and the United Nations," in *China Joins the World: Progress and Prospects*, ed. Elizabeth Economy and Michel Oksenberg (New York: Council on Foreign Relations, 1999).
8. Hayhoe, *China's Universities and the Open Door*, p. 161.

Table 5.1   UNDP Funds Expended in China, 1981–2000 (million $)

Program	Years	Funding
CP1	1981–85	79.6
CP2	1986–90	147.8
CP3	1991–95	171.6
Country Cooperation Framework I	1996–2000	95.2
TOTAL		494.2

Source: UNDP Country Office in China, 1998.
Note: Includes counterpart funding from Chinese side, which in 1996–2000 was valued at over $37 million. CP, Country Project; UNDP, United Nations Development Program.

Program (UNDP) (table 5.1) and World Bank aid (table 5.2),[9] while Japan's assistance to China surpassed that of the World Bank.[10] As of December 2000, the Asia Development Bank had committed to loans totalling $10.3 billion.[11]

Alternative empirical measures might include foreign aid and concessionary loans as a share of investments in fixed assets, reflecting the share of aid being used to sustain economic growth. Or we might look at ODA as a share of total investment in specific sectors, such as public health, education, or management training. A regional analysis would look at the amount of foreign aid in poverty alleviation as a percentage of total investment in poverty alleviation in a single province or county. For example, Yunnan Province, where many foreign NGOs are working on rural poverty, may be seen as more internationalized than other provinces in which donors have more limited access.

However, because my definition of internationalization entails both high levels of transnational flows and decreased regulatory controls, I focus here on the strength of administrative controls and the extent to which state bureaucrats regulated the aid process, hypothesizing that less bureaucratic control and more donor control increased internationalization. Therefore, we first look at the domestic demand for aid, the channels of global trans-

9. In terms of combined International Bank for Reconstruction and Development loans and International Development Agency (IDA) credits, China, as of 1990, was sixth in the world. As of 1993, China became the World Bank's largest customer. See World Bank Resident Mission in China, *The World Bank Group in China: Facts and Figures* (Beijing, 1997), p. 1.
10. By 1995, China had received three loans from Japan, totaling approximately $10.1 billion. The fourth loan (1996–2000) was for approximately $10 billion in current dollars. See Susan J. Pharr and Ming Wan, "Yen for the Earth: Japan's Pro-Active China Environment Policy," in *Energizing China: Reconciling Environmental Protection and Economic Growth*, ed. Michael B. McElroy, Chris P. Nielsen, and Peter Lydon (Cambridge, Mass.: Harvard University Press, 1998), pp. 601–38.
11. "A Fact Sheet: People's Republic of China and ADB," http://www.adb.org/Documents/Fact_Sheets/PRC.

Table 5.2   World Bank Assistance to China, 1981–2000 (million $)

Year	World Bank	IDA	Total
1981	100.00	100.00	200.00
1982	0.00	60.00	60.00
1983	392.16	150.39	542.55
1984	600.46	421.40	1,021.86
1985	573.31	437.26	1,010.57
1986	668.61	449.49	1,118.10
1987	863.54	553.78	1,417.32
1988	842.89	639.21	1,482.10
1989	833.40	515.00	1,348.40
1990	0.00	590.00	590.00
1991	452.07	977.80	1,429.87
1992	1,577.70	948.60	2,526.30
1993	2,155.00	1,017.00	3,172.00
1994	2,145.00	925.00	3,070.00
1995	2,369.50	630.00	2,999.50
1996	2,490.00	480.00	2,970.00
1997	2,490.00	325.00	2,815.00
1998	2,323.00	293.40	2,616.40
1999	1,649.40	407.60	2,057.00
2000	1,672.50	0.00	1,672.50

Source: World Bank Resident Mission in China, *The World Bank Group in China: Facts and Figures* (Beijing, June 1997 and July 2000).
Note: IDA, International Development Agency.

action established by the state, and then the demand of foreign donors for access to China. These three factors set the context within which overall country programs were negotiated and determined whether donors or China's central administrators controlled the allocation of funding. Second, we look at specific projects, to determine whether China's bureaucratic agents, particularly counterpart agencies (CPAs) established to control foreign donors, or the donors' representatives controlled the key decisions about funding allocations. Finally, we assess whether Chinese government agents, such as CPAs, continued to monitor relations between donors and Chinese society and argue that the more direct the relationship, the deeper the level of internationalization. My data come from detailed interviews with officials in four donor agencies—the UNDP, World Bank, Canadian International Development Agency (CIDA), and Ford Foundation—and more detailed studies of a sampling of their aid projects.

This chapter differs from the other sector studies in several critical ways. First, it does not address a specific industrial sector such as rural industry, a system such as the educational hierarchy in China, or specific localities

such as cities and their zones. ODA went to various systems and regions of
the country, making the analysis of this sector much more diffuse. Nevertheless, a significant amount of these funds were directed at strengthening
China's administrative capacity, making bureaucrats themselves the beneficiaries of the flow of capital, goods, and services. Also because foreign
forces have used aid to influence domestic politics in developing countries
and because China has insisted so strongly on controlling and not formally
decentralizing the sector, I feel it is important to look at aid as a potential
critical case that could challenge my overall hypothesis. If China maintained control over ODA, then at-the-border institutions or the level of
decentralization were critical, but, if China also lost control in this sector,
then international forces were indeed omnipotent.

Domestic Demand for Overseas Development Assistance

The Cultural Revolution decimated China's central bureaucracy, creating
a severe shortage of foreign and domestic capital, equipment, information-
retrieval capabilities, and talented officials. The central government also
lacked the administrative capacity to deal with foreign bureaucracies and
aid agencies, in part due to a shortage of people with foreign language
skills. Technical needs in the early 1980s were so extensive that a shopping
list presented in 1980 to UNDP by the Ministry of Foreign Economic
Relations (MOFER) frightened UN officials.[12]

China's participation in the UN, its role as a UNDP donor, and long-
term observations by the United Nations Small Group[13] had created a constituency in China's foreign-oriented bureaucracy that believed China, its
bureaus, and its officials could benefit from and manage foreign aid and
loans. They encouraged top leaders to accept aid. In late 1977, after Deng
Xiaoping returned to power, MOFER officials in China's UN mission began
debating the merits of UNDP assistance. MOFER's Minister, Chen Muhua,
who understood the long-term advantages of UNDP aid, approved a draft
report outlining the benefits of UN technical assistance[14] (table 5.3).

Still it was not an easy decision for China's leaders to accept foreign aid.
In 1979, China's top leaders, Deng Xiaoping, Chen Yun, and Li Xiannian

12. Interview with Nessim Shallon, UNDP headquarters, New York, 1992. Since the 1970s,
the ministry in charge of foreign trade and aid has been called MOFER (Ministry of Foreign
Economic Relations), MOFERT (Ministry of Foreign Economic Relations and Trade), and
MOFTEC (Ministry of Foreign Trade and Economic Cooperation). In the text, I use all
three names depending on what it was called at that particular time.
13. Jacobson and Oksenberg ascribe an important function to this organization, which was
originally established in the Bank of China in 1972, but one of my Chinese informants who
had been involved in early discussions on UNDP had never heard of the UN Small Group.
14. Interview FPASSY, New York, 1991.

Table 5.3   Periodization of China's Policy on Overseas Development Assistance, 1971–1995

October 1971	China joins the United Nations
1972	China sets up United Nations Small Group in the Bank of China
1974	China becomes donor nation under UNDP
August, 1978	Chinese State Council decides to accept UNDP assistance
January 1979	China formally accepts UNDP assistance
1979	OECD decides to include China among acceptable donors
May 1980	China joins the World Bank
July 1981	Canadian International Development Agency program approved for China
1984	China establishes CICETE as counterpart agency for UNDP and UNIDO
1986	China joins Asian Development Bank; first loans accepted in 1987
1988	Ford Foundation opens its office in Beijing
1989	Tiananmen crackdown leads to freeze on World Bank and other donor programs
1993	Upsurge in the number of foreign NGOs
1995	Environmental protection and sustainable development become new global development paradigm for the UNDP

Note: CICETE, China International Center for Economic and Technical Exchange; OECD, Organization of Economic Cooperation and Development; NGOs, nongovernmental organizations; UNDP, United Nations Development Program; UNIDO, United Nations Industrial Development Organization.

agreed that China could receive UNDP aid before the State Council made the formal decision. At that time, serious fears had remained about the price of engagement, in terms of disclosure of state secrets and China's vulnerability to international capitalism. So before joining the World Bank, China consulted with Yugoslavia and Romania, two socialist comrades, about the level of transparency that was necessary to receive World Bank loans. Ideologically, too, it was difficult to jettison Mao's concept of self-reliance. But within China, the potential beneficiaries of aid, such as local governments, bureaucratic agencies, and producers and end users, all had great need for foreign goods, services, and overseas access.

In the case of Canadian aid, the proliferation of contacts between departments in the federal government, provincial governments, universities, business community, and their counterparts in China throughout the 1970s already "were providing China with something very close to development assistance," and these Canadian interests were "knocking at CIDA's door, seeking financial support to breathe some life into these arrangements."[15] So, in early 1980, when Bo Yibo signaled China's interest in receiving Canadian aid, Canada responded quickly.

First and foremost, ODA meant foreign exchange for overseas training, travel, and the acquisition of foreign technology and management skills.

15. Jack Maybee, "The China Program of The Canadian International Development Agency" (paper presented at the Conference on Canada-China Relations, Montebello, Canada, May 1985).

From the late-1970s through the mid-1990s, the demand for foreign capital in China by administrative agencies that had no income-generating capability was tremendous. CPAs that managed foreign aid could increase their own power by strategically allocating these monies. Revolving funds, a form of endowment set up with foreign funds under some ODA projects, became a lifeline by which Chinese units could survive after the project, and the flow of foreign capital, ended.

For years UNDP aid was highly valued because it transferred state-of-the-art technology to SOEs needing technical upgrading; audiovisual equipment offered administrative units a new medium for transferring knowledge and running profit-making seminars. Vehicles, such as Land Rovers, were needed to deliver programs to remote rural areas, but they also raised the status of local officials who drove in them; so new vehicles often became part of the price of insuring local government participation in a project. Also, aid-related technology (or vehicles) could be imported duty free, increasing incentives for local governments or production units to seek a foreign aid project.

Foreign aid improved the institutional capacity and competitiveness of government agencies. Through management or language training programs, and by supplying technical equipment, such as faxes, computers, telephones, and photocopiers, many donors first strengthened the administrative capabilities of their CPA to insure the effective management of their overall program. But after such training, the CPA's staff could build its own international networks, write more competitive grant applications, and get more foreign aid on its own.

ODA moved human resources into and out of China. Many donor countries sent senior administrators on international study tours to transform their insular worldview or influence their selection of technology to import. In other cases, trips were a pay-off to bureau chiefs who had not been abroad.[16] CPAs also used overseas trips to build relations with other bureaus in China. Younger staff, on the other hand, often wanted one- or two-year training programs because they need diplomas to be promoted. In either case, savings from the subsistence allowances from such trips were enormous compared to domestic salaries; and until 1993, as described in chapter 4, anyone going abroad could buy several appliances upon his or her return.

In China, foreign teachers internationalized domestic training programs, increasing their attractiveness and marketability. Canadian teachers supplied by CIDA to Nankai University improved the competitiveness of the school's training program, despite teaching for only two weeks of a

16. The high demand for study tours is a problem with much Third World aid; UN officials also use aid projects to justify overseas travel. See Graham Hancock, *The Lords of Poverty: The Power, Prestige and Corruption of the International Aid Business* (New York: Atlantic Monthly Press, 1992), p. 117.

twelve-week program. As one program coordinator put it, "We are a kind of sweetener, and we give it a certain international cache that helps make it attractive."[17] Similarly, one university forced its UN Volunteers, who were sent to teach in their foreign programs, to participate in domestic courses so they could be marketed as foreign training programs.[18]

ODA attracted domestic capital from national or local budgets. Aid recipients had to contribute counterpart funding (*peitao zijin*) to a project, forcing the State Planning Commission or Ministry of Finance at various levels of the system to transfer funds to the benefitting unit, giving ODA the "power of attraction of things foreign." According to one UNDP official,

> once a unit got UNDP assistance, it immediately wrote a report to its ministry or the State Council, saying that the UN has decided to give it a half million in technical assistance; but to make the best use of the limited resources, it needed counterpart contributions—how much office space, how many people, how much of a budget. China wants face. With this hat on, a unit gets priority and privileges. . . . Some people are very frank with us, saying that they know that their project is not a priority area or is not so important; so they ask us to reduce the budget but keep the project on the list so they can get more money from the ministry budget.[19]

A leader of the All-China Women's Federation (ACWF) admitted that only through ODA could the ACWF get more central government funds.[20] When some units got Japanese loans, the State Planning Commission let them issue domestic bonds to raise funds for the project.[21] In some cases, access to counterpart funding was more important to the recipient than the project itself. For example, because it received foreign aid for a training center, Kunming Normal University also received funds for a five-story building, a fax machine, a photocopy machine, and a language lab in the building. Therefore, "they were more concerned with getting the center and the equipment than about training teachers or using Chinese teachers trained in Australia to train other Chinese."[22]

Foreign aid offers bureaucrats promotions, additional personnel, or the chance to set up new bureaus or companies. Although low salaries and recurrent business fevers depressed the value of bureaucratic posts, new bureaus expand bureaucratic power and create new leadership posts, allowing officials promotions with the perquisites that followed. When the

17. Interview COCPint.1.
18. Interview UNVZJZ, 1992.
19. Interview UNDPYSS2, 1991.
20. Interview, All-China Women's Federation, Beijing, summer 1993.
21. Interview on Japanese aid, Cambridge, Mass., 1995.
22. Interview UNDPUNZJZ, 1994.

Agricultural Bank received a World Bank loan, it established a new section to manage that loan without much difficulty. Why? "If you can argue that you can get foreign money, they let you set up the section. But sometimes you have to get the money first. In China, if you deal with foreign money, you must be important, so there is no problem getting the *bianzhi* [positions]."[23] Foreign aid allowed administrators to create organizations—such as banks, credit coops, management training centers, production units, and even new government bureaus—that drew their sustenance from foreign capital and the donor's moral support. One official working on rural China had long wanted to set up a company that could loan money to improve the infrastructure in rural China. But only after the World Bank gave China a structural readjustment loan worth over $200 million was he able to persuade top officials in the State Council to let him set up such a company. Without that money his efforts would have been blocked.

ODA created new higher paying jobs for Chinese bureaucrats who staffed the donor's resident offices. Most of the staff in the Ford Foundation's Beijing office were seconded from the Chinese Academy of Social Sciences (CASS), and although the staff might not get much larger salaries, CASS earned extra income from their labor. Similarly, the Chinese International Center for Economic and Technical Exchange (CICETE) helped staff the UNDP office, and one British volunteer organization, Voluntary Service Overseas (VSO), recruited its own staff, but still had to hire them through the Foreign Expert Service Company, which was notorious for taking the vast majority of these foreign-paid salaries. Such material benefits for bureaus were strong incentives to support an influx of foreign donors.

Finally, ODA helped China and many of its local governments deal with the deeply entrenched poverty in western and southwestern China. Poverty alleviation has remained a priority for many foreign governments and for foreign NGOs, and the funds proffered by foreign donors for such programs are significant. The World Bank program for China has always directed much of its funds toward poorer regions of China. Beginning in the mid-1990s, many local governments in poorer regions of China were very keen to establish ties with smaller foreign donors whose financial and technical support could help alleviate their economic and political problems.

Counterpart Agencies: The Channels of Global Transaction

Throughout the 1980s and well into the 1990s access to foreign aid for domestic actors and access to Chinese society for foreign donors were con-

---

23. Interview AMML-1993.

strained by a thick coterie of CPAs (*duikou danwei*), the channel of global transaction for ODA. As in other developing countries, donors in China, particularly bilateral and multilateral agencies, were expected to work through these agencies—bureaus, banks, and research centers—as the price of admission.[24]

From the state's perspective, CPAs protected national security and the prestige of China; monitored the flow of foreign exchange, technology, and foreign values; forced donors to conform to China's national priorities; and limited foreign interests. They were expected to insure that Chinese officials met the requirements under the various loans, grants, and international agreements that had brought donors to China. And, in general, they helped define the country programs and project content, as well as filtering the inflow of foreign resources and foreign influence, determining in many cases the final resting place of the foreign personnel, funds, and technology.

Thus in 1979, the Ministry of Finance became the World Bank's CPA to insure that borrowing from the World Bank did not threaten China's balance of payments and because the Ministry of Finance had to become the legal guarantor of these multimillion dollar loans. Similarly, when the UN's program for China began in 1979, the State Council decided that MOFER would handle the UNDP and the United Nations Industrial Development Organization (UNIDO), the State Council's Population Leadership Small Group would handle the UN Fund for Population Activities (UNFPA), and the All-China Association for the Protection of Children (*Quanguo baowei ertong weiyuanhui*) would manage UNICEF. And although the State Council gave MOFER a monopoly on most UN aid in 1981, in 1983 it decided that MOFER could remain the CPA to UNIDO and UNDP, but that ministries that had benefited from UN specialized agencies would become the CPAs for those agencies in China.[25] Almost every ministry, commission, or central organization in China set up foreign affairs offices, departments (*ju*), or sections (*chu*) to handle the donor's activities, or new organizations sought to control or monopolize the flow of goods and services from a specific donor or category of donors.

Although the power of the purse and the ability to set the national priorities for the Five-Year Plans gave the State Planning Commission and the Ministry of Finance (which allocated foreign and domestic capital,

---

24. Even The Gambia, however minute, pushed all donors, particularly NGOs, into one CPA that monitored and controlled foreign aid. See Deborah Brautigam, "State, NGOs, and International Aid in The Gambia," in *The Changing Politics of Non-Governmental Organizations and African States*, ed. Eve Sandberg (New York: Praeger, 1994). According to Robert Meagher, strong states generally control this process, making China's case less than unique. Personal communication.

25. *Dangdai Zhongguo dui wai jingji hezuo* [Contemporary China's external economic cooperation] (Beijing: Chinese Social Sciences Publishing House, 1989), p. 506.

respectively) great influence over which aid projects were approved and would receive counterpart funding, central control was compromised by the distribution of donors among ministries, commissions, bureaus, and professional organizations. The problems of monitoring were endemic, especially as the number of donors and CPAs proliferated. But this strategy also expanded the number of domestic stakeholders in China who supported foreign aid. Had only a few ministries benefited, more opposition to this ideologically charged policy could have emerged. Also, controlling linkage channels in related fields allowed CPAs to strengthen their institutional capacity and increase their ability to deliver services to constituencies in China, and allowed China to compete with other countries for more international assistance.

UNDERSTANDING COUNTERPART AGENCY INTERESTS

The fiscal well-being and long-term survival of a CPA was based on its ability to exploit its position as a channel of global transaction, so how it dealt with foreigners, domestic agencies, and recipients was as much the product of its own defined needs as of those of the Chinese nation. The behavior of CPAs was only loosely monitored by administrative superiors and CPAs also were not subject to public oversight by China's populace; so if foreigners did not complain, CPAs could act as they pleased.[26] As a result, some CPAs used ODA more to build their own institutional capacity than to directly assist recipient units.

Initially, the value of these channels was not clear to China's bureaucrats.[27] In 1971, when Premier Zhou Enlai called a meeting to divide the UN agencies among China's ministries, few participants knew what these agencies did; MOFER had to send a team to the Beijing Municipal Library to find out. Even in 1978, when the Foreign Ministry recommended that the powerful State Planning Commission control all UN activity in China, the State Planning Commission declined this opportunity because it lacked the English speaking staff to deal with the UN. According to one former MOFER employee, "no one wanted to take on this work; it was a burden. No one could see the direct benefits or profits, and the big headache was the amount of paperwork in English; this was really a big headache." But over time, bureaucrats learned the benefits of controlling an aid channel and through the 1980s competition among Chinese agencies over these organizations and their resources intensified.

The authority to allocate global resources gave CPAs certain power. MOFERT's Department of International Relations determined which

26. Dennis Rondinelli, *Development Administration and U.S. Foreign Aid Policy* (Boulder: Lynne Reinner, 1987), p. 179.
27. This paragraph is based on an interview with a former MOFER employee in New York, 1992.

localities could request loans from foreign governments, and permission to do so did not come cheaply. In 1993, an official in Yantai Municipality in Shandong Province told me that in order to request a foreign loan, they had to spend 50,000 RMB on gifts, travel, and writing proposals to lobby the provincial branch of MOFERT and the Department of International Relations in Beijing. One cynical Canadian aid official speculated that MOFERT actually auctioned off Canadian projects to the highest bidder in the Chinese bureaucracy.

CPAs often acted as if they owned projects and the channels through which they flowed. According to one Department of International Relations official, the State Education Commission saw Canadian human resource development projects as "theirs, and they do not let other people participate in them."[28] The right to charge fees for managing projects, which was allocated to some CPAs by the Chinese government, strengthened this ownership-rights consciousness, and so CPAs blocked other bureaus from establishing direct long-term ties with their donor. For example, the Department of International Relations insisted that a Chinese in the foreign affairs office of the State Family Planning Commission who had tried to work directly with UNFPA be fired. Similarly, CICETE strictly controled the allocation of UN Volunteers, which sends older specialists as part of UNDP technical cooperation programs. According to one observer, UN Volunteers is wonderful for expanding CICETE's *guanxi* (relationships). And although CICETE's official authority over the allocation of these volunteers is limited to UNDP projects, they blocked UN Volunteers postings to projects outside the UNDP system, such as to UNESCO, in order to maintain their monopoly over this valuable human resource.

Because so much money in these projects goes to consultants, CPAs tried to stop donors and their executing agencies from employing foreign advisors. The salaries paid to international consultants on aid projects are considerable; on a yearly basis they easily surpass $100,000. Chinese agencies wanted to allocate these opportunities to their own citizens, not to foreigners. Thus CICETE closed down one joint UNDP–World Bank project focusing on water supply and sanitation largely because so much money went to foreign advisors. But CICETE was not alone in this perspective. A Chinese doctor in the Ministry of Public Health involved in this project also complained that after working for ten years on related projects, he could easily manage it; there was no reason to pay a foreigner to run the project.

Conflicts over project ownership increased in the 1990s after the central government cut the subsidies of many state agencies. Now forced to pay their own administrative costs,[29] CPAs saw projects as a way to establish a

---

28. Interview BJDIR, summer 1993.
29. The policy encouraged these agencies to *chuan shou* (earn incomes). Yi-min Lin and Zhanxin Zhang, "Backyard Profit Centers: The Public Assets of Private Agencies," in *Property Rights and Economic Reform in China*, ed. Jean C. Oi and Andrew G. Walder (Stanford: Stanford University Press, 1999), pp. 203–25.

permanent source of capital. For example, as we see later, when the All-China Women's Federation used CIDA aid to poor women to build a fashion center to fund ACWF programs, the Canadian agency resisted.

External Demand and China's Opening to Overseas Development Assistance

The domestic demand for ODA explains only part of the story. The level of internationalization was also determined by the willingness or ability of donors to influence the terms under which they established their program and projects. One critical explanation for the variations in the degree of domestic versus foreign control is the type of donor. Multi-lateral agencies, bilateral agencies, and international NGOs have different constituencies, different levels of funding, and different management styles. Thus, if we characterize the level of Chinese control over the aid process as a continuum, running from very tight control to quite limited control, China exerted the greatest control over multilateral donors, less control over bilateral donors, and the least amount of control over foreign NGOs.

Donors who came to China in the late 1970s and in the 1980s were keen to be there for a host of strategic, economic, institutional, and humanitarian reasons.[30] For example, Canada's Prime Minister Pierre Trudeau, long fascinated with China, had generated considerable strategic thinking in his government about how to get China to open up and become a meaningful geostrategic partner. In line with that goal, aid was seen as an important strategy for Canada "to contribute to China's developmental efforts; to help strengthen the tendency within China towards more open, tolerant policies; and to cultivate China as a partner in development, commerce and international geo-politics."[31] China's potential market also played a role for bilateral donors, although in Canada's case CIDA was careful not to justify the entire program on economic terms, in case the trade benefits did not materialize. Canada also had a specific strategy based on the "multiplication of contacts at the thinking level."[32] By engaging China's current and future leaders in policy dialogues, Canadians hoped to open leaders' minds to the global community and influence future events. "Our

---

30. Japanese aid was intended to foster pro-western forces in China and keep China open. Qingxin Ken Wang, "Recent Japanese Economic Diplomacy in China: Political Alignment in a Changing World Order," *Asian Survey* 32 (June 1993): 625–41. For a study that assesses the relative roles of strategic factors, economic interests, and cultural compatibility as key determinants of aid, see Peter J. Schrader, Steven W. Hook, and Bruce Taylor, "Clarifying the Foreign Aid Puzzle: A Comparison of American, Japanese, French, and Swedish Aid Flows," *World Politics* 50 (January 1998): 294–323. For the humanitarian argument, see Sarah J. Tisch and Michael B. Wallace, *Dilemmas of Development Assistance: The What, Why and Who of Foreign Aid* (Boulder: Westview Press, 1994), p. 84.

31. See CIDA, *China: Country Program Review, 1985–90*, December 1984.

32. Marcel Masse, then president of CIDA, February 1981.

job was to deal much more with changing people's way of seeing the world, and supporting development, rather than disbursing money."[33]

Multilateral agencies, such as the World Bank, and myriad UN agencies could not argue that they were global organizations if they were not in China. They, too, wanted to integrate China into the global community. Robert McNamara, president of the World Bank, had been trying for years to get China to join; in 1979, the managing director of the IMF reportedly told a delegation going to China to "do anything you can" to convince China to join.[34] China's decision to accept UNDP aid was also relatively easy because UNDP officials themselves worked very hard to persuade China to become an aid recipient.[35] For organizations, such as the UNFPA, helping China manage its expanding population size was exactly what the agency was founded to do.

Being involved in China offered donors a China strategy for advancing organizational or individual prestige, influence, and resources. According to Sarah Tisch and Michael Wallace, "donor agencies live with contradictions resulting from their multifaceted agenda to promote their own bureaucratic objectives, advance state political and economic interests, extend humanitarian development aid, and contribute to international stability."[36] China programs increased budgets and consulting opportunities. For example, UN specialized agencies received 13 percent overhead for administering projects, so increasing the scale of aid by moving into China gave UN agencies a dramatic new source of revenues. According to Kim Nossal, Canadian aid maximized the international prestige of policy makers, maintained bureaucratic posts, and limited the costs of foreign policy by spending aid on Canadian firms.[37] The multitude of foreign NGOs that flowed into China beginning in the late 1980s and increasing significantly in the mid-1990s were motivated by similar forces. According to one observer of international NGOs in China, "most of them feel that they ought to be in China. It's part of their legitimacy; if you are a large donor but don't have anything to contribute to the largest country in the world, then that challenges your legitimacy as a donor."[38]

This strong desire to be in China, as well as the emphasis on China's strategic value to the West, helped China in the struggle for control over broad aid agendas and specific projects, weakening the donor's leverage in its negotiations with China and improving the terms of engage-

---

33. Interview with an official who worked on the early China program, Ottawa, Canada, 1994.
34. Jacobson and Oksenberg, *China's Participation in the IMF.*
35. Interview at UN headquarters, New York, 1991.
36. Tisch and Wallace, *Dilemmas of Development Assistance*, p. 84.
37. Kim M. Nossal, "Mixed Motives Revisited: Canada's Interest in Development Assistance," *Canadian Journal of Political Science* 21 (March 1988): 35–56.
38. Interview, BJYN, Beijing, November 1999.

ment.[39] UNDP was reportedly "delighted" when China agreed to accept its aid, and "agreed to practically everything China requested at that time."[40] Particularly in the 1980s, many bilateral and multilateral donors did not press China greatly to alter its policies. As one UNDP official commented, "UNDP is not an NGO, and one must take China's wishes into account. Especially when China defines its wishes so clearly, its harder to say no."[41]

In 1999, one critic of the UN in China still believed that its agencies were unnecessarily docile in their dealings with China. "UN agencies let the Chinese set their agenda and control much of the projects because they want the ear of the government. They are more like diplomatic units, not aid units. This is especially true for UNICEF which never says anything bad about China. . . . They believe they can't control the program, so they just want the government's ear to discuss what they see as sensitive topics. They praise everything in China so that they can express their private concerns about problems."[42]

China's use of force to end the Tiananmen protests altered the attitude and behavior of many bilateral donors. Canadian citizens began to ask why their taxes were being used to support an authoritarian regime that killed its own citizens. To justify the program, CIDA had to increase the pressure on China to accept more sensitive projects, such as those related to good governance, judicial reform, or the promotion of a civil society. After Tiananmen, even the UNDP introduced a more reform-oriented policy agenda.

Changes in the 1990s in the global agenda, particularly the rise of environmental issues and sustainable development, affected the type of projects that donors brought to China, increasing pressure on China to address some issues earlier than they might have otherwise. In particular, in the 1990s, Japan pressed China to accept many more environmental projects under its fourth aid tranche. The UNDP's new emphasis on the global environment and sustainable development also shifted a significant amount of funds into these two categories.

In addition, the arrival of foreign NGOs changed the nature of foreign aid and the internal-external balance. Although many foreign NGOs came in the late 1980s, more entered in the early and mid-1990s. Unlike multilateral or bilateral donors, who begrudgingly accepted the many controls imposed by China's government, NGOs behaved more like network capital,

---

39. States giving aid for political or strategic reasons have much less leverage over the recipient's economic agenda. For example, despite the enormity of its aid program, U.S. strategic interests in Egypt gave the United States little leverage over Egypt's economic reform. Denis J. Sullivan, "Bureaucratic Politics in Development Assistance: The Failure of American Aid in Egypt," *Administration and Society* 23 (May 1991): 29–53.
40. Interview FPASSY, New York, 1991.
41. Interview UNDPBNY, New York, 1991.
42. Interview BJYN, Beijing, November 1999.

in search of strategies for circumventing government controls. By their very nature, these foreign NGOs wanted to go directly to the grassroots and work with social organizations, not state agents. Thus in the 1990s, de facto decentralization occurred in the aid sector, allowing NGOs to work directly with local governments or local agencies and at times to completely ignore all bureaucratic controls.

Regulating the Donors: The Struggle for Control over Foreign Aid

Did CPAs control donor activities in China? To assess their relative strengths, we explore here the overall allocation of funding for the three types of donors, whether foreigners or Chinese were the executing agency for specific projects, whether the foreign donors worked through CPAs or contacted Chinese ministries and local governments directly, and how funding was spent on specific projects.

MULTILATERAL AGENCIES

Of the three donor types—multilateral, bilateral, and foreign NGOs—multilateral agencies were the easiest to control. China was often a member of their governing body, giving it great influence. The scale of multilateral contributions were very large, so China had to be vigilant in protecting its economic sovereignty. The next sections evaluate the level of foreign versus domestic control over the aid process at the UNDP, UNFPA, and World Bank.

United Nations Development Program

In the initial stages of the China program, China did not exercise effective control over UNDP funding because the UN, needing to feed its own agencies, channelled much of the early funding their way. Hoping to gain a share of the initial $15 million aid package established in 1979, Chinese nationals working in UN agencies lobbied their counterpart line ministries in China to propose projects that would channel UN funds to these UN agencies. So, projects proposed by Chinese ministries were warmly received by UNDP, but most funding went to the UN organizations that became the executing agencies for the projects.

China increased control over the content of its first formal Country Program (CP1), designed in late 1981 and early 1982, because it was written in coordination with the State Planning Commission, the Ministry of Finance, and the Ministry of Foreign Affairs. Nevertheless, the UN specialized agencies actively sought a share of the emerging China program. UNIDO and China's industrial ministries prepared a long list of large and well-defined projects and, due to links with the key bureaus in MOFER,

Table 5.4   Budgets for UNDP's Changzhou Entrepreneur's Center

Component	Original Budget		Revised Budget		Change (% of budget)
	Amount (thousand $)	Percentage of Total	Amount (thousand $)	Percentage of Total	
Foreign consultants	294.8	45.5	361.7	48.6	+3.1
Chinese training and Domestic costs	113.5	17.5	95.0	12.8	−4.7
Equipment	203.7	31.3	150.0	20.0	−11.3
Revolving fund	—	—	100.0	13.4	+100.0
Meetings in China	30.0	4.6	0.0	0.0	−100.0
Other miscellaneous	8.0	1.2	38.0	5.1	+3.9
Total budget	650.0	100.0	744.7	100.1	

Source: UNDP Documents, Beijing.

they received a significant number of projects. Again the Chinese line ministries, who had expected that their bureaus would be the executing agencies, "were surprised that after they had made the proposals, the UN agencies got to implement the project."[43]

The history of the Changzhou Entrepreneur's Center illustrated this tendency. Established in 1989 by UNDP and CICETE, the project was controlled by the International Labour Organization (ILO), which was selected over a local cadre management school to train the center's consultants. Although younger officials in CICETE had wanted to run the project, leaders in CICETE and the UNDP decided to make this a model project, and after a UNDP consultant reported that teachers at the cadre management school were poorly trained, the ILO was hired.

This decision ensured that a large amount of funds went to goods and services delivered from overseas (table 5.4). In the original budget, 45.4 percent of the UNDP's total contribution was to be spent on foreign consultants and their travel. Foreign equipment made up 31.3 percent, and 22.1 percent was to be spent on training Chinese inside and outside China. In return, China would supply 3.5 million RMB, primarily on remodeling the facilities for the center. After revisions, the total allocated to foreign consultants increased by 3.1 percent to 48.6 percent, equipment for China was cut by 20.2 percent, and training for Chinese and other expenditures for domestic advisers dropped 4.7 percent. Although part of this reallocation was done to create a revolving fund of $100,000 (13.4% of the budget) to help promote the Changzhou Entrepreneur's

43. Interview FPASSY, New York, 1991.

Center consultancies and improve its sustainability, a foreign agency, the ILO, and consultants in its network were the projects' largest financial beneficiary.

By the mid-1980s, China increased control over it own country program due both to the UNDP's preference for national execution and the aggressive efforts of its CPA, CICETE. Under national execution, the UNDP voluntarily gave up control over its programs to CICETE and other domestic agencies. As articulated by its first resident representative, Nessim Shallon, the UNDP always sought to increase the institutional capacity of organizations in the host country so that they could implement their own programs.[44] Thus by 1990, the share of programs under national execution had increased significantly, reaching 32 percent of all UNDP projects, undermining the influence of the UN specialized agencies. By 1993, it reached 72 percent and by 1996 98 percent.[45] As national execution became more widespread, CICETE took a greater initiative in managing the program. According to one UNDP official, "in the early days of UNDP in China, before government execution, there were less efforts [by UNDP officials] to control the Chinese, but the Chinese were also more willing to listen to the resident director and UNDP's suggestions." Why? "Because as the key to money, he [the resident representative] had a great deal of influence, but now they [CICETE] know the UNDP and the UN system and are not afraid of becoming dependent."[46]

The regional distribution of UNDP aid showed the dominance of CICETE's (and perhaps China's) normative approach to technical transfer and aid. Speaking to the donor's group in Beijing in 1992, Long Yongtu, former deputy director of CICETE and then director general of the Department of International Relations in MOFERT, argued that technical assistance should go to more advanced areas in China, which could best absorb it. Because technical assistance should improve institutional capacity and aid management, the Department of International Relations' "primary emphasis will be to improve the skills of those people who are actively dealing with foreign partners, to make them equal partners with their foreign counterparts." Recognizing that this emphasis on advanced regions "is not in line with the internal policies of all donors," Long noted that aid to advanced areas often expands tax revenues for the central government, which can then increase aid to poor and remote regions.[47] Through 1992, CICETE resisted any focus on poorer regions or poverty alleviation. According to a former UNDP official, "CICETE made it

44. Interview with Nessim Shallon.
45. See United Nations, *Situational Analysis of the UN System in China for 1990–96* (Beijing: United Nations, 1995), p. 10.
46. Interview UNBJRC, 1992.
47. "Report of Donor Meeting," UN Conference Room, Beijing, 1 April 1992.

very clear to the Resident Representative that this issue was not open for discussion."[48]

According to the UNDP's own evaluation, only 10 percent of its resources for its second Country Program (CP2) went to poor provinces and autonomous regions, while most funds were spent in Beijing.[49] Of approximately two hundred projects, 106 or 60.1 percent of the total funding ($163.1 million) for CP2 went to Beijing. No doubt, the UNDP's focus on technical transfer helps explain the program's stress on the wealthier, more advanced areas. As the UNDP report states, CP2 was "heavily focused on the relatively advanced areas of the country which are endowed with greater absorptive capacity both in terms of the qualifications of project personnel and the ability of implementing agencies to live up to counterpart obligations. Because of the relatively advanced nature of the recipient institutions, most projects have emphasized the transfer of sophisticated technologies. As one of the goals of CP2 was the acquisition of high technology for China, this emphasis was appropriate."[50] By 1991–92, however, UNDP wanted to change its priorities for the third Country Program (CP3), arguing that targeting "the poorest sections of the population, and minority groups is both in line with UNDP's mandate and its comparative advantage."[51] Thus, "UNDP should directly assist the most disadvantaged sections of the population" and "concentrate more of its assistance on poorer and remote areas that are as yet unable to absorb technology from elsewhere in China."[52]

This shift in strategy met serious opposition from CICETE. When the UNDP tried to develop a World Bank pilot project that helped poor regions manufacture and install inexpensive water pumps and highly sanitary latrines, CICETE fought back. Why? First, the project employed many foreign advisors. Of a total budget of $494,000, $248,000 (50.1 percent) was allocated for salaries for foreign consultants or their travel.[53] Second, the unit selected as the executing agency was a bureau affiliated with the Ministry of Public Health, not a unit with close ties to CICETE. Third, CICETE may have opposed the use of UNDP funds to create domestic low-technology solutions to development problems; it would have preferred to use the funds to import modern technology. In 1992, UNDP officials in Beijing and foreign officials working on this project criticized CICETE's efforts to insure a continued flow of UNDP technology into

---

48. Interview UNBJRC, 1992.
49. *UNDP Advisory Note on the Third Country Program, for the People's Republic of China, 1991–1995* (Beijing: January 1990), p. 6.
50. Ibid., pp. 5–6.
51. Ibid., p. 12.
52. Ibid., p. 10.
53. *UNDP, Project Document, Low-Cost Rural Water Supply and Sanitation, 1988–1991,* CPR/88/011/A/01/99, p. 32.

China's advanced coastal regions. From their perspective, CICETE wanted to insure that foreign resources went to units that could pay its 3 percent management fee and did not want the UNDP to get involved in poverty alleviation.

However, in the mid-1990s, CICETE's control over the UNDP's agenda weakened. Shifts in UNDP priorities and budgetary allocations, particularly toward environmental protection, sustainable development, and poverty alleviation, altered the context of the CICETE-UNDP debate.[54] In 1995–96, under "its new director general, Gus Speth, the paradigm began to emerge of sustainable human development as UNDP tried to redefine its mandate. Sustainable human development didn't lend itself to technology transfer." Also China's need for technology was being met by massive amounts of FDI, which in 1993 reached $40 billion per year. The UNDP's main donors advocated a socially oriented agenda, focusing on poverty alleviation, education, health—"the places where private investment wasn't giving any help."

This shift in focus at the UNDP allowed a new, more assertive resident representative to change UNDP activities in China. In his passion for poverty alleviation, this UNDP official reportedly had the support of his counterpart at CICETE who was also concerned about social equality and poverty alleviation. According to the resident representative, "here in the PRC [People's Republic of China] bureaucracy you can talk about greater equality and people listen. They are concerned about socialism. I used this argument in 1994–95, even before the new UNDP policy was officially introduced, and the head of CICETE was concerned about helping the poor parts of the country. We had an agreement on this."[55]

Funds were moved from core programs, which remained subject to CICETE's control, into projects funded by the Montreal Protocol and the Global Environment Facility. These monies, according to the Chinese State Council, were to be managed by the National Environmental Protection Agency and the Ministry of Finance, respectively. As we can see from table 5.5, between CP3 (1991–1995) and the Country Cooperation Framework I (1996–2000), the UNDP funds for the core program dropped from 67 percent to 30 percent; the share of funds going to the Global Environment Facility and the Montreal Protocol rose from 22 to 51 percent during this time. Even within the core resources, the amount of funds allocated to the more high-tech sectors favored by CICETE, such as industry, transport, and telecommunications, were ended, while funds going to environmental governance, women, and poverty alleviation increased.

CICETE's influence declined as well due to internal problems. Saddled with over 150 retirees who had worked in the hotel that CICETE had taken

54. This paragraph draws on interview, UNDP1998.int.
55. Ibid.

Tale 5.5 UNDP Core and Noncore Resources, 1991–2000

	Third Country Program (1991–95)		Country Cooperation Framework I (1996–2000)	
	Amount (thousand $)	Percentage	Amount (thousand $)	Percentage
Contributions				
Core	115,045	67	57,542	30
Cost-sharing	19,175	11	37,645	19
Global Environment Facility	14,604	8	48,890	25
Montreal Protocol	24,300	14	50,000	26
TOTAL	173,124	100	194,077	100
Assistance by Sector				
Education and health	5,996	3	5,740	3
Women	300	0	3,305	2
Governance	17,300	10	31,500	16
Sustainable energy	35,979	21	39,810	21
Environment	26,755	15	81,890	41
Agriculture and forestry	34,385	20	10,986	6
Poverty alleviation	2,696	2	14,880	8
Industry, transportation, and telecommunications	49,714	29	—	—
Others and uncommitted	—	—	5,967	3
TOTAL	173,124	100	194,078	100

Source: UNDP, *United Nations Development Programme in China: Sustainable Human Development* (Beijing, August 1998).
Note: UNDP canceled the category of industry, transportation, and telecommunications for its Country Cooperation Framework I.

over as its headquarters in the 1980s, it needed to find new ways to gen-erate income, so, it set up twelve new companies, all of which failed. CICETE's capacity to deliver UNDP programs also declined. According to a UN study in March 1995, "CICETE's project execution capability, expressed as delivered expenditure against project budgets, has steadily deteriorated in the last few years. The decline in execution capacity is evident in the following project delivery rates: 75.6 percent in 1992, 65 percent in 1993, 49 percent in 1994, and an estimated 50 percent for 1995."[56]

In 1997, the UNDP resident representative told me that the UNDP had pulled free of CICETE control. "These days we are much more casual in where we go. . . . I have more flexibility to work outside CICETE, so we do that to the hilt. . . . CICETE doesn't gatekeep a lot of what we do."[57]

56 R. H. Gecolea, "Building National Execution Capacity in China," Consultant Report, UNDP Beijing, cited in United Nations, *Situational Analysis*, p. 11.
57. Interview BJUNDP1998.int.

However, CICETE officials say that significant authority remains in their hands. Although the resident representative had asked several ministries to do projects with the UNDP directly, pulling an end run on CICETE, and had tried to get CICETE to select projects only from either China's Agenda 21 program (its new environmental program) or poverty-alleviation projects, CICETE reportedly resisted, arguing that it had to accept a wide assortment of projects from the line ministries based on the Ninth Five-Year Plan. "We must consult with the State Planning Commission—that is the basic principle of UNDP's agreement with China—and we have to respond to the government's needs and follow the Ninth Five-Year Plan, not follow Agenda 21."[58] Also, under pressure from the Ministry of Foreign Trade and Economic Cooperation (MOFTEC), the ministries did not respond; Long Yongtu may even have told the resident representative to stop these activities. Still with a significant amount of UNDP funding shifting to issue areas other than technology transfer, CICETE's monopoly over the UNDP was over.

United National Fund for Population Activities

Not all UN agencies were as tightly controlled or as passive as the UNDP. The UNFPA was much more assertive and interventionist in pursuing its goal of raising the status of women and insuring that birth control policies were carried out in a humane manner. Its director was proud of having resisted efforts to make CICETE its CPA; when this was first proposed, he threatened to pull UNFPA out of China. As a result, UNFPA worked with the Department of International Relations under MOFERT, in a relationship that increased its flexibility. This more aggressive attitude shows the importance of the resident representative in determining the relationship between the UN agency and the Chinese government. Also, because the services provided by UNFPA—training China to control its population size more effectively—were critical for the Chinese central government and local governments and because UN funding for population control is so political, UNFPA could take tough stands in its negotiations and succeed.[59] For example, because of the risk that they would be used to identify female fetuses (which would then be aborted), UNFPA refused the Ministry of Public Health's request that it buy each county an ultrasound machine. Similarly, the UNFPA rejected any request for modern equipment that did not include a major training component to insure that Chinese personnel would be able to use the equipment effectively. UNFPA also constantly talked with the Chinese government about human rights.

Projects established by UNFPA were also more intrusive, using foreign exchange to challenge the attitudes, norms, and behavior of local govern-

58. Interviews in Beijing, 5 November 1999.
59. Interview, UNFPA, Beijing, 1993.

ment officials toward women. One project stands out—the Women, Population and Development Programme. This program gave four counties a revolving fund of 942,000 RMB to invest in township and county-owned enterprises,[60] but in addition to paying back the loan over three years, local governments had to fulfill several requirements if they wanted access to the loan: donate 4 percent of the value of the original loan to a social development fund to be used by local autonomous women's groups;[61] establish maternal health and family planning centers, including care for pregnant women, day care centers, nutrition programs for children under five, and basic medicine and contraceptive services at the factory and surrounding villages; establish targets to increase the number of women at management and supervisory levels and be accountable for compliance; intensify and regularize seminars on women's rights and welfare; and improve the amenities and services for women in the factory. This way, UNFPA altered the incentives for county governments and improved the quality of life for rural women.

World Bank

The most significant multilateral donor, the World Bank, brought billions of dollars to China. As of the end of 2000, a total of $34.3 billion had been loaned and given as development assistance.[62] Yet it has been tightly controlled by its CPA, the World Bank Bureau in the Ministry of Finance. China has controlled the program because the leaders of the World Bank and the IMF were very keen on having China rejoin the bank and borrow their funds. Despite U.S. government efforts to delay negotiations, the IMF delegation and its Chinese interlocutors who met in 1979 quickly agreed on general principles, and two weeks later the IMF's Executive Board agreed that the government of the People's Republic of China in Beijing, rather than the government of the Republic of China on Taiwan, would occupy the Chinese seat in the IMF. The IMF gave China access to approximately $1 billion in loans with very few conditions, and the World Bank agreed to find uncommitted funds and to identify projects for which the usual feasibility studies could be shortened. In return, China had to provide information on its economy and external finances and accept an IMF decision to disperse some gold to Taiwan.[63]

---

60. See Felicidad L. Villareal, "Creating Positive Synergy: Women, Population and Development," Program on Women, Population and Development, UNFPA, Beijing, China, April 14, 1993, pp. 15–16.
61. Using UN funds to create autonomous women's groups was highly controversial because China greatly resists these kinds of civil society organizations. No doubt, conflict would emerge with the local branch of the ACWF.
62. *World Bank Group in China.*
63. Jacobson and Oksenberg, *China's Participation in the IMF.*

Bank officials stress that China, not the World Bank, controls the agenda. According to Pieter Botellier, one-time chief of the World Bank's Resident Mission in China, "More than anywhere, they have used us and they have always been in the driving seat."[64] Thus, the World Bank avoids antagonizing China. According to one source, in 1998 a critical report on China's social welfare policies was toned down under pressure from the Chinese government before it was published as the *China 2020* book on health financing. Similarly, a World Bank official I interviewed in February 1998 stonewalled the interview, refusing to admit any differences between the World Bank and the Chinese, despite a well-informed observer's having told me of a major issue. In a throwback to the days when China was closed, a Chinese citizen from the World Bank's Public Affairs Office took notes of the entire conversation. Other Chinese World Bank employees confirm that the Bank is quite secretive about its dealings with China, particularly about any problems it faces.

Given the large scale of the borrowing available under the World Bank's China program and the Ministry of Finance's responsibility to guarantee these loans in hard currency, China was wise to keep control over the World Bank's program by running all projects through the World Bank Bureau in the Ministry of Finance. In this way, it avoided any serious foreign debt crisis, which could have increased the IMF's leverage over China's domestic and foreign economic policies. Also, because large-scale infrastructure projects need significant complementary funding, World Bank projects have to fit into China's overall planned allocation of investment and capital. According to a World Bank official, the scale of the loans meant that the State Planning Commission, more than the Ministry of Finance, was the Bank's real interlocutor, and the State Planning Commission is a difficult negotiator.

Nevertheless, the World Bank does not always check its China projects very carefully. According to an official from an agricultural college in central China, before the World Bank's investigation group visited his school, officials there wrote the report that the college's World Bank project director was to read to World Bank officials. Other school officials were warned not to say anything to the World Bank officials about the project, other than to praise it. Yet, according to this Chinese citizen, who was deeply troubled by this state of affairs, World Bank officials simply accepted the report and made no serious effort to check its validity.

The history of Rural Structural Adjustment Loan (RSAL), given to China in the mid-1980s, illustrates that the World Bank was, at times, more interested in getting China to accept its funds than it was in monitoring how China used them. In 1987, a World Bank economist working on China

64. In "World Bank: China 'Always in the Driving Seat,'" *China Development Briefing* 1 (March 1996): 5. Of the $22 billion dispersed by mid-1997, $13.7 billion were commercial loans, and $8.4 billion were interest free, repayable over thirty-five years.

proposed a $300 million loan and that the 1.2 billion RMB earned from the sale of imported fertilizer, pesticide, and other products be used to cushion China through difficult reforms in agricultural prices, marketing, and rural finance. According to a World Bank official, such policy loans are "a sophisticated form of bribery to get countries to deregulate their agricultural sectors."[65]

However, unlike RSALs for most less-developed countries, which give the World Bank the leverage to introduce reforms, the World Bank viewed China's macroeconomic policies, its lack of public sector debt, and its exchange rate as quite positive.[66] Instead, this loan was seen "by both the PRC government and Bank staff to be a positive reinforcement for a job already well done."[67] The World Bank did not place strong restrictions on the use of the funds, although some World Bank officials believed that conditions would be useful. In fact, the perception in China was that the World Bank did not care how the money was used.[68] The World Bank did try to dictate which products should be purchased with the loan, "but the funds, once they come into the country are called a 'counterpart loan' and are not controlled by us."[69]

The funds went to support reform experiments that were already underway, as well as some new experiments. The World Bank's implementing agency, the Research Centre on Rural Development (RCRD), under the State Council and its Development Institute, was already managing a program, approved by the State Council and the Party Secretariat, to carry out rural restructuring in nineteen experimental zones, focusing on land holdings, rural finance, grain production and marketing, TVE ownership structure, and structures of rural cooperation.[70] But some officials in the Development Institute had long wanted to set up an investment company to finance rural infrastructure and, now that they had the foreign cash, they established the company. Although some ministries challenged the company because the Ministry of Finance had to put up 20 million RMB as initial capitalization, a loan of $200 million was a strong incentive for the Ministry of Finance; so the State Council established the China Agribusiness Trust and Investment Corporation (CATIC), whose official function was to provide financial services to the rural informal sector.[71]

65. UNDPWSSP.in3, 1993.
66. World Bank, "Policy-Based Lending in Agriculture: Rural Sector Adjustment in The People's Republic of China" (unpublished and undated report), p. 16.
67. Ibid.
68. Interview no.1, RCRDWB, 1990.
69. Interview WBBE, July 1990.
70. See Guowuyuan nong yan zhongxin shiyan qu bangongshi [State Council Rural Research Centre's Experimental Zone Office], *Gaige shijian lu* [A recording of the experience of reform] (Beijing: Zhongguo zuoyue chuban gongsi, 1990), p. 19.
71. The company was originally called the China Rural Investment and Trust Corporation.

Interviews suggest that the World Bank did not try to influence the way the funds were used. In a conversation with Du Runsheng, head of the RCRD and Zhao's leading advisor on agriculture, a vice-president of the World Bank reportedly said that "China is a very big country, and the World Bank cannot use a small amount of money to force China to do anything. This is your reform and we just support your plan."[72] This statement, repeated to top Chinese leaders, Yao Yilin and Li Peng, created high-level support for the loan. Also, despite strong concerns that the distribution of funds to China had proceeded too quickly and that some penalties for non-compliance should be introduced, and despite the fact that this loan ran counter to the emerging trend in the World Bank that large loans be given over time in tranches so that compliance could be monitored, no conditionality was imposed because some World Bank officials feared that Chinese leaders would be insulted and reject the loan altogether.[73] Leverage was claimed to exist in the idea of a second RSAL which, it was argued, would insure China's compliance. Clearly, persuading China to accept the loan was a top World Bank priority, which essentially left China free to act as it wished.

There were problems, however, with how the funds were used. Of the initial $100 million, valued at 400 million RMB, CATIC took 300 million RMB and gave 100 million RMB to the experimental zones. Of the second $200 million, $100 million also went to CATIC and $100 million went to the Ministry of Finance to deal with China's financial crisis of summer 1988. Thus almost 60 percent of the loan went to CATIC, and only 8 percent went to the Experimental Zones Office. CATIC then loaned millions of renminbi to an automobile factory, which in return sold CATIC cars at a discount. CATIC resold these cars to pay the World Bank for the loan. CATIC reportedly also loaned 100 million RMB to a clothing factory in central China and developed property in Hainan Province. The World Bank reportedly did not lodge a complaint, but Tian Jiyun, a Politburo member responsible for agriculture, pressured CATIC to recall the funds. Thereafter, CATIC was more careful; however, in 1997, fifteen of its officials were arrested for corruption and bad investments and the trust company was closed.

The 100 million RMB that went to the Experimental Zone Office was used to sustain agricultural experiments that had been under way for eighteen months, such as price liberalization, which needed financial support so that floating agricultural prices did not generate unrest. In fall 1988, however, when conservative leaders reined in the economy, cash-strapped localities inundated the Development Institute with less-than-exemplar proposals covering an assortment of reform initiatives. The Experimental

72. Interview no. 1, RCRDWB, 1990.
73. World Bank, "Policy-Based Lending in Agriculture," p. 15.

Zone Office then expanded the initial fourteen sites to nineteen and quickly disbursed over 80 percent of funds. Rather than link the loan to specific topics and then offer the funds to localities that tried such experiments, it simply gave the funds to localities that promised some future reform. According to one observer, these reformers "were not very familiar with how to use this money."[74] In fact, the rapid disbursement of foreign exchange under the RSAL so surprised World Bank officials that they reevaluated their earlier enthusiasm. In its own analysis, the World Bank admitted that "the attraction of moving forward on policy-based lending in China may have convinced the Bank to compromise its own policies,"[75] allowing China to dominate the allocation of funds entirely.

Similarly, China, not the World Bank, determined the content of the World Bank's program with the SEDC that supports higher education. Although World Bank policy stresses primary school and nonformal education,[76] China insisted that three of nine education loans go to higher education, with the first university loan program going to China's elite universities. According to Hayhoe, "China's success in persuading bank advisers to concentrate so many loans in higher education is rather remarkable given the bank's educational lending policies."[77]

Despite these cases, the World Bank did insure that its projects reflected the World Bank's commitment to resolving rural poverty established by McNamara in the 1970s.[78] To do so, however, it had to move more of its projects into the inland regions. To the World Bank's credit, the data show that as of mid-1997, 52 percent of aid went to noncoastal regions (figure 5.1). Similarly, David Denny found that the World Bank had a regional orientation almost exactly opposite to private investors, favoring poorer parts of China.[79] Perhaps Long Yongtu's suggestion that infrastructure loans go to inland regions (and technology imports go to the coast) explains this investment in poor areas. In 1998, a key conflict revolved around China's refusal to use International Bank for Reconstruction and Development (IBRD) loans, which must be repaid with interest, for social development, particularly in poorer regions. Previously, China had used only IDA funds, which are interest free, on social sector development, but with China on the verge of losing its eligibility for IDA funding, World Bank

---

74. Interview no. 1, RCRDWB, 1990.
75. World Bank, "Policy-Based Lending in Agriculture," p. 23.
76. Robert L. Ayres, *Banking on the Poor: The World Bank and World Poverty* (Cambridge, Mass.: MIT Press, 1983), pp. 5–6.
77. Hayhoe, *China's Universities and the Open Door*, p. 161.
78. Ayres, *Banking on the Poor.*
79. David Denny, "Regional Economic Differences During the Decade of Reform," in Joint Economic Committee, U.S. Congress, *China's Economic Dilemmas in the 1990s: The Problems of Reforms, Modernization, and Interdependence* (Washington, D.C.: U.S. Government Printing Office, 1991), pp. 202–4.

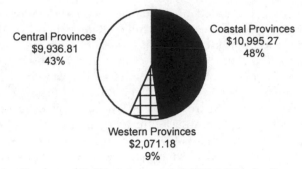

Figure 5.1   Regional Distribution of World Bank Projects in China, 1981–1997 (million$)

Note: Coastal provinces include Guangxi, Guangdong, Fujian, Jiangsu, Shandong, Hainan, Liaoning, Hebei, and the municipalities of Shanghai and Tianjin. Western provinces include Gansu, Ningxia, Qinghai, Xinjiang, Guizhou, and Shaanxi. There were no data for Tibet. Central provinces include Anhui, Shanxi, Inner Mongolia, Jilin, Heilongjiang, Jiangxi, Henan, Hunan, Hubei, Sichuan, Yunnan, and the municipality of Beijing.

officials were deeply concerned that China would stop using its funds for poverty alleviation and social welfare projects.[80]

In the distribution of World Bank loans to universities, with 185 participating universities, 48.6 percent of the projects went to the central and interior provinces, 25 percent went to coastal provinces, and another 25 percent went to Beijing, Shanghai, and Tianjin.[81] But because the SEDC officials involved in these loans were imbued with Maoist egalitarianism and concerns for China's less developed regions,[82] this outcome may be due as much to the values of China's officials as to the fulfillment of the World Bank's goals. Also, since the 1950s, China had actively developed tertiary education in inland cities, such as Wuhan, Chengdu, and Xian, so the distribution of funds to top universities naturally went to these inland cities.

BILATERAL DONORS

Bilateral donors need to convince taxpayers that aid is beneficial to their national interests and to channel a large part of their funding to their own national NGOs in order to develop a constituency of stakeholders in their overall aid program. But bilateral arrangements were negotiated with China's Ministry of Foreign Trade, and national governments were legally bound by these arrangements. If they tried to move outside those agreements, the Chinese government could limit their activities. Also, in the 1980s, many countries were very positive toward China, so they willingly

80. Interview with World Bank official, February 1998.
81. Hayhoe, *China's Universities and the Open Door*, p. 169.
82. Ibid., pp. 164–65.

helped China in those sectors that China considered as it own priorities. CIDA felt bound by its Memorandum of Understanding on development assistance, so it accepted projects proposed by MOFERT as long as they fit the bilaterally determined guidelines. According to a CIDA official, "We are more responsive, reactive, to the Chinese requests, all through the 1980s, even up to now. . . . All those projects were what we would call 'responsive'; the Chinese give us many proposals and we responded to them. . . . This is why we call it development 'cooperation,' rather than development assistance."[83]

Nevertheless, the case of CIDA shows that although bilateral agencies must mesh their overall development program with China's interests—otherwise China will not accept the program—the allocation of funds under specific projects is often greatly affected by the donor country. The Canadian program was greatly influenced by the goal of using its funds to strengthen the capacity of Canada's NGOs to compete globally and to give these agencies some financial support. Thus, whenever possible, CIDA tried to appoint a Canadian Executing Agency, even though doing so might anger the Chinese. What follows are three case studies of CIDA projects, with the key focus on who controlled the project.

Management Training Centers
The development of two management centers built with CIDA funds, one in Chengdu, capital of Sichuan Province, called the Canada-Chengdu Management Training Center (CCMTC), and a second in Hefei, Anhui Province, called the Anhui Management Development Center (AMDC), were projects for which the Canadian Executing Agencies controlled the flow of funds very tightly and insured that much of the money was spent on Canadian advisors and strengthening Canadian NGOs.

In Chengdu, through the first two of three project cycles, "the Canadians kept complete control over those funds and decided on their own which projects would and would not be run."[84] According to the project's termination report, the Canadian executing agency, the Association of Community Colleges of Canada (ACCC) was in the driver's seat: "Administrative and financial control rested with the ACCC until the end of the project."[85] So, although the CCMTC wanted consultants from China or Hong Kong, who were cheaper than foreign experts, "ACCC needed to keep sending people from the community colleges."[86] The Chinese side learned to work within these constraints and still gain important financial

83. Interview FFX-CIDA-1993.
84. Interview Chengdu no. 4, 1993.
85. Joan Bell, "Chengdu Enterprise Development Project—Phase III," *CIDA Asia Branch Termination Report*, November 1996, p. 6.
86. Interview, Chengdu no. 4, 1993.

benefits from the Canadian funds. How? CCMTC translated the foreign advisors and their large salaries into direct financial returns by pushing for more short-term training programs whose international content could attract many Chinese participants and their tuition fees.

But in phase III, as the end of Canadian support loomed, CIDA invested more in sustainable income-generating activities, such as a Consulting Office, which increased the share of project funds spent in China (see table 5.6). Under phase III, CIDA committed CDN$107,000 for the Consulting Office, of which 60 percent (CDN$77,134) went to promote its services, and only 29 percent (CDN$30,178) went to Canadian trainers. Significant funding went to developing personnel management (CDN$62,505) and other administrative skills (CDN$133,610), including a database and library facilities (CDN$229,568).

Still, of a total budget of CDN$4.3 million, 22.2 percent went to in-Canada project management, 21.9 percent went to salaries for Canadian management in China, and another 12.2 percent went to Canadians for consulting, training, and teaching the Chinese. In total, almost 59 percent of funds went directly to Canadians and only 41 percent went to Chinese.

The second center, AMDC, received no money from Canada. According to its Chinese director, the Fund for International Training, the Canadian executing agency, controlled all the money—"they like money so the money goes to F.I.T."[87] In return, the Fund for International Training helped AMDC become a modern, open-minded training center running management courses that meshed with China's domestic needs. Thus AMDC controlled the content of the training; this was acceptable to its leader who believed that "if I can control the content, then I can make money."[88]

Coastal Open Cities Project

Under the Coastal Open Cities Project (COCP), a significant amount of funds were used to support Canadian NGOs. The main executing agency was the Federation of Canadian Municipalities (FCM), a lobbying group for Canadian cities whose leaders in the mid-1980s decided that to thrive, it had to help Canadian cities market their management skills overseas. According to the first mid-term review of this project, "the most apparent impact of the project has been on FCM."[89] International projects dramatically increased FCM's workforce—by 1993, one-third of its employees worked on international projects—and strengthened its links with its

87. Interview of staff at AMDC, June 1993.
88. Ibid.
89. Jackson and Associates, "Common Understanding, Common Benefit: Report of the Mid-Term Evaluation of the Chinese Open Cities Project, Phase I," E. T. Jackson and Associates, Ltd., Ottawa, 1991, p. 137.

Table 5.6   Canada-Chengdu Management Training Center, Estimated Budget, Phase III, 1991–1996 (CND$)

Items	Amount
Funds Allocated in Canada or to Canadians	
In-Canada Project Management	956,782
In-China Project Management (to support Canadian co-manager and project officer and Canadian consultants, teachers, staff, specialists)	943,775
Project consultants (Canadian) and resource persons (in China)	225,916
Joint Project Steering Committee meetings (in Canada)	90,411
Canadian consultants and office	30,178
Canadian management; training specialists to strengthen center administration	23,920
Canadian-taught programs (in China)	
salaries	131,700
expense allowance for Canadian teachers	116,287
Funds Allocated in China or to Chinese	
Strengthen consulting services	77,134
Equipment (source not necessarily from Canada)	720,000
Develop personnel management	62,505
Strengthen management and administration skills	133,610
Publications and library	229,568
Research and development training	32,629
Faculty training	
in China	175,139
abroad or in Canada	38,756
Academic/administrative support services (including staff in China)	22,165
General support staff	87,995
Office printing equipment	81,000
Publicity and promotion	87,800
Joint Project Steering Committee meetings (in China)	26,067
Total Budget	
Total funds allocated to Canadians or in Canada	2,527,969
Funds to Canadians (% of total budget)	59
Total funds allocated to Chinese or in China	1,774,368
Funds to Chinese (% of total budget)	41

Source: Joan Bell, "Chengdu Enterprise Development Project–Phase III," (Project 282/16723) 1991–1996, *CIDA Asia Branch Termination Report*, November 1996.
Note: This table is in Canadian dollars, which were worth .87 U.S. dollars in 1991, when this budget was established. See http://www.bankofcanada.ca/en/exchange-avg.htm.

constituents because the projects expanded the cities' global business opportunities. International projects also improved staff quality; it could not fire long-time employees, but new programs, with higher salaries, brought in new talented people.[90]

Another key beneficiary was the Canada-China Business Council (CCBC), whose role is to promote Canadian business interests in China. According to one observer, "a big chunk of their revenue is this project."[91] Unlike the U.S.–China Business Council, which has thousands of members, the CCBC cannot survive as a consulting firm, and without CIDA's support the CCBC might have closed down. "CCBC is always in trouble because they don't make enough on revenues, so CIDA was using its money to support CCBC to develop a more active profile."[92]

This project funneled CIDA money to the CCBC (table 5.7). In 1991, over 50 percent of CCBC's total revenue (part A) came from its services to members and nonmembers, and in 1990 45 percent did. Yet as part B shows, final revenue (revenue – expenses) from the COCP project in 1991 (CDN$179,042) was 48 percent of the total final revenue from services to members and nonmembers (CDN$375,355). Similarly, in 1990, final revenue (CDN$130,809) was 40 percent of the total final revenue from these services (CDN$321,680). These are enormously high rates of profit, which strongly suggest that CIDA was paying CCBC far more than it needed to for this project. Yet, even with these subsidies, CCBC made only CDN$25,843 in 1990, and lost CDN$51,381 in 1991.

The project helped the CCBC station another person in China—the Chinese counterpart for the COCP project paid his housing costs—and paid part of the CCBC's office rent. Also, to help CCBC build its consulting practice in Beijing, the home office told its Beijing staff members to spend at least half their time consulting on trade projects but not tell the FCM.

In 1995, FCM officials convinced CIDA that the CCBC's role was no longer important. According to CIDA officials, by 1997 CCBC's participation was seen in retrospect to have been the result of some internal intrigue between CIDA and the CCBC, and all along CCBC had been struggling for an identity in the project.[93] Nevertheless, in 1997 it still got a monthly stipend from the project and was involved in project events. CIDA wanted to keep this stakeholder afloat.

Yet the COCP shows how a powerful Chinese CPA can influence the allocation of funding for bilateral projects. The key Chinese CPA was the Special Economic Zone Office (SEZO) of the State Council. Canadians hoped that by working with SEZO, which drafted policy on international-

90. Interview CIDACOCP.in2, 1993.
91. Interview CIDACOCP.in1, 1993.
92. Ibid.
93. Interview CIDACOCP.in7, 1997.

Table 5.7   Role of Coastal Open Cities Project in the Canada-China Business Council Budget, 1990–1991 (CDN$)

A. Revenue, Expenses, and Budgetary Surplus

	1991	1990
Revenue		
Membership Fees	181,644	174,681
Services to members and nonmembers[a]	375,355	321,680
Federal government grant	150,000	200,000
Miscellaneous	3,592	17,521
Total revenue	710,591	713,882
Expenses	761,972	688,039
Excess (deficiency) of revenue over expenses	(51,381)	25,843

B. Services to Members and Nonmembers

	COCP	Other Projects	Seminars and Services	Research Proposal	Total
1991					
Revenue	261,336	215,179	25,954	74,302	576,771
Expenses	82,294	77,758	19,470	21,894	201,416
Final Revenue	179,042	137,421	6,484	52,408	375,355
1990					
Revenue	244,155	276,431	10,563	—	531,149
Expenses	113,346	85,257	10,866	—	209,469
Final Revenue	130,809	191,174	−303	—	321,680

Source: Canada-China Trade Council Annual Report, 1991.
Note: COCP, Coastal Open Cities Project. Table is in Canadian dollars, which were worth .86 U.S. dollars in 1990 and .87 U.S. dollars in 1991. See http://www.bankofcanada.ca/en/exchange-avg.htm.
[a] Minus expenses; see part B.

ization for the State Council and prepared cities for internationalization, Canada could influence China's urban development on issues such as environmental protection, urban planning, and foreign trade, in which Canada had comparative advantage.

Despite these diverse interests, there were few disputes over budgetary reallocations on this project because CIDA, FCM, and SEZO all wanted to spend more money on the mayors' tours to Canada. These tours helped SEZO manage relations with cities and provinces in China by dispensing overseas trips to its major constituency, the mayors of open cities. According to one observer, "everyone in their own system needs a stick and a carrot, and Canada provided the carrot for SEZO."[94] SEZO strengthened its ties with top ministries and commissions in Beijing by placing them on

94. Interview CIDACOCP.in3, 1993.

Table 5.8   Budgets for CIDA's Coastal Open Cities Project, 1988–1992

| Component | Original Budget | | Revised Budget | | Change (% of budget) |
	Amount (thousand CDN$)	Percentage of Total	Amount (thousand CDN$)	Percentage of Total	
Project management	1,982.5	28.3	2,138.5	30.5	+2.2
Study tours in Canada	953.5	13.6	1,740.0	24.9	+11.3
Training in Canada	830.0	11.9	1,490.5	21.3	+9.4
Seminars, lectures, workshops in China	1,595.0	22.8	896.0	12.8	−10.0
Support to twinnings	528.8	7.5	329.0	4.7	−2.8
Training advisor	100.0	1.4	146.0	2.1	+0.7
Audiovisual[a]	895.3	12.8	—	—	—
Conferences in China[a]	115.0	1.6	260.0	3.7	−10.7
TOTAL[b]	7,000.1	99.9	7,000.0	100.0	

Source: Data collected from CIDA documents.
Note: Table is in Canadian dollars which were worth approximately .86 U.S. dollars in 1990. See http://www.bankofcanada.ca/en/exchange-avg.htm.
[a] For the revised budget, CIDA combined audiovisual and conferences into a new category called Training and Business Development. Therefore the decrease of 10.7 percent is for both categories.
[b] Totals are slightly off due to rounding.

the project's Joint Planning Steering Committee and inviting them to meetings in Canada every other year. Finally, SEZO wanted to teach mayors and urban administrators in newly opened cities novel ways to manage their cities. In fact, as the number of open areas increased and SEZO faced an ever-increasing demand for overseas travel and training, it tried to halve the four-month training course under the program in order to double the number of people they could send overseas. The Canadians, however, rejected this idea, arguing that the quality of the training was as important as the quantity of people trained.

So after a 1991 evaluation report, the mayors' study tours received 11.3 percent more funding (table 5.8). Also, despite Tiananmen and defections by Chinese on many CIDA projects, training in Canada jumped 9.4 percent. These two components now totaled over 45 percent of project funds. The rise in project management also reflected the desire to expand study tours because CIDA had underestimated the costs of managing such tours. As a result, cutting CDN$700,000 from seminars, lectures, and workshops in China and canceling the audiovisual equipment generated no opposition from SEZO.

One conflict was over the project's geographic spread, but this issue was resolved in a manner acceptable to both sides. Recognizing that there was little to show after the first round of the project, CIDA tried to decrease the number of target municipalities. However, this effort came just as cities from Nanjing to Chongqing were opened following the 1992 internation-alization of the entire Yangzi River. So SEZO was under domestic pressure to expand the number of cities in phase II from 22 to 88. CIDA responded with a new concept—city regions—which shrank the total number of targets to fewer than 22, even as SEZO became free to expand project activities to many small cities in each region.[95] Thus a project team succeeded in getting "the number of cities both down and up."[96]

SEZO prevented Canada from linking directly with other domestic agencies on this project. When the FCM suggested farming out part of the project to the Ministry of Urban Construction's Mayor's Association because it was an appropriate counterpart to FCM, the idea went nowhere. In fact, some Canadians explained SEZO's preference for trade over urban development as a strategy to keep the Ministry of Urban Construction at bay. Similarly, SEDC, SEZO's co-executing agency under the original Memorandum of Understanding, was squeezed out of the project entirely. According to one insider, SEZO wanted to maximize the amount of Canadian funds available for the mayors' tours—the project's most valuable contribution to SEZO's *guanxi* building efforts—and limit CIDA investments in any SEDC university.[97]

SEZO tightly controlled the twinning relationships between Canadian and Chinese cities. Although coastal cities in China had hoped to establish direct relationships with their Canadian counterparts, and to arrange funds and training programs without SEZO, all twinning activities proposed by the Chinese had to go through SEZO, which then presented them to FCM.

Canadians recognized SEZO's influence over the project. "SEZO has a veto power over everything,"[98] remarked one Canadian, and even FCM officials admitted that "we push the Chinese, but we realize in the final analysis, on the big issues, the decisions will lean in their favor."[99] Despite CIDA's desire to restructure the project in phase II, one observer commented that "the project goes on at the pleasure of the Chinese."[100]

Canada-China Women in Development
The Canada-China Women in Development (CCWID) project shows how China's changing political economy pushed the Chinese beneficiary

---

95. Interestingly, when a new CIDA project officer took over the project in 1993, the FCM did not inform him that the geographic spread of the project had been an issue, so he did not protest when SEZO expanded the number of cities that were sending mayors on the study tours.
96. Interview CIDACOCP.int8, 1997.
97. Interview CIDACOCP.in2, 1993.
98. Interview CIDACOCP.in2, 1993.
99. Interview CIDACOCP.in1, 1993.
100. Interview CIDACOCP.in8, 1997.

to fight vigorously over the allocation of Canadian funds for China. Facing major budget cuts, and under pressure to develop income-earning activities, the ACWF (All-China Women's Federation) saw the funds available under this project as a marvelous opportunity to secure its own long-term development. But to do so, it needed to control where funds were spent.

Thus the struggle between CIDA and the ACWF over the executing agency figured prominently in this case. ACWF wanted to handle the project itself, fearing that too much money would be spent on a foreign chief technical advisor. But although CIDA "forced it [the ACCC] down the throat of ACWF,"[101] the insertion of a Canadian executing agency caused "a certain tension in the project and perhaps has resulted in the ACWF taking less ownership of the project than it might have otherwise."[102] Rather than placing the CCWID project office under its International Liaison Department, which managed aid projects, the ACWF banished it to a rented space down the road from ACWF headquarters. The ACWF codirector did not work in the project office, but stayed instead in her ACWF office. This physical and psychological distance reflected both the ACWF's desire to keep foreigners entirely out of the ACWF and their revenge for Canadian insistence that the project have both a Canadian executing agency and a Canadian chief technical advisor on site in Beijing.[103]

The Chinese also won an intense battle over the ACWF's desire to use 50 percent of the CND$2.2 million CCWID fund, earmarked for medium-size projects, to set up a garment center in Beijing, complete with fashion design facilities, production facilities, and a training center. CIDA officials, who had wanted to reject the garment factory as a traditional women's project involving little poverty alleviation,[104] had always avoided telling the Chinese a flat no.[105] Instead, at each Joint Project Steering Committee Meeting they asked for a feasibility study for the center, which the Chinese took as form of assent.[106] But, "unless you really say a flat square no, which would be very undiplomatic, and even if they know that you are saying no, they keep coming at it over and over. . . . So at the beginning, the early

---

101. CCWID, int.1, 1994.
102. Jackson and Associates, *Common Understanding, Common Benefit*, p. 7.
103. ACWF officials said that they needed to separate the project office, with its income-generating potential, from the International Liaison Department, which had social welfare functions, because they feared criticism by conservative elements in the ACWF that they were using foreign funds to promote business projects. So the project was placed within the Women in Development/Rural Development section, which according to ACWF norms was allowed to explore business opportunities for women.
104. Jackson and Associates, *Common Understanding, Common Benefit*, p. 13.
105. CCWID interview no. 1, 1994, p. 23.
106. Most Chinese feasibility studies do not determine whether a project will go forward; rather they are done after a project has been approved to justify the decision. See Samuel Ho, "Technology Transfer to China during the 1980s: How Effective? Some Evidence from Jiangsu," *Pacific Affairs* 70 (spring 1997): 85–106.

decision was something like, 'these projects need feasibility studies, and for us approval is conditional on a positive conclusion of the feasibility study.' Their interpretation was, well, we just have to write the feasibility study and the Canadians will be happy."[107] In fact, following the request for a feasibility study the Chinese began to invest in the project, buying land and hiring eighty people. Moreover, the feasibility study, done by the CCMTC in Chengdu, downplayed the factory's role in the project, emphasizing the training component, even though 30 percent of project funds would go to buy machinery and cloth for the plant. It never listed where the poor trainees would come from or how they would use their newly learned skills. It presented only a very minimal market survey, although it recognized the highly competitive nature of the textile and apparel industry. Its primary purpose was to explain what the report called, the "necessary" nature of the project.[108]

The ACWF trapped the Canadians into accepting this fait accompli. "Had we said a flat 'no' . . . , I think we would have compromised the whole project, the whole relationship and everything. . . . By the time it's on your desk, and they've spent money and all that, it's very hard to say no. They know how to corner you."[109] So Canadian officials decided to redesign the project, hold their noses, hoping it did not become a disaster, and then let the ACWF go forward.

Although the ACCC, which developed the CCMTC, ran this project as well, the majority of project funds were spent in China for four reasons. First, although the project originally included long-term study in Canada, after Tiananmen the ACWF so feared defections that they refused to send unmarried women overseas even for short study tours; so overseas study or training was set aside.[110] Second, because it was more relevant for women from inland regions to see how women in coastal China managed projects and asserted themselves than to learn about the conditions and efforts of women in Canada, the Canadian project director favored in-China training. Third, the CCWID Development Fund, which made up 44 percent of project funding, by its very nature had to be spent in China, and, given the small scale of most projects, could not support overseas components that would have transferred funds to Canadians. Finally, most of the institutional strengthening component (table 5.9), in particular training ACWF cadres and trainers, went to train women in less developed parts of China. Only training CCWID staff and technical assistance involved monies for foreigners or for overseas travel.

107. CCWID interview no. 1, 1993.
108. Feasibility Study on the Project of China Women and Children Garment Centre, by Consulting International, China Enterprises Management Training Centre at Chengdu, 1 April 1993, p. 28.
109. CCWID, interview no. 6, 1993.
110. Ibid.

Table 5.9   Canada-China Women in Development Budget, 1992 (CND$)

Inception mission		20,989
Women in Development Fund		2,065,765
Institutional strengthening		1,417,750
training ACWF cadres	627,700	
training ACWF trainers	445,800[a]	
training CCWID project office staff[b]	184,840	
technical assistance[c]	159,415	
Project management		1,161,080
in China	499,350	
in Canada	348,015	
other[d]	273,560	
TOTAL		4,665,584

Source: "Management Plan: Canada-China Women in Development Project, August 15, 1992," Canadian International Development Agency, p. 25.

Note: ACWF, All-China Women's Federation; CCWID, Canada-China Women in Development. The Canadian dollar was worth .83 U.S. dollars in 1992. See http://www.bankofcanada.ca/en/exchange-avg.htm.

[a] Increased subsequently to CDN $550,100.

[b] Training included 16 months of study abroad for two candidates, as well as study tours and training programs mainly in China. Experts who gave training are all from within China.

[c] Primarily consultants from outside China or expatriates living in China.

[d] Overheads of 53% and 30% for miscellaneous services, plus federal sales tax.

The ACWF influenced the regional distribution of these funds. Despite CIDA's preference for empowering women in poor parts of China, the ACWF also allocated funds to wealthy regions, reflecting its need to share monies uniformly. According to CIDA officials, "We had a confrontation at a very early stage over the fact that they wanted one project per province. They wanted to be able to give out rewards and they saw these things as rewards, including the travel. To give each province a separate pot was their way of dispensing the goods. Of course, we didn't see it that way at all. We wanted to focus on fewer provinces. We didn't want to have any geographic limitations apart from the smaller spread. We wanted to choose on the basis of good proposals and what was good development and good aid. We were constrained from doing that because they wanted to distribute the 'goodies' equally."[111] The ACWF countered that even richer provinces had poor regions deserving support. So when it wrote the Guiding Principles of the CCWID Project in Chinese for its Chinese constituency, it added the

111. Ibid.

statement that "isolated and poor areas existed not only in poor provinces and cities but in rich provinces and cities as well."[112] Once approved by both sides, this document justified distributing a project to each province.

The three case studies presented here suggest that there is no uniform pattern to who controls bilateral aid projects. But the dynamics are clear. The Canadians entered these projects with a collaborative mindset, but tried to maintain as much control as possible over the allocation of funds in order to maximize the flow of Canadian resources to Canadian NGOs. Still, when the Chinese side pressed, the Canadians yielded rather than harm ties with their Chinese counterparts.

INTERNATIONAL NONGOVERNMENTAL ORGANIZATIONS

Although China tightly regulated multilateral agencies, and channeled the actions of bilateral donors, it had less success controlling international nongovernmental organizations (international NGOs). Unlike the UNDP or the World Bank, China is not a powerful member of these organizations' boards, nor is the relationship constrained by government-to-government protocol, which limits the flexibility of bilateral donors. No doubt, most international NGOs that entered China after a long hiatus worked closely with the Chinese government in selecting their projects. In some cases, they simply gave the funds to a Chinese organization and then worked with it to establish the program. But some international NGOs that entered China in the 1990s were committed to linking directly with the society, were relatively resolute about doing so, and, in fact, were much freer in selecting their own CPAs, if they selected one at all.

International NGOs were particularly threatening to China. Most international NGOs came from the "northern" or developed world and challenged China to alter its domestic political arrangements.[113] They advocated expanding civic participation in development projects and worked to strengthen civil society organizations that could threaten local government's monopoly on services. They pointed up the government's inability to resolve the problems of the poor. Yet governments in poorer regions needed financial and organizational help to alleviate entrenched poverty and therefore proved receptive to international NGOs. The trick for the local government was to get the help without losing control. Also, as a share of total foreign aid, international NGO contributions are not large. World-

112. "Zhong jia funu canyu fazhan xiangmu zhidao yuanzi" [Guiding principles of the Canada-China women in development project], *Zhong jia xiangmu gongzuo huiyi wenjian zhi er* (Document no. 2 of the working meeting of the China-Canada project), undated, p. 2.
113. Paul Streeten, "Nongovernmental Organizations and Development," *Annals of the American Academy of Political and Social Science* 54 (November 1997): 193–210.

wide, they contribute only approximately 13 percent of the net disbursements of official aid.

Conceptually, however, international NGO activity in China is highly relevant to our study, because here again we can see how local government interests undermine state controls. Local governments knew that if they refused aid from an international NGO because the central government frowned on direct links between donors and local governments or because the international NGOs might threaten the local state's own power, the international NGO could find another partner government that would accept its assistance despite the risks. As a result, a link emerged between international NGOs and local governments that was not mediated by a CPA, undermining the central state's control over the ODA sector.

The Ford Foundation's ties in China are a good case in point. Knowing that the Chinese government would insist on them having a CPA, they proposed that the Chinese Academy of Social Sciences (CASS), which had benefited from many of Ford's training programs and exchanges, become their CPA, ignoring entreaties from SEDC and CICETE. The Ford Foundation feared that these other units would constrain their freedom of action. The core issue was that the CPA have no veto power over projects. "We made it clear that we would not accept an arrangement under which we would be required to seek prior clearance. We knew from our operational experience that counterparts who have to grant clearance become administrative obstacles which undermine our efforts. We told CASS that we would be willing to keep them informed, but we did not want to ask for clearance. We also didn't want a purely administrative unit or one that would limit the types of units in China that we could work with—we also wanted an institution that understood the issues."[114] CASS understood Ford's terms and lobbied the State Council to let them become the CPA. "This was not an easy choice, as they were only one candidate among others, so we explored with them whether they would restrict us. We talked quite openly with them. They understood us and saw the benefits that would come to them, so they took the lead in helping us get approval and were critical in getting the State Council to grant us permission to work in China." When Ford opened its Beijing office in 1988, CASS became its CPA.

CASS imposesd few controls on the Ford Foundation. Ford went directly to agencies to run programs. It worked directly with Yunnan Province and other organizations in Beijing on poverty alleviation, and it worked directly with the Ministry of Civil Affairs on village democracy. In fact, most of Ford's China budget does not pass through CASS. According to a 1996 report, between 1988 and 1995 Ford spent approximately $40 million on its China program, although some of this was for projects outside the

114. The comments and the analysis here are based on interviews with numerous Ford Foundation officials in 1993–95 and 1998.

country. During this period, CASS received grants totaling $6.5 million, or about 16 percent of Ford's total China program.[115] Because most Ford projects did not need counterpart funding, its programs did not have to mesh, programmatically or fiscally, with China's Five-Year Plan. Also, because it was not constrained by bilateral government agreements, Ford, after informal consultations, decided on its own which sectors in China to support. In fact, Ford did not consult with CASS when it set its yearly China budget; instead it outlined the projects it had run that year in a two-page letter to the CASS president, which he simply acknowledges.[116]

Still, CASS benefited greatly from the relationship. According to a former field officer, who denied that there was a policy to give CASS a fixed percent of the budget, "we are sensitive that they are our host, and we want to be attentive to their interests and want to support them in their fields where they are making contributions. And since our activities are generally in the social science and humanities, they get a certain amount of the business."[117] The CASS staff was often included in projects that CASS itself did not run. The Ford Foundation also strengthened CASS's institutional capacity by training its researchers and staff overseas. "We gave them the money and the power to decide who to send abroad—we explained that we would not look over their shoulders. But if they misused it, we would stop our support."[118] CASS supplied the staff for Ford's Beijing office, which increased the salaries of the CASS staff and CASS's coffers, but because many of these people had been trained by Ford, they were a highly motivated, professional staff.

International Nongovernmental Organizations in the 1990s

After 1992, China gave up efforts to control a number of foreign NGOs who had moved into China. Due to weak regulations governing their behavior, creating a partial regulatory vacuum, international NGOs were signing memoranda of understanding directly with local governments at the prefectural or county level, escaping the bureaucratic structure erected by the central state to monitor and control their activities. For example, Médecins Sans Frontières worked directly with the Public Health Bureau in Guangxi Province and the Bureau of Foreign Affairs in Shaanxi Province. According to their director, "we are not working within a regulated framework, we are not registered as an NGO. . . . Our staff get a one year working permit, which has always been renewed when requested. In that sense,

---

115. "Ford Foundation," *China Development Briefing* 1 (March 1996): 15–16.
116. While one informant said that the president of CASS did not respond to the Ford Foundation's letter (Interview Ford 1998.in1), another observer suggests that the CASS president acknowledges the letter in writing but does not comment on it. Communication with the author, 17 October 2001.
117. Interview Ford, New York, 1995.
118. Ibid.

there is no official acknowledgement of our presence and we mainly rely on the willingness of some Chinese officials to improve the situation of the people."[119] Surprisingly, other countries where Médecins Sans Frontières had worked were much more restrictive than China. "I myself have been working with MSF in other countries where the local administration was extremely heavy, and much more demanding than here in terms of monitoring, reporting, taxation, etc. . . . Here, we face none of these constraints, we have never been asked for any tax, nor any reports of our activities after 4 years of cooperation."[120] Moreover, in several cases where foreign NGOs found CPAs constraining them or charging a 3 percent management fee, they simply broke off the ties and went directly to the localities.

The official guidelines, set out in a 1987 State Council document, designated CICETE's NGO Division as the sole official organization empowered to handle foreign NGOs in China. But CICETE's own officials admit that the decentralization of the ODA sector, whereby international NGOs go to the provinces directly, "just happened."[121] Foreign NGOs set up project offices (*xiangmu bangongshi*) without formally registering with the Ministry of Civil Affairs. And as long as they did not establish a representative office or call themselves a national office, they could start another project after completing the first one. According to Chinese officials, "the central government is aware of this, but there has been no new document or regulation to prohibit it."[122] As a result, foreign NGOs were direct executing agencies for some projects and there was no Chinese CPA monitoring their activities.

As in the education sector, the number of Chinese organizations hoping to service foreign donors and manage their funds multiplied in the 1990s, with many of them situated at the provincial level, making aid a competitive market industry. In addition to CICETE, organizations such as the Amity Foundation in Nanjing and Caritas-Hong Kong ran aid projects for other NGOs in China. With the emergence of a real labor market in China, foreign NGOs could hire staff on their own. The Foreign Enterprise Service Company, which had previously supplied all employees for foreign companies and kept up to 90 percent of their foreign salaries, now simply registered the Chinese employees and charged a 400 RMB management fee. The Foreign Enterprise Service Company also helped foreign NGOs register in Beijing. In this way a foreign NGO could enter China, open a project office, hire domestic staff, and never come under the control of a central CPA.

119. Email message from Médecins Sans Frontières, 12 November 1999.
120. Ibid.
121. Interview, CICETE, 1999.
122. Interview, CANGO, 1999.

Because of budget cuts and the fact that they could now legally charge aid recipients or donors a 3 percent management fee, many former Chinese government bureaus declared themselves to be nonprofit social organizations (*shehui tuanti*)—as opposed to state organs—and called themselves international NGO societies. At the provincial level, these provincial international NGO societies were spun out of the provincial department of MOFTEC.

The model they emulated was the China Association for Non-Governmental Organizations (CANGO), created by CICETE's NGO Division in 1992. Registered in 1993 as a social organization affiliated with MOFTEC,[123] this organization had a roster of potential development projects proposed by forty-three domestic NGOs and local governments, which it presented to foreign donors as possible aid recipients and project locations. "CANGO basically has a warehouse (*ku*) of projects, a project roster, and we sell the projects to INGOs [international NGOs] and get them to put their project funds into one of these projects. If they tell us that they are interested in Tibet, and today many donors are interested in Tibet, we have a database and can help them set up a project there."[124] CANGO's staff ran seminars for domestic NGOs and local governments about managing aid projects. But CANGO officials recognized that "it is now a market society—we can no longer monopolize this process."[125]

The proliferation of donors, the supply side of this equation, came about after Deng's southern trip and the need by these organizations to show that they were working in China. As of 1999, total funds invested in China by foreign NGOs was estimated to be over $100 million, more than the total annual budget of all the UN agencies, including the UNDP.[126] The total number of such organizations was estimated to be over two hundred, with the bulk of them working in China's poorer provinces. As figure 5.2 shows, of the 120 donors listed in one directory, the majority were either in China before 1987, having established a foothold before 1949, or they came into China after 1992. In fact, 56 percent of these 120 NGOs entered China in or after 1992, with almost 30 percent of all donors arriving in 1993–95. (See the left column, which presents the INGOs entering China each year.)

Local demand for financial aid drove this process. With budgets slashed and few new sources for taxation, provincial and county governments in poor areas saw foreign donors, particularly those with poverty-alleviation agendas, as God-sends. "Local governments understand that donors are

---

123. According to Chinese regulations, all domestic organizations must be affiliated with a government organization.
124. Interview, CANGO, 1999.
125. Interview, CANGO, 1999.
126. The data are from Fong Ku, ed., *2000: Directory of International NGOs Supporting Work in China* (Hong Kong: China Development Research Services, 1999).

Number for the year  Cumulative number

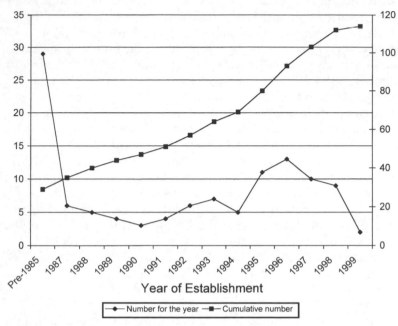

Figure 5.2   International Nongovernmental Organizations in China, 1985–1999

Source: Fong Ju, ed. *2000 Directory of International NGOs Supporting Work in China* (Hong Kong: Development Research Services, 1999).
Note: There were 6 organizations whose date of establishment in China could not be determined. Therefore, the total number is 114, not 120. There were 29 INGOs in China before 1986.

looking for a big return on a small investment—which may still be a large amount of money for a county—so they try to sell China and . . . promise to help the donor create a model—this is a fairly standard line from the Chinese when they put forward a proposal to the donor agency."[127]

Bureaucratic agents tried to reassert control over foreign NGOs, both for mercenary reasons and to regulate a truly unregulated sector. In many ways, provincial international NGO societies were one strategy by which MOFTEC—or at least its agents—could reassert some administrative control and establish a unified system for receiving NGO assistance. In Yunnan Province, which is the site of the most freewheeling donor activity, the director of the provincial international NGO society was determined to get all the foreign NGOs under his control. At a meeting in the late 1990s of approximately twenty international NGOs, "he passed out a piece of

127.   Interview BJYN, Beijing, November, 1999.

paper that said that he had met with the Vice Governor of Yunnan, who had authorized him to tell everyone present that 'it had been decided that all international NGOs in Yunnan had to register with YINGOS [Yunnan international NGO Society]. . . . But there was no regulation, so this was merely a case of empire building and efforts to bully these organizations."[128] Similarly, the Yunnan provincial international NGO society was reportedly quite keen on capturing OXFAM–Hong Kong, but OXFAM resisted its efforts.

How long this regulatory vacuum will persist remains unclear. In fall 1999, the bureau on NGOs in the Ministry of Civil Affairs was drafting a new set of regulations for foreign NGOs that might force them all to register with the ministry. This was "very bad news," according to one observer, because the bureau, which knows nothing about what foreign NGOs do, was drafting the regulations without consulting any donors.[129] Concerns over legitimizing domestic NGOs meant that, as of fall 2001, the draft law on international NGOs was not likely to be tabled very soon.[130] Nevertheless, in its *White Paper on Rural China's Poverty Reduction*, the Ministry of Civil Affairs dedicated a specific section to international cooperation.[131]

Undermining the Constraints: The Demand for New Transnational Linkages

Although there is no indication that local governments lobbied the central government to expand the scope of foreign aid, it is clear that within projects the beneficiary units often pressed the Chinese CPA or the foreign executing agency to increase the opportunities to go overseas under their specific project. And this pressure, in some cases, did lead to the expansion of those channels. In this way, efforts to control the flow of human resources were undermined by unorganized collective interests from within the domestic ODA sector. No doubt, overseas training programs were very important if CPAs and China's bureaucrats were to improve their institutional capacity. But because state bureaucrats could barter exchange opportunities for other political and economic resources, they had strong reasons to press for more resource flows and a widening of overseas channels.

Although this generalization may not hold true for all projects, and clearly does not apply to the period right after the spate of post-Tiananmen defections, Chinese officials and citizens were constantly pressing CIDA to

128. Interview BJYN, Beijing, 6 November 1999.
129. Ibid.
130. Josephine Ma, "Sect Fears Put New NGO Laws on Hold," *South China Morning Post*, 15 October 2001, p. 8.
131. Josephine Ma, "Foreigners Backed in Poverty Battle," *South China Morning Post*, 16 October 2001, p. 11.

expand the number of people going overseas. The management training centers in Chengdu and Hefei both became pathways for overseas travel because much of the training occurred in Canada, until too many trainees opted to remain overseas after Tiananmen. These defections harmed both projects: by 1993, only twelve of forty-six people from CCMTC in Chengdu trained in Canada remained at the center—twenty-six had stayed in Canada—and AMDC in Hefei was left with only twenty staff after seven senior trainees did not return. According to one estimate, these defections cost CIDA over CDN$600,000 in direct training expenses, "and substantially more when examined in relation to the project overall."[132]

As with Chinese universities, these centers needed overseas training programs to attract talented staff. Before 1989, CCMTC administrators insisted that the ACCC provide more overseas spots: "They wanted to make sure that as many people as possible could go to Canada. Promises had been made when these folks were hired that they were going to have a chance to go to Canada, so they had an expectation now. The directors of the center had this project in their pocket and there was certain number of tickets to Canada that was part of the package. So they could use that as an inducement to get the right people, to get the good people."[133] For the AMDC, international ties were also critical, driven by economic demand for establishing global linkages. The AMDC made its money organizing trips to Canada for managers of medium-size enterprises in Anhui Province who were looking for JV partners. For the Anhui Provincial Economic Commission, which sponsored the project, the AMDC was a "window to the outside world" for this isolated province and its SOEs, which had few transnational contacts.[134] Also as we have seen, pressures from SEZO expanded the number of mayor's tours under the COCP. In this small way, domestic pressure again contributed to opening the Chinese system.

Conclusion

State agents had strong vested interests in monitoring, controlling, and promoting overseas development assistance. As government officials, their job was to protect China from unwanted foreign influences and prevent dependency on foreign aid, while at the same time attracting aid that would modernize China on the best terms possible. They also had their own interests. As CPAs, they wanted to control resource channels. Changing property rights and decreasing administrative budgets encouraged CPAs to *chuan shou* (earn incomes) by charging fees for redirecting aid to

132. Bell, "Chengdu Enterprise Development Project," p. 8.
133. CCMTC, interview no. 2, 1993.
134. Interview, Anhui Provincial Economic Commission, summer 1992.

specific units or localities. Trips overseas were commodities that could be bartered for political or economic favors. Foreign aid increased these units' institutional capacity, and expanded their bureaucratic sinecures, helping them compete for other domestic and global resources. Finally, some units simply used the aid to establish new companies or enterprises that could bring them or their bureau important financial benefits. Although these monitors did not become a class of internationalists who favored external interests over those of the Chinese state,[135] they did have strong incentives to expand the amount of foreign aid passing through their bureaus.

Through the early 1990s, domestic demand for aid remained under relatively tight institutional control. As long as channels of global transaction were not decentralized, local governments, enterprises, and research and academic institutions could only lobby CPAs to allocate projects to them. As a result, no aid fever emerged. Also these units did not lobby the center, and direct contacts with donors remained difficult in this highly centralized environment. In this way, all donors' roads led through Beijing, leaving China in control of its transnational relations. But the benefits of aid to a locality or local bureau were immense, creating an enormous pent-up local demand. Any aid recipient, once awarded a project, and foreign resources, also received new domestic funding, giving ODA a great power of attraction over domestic resources. Because much of the aid was either free or loaned on easy terms, aid projects were a significant boon to local development. In particular, the concern of many foreign NGOs with poverty alleviation and their willingness to pour money into poorer rural counties created a great deal of support for a more liberal ODA regime in China's poorer provinces.

Yet even in these stricter times, donors influenced the aid process. In the cases presented in this chapter, the UN's specialized agencies directed the early China projects into their own bailiwicks and insured their 13 percent fee. Similarly, CIDA was able to channel the allocation of funding under several of its projects to Canadian NGOs.

The situation changed in the 1990s, as a new global agenda—sustainable development, environmental protection, poverty alleviation, and good governance—led to a restructuring of China's ODA system, undermining the monopoly of the traditional CPAs. The more negative view of China following Tiananmen led foreign actors to demand greater freedom from the Chinese bureaucracy and greater access to Chinese society. When massive levels of FDI began to flow into industrial coastal China, donors insisted on helping China's poor. In this way, global pressure shifted the balance between China and the global donor community. Also, increased domestic demand for foreign assistance for poverty alleviation and the weakening of

---

135. Broad, *Unequal Alliance.*

the constraints regulating contacts between local governments and foreign NGOs allowed the number of channels between foreign donors and domestic actors to expand significantly.

No doubt, China's leaders made the first critical decisions to open domestic China to foreign aid. The system they established, in which state agents negotiated country programs based on China's Five-Year Plans, with a coterie of CPAs monitoring these programs, was expected to enable the state to contain foreign influences. And in fact, official large loans from organizations such as the World Bank and the Asia Development Bank, as well as assistance from many multilateral donors in the UN system, have remained under tight control. But although multilateral donors live in a highly regulated world, bilateral donors have earned some freedom to maneuver and have pushed China in directions more in line with their norms than with the Chinese government's own preferences. And foreign NGOs are now entering China with few constraints and moving freely around China. As the new millennium dawns, foreign forces in the form of ODA play a more aggressive role in China, pushing for the adoption of new global norms. It has been a winding road, but international forces, encouraged by local demand, have pushed China into a more interdependent, more market-oriented global system.

Conclusion: Bringing Down the Barriers

Global markets are driving down regulatory barriers across much of the world, and China has not proved exempt from these pressures. International economic forces and domestic interests have collided and colluded with bureaucratic agents all along China's administrative borders, as goods, services, and both financial and human capital have sought their most profitable location. The historic WTO agreement between the United States and China, signed on November 15, 1999, further weakened many regulatory constraints that had sheltered China from international competition, showing the enormous power of global markets. Throughout the 1980s and much of the 1990s, the ultimate victor in this war remained unclear. Entrenched bureaucratic interests and mercantilist values proved resilient against attempts at the wholesale dismantling of their control channels. But the opportunities arising from differences in the relative value of goods and services on either side of the Chinese border and the benefits derived from facilitating transnational exchanges triggered a hunger for global linkages within China. Societal interests proved a worthy opponent for the bureaucrats in this historic struggle for the future.

The China that entered the new millennium had changed dramatically over two decades. China's top leaders are now less mercantilist and more comfortable with market forces. They talk about China's need to adjust its external behavior to meet global economic norms.[1] They have moved beyond partial integration, which viewed participation in the global economy as practical, desirable, but needing careful control, and now favor deeper integration, whereby domestic laws must conform to international practice.[2] Aware that protectionism could scare off FDI and the transfer of technology and complicate recovery from the East Asian financial crisis, President Jiang Zemin and Premier Zhu Rongji agreed to open China's

1. Thomas G. Moore, "China and Globalization," in *East Asia and Globalization*, ed. Samuel S. Kim (Lanham: Rowman and Littlefield, 2000), pp. 105-31.
2. Margaret Pearson, "China's Integration into the International Trade and Investment Regime," in *China Joins the World: Progress and Prospects*, ed. Elizabeth Economy and Michel Oksenberg (New York: Council on Foreign Relations, 1999), p. 162.

domestic market to overseas investors. They also realized that deregulating transnational barriers would help in their struggle against system-threatening corruption.

Foreign interest in China's market, limited in the 1980s, grew dramatically in the 1990s. After 1989, Taiwanese businessmen swarmed to China's mainland. Deng Xiaoping's 1992 southern trip led to a feverish flow of foreign direct investment (FDI) in 1992–95, as multinational corporations feared that early entrants in the China market would establish monopoly positions. In the 1990s, the number of international NGOs grew, reflecting a worldwide attitude that you were not a global player unless you were in China.

Cowed into passivity in 1989 by the harshness of the Communist Party's response to the Tiananmen movement, Chinese society erupted in 1992–93 in a paroxysm of business acumen, risk taking, and local government entrepreneurship that catapulted China's economic growth. With so many benefits based on international transactions, the desire for global linkages undermined many barriers to transnational flows imposed by the central state.

The century has turned and the picture is more complex. Many domestic forces no longer advocate greater internationalization. The price for entering the WTO involves dismantling subsidies and deregulating markets in politically powerful or sensitive sectors. Some winners under segmented deregulation, whose benefits will erode under deep integration, oppose any movement beyond the partial reform equilibrium that has emerged.[3] For example, bureaucratic and regional interests want to protect the rents and extra-normal profits they have been earning, while foreigners who have already penetrated China's market, particularly those who received supralegal privileges from Chinese governments, could oppose a further opening that erodes their preferred market position.[4] In addition, resurgent nationalism opposes new concessions to external interests.[5] As China emerges as a major global power, 150 years after western imperialism first began to undermine the Qing dynasty, powerful forces still fear a foreign conspiracy to keep China down. These proto-nationalists ally with bureaucrats and other anti-WTO forces to resist globalization. The gateway to full participation in the world economy is being constructed and the road beyond it is being paved; but only strong leadership can overcome these entrenched domestic and transnational interests.

3. Joel S. Hellman, "Winners Take All: The Politics of Partial Reform in Postcommunist Transitions," *World Politics* 50 (January 1998): 204.
4. Daniel H. Rosen, *Behind the Open Door: Foreign Enterprise in the Chinese Marketplace* (Washington, D.C.: Institute for International Economics, 1999).
5. Yongnian Zheng, *Discovering Chinese Nationalism in China: Modernization, Identity, and International Relations* (Cambridge, UK: Cambridge University Press, 1999).

Why Did China Open Up?

The four sector studies show that the determinants of China's opening were complex. The behavior of four key actors—external political and business interests; China's ruling elites; bureaucratic agents; and local communities, organizations, and individuals—was affected by differences in relative prices, the nature of the regulatory regime controlling transnational exchanges and whether those control mechanisms were formally decentralized, and the nature of property rights in their sector. In the following sections, I discuss these issues and suggest how the process of internationalization has shaped China's current political economy.

INTERNATIONAL FORCES: GLOBAL MARKETS AND THE RELATIVE VALUE OF RESOURCES

International forces—external powers and markets—led elites, bureaucrats, and local actors to behave in ways that undermined the regulatory regime that controlled China's transnational exchanges. As Frieden and Rogowski predict,[6] the relative value of labor led to the internationalization of China's countryside and its universities. Zhao Ziyang attributed his decision to open rural China to both exports and FDI to rising labor costs in East Asia, which created a comparative advantage for rural China in foreign trade. Also, by 1987 he had learned that, contrary to his expectations, state-owned enterprises (SOEs) could not lead China's export drive; that task belonged to rural China. And once he opened the door to rural China, network capital from Taiwan and Hong Kong swarmed to the coastal countryside searching for cheap labor and colluding with local officials to evade regulations governing joint ventures (JVs) and foreign trade. Similarly, superior graduate training, the relative value of overseas employment, plus foreign capital in the form of graduate and postdoctoral fellowships provided by foreign universities and companies, pulled Chinese students and scholars abroad. Lacking capital to train its lost generation of scientists, the central state in 1983–85 loosened controls on overseas study, introducing the category of self-paying students and letting universities expand linkages on their own. In 1992–93, in order to attract back foreign-trained Chinese who had become the repositories of foreign technology and foreign networks, the state relaxed its rules on overseas studies.

But contrary to the assertions of Frieden and Rogowski, changes in relative prices offer only part of the explanation for China's brain drain and the demand for global academic exchanges. The relative value of working

6. Jeffry A. Frieden and Ronald Rogowski, "The Impact of the International Economy on National Policies: An Analytical Overview," in *Internationalization and Domestic Politics,* ed. Robert O. Keohane and Helen V. Milner (Cambridge, UK: Cambridge University Press, 1996), pp. 25–47.

or studying overseas, compared to staying in China, existed long before China internationalized its educational and research and development sector. Teachers in China were always underpaid and a large cohort of academics trained in the 1960s were available to go overseas before 1978. Had they been allowed to go, western intellectual enterprises would have supplied funds for travel and training. But as Shirk and Evangelista show, tight regulatory controls by the Chinese government prevented Chinese from knowing their interests, and, despite the enormous financial gains that could come from studying or working overseas, there was little liberalization in this realm before 1978.[7]

What changed was not the price of Chinese labor or even the value of overseas study, although that did rise in the 1980s, but the ease with which individuals could pursue their interests. Once universities were allowed to establish their own exchanges or individuals could go abroad through their own channels, the flow overseas increased dramatically. This incipient marketization of China's transnational labor market, due to an easing of governmental constraints, and the demand by western academic and research institutions for Chinese students and scholars, pulled more and more students and scholars overseas.

So, too, with overseas development assistance (ODA). It was not so much a change in the value of foreign resources that triggered the growth of transnational exchanges outside the state's regulatory regime; Chinese had long coveted foreign resources. What was new was that foreign NGOs arrived on the scene with millions of dollars for China's impoverished localities who were hungry for international assistance and that the central government acceded to their desire to work at the grassroots. Also changes in global norms weakened administrative controls as the new stress on sustainable development and environmental degradation let the UNDP pry itself loose from its counterpart agency (CPA) and retarget its aid to a multiplicity of beneficiaries.

Finally, China's increased dependence on exports and FDI in the 1990s contributed to internationalization. Following the Tiananmen crackdown, worldwide sanctions increased China's dependence on exports to the United States, giving the U.S. trade representative leverage to bring down China's protective walls on intellectual property rights and market access, and tariff and nontariff barriers. The United States also used China's desire to enter the WTO to demand more trade and investment liberalization, and a series of deregulations among East Asian states pressured Jiang

---

7. Susan Shirk, "Opening China to the World Economy: Communist Institutions and Foreign Economic Policy Reforms," in *Internationalization and Domestic Politics*, ed. Robert O. Keohane and Helen V. Milner (Cambridge, UK: Cambridge University Press, 1996), pp. 186–208; Matthew Evangelista, "Stalin's Revenge: Institutional Barriers to Internationalization in the Soviet Union," in *Internationalization and Domestic Politics*, ed. Robert O. Keohane and Helen V. Milner (Cambridge, UK: Cambridge University Press, 1996), pp. 159–85.

Zemin to lower China's own tariffs. Finally, the drop in FDI during the East Asian financial crisis and an awareness among China's leaders that foreigners would go elsewhere if the investment climate were not inviting, led China's leaders to yield further on market access.

Future analysts may view China's opening as part of the global sweep that liberalized the world economy after the Margaret Thatcher and Ronald Reagan conservative revolutions.[8] Given the tectonic shifts in financial markets,[9] the expanded influence of transnational organizations,[10] the lower transport costs, the ability of manufacturers to move swiftly to regions with cheap labor, and the increased influence of both a hegemonic United States and international regimes such as the WTO, perhaps no nation, not even mercantilist China, could have resisted the pressures of globalization in the 1980s and 1990s. From this perspective, the world opened China, rather than China opening to the world.

Elites and Bureaucrats under Internationalization

But just as I reject a unidimensional political explanation for the opening, I also challenge the international political economy literature's overemphasis on external forces. For internationalization to ensue, central elites, state bureaucrats, and societal interests (often categorized as domestic structures) had to play a clear role in determining the process of deregulation and the pace, depth, and geographic spread of China's internationalization.

Because state ideology legitimized barriers to global exchange and economic and political interests had solidified around them, reformers had to overcome the pro-protectionist conservatives if ideological constraints were to be undone.[11] Without Deng's agency in 1978–79 and 1992, Zhao's assertiveness in 1984–85 and 1987–88, and Zhu Rongji's efforts in 1998–99, liberalization in each period would not have occurred. Yet these leaders themselves had to develop a less hostile view of the world economy that would allow them to trade some of China's sovereignty for access to global technology, foreign investment, and international markets. Without the strategy of these pro-market leaders, which both motivated local elites and Chinese citizens to seek global opportunities and offered bureaucrats incentives not to oppose deregulation, domestic demand for global links would have remained stifled by internationalization's opponents. Had

8. Daniel Yergin and Joseph Stanislaw, *The Commanding Heights* (New York: Simon and Schuster, 1998).

9. Barbara Stallings, "International Influence on Economic Policy: Debt, Stabilization, and Structural Reform," in *The Politics of Economic Adjustment*, ed. Stephan Haggard and Robert R. Kaufman (Princeton: Princeton University Press, 1992), pp. 41–88.

10. Susan Strange, *The Retreat of the State: The Diffusion of Power in the World Economy* (Cambridge, UK: Cambridge University Press, 1996).

11. Leonard Cheng made this point during a lecture I gave at the Hong Kong University of Science and Technology, September 1999.

elites made poor choices, such as supporting only import-substitution industrialization without shifting to export-led growth, or following Hua Guofeng's state-led opening of the late 1970s, huge debts would have made China's pathway from the periphery just as torturous as it has been for many other developing countries.[12]

Bureaucrats, too, facilitated internationalization, largely out of self-interest. Rather than block exchanges, many of them "slept with the enemy" (i.e., the global market), translating regulatory authority into economic gain for themselves and their bureaus.[13] In all four of our sectors, the regulators facilitated exchanges; otherwise control over transnational channels had little value—again, "no flow, no dough!" They also granted foreigners access to the domestic market, fearful that if they did not, foreign capital would simply move elsewhere. But in doing so, bureaucrats undermined the very sovereignty that empowered them. Although regulations created rents, the growth of multiple channels for global linkages generated market-oriented internationalization that weakened their leverage over those who used their channels.

But bureaucrats did not simply wilt under pressure; their preferences, like those of many top elites, were fluid. If internationalization increased their incomes and opportunities, they supported it. But in sectors, such as agriculture, pharmaceuticals, telecommunications, and automobiles, they fought ferociously to protect their enterprises and their interests from global competition in the face of WTO access and, where possible, even to expand regulatory constraints if it was in their economic interests.[14]

REGULATING INTERNATIONALIZATION

We could argue that China needed more, not fewer, regulations, especially rules and norms that forced transnational exchanges to follow market principles and kept predatory officials at bay.[15] Secrecy gives officials great flexibility in interpreting regulations and forcing foreigners to cooperate with them. Decentralization compounded this agency problem as local governments with vested property rights in enterprises and firms implemented

12. Stephan Haggard, *Pathways from the Periphery: The Politics of Growth in the Newly Industrializing Countries* (Ithaca: Cornell University Press, 1990).

13. Victor Nee and Peng Lian, "Sleeping with the Enemy: A Dynamic Model of Declining Political Commitment in State Socialism," *Theory and Society* 23 (1994): 253–96.

14. In 1999, foreign sealant importers were forced to sell their products through one company set up by the State Economic and Trade Commission and staffed by commission bureaucrats. When this company imposed tariffs of 100 percent on imports and then further limited imports based on alleged quality issues, imports dried up, allowing domestic firms to reestablish their market share. Ian Johnson, "China Continues to Hobble Foreign Firms," *Asian Wall Street Journal*, 23 March 2000, pp. 1, 5.

15. Steven K. Vogel, *Freer Markets, More Rules: Regulatory Reform in Advanced Industrial Countries* (Ithaca: Cornell University Press, 1996).

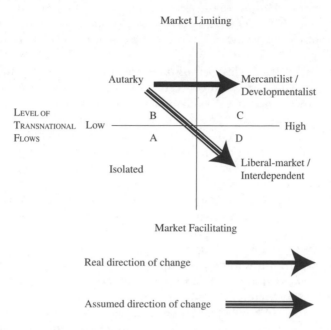

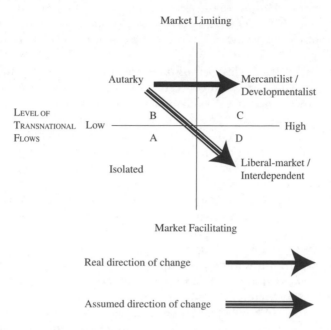

TYPE OF REGULATORY CONSTRAINT

Market Limiting

Autarky → Mercantilist / Developmentalist

LEVEL OF TRANSNATIONAL FLOWS   Low   B   C   High
                                       A   D

Isolated   Liberal-market / Interdependent

Market Facilitating

Real direction of change →

Assumed direction of change ⇒

Figure C.1   Pattern of Transnational Linkages II

these rules relatively unmonitored. Also, by limiting market flows and foreign access, regulations created large rents in China's highly protected markets. Personal relations (*guanxi*), the grease of the bureaucratic wheel, increased in value as actors sought to benefit from the differences in relative prices that were created by these regulatory constraints.

Borrowing from Steven Vogel, I now revise my original matrix, figure 1.1, by changing the nature of the vertical axis (figure C.1).[16] Rather than focusing on the extent to which transactions were regulated—as I did in my original matrix—we focus on the type of regulations that were established and whether those regulations facilitated market-oriented transnational exchanges. Since 1978, the state has deregulated many aspects of its global linkages. Although deregulation can decrease costs and increase exchanges, markets dominated by personal ties, rather than impersonal rules or norms, may be inefficient and unpredictable for many foreign investors and harmful to China's polity. Therefore, decentralization and deregulation, without good market-facilitating rules, might be highly

16. Ibid.

problematic.[17] As we look back at the four sectors, we need to see whether reforms left the sector well regulated or simply poorly regulated. If the former has occurred, then China is well on its way to stable market-oriented internationalization; if the latter, corruption may rule the day.

The strength or effectiveness of the regulatory regime in China varied across sectors, and the weakness of the rules or their lack of clarity contributed both to corruption and de facto internationalization. The rules governing administrative behavior in the zones were particularly vague,[18] allowing bureaucrats to sell access to the domestic market in return for more FDI. In Chengdu even the boundaries of zones were abstract; suburban universities and laboratories were incorporated into the downtown high-tech development zone (HTDZ), functioning in a more deregulated economic environment without ever moving into the city. Similarly, to encourage Taiwanese investment, rural leaders re-interpreted the guidelines stating that preferential policies went only to those who exported 70 percent of their output, calling the target firms "firms facing difficulties" (*kunnan qiye*). In this way, they brought in more FDI and gained access to both foreign and domestic markets. In the aid sector, regulations were bifurcated. Tight conventions constrained multilateral and bilateral donors, but foreign NGOs that entered China in the 1990s found a regulatory vacuum, because rules introduced in the 1980s were simply not enforced.

Only in the education sector did the rules governing exchanges and movement across China's borders appear well-regulated. (After all, we are talking about migration, a process that states control carefully.) Nevertheless, who was eligible for travel overseas and under what terms they could go shifted constantly, as the Ministry of Education (MOE) tried to balance the danger of the expanding brain drain against the need to send people abroad. Stricter regulations limiting overseas study actually intensified the demand to go abroad, and state efforts to redirect students away from the United States were circumvented. Regulations allowing individuals to go overseas as self-paying students also weakened bureaucratic control over these population flows. Therefore, a dual process emerged here as well: informal exchanges, based on an individual's gaining his or her own funding from overseas and monitored only by the local police; and bureaucratically managed exchanges, controlled by academic administrators and monitored closely by universities, research labs, or state agents in Beijing or the provincial government.

---

17. Some of the ideas expressed here are responses to arguments raised by Leonard Cheng, David Dodwell, and Gu Xin, who attended seminars I gave on this book.

18. David Wall, "Special Economic Zones in China: The Administrative and Regulatory Framework," *China Paper 91/7*, Economics Division–Research School of Pacific Studies, National Centre for Development Studies, Australian National University, 1991.

As China deepened its global links, clear and effective rules governing those ties were often in short supply. Some regulations, born from a spirit of mercantilism or bureaucratic preference for monopolies, constrained foreign access to the large rents available in China's highly protected markets. But such profits were too valuable to ignore; so Chinese bureaucrats took advantage of the weak rules sheltering the domestic market and either expropriated the rents themselves or traded access to them to foreigners in return for foreign markets, technology, or investment capital. In the end, these unclear rules, which Lu and Deng call China's soft-authority constraint, facilitated China's initial internationalization.[19] Yet, under WTO, clearer rules, greater predictability, and a more stable market that is open to foreign investors will now deepen internationalization.

Once the state decentralized authority over transnational exchanges to lower-level officials, allowing more of the benefits of exchanges to accrue locally, horizontal flows proliferated, the demand for exchanges intensified, and linkage fevers emerged. The periods 1984–85, 1987–88, and 1992–93 were critical for the sectors. In 1985, universities were empowered to establish their own exchange programs. Also in 1985, the autonomy of local foreign trade companies was established, intensifying in 1988, and in 1984 and 1988 formal export-processing zones and HTDZs respectively, were created. In 1988 many rural areas in coastal China were opened to FDI and their local governments were given the authority to approve most foreign investment projects that came their way. Finally, in 1992–93, the number of zones and rural JVs proliferated.

Formal decentralization appears to explain weakened state control over transnational flows in the first three sectors. But the data on foreign aid show that even without formal decentralization, weak regulations still allow local governments to ally with foreign donors to undermine the regulatory regime. This lack of formal regulations decentralizing controls over foreign aid probably prevented a foreign aid fever because bilateral and multilateral donors do not work directly with local governments, and the number of international NGOs is limited; but foreign NGOs and local governments have still been able to link on their own. Therefore, where decentralization occurred, internationalization was more likely. But even without it, weak rules or unclear regulations allowed local governments, hungering for relief from poverty to grant foreigners access to domestic China.[20]

---

19. Ding Lu and Zhimin Tang, *State Intervention and Business in China: The Role of Preferential Policies* (Cheltenham, UK: Edward Elgar, 1997).

20. Similarly, rules prohibiting provinces or municipalities from borrowing overseas without central government approval were circumvented when local governments set up their own international trade and investment companies (ITICs), which did the borrowing for the governments. Weak regulatory controls also allowed many of the 256 ITICs established in the mid-1990s to go into debt.

PROPERTY RIGHTS AND INTERNATIONALIZATION

Property rights in China have undergone dramatic transformation. If we define property rights as a bundle of rights, including the right to sell a firm, the right to its profits, and the right to allocate resources within it,[21] the state in the mid-1980s clarified the property rights of enterprises, the governments that controlled them, and government bureaus and universities by granting them control over part of their income or profits. And because global exchanges were a key source of profits, these agencies were encouraged to deepen the level of internationalization.

In the countryside, the financial responsibility system (*caizheng baogan*) gave developmental communities, with corporate networks of government, party, and enterprise leaders who controlled a pool of cheap rural labor, strong incentives to move into export-led growth. Zone directors, too, had strong incentives to attract domestic exporters and foreign investors because the zone's income and the amount of money a zone director could allocate expanded along with the scale of business. In both cases, however, greater profits could be made by selling foreigners access to domestic markets. Similarly, the 1985 educational reform, which encouraged universities to expand their incomes through commercial endeavors, triggered a plethora of new organizations owned by the university, which sought financial benefit from global linkages.

On the downside, unclear property rights over land generated the wasteful zone fever of 1992–93. Given the paucity of funds for urbanization, gleaning capital from land was necessary to defray the costs of creating a hard environment that could attract foreign investors. But weak property rights over land and unclear lines of financial responsibility for zones that were not completed or successful made expropriating land an acceptable strategy for gaining lower tax rates or ill-begotten wealth. In the ODA sector, the emerging property rights regime, whereby many bureaus or organizations had to finance their own expenses, led several CPAs to channel aid monies to projects that would earn incomes and insure their bureau's own long-term welfare. Because most donors preferred to help the very needy, the result of this behavior was bad blood between donors and their CPAs.

Domestic Demand and Linkage Fevers

The four sectors show that opportunities under internationalization led domestic actors to undermine the state's barriers to deeper integration. And here lies this book's special story—how the domestic hunger in China

21. Janos Kornai, *The Socialist System: The Political Economy of Communism* (Princeton: Princeton University Press, 1992).

for global linkages, generated in part by foreign market forces and the state's own regulations, brought down institutional impediments to transnational relations and weakened the state's control over its citizens, resources, and sovereignty far more rapidly and completely than the elites and bureaucrats had anticipated. True, organized collective action, as understood by social scientists, did not drive this process.[22] Instead, enormous economic and political incentives for local governments, communities, companies, universities, and individuals to increase the scale of transnational linkages generated unorganized collective action, whereby autonomous actors, sharing similar institutional constraints, pressured the state to deregulate its barriers to transnational exchanges.

Concerned that opportunities would diminish if many others engaged in the same activity, individuals and collectivities aggressively sought those benefits. But their individual actions had a multiplier effect; in the words of Schelling, people react "to a totality of which they are a part."[23] Demand for global linkages intensified as each individual or organization sought to link before others could. Cities prepared development zones, fearful that other localities would beat them in the race for preferential policies and domestic and foreign investors. Suddenly they became part of a widespread macrobehavior pattern—a zone fever—that pressed the state to expand the number of formal zones, liberalizing the overall trade and investment regime. Counties, townships, villages, and town and village enterprises (TVEs) in Jiangsu, Zhejiang, and Guangdong provinces, eager for FDI and export channels, did not lobby the central government to deregulate the foreign trade and investment regime under which they functioned. Instead they established thousands of JVs in the early and mid-1990s and eased constraints on foreign-oriented activity on their own, granting foreigners access to the domestic market on relatively easy terms. Students and scholars, fearful that escape routes might suddenly close, or recognizing that, in the competition for advancement in an internationalized China, overseas training was essential, pressured Chinese universities to expand the number of transnational channels. These schools then either pressed the state to grant them more exchanges or established thousands of bilateral agreements with foreign universities. Only in the ODA sector were popular fevers suppressed because access for provincial and local governments to large multilateral and bilateral donors remained tightly constrained by

---

22. There are some instances of organized collective action. In the mid-1990s, investor associations may have openly advocated trade liberalization. Dali Yang, personal communication, 1998. Also, the WTO debate has created an informal lobby opposed to further liberalization. See John Pomfret, "Chinese Are Split over WTO Entry: Monopolies Fear Western Influence," *Washington Post Foreign Service*, 13 March 2000, p. A01. Associations of returnee overseas students also advocate collective interests on policies related to their treatment in China.

23. Thomas C. Schelling, *Micromotives and Macrobehavior* (New York: W. W. Norton, 1978), pp. 77–78.

central counterpart agencies. Still, by the mid-1990s, local governments, eager for funds for poverty alleviation, linked with foreign NGOs in dozens of unregulated relationships.

State bureaucrats were well served by unorganized collective action. Because bureaucrats manned the channels of global transaction and because most lobbying for preferential policies, deregulation, or favorable interpretations of existing regulations occurred on a one-to-one basis, localities became the supplicants of state administrators, who dominated the negotiations. As a result, linkage fevers brought some benefits of increased transnational flows to central bureaucrats, even as the proliferation of local horizontal channels weakened their controls.

Opposition to Internationalization and the World Trade Organization

As internationalization deepened, a strong antiglobalization movement emerged in China. Much of it targeted the enormous level of deregulation and the further anticipated deregulation that will ensue due to WTO accession.

But first, why was opposition to deeper internationalization muted for so long? Many sectors of society benefited from China's early internationalization; there were very few losers. Opposition in the 1980s was primarily ideological and bureaucratic. TVEs moved into international markets that were inaccessible to SOEs due to the their high labor costs, so China and TVEs moved forward on the trade frontier without transferring wealth or investment away from SOEs. Also, network capitalism was uninterested in SOEs. Therefore, rural internationalization progressed without much of an overt challenge from SOEs or their bureaucratic protectors. Also, although TVE exports benefited only a few coastal provinces with industrialized rural areas, agricultural regions of China suffered no direct loss.

China managed its foreign aid well, affording foreign donors little leverage over China's domestic policies. So no opposition to foreign aid emerged. Similarly, the influx of foreign NGOs into poverty-stricken regions, without reducing or redistributing existing multilateral or bilateral aid flows, created a win-win situation. Coastal regions still received the lion's share of official foreign loans, even as the deregulated aid flowed into poorer western regions that the central government wanted to help. So only bureaucrats who wanted to maintain their monopoly over foreign aid had an incentive to stop foreign NGOs from dealing directly with local governments.

Although China's brain drain threatened the internationalization of the education system, China's leaders and administrators realized that technology would not flow inward if people were not allowed to flow out. Hence Zhao Ziyang's comment about "storing brain power overseas."[24] Moreover, the cohort that returned from overseas in the early and mid-1980s brought such a great benefit to China's scientific development that it was hard to contemplate stemming the flow. Academics who had not gone abroad opposed the preferential policies that were used to attract overseas scholars back; there they felt a direct loss. But rather than have the door closed, they now sought postdoctoral fellowships that would give them stronger global linkages.

Only the yawning regional imbalance created by segmented deregulation and China's pro-coast, tilted development strategy triggered a strong outcry for policy reassessment. But again, few voices called for an end to internationalization; instead the need for greater equality in public policy culminated in the call in March 2000 to deregulate western China in order to increase the flow of FDI into these long-ignored regions.

But in the mid-1990s a more powerful challenge to internationalization emerged as nationalism replaced Marxism as the ideological and mobilizational source of opposition to deeper global links.[25] According to some intellectuals, globalization had undermined China's power in several ways. Deep integration left military and technological modernization dependent on the strategic interests of other countries and their often volatile attitudes toward China. In particular, they saw U.S. hegemonic interests, the cornerstone of the global economic system, limiting China's access to technology and forcing economic sectors that could form China's global competitors in the twenty-first century to open prematurely.[26] Also, fearing national fragmentation and supportive of greater state power, nationalists preferred centralization to the decentralization that had allowed for a proliferation of global linkages.[27] As a late modernizer, they argued, China must maintain a neomercantilist strategy (figure C.1, quadrant C), protect its domestic economy and national industries, and build an independent and relatively self-sufficient industrial and scientific system.

Beginning in 1995, nationalists challenged the concept of comparative advantage, a key component of China's export-led growth strategy and of the opening of the other sectors discussed in this book.[28] For export-

24. Lecture by Xu Lin, Fairbank Center, Harvard University, December 1989.

25. Nationalism initially influenced the decision to adopt a mercantilist strategy in the late 1970s and early 1980s, but waned as a force after the second wave of reform (1984–85) was justified by Zhao Ziyang on the premise of national self-strengthening.

26. Susan Lawrence, "The Say No Club," *Far Eastern Economic Review*, 13 January 2000, pp. 16–18. See also Fang Ning, Wang Xiaodong, and Song Qing, *Quanqiuhua yinxiang xia de Zhongguo zhi lu* [China's road under the influence of globalization] (Beijing: Zhongguo kexue chubanshe, 1999).

27. Zheng, *Discovering Chinese Nationalism in China*, pp. 38–39. See also Wang Shaoguang and Hu Angang, *The Political Economy of Uneven Development: The Case of China* (Armonk: M. E. Sharpe, 2000).

28. These issues are discussed in Zheng, *Discovering Chinese Nationalism in China*, pp. 58–61.

processing zones, TVE exports, academic exchanges, and technology transfer to succeed, U.S. markets must remain open to China. Because closing those markets would imperil China's overall development, export-led growth intensified western leverage over China. These concerns came to the forefront during the 1998–2000 debate over entry into the WTO.

It is possible to assert that the historic WTO agreement of November 15, 1999, with the U.S., and the deep integration that will take place in China thereafter, negates my overall thesis—that signing the agreement demonstrated China's leaders' support of deep integration and internationalization (figure C.1, quadrant D), not neomercantilism (quadrant C). However, my explanation of China's internationalization has suggested all along that differences in the relative value of goods and services, domestic interests, and elite activism increased the interdependence of the 1980s and mid-1990s and weakened China's resistance to further integration. On the other hand, although domestic and bureaucratic interests propelled China's internationalization in the sectors I have discussed, the impact of internationalization varied across sectors. Where entry into the WTO harms powerful vested interests, leadership must overcome the resulting resistance.

By the mid-1990s, many potential beneficiaries of internationalization had pushed down the barriers in their sector and engaged global markets. But in the sectors most deeply affected by WTO there is little domestic demand from local communities, enterprises, or citizens for greater internationalization. The WTO's demand for greater transparency threatens bureaucratic discretionary power based on unclear regulations and undermines the rent-access positions generated by mercantilism. Also, entry into the WTO involved public concessions to external forces—such as the United States—not surreptitious undermining of China's sovereignty by a local government alliance with ethnic-Chinese network capital. China's assertive nationalism suddenly had an overt foreign target—the hegemonic United States and the WTO—making it a viable mobilizing principle for recentralization and neomercantilism.

In addition, although internationalization in 1978–95 did not threaten various inefficient sectors, entry into the WTO does. So, SOEs and their ministerial allies fight the dismantling of their monopolies, and sunrise industries—China's newly emerging enterprises—want to protect their domestic market share from foreign corporations until they are able to compete globally. Similarly, agriculture, which did not suffer directly during the first decade and a half of the opening, now faces enormous threats from western agribusiness. With most crops in China selling above world prices,[29] opening the domestic food market to U.S. and European interests could devastate many regions of rural China.

---

29. Yang Shengming, "Some Ideas on Counter Measures that Our Government Must Utilize after 'Entering the WTO,'" *Guangming ribao* [Guangming daily], 9 May 2000, p. 2.

With mostly short-term losers and few long-term winners, the decision to join WTO on U.S. terms was highly political. Only Zhu Rongji's leadership with Jiang Zemin's support could have pushed the WTO deal through. Yet the fact that China's leaders overrode strong domestic opposition—in the words of Pearson, "opposition in China was not won over . . . but rather was run over"[30]—must have convinced nationalists, neoauthoritarians, and ideologues that internationalization has increased China's vulnerability to external influences. U.S. threats of market closure, the East Asian financial crisis (which shrank foreign investment and exports), a deflating economy, and rising social unrest suggested that China's only escape route was to concede even more ground to the foreigners, precisely what the critics of deep integration predicted. Clearly, maintaining sovereignty in a global economy—staying in quadrant C—even for a state with relatively thick institutions is difficult once a certain level of internationalization has been attained.

Process versus Outcome: How We Get There is as Important as Where We Are Going

This study is more about process than outcome.[31] Liberals may care mostly about the end point—whether China liberalized or not. But the process by which the state deregulated its controls over transnational exchanges explains key problems China faces in 2001. This is not simply a case of same outcome, different path. Leaving autarky (figure C.1, quadrant B), through segmented deregulation, decentralization, re-regulation, and a host of weak laws and norms, generated distortions, false expectations, pathologies (especially corruption), and inequalities that have long-term implications for China's present and future.

Segmented deregulation and preferential policies exacerbated regional inequality by allowing some regions to link with the global economy first. In this way, economic growth was in part the product of state policy because deregulation created a comparative advantage for some and a "comparative disadvantage" for others.[32] Although vested interests, in the form of path dependence, also led these disadvantaged regions to eschew the risks and benefits of internationalization, the continuing influence of supralocal

---

30. Margaret Pearson, "The Case of China's Accession to GATT/WTO," in *The Making of Chinese Foreign and Security Policy in the Era of Reform, 1978–2000*, ed. M. David Lampton (Stanford: Stanford University Press, 2001), p. 364.

31. This section is a response to comments by Jonathan Kirshner on my "Hungry for Linkages: Domestic Interests and China's Internationalization" (paper presented at the Conference on International Relations Theory and Chinese Foreign Policy, Harvard University, June 1998).

32. Dorothy J. Solinger, "Despite Decentralization: Disadvantages, Dependence and Ongoing Central Power in the Inland—the Case of Wuhan," *China Quarterly* 145 (March 1996): 1–34.

authorities undermined the vision and entrepreneurship of the more constrained regions, preventing them from pursuing their interests, even after they understood them.

But, as the neo-liberal model predicts, inequality arising from rapid growth in entrepreneurial localities that quickly established global linkages illuminated the high cost of path dependence and protectionism, leading citizens in less integrated areas to push their elites for greater internationalization. The comparison of Nantong and Zhangjiagang in chapter 3 is most instructive. Despite its early opening in 1984 and its State Council export-processing zone, Nantong as of 1992 had still not placed international trade and investment at the core of its development strategy. Nantong leaders were crusty and unpopular. But the boom in southern Jiangsu, where communities such as Zhangjiagang established strong global linkages, and rapid growth in other parts of coastal China after Deng's 1992 trip forced new leaders in Nantong in 1994 to maximize the city's riverine resources and development zone, making it truly an export-oriented city.

Segmented deregulation led to other distortions. Localities drove farmers off arable land in order to lobby the state for open zones and preferential policies; the land, however, remained fallow. The benefits granted to JVs made round tripping a rational strategy that allowed them to minimize constraints and taxes, increase profits, and import cars duty free. In the education sector, preferential policies supplied by China's government to attract those with transnational capital back to China, such as larger flats, new cars, faster promotions, expatriate packages, or special research grants, exacerbated the fever to go abroad as it became clear that the path to success in Chinese academia involved treading on foreign soil. But given the low return rates for overseas sojourners, any policy that prompted a fever to go abroad magnified the brain drain as well.

Internationalization through decentralization empowered the local state vis-à-vis the center by creating a coterie of developmental communities whose horizontal linkages with network capital supplied them with an alternative source of resources and status outside the purview of Beijing. This expanded freedom from administrative authority could have seriously undermined the regime's political authority,[33] but instead more wealth improved the local government's leverage vis-à-vis both the central government and local society. Despite the leftist critique that FDI undermines Third World states, the global linkages and wealth brought to rural China by foreigners apparently strengthened the local state; foreign penetration increased, not weakened, CCP control.

33. Andrew G. Walder, "The Quiet Revolution from Within: Economic Reform as a Source of Political Decline," in *The Waning of the Communist State: Economic Origins of Political Decline in China and Hungary*, ed. Andrew G. Walder (Berkeley: University of California Press, 1995), pp. 1–24.

Perhaps the greatest downside to China's transition through mercantilism is the institutionalization of corruption. As the critics of government regulation predict, expanding transnational linkages, such as foreign trade and educational exchanges, amid continued regulatory controls and large differences in relative prices, created enormous rent-seeking opportunities. No doubt, rents and extra-normal profits, created by regulations left over from the planned economy, were often undermined by new market entrants. Also, channels of global transaction often failed to limit the flow of goods, services, and people across China's borders: many flooded through or circumvented those channels, reducing the value of the rents. But the existence of regulations whose main purpose was to create rents and that fostered a bureaucratic culture based on regulatory constraints was highly problematic because personal relations (*guanxi*), bribery, or bureaucratic fiat usually determined domestic access to the global economy and foreign access to the domestic economy. And bureaucrats preferred it that way; their power and patronage grew from their right to parcel out global access.

If the gap between international and domestic prices is so large that, even after payoffs are made, transnational exchanges remain profitable, few actors in the transnational sector, particularly bureaucrats, have strong incentives to make de jure changes to the regulatory regime and therefore little reason to shift from quadrant C to D (figure C.1). Thus instead of relative prices easing institutional constraints, regulators may win out as both sides resort to de facto liberalization—smuggling, payoffs, and bribery—leading to "revenue leakage" in the import sector.[34] In fact, for much of the 1990s, China's import revenues were only one-sixth of that expected given the tariff schedule and structure of imports. Half the revenues was lost through various official exemptions bequeathed to foreign investors; the other half was lost to corruption.[35]

Opportunities for corruption and rents, created by regulatory constraints, lead bureaucrats to prefer partial reform and partial deregulation (quadrant C) over deeper global integration (quadrant D). Rents generated by institutional constraints under conditions of significant differences in relative prices—so that there are lots of transactions with most passing through bureaucratic agencies—is the bureaucrat's utopia.

Here the rent-seeking and liberal hypotheses predict very different outcomes. If the state maintains many institutional constraints, so that the number of participants and the scale of benefits increase, "disintegrative" corruption could emerge, leading to a political crisis.[36] If the state becomes

---

34. World Bank, *China Foreign Trade Reform* (Washington, D.C.: World Bank, 1994), p. 59.
35. Ibid.
36. Meany and Johnson differentiate between "disintegrative" and "market facilitating" corruption. Under the later, corruption helps resources cross bureaucratic constraints that would otherwise undermine transactions, efficiency, and growth. See Connie Squires

predatory (i.e., creates policies that purposely increase bureaucratic rents and profits, rather than promoting national development) the risks to its survival intensify.

Fortunately, mercantilism (quadrant C) may not be the equilibrium point in China's global economic relations.[37] Domestic and international market pressures have pushed parts, if not all, of China into quadrant D, deepening global interdependence. Continued demand by China's citizens for improved access to global markets, better and cheaper products, lower transaction costs, and new opportunities create pressure for continued deregulation. Moreover, Jiang Zemin and Zhu Rongji have brought China into the WTO precisely because entry will precipitate further deregulation, cut tariffs, and decrease the incentives for smuggling and corruption.

The framework driving this book (figure 1.1) suggests that without the WTO and significant re-regulation to create a more stable and transparent transnational regime, China will find itself either stuck in a world where corruption reigns supreme (quadrant C) or in an incipient market environment, where few rules govern economic behavior (quadrant D). Neither position is optimum for the long-term viability of the regime. Therefore, enormous benefits may come to China from its entry into the WTO, especially if the external pressures brought by membership force the state to impose the rule of law on its own transnational system (figure C.1, quadrant D).

CHINA AND INTERNATIONAL POLITICAL ECONOMY

The China case reconfirms the popular argument that states are not omnipotent. Long ago, Raymond Vernon alerted us to the impact of multinational corporations on the sovereignty of states and their ability to control their internal political economies.[38] Susan Strange reaffirmed that argument by showing how telecommunication companies, the Mafia, and the six largest insurance companies act as if national boundaries no longer exist.[39] In Kenichi Ohmae's "borderless world," regional governments, firms, and entrepreneurs, but not the central state, are becoming the key

Meany, "Urban Reform and Disintegrative Corruption in Urban China," in *Reforms and Reaction in Post-Mao China: The Road to Tiananmen*, ed. Richard Baum (New York: Routledge, 1991), pp. 124–42; Michael Johnston, "The Political Consequences of Corruption: A Reassessment," *Comparative Politics* 18 (July 1986): 464–65.

37. Sam Ho raised this point during a seminar I gave at the University of British Columbia in January 1998.

38. Raymond Vernon, *Sovereignty at Bay: The Multinational Spread of U.S. Enterprises* (New York: Basic Books, 1971).

39. Strange, *Retreat of the State*.

economic actors who must respond to popular demand for better standards of living.[40]

The China case shows that domestic and global interests, particularly local communities and new corporate organizations that benefit from transnational linkages, can undermine even strong authoritarian states that try to control their global exchanges as they open to the outside world. Keeping control is easy when domestic actors do not know their interests, but once leaders allow transnational flows and global communications begin to penetrate the domestic economy, demands for exchanges increase as those with a comparative advantage in transnational exchanges seek to expand their linkages. Global and domestic pressures for lower transaction costs begin to affect the regulatory regime, creating pressure for its simplification.

The form that domestic pressures take may be greatly influenced by domestic political institutions. In democracies, lobbies, independent trade unions, and commercial associations possess the legal authority to pressure the government to alter its trade regime. In authoritarian systems, even when interests are clarified, collective action remains difficult if not illegal. But as this book shows, once states reject autarky and adopt developmental strategies based on expanded transnational exchanges, independent actions by domestic actors can combine to exert strong pressures on the states to adjust their regulatory regimes and lower their barriers to global linkages.

Even so, bureaucrats in authoritarian (and even in some democratic) states can control many international transactions for a long period of time. Regulators remain powerful guardians of these global channels and can stop, monitor, or facilitate those flows. As long as states maintain those channels and do not adjust the regulatory regime governing market forces, shutting off transnational flows remains easier. But how states open to the outside world and manage or control deregulation greatly affects the pattern and politics of internationalization and ultimately the nature of the regime. The interests of regulators shift over time as they recognize that more can be earned by abetting exchanges than blocking them, but they have strong incentives to both maintain regulatory controls and facilitate exchanges that pass through their bureaus. Still, self-interested citizens and far-sighted leaders can pressure those with vested interests in preserving a semiregulated trade and investment regime to give up most controls. Otherwise, crony capitalism will be the country's long-term future, generating corruption, undermining growth, and preventing a more definitive shift to market forces and the wealth and prosperity that such markets bring.

40. Kenichi Ohmae, *The Borderless World: Power and Strategy in the Interlinked Economy* (New York: Harper Business, 1990).

Index

The Political Economy of Policy Coordination: International Adjustment since 1945
  by Michael C. Webb

The Myth of the Powerless State
  by Linda Weiss

The Developmental State
  edited by Meredith Woo-Cumings

International Cooperation: Building Regimes for Natural Resources and the Environment
  by Oran R. Young

International Governance: Protecting the Environment in a Stateless Society
  by Oran R. Young

Polar Politics: Creating International Environmental Regimes
  edited by Oran R. Young and Gail Osherenko

Governments, Markets, and Growth: Financial Systems and the Politics of Industrial Change
  by John Zysman

American Industry in International Competition: Government Policies and Corporate Strategies
  edited by John Zysman and Laura Tyson